CHINA IN THE MIX

CHINA
IN THE
MIX

Cinema, Sound, and Popular Culture in the Age of Globalization

YING XIAO

University Press of Mississippi / Jackson

www.upress.state.ms.us

The University Press of Mississippi is a member of
the Association of American University Presses.

Copyright © 2017 by University Press of Mississippi
All rights reserved

First printing 2017

∞

Library of Congress Cataloging-in-Publication Data

Names: Xiao, Ying (Professor of film studies) author.
Title: China in the mix: cinema, sound, and popular culture in the age of
globalization / Ying Xiao.
Description: Jackson: University Press of Mississippi, 2017. | Includes
bibliographical references and index. |
Identifiers: LCCN 2017012504 (print) | LCCN 2017028709 (ebook) | ISBN
9781496812612 (epub single) | ISBN 9781496812629 (epub institutional) |
ISBN 9781496812636 (pdf single) | ISBN 9781496812643 (pdf institutional)
| ISBN 9781496812605 (hardback)
Subjects: LCSH: Sound motion pictures—China. | Motion
pictures—China—History. | Sound in motion pictures—China. | Motion
pictures and music—China. | Popular culture—China—History—20th
century. | Popular culture—China—History—21st century. | Popular
music—Social aspects—China—History—20th century. | Popular
music—Social aspects—China—History—21st century. | BISAC: SOCIAL
SCIENCE / Media Studies. | PERFORMING ARTS / Film & Video / History &
Criticism. | SOCIAL SCIENCE / Popular Culture.
Classification: LCC PN1995.7 (ebook) | LCC PN1995.7 .X56 2017 (print) | DDC
791.4302/4—dc23
LC record available at https://lccn.loc.gov/2017012504

British Library Cataloging-in-Publication Data available

For August-烁尘, who sparks me to cross the ground

CONTENTS

ix   Acknowledgments

3   **Overture**
Sound, Image, and Popular Media at the Nexus of Global-China

18   **Chapter One**
Northwest Wind: Folklore, Vernacular, and the Chinese New Waves

52   **Chapter Two**
The Convergence of Popular Music-Film: Zhang Yimou-Zhao Jiping and Spectacles of Sound

75   **Chapter Three**
"Rock 'n' Roll on the New Long March": Cui Jian and the Voices and Moving Images of Chinese Rock Kids

112   **Chapter Four**
"At the Intersection of Film and Music": Jia Zhangke and Urban Youth Cinema

142   **Chapter Five**
National Anthem at *Guangchang*: Languagescape, Ideoscape, and Mediascape in the Time of Global Picture

195   **Chapter Six**
"Hip Hop Is My Knife, Rap Is My Sword": Hip Hop Network and the Changing Landscape of Image and Sound Making

233   **Finale**
A Shift in Perception

239   **Appendix I**
Music and Sound in Jia Zhangke's *Platform* (*Zhantai*, 2000)

249 Appendix II
Box Office Overview of Mainland China, 1985–2012

257 Notes

283 Chinese Glossary

289 Filmography

295 Bibliography

311 Index

ACKNOWLEDGMENTS

When I crossed the Pacific Ocean and set out on a new venture on the Western Hemisphere at the turn of the twenty-first century, I knew that I wanted to study and write about my journeys, my life, and my negotiations in different cultures and settings. This gives me great cause to embrace my upbringing and get in touch with new grounds in a more thoughtful and critical way. It has been my privilege to have studied in Cinema Studies in New York University, which has shaped my intellectual mindset and paved my way into scholarly exploration. I am especially grateful to Zhang Zhen, who has always guided me with her insights, profound knowledge, and expansive life experience. Her unwavering dedication to substantial scholarship and her extraordinary knack of building a sound, energizing professional-parental life continue to inspire me and have a significant impact on my work and career choices. I am also indebted to many other professors who have set me on the path, encouraged me to go on and go further on this voyage of boundless learning, and supported me all the way along: Dana Polan, Anna McCarthy, Robert Stam, Richard Allen, Robert Sklar, Ed Guerrero, and Chris Straayer at New York University; Sung-sheng Yvonne Chang, Wen-Hua Teng, S. Craig Watkins, and Mary Celeste Kearney at the University of Texas at Austin; Claudia Gorbman at the University of Washington Tacoma; Jiayan Mi at the College of New Jersey; Jonathan Kahana at University of California Santa Cruz; and Han Yuhai, Zhang Yiwu, Cao Wenxuan, Li Yang, and Dai Jinhua at Peking University. Their wisdom, expertise, and generous help have continuously nurtured me since I was student and became an academic myself.

Special thanks also go to my excellent colleagues at the Department of Languages, Literatures, and Cultures, Center for Film and Media Studies, Center for Gender, Sexualities, and Women's Studies Research, College of Liberal Arts and Sciences, College of Journalism and Communications, School of Art and Art History, and School of Music at the University of Florida: Mary Watt, Ingrid Kleespies, Richard G. Wang, Guolong Lai, Mario Poceski, Brigitte Weltman-Aron, Barbara Mennel, Maureen Turim, Scott Nygren, Eric Kligerman, Sylvie Blum-Reid, Youssef Haddad, Sarra Tlili, Franz Futterknecht, Ann Wehmeyer, Malini Johar Schueller, Churchill Roberts, Sophia Krzys Acord, Welson Tremura, among others. This work would not have been completed without their support. I relish the amiable atmosphere and dynamic of working with them—as well as with my students, whom I have laughed with, talked with, and learned from.

I have benefitted greatly from the valuable suggestions and input of many colleagues and friends who made time to listen to my ideas, read my drafts, and offer their perceptive comments. There are too many to name here, but they include: Xiaobing Tang, Ban Wang, Sheldon Lu, Yomi Braester, Hui Faye Xiao, Haomin Gong, Xin Yang, Jin Liu, Qi Wang, Fan Yang, Keith B. Wagner, Chang Tan, Jun Ren, Hongmei Yu, and Hongmei Sun. Thanks also go to the Dean's Office, Office of the Vice President for Research, College of Liberal Arts and Sciences, and the Center for the Humanities and the Public Sphere at the University of Florida, the Freeman Asian Studies Fund, NCTA Grant, the Lieberthal-Rogel Center for Chinese Studies at the University of Michigan, and the International Center for Studies of Chinese Civilization at Fudan University for having facilitated and funded my research efforts. Since my research has expanded and gone further, I have communicated related notions in articles in the *Oxford Handbook of New Audiovisual Aesthetics*, *Neoliberalism and Global Cinema: Capital, Culture, and Marxist Critique*, and *Paradoxa: Studies in World Literary Genres*, where the materials in several of my chapters have originally appeared.

My gratitude also goes to Kimberley Monteyne and Mika Turim-Nygren for their penetrating commentary and meticulous edits on the drafts of this work at various phases. Debing Su deserves special mention for preparing images and for providing prompt and untiring technical support for this project. As I completed the manuscript, I was very fortunate to work with the team at the University Press of Mississippi, which has been such an incredibly positive and pleasant experience. I thank particularly Leila Salisbury, Lisa McMurtray, and Vijay Shah for their enthusiasm, efficiency, and truly outstanding professional work. I also want to acknowledge Norm Hirschy, Christopher Ahn, Lian Sun, Patrice Petro, Lisa Boyajian, and the anonymous readers for their keen interest and important feedback on this project. I appreciate Pingjie Michael Zhang and Reel China for providing me unique and exciting opportunities to interact and work with many filmmakers and cultural institutions, which has greatly complemented and enriched my study. I thank especially director Zhang Yang for his gracious support and for generously offering his film image to be used for the cover artwork of my book.

Most of all, I owe my family in China and in the States a great deal for their unfaltering love, support, and belief wherever I am and whatever I do. In 2015, a decade after journeying to New York, I wrapped up the last chapter, packed up my baggage, and returned to China through my life dream journey of the Trans-Siberian Railway. I then knew that my research and writing meant more than a daily routine—and an academic job—to me. (The other reason for the trip was that we high-school classmates promised each other to meet and chant again in twenty years on the top of Mount Heng to relive the memories of our youth.) So much has changed. Yet nothing has really changed. This book will be a witness to my lifelong fascination and endeavor in visual arts, popular music, and youth culture. As Shania Twain sings in the song "You've Got a Way" (a remixed version of which appeared in *Notting Hill*):

> You've got a way with me
> Somehow you got me to believe
> In everything that I could be . . .
> You gave me faith to find my dreams

I dedicate this book to all of you who made my way.

CHINA IN THE MIX

OVERTURE

Sound, Image, and Popular Media at the Nexus of Global-China

> Music, the quintessential activity, like the crowd, is simultaneously a threat and a necessary source of legitimacy; trying to channel it is a risk that every system of power must run.
> —**Jacques Attali**, *Noise: The Political Economy of Music*[1]

This book originated from my initial philia toward both film and music and thence from my cumulative intellectual discovery of the alliance, analogy, and conjoining between the two entities, visual and aural, cinema and other forms of screen arts and popular mediums, all of which are quintessential embodiments of mass culture and of power relations, as Jacques Attali has illuminated above. In brief, my book is an inquiry into the connections and intersections of film, media, music, and popular culture in contemporary China under postsocialist reform, capitalist globalization, and hybridization. The nexus and relationship I build in the book are, therefore, twofold. First, it seeks to spell out the complex, evolving interplay of expressions, elaborations, and experiences in a particular social, symbolic time and space and show how they reflect and engage the important cultural and socio-historical shifts in contemporary China and the large current of globalization. Second, the investigation of *China in the Mix* attempts to complement, redress, and re-envision studies of Chinese cinema and media by weaving out a broad picture of Chinese expression and culture from a unique, cohesive acoustic angle. In other words, the prime aim of this book is to explore the articulations and representations of mass culture and everyday life, with particular concentration on their aural/oral manifestations in contemporary Chinese cinema and in a wide spectrum of media and cultural productions.

To this end, the first nexus I craft in this book is significantly spatiotemporal, that is, the interaction of China and the global movement at the turn of the twenty-first century. The various films, music trends, and cultural phenomena I analyze in the book are discursively placed under the postsocialist rubric, roughly spanning from the release of Chen Kaige's *Yellow Earth* in 1984 to Hollywood's re-entry into China in 1994 to China's accession to WTO in 2001 until the second decade of the twenty-first century. The year 1984 marked a breaking point in Chinese film historiography when films in the Chinese New Wave, such as *Yellow Earth*, started to make appearances on the international circuit. The worldwide salute made Chinese cinema, which had been barely known or dismissed largely as a propaganda tool in the West, a worthwhile subject for appreciation and academic study. It is no surprise that the expeditious formation and institutionalization of Chinese film studies and criticism are a direct outcome of the surge of festival-going, prize-winning films, and, quite simply, a product of transnational circulation and consumption in the new era. In the midst of a large-scale opening-up and marketization and the postsocialist sea change, artistic films of the Fifth Generation and the Sixth Generation garnered critical attention and awards from the West with the ethnic and cultural images of indigenous China, whereas Hollywood's entertainment-oriented mega-productions reached out their hands to the Chinese market and took hold of a mass audience with spectacle, sensuality, action, and "true lies" of Western modernity.

The year 1994 was another turning point when Hollywood films such as *True Lies* (dir. James Cameron, 1994) started to re-enter the Chinese film market that set off the immediate and far-reaching encounters between Chinese national cinema and Hollywood, and that coincided with Chinese film industry's internal reform to displace the state-planned filmmaking with the capitalist mode of production, management, and commercialization. Starting with *The Fugitive* (dir. Andrew Davis, 1993), China reached agreements with Hollywood studios to import ten "excellent" foreign films on a revenue-sharing basis every year. This historical deal to crack open the Chinese film market again to Hollywood—after its monopoly during the Republican period and its utter disappearance in Maoist China—has generated a second golden age for Hollywood, but has also unwittingly intensified the deep crisis of the already troubled, frail Chinese film industry. For instance, moviegoers filled theaters for *Titanic* (dir. James Cameron, 1997), a record-breaking Hollywood blockbuster that accounted for more than one fourth of the total national box office in 1998.

The turn of the twenty-first century marked the third milestone in that it saw successively the fiftieth anniversary of the founding of the PRC (1999),

China's successful bid to host the 2008 Olympics (2001), and China's accession to WTO (2001), signifying China's further step toward globalization. Prior to China's WTO accession, with the signing of the Sino-US bilateral covenant, the two came to an agreement in 1999 to double the annual quotas of imported revenue-sharing films from ten to twenty, which has been elevated again to a total of thirty-four in 2012.[2] Against the decade-long rivalry with the all-powerful Hollywood, Chinese domestic film business went into a downward spiral in the late 1990s, but ascended at a blistering pace with blockbusters of its own in the new millennium. It should be noted that since 2012, the country soared to the second largest film market. Eight of the ten highest-grossing films in China were domestic productions in 2013, five in 2014, and seven in 2015.[3] In February 2015, China's box office hit a record high of $650 million, overtaking that of the US to become the world's largest film market.[4] Shall this be seen as an alternative or a reversal of the century-long Hollywood hegemony? How Chinese cinema confronts the likes of Hollywood and the prospects of it en route to the second centennial remains to be seen, but one thing is unquestionable: the interplay between China and Hollywood and the world will remain, widen, and deepen in this inescapably interconnected age and in a "polycentric world," in the words of Zhang Yingjin.[5]

For me, the above sketch of Sino-Hollywood relation provides a springboard to begin my quest of the complexity and complications of image exchange, musical exchange, and cultural exchange in postsocialist, globalized China. It remains as an undergirding narrative and a fundamental "leitmotif" throughout my arguments. Drawing on yet different from Miriam Hansen's formulation of "vernacular modernism" that implies a hierarchic relationship between Hollywood and other national practices,[6] I propose "global vernacularism" as a new perspective to re-examine and re-evaluate Chinese local experiences in relation to the widely dispersed model of Hollywood and to a wide range of sociocultural phenomena, perceptions, and media affected by the so-called process of modernization and globalization. My focus is on the balancing and "synchresis" between the local, the global, and the national that make out a multidirectional and "polyphonic"—instead of centrifugal-characteristic—movement in today's mixing, ever-unfolding soundscape, visualscape, and mediascape.

"Synchresis" is a term I adopt in citation of Michel Chion's treatise of the intrinsic and integrated relationship between image and sound in cinema. As Chion asserts: "*Synchresis* (a word I have forged by combining *synchronism* and *synthesis*) is the spontaneous and irresistible weld produced between a particular auditory phenonmenon and visual phenonmenon when they occur at the same time . . . Synchresis is what makes dubbing, postsynchronization, and sound-effects mixing possible, and enables such a wide array of choice in these processes."[7] In this book, I explore the specific form of "synchresis" as presented in diverse Chinese film, music, and media texts. Additionally, this trope is deployed evocatively to facilitate my discussion of the discursive strategy of "synchresis" (or what I call "mixing") at a particular historical moment and in a broader sociocultural context of contemporary China. I borrow the term "polyphony" from Mikhail Bakhtin with the intent to restore globalism back to its vernacular origin and to shed light on my own speculations about the mixed and hybrid nature of Chinese film, music, and culture. "Polyphony," a concept derived from music and further developed by Bakhtin in his originative analysis of the narrative, is the multiple voices, each of which has its own perspective, its own autonomy, and its full validity, and which can be "applied to the construction of the whole."[8] In sum, polyphony "is precisely what happens *between various consciousnesses,* that is, their interaction and interdependence."[9] Thus, in my study, not only has the use of popular music and modern standard language become a recurrent theme and a stylistic mode in many contemporary Chinese films, but other linguistic-sonic features—such as vernaculars, dialects, local idioms, and foreign inflections—are constantly heard and employed by a considerable number of Northwest Wind, rock 'n' roll, and Leitmotif films in their respective chapters. Moreover, an act of choosing and switching between different language codes and repertoires, as my chapters on Northwest Wind and Chinese hip hop also convey, present this postsocialist soundscape as a plural, contested, and dialogically connected space in the sense of Bakhtin.

The subject matter of Chinese film and media has been examined in many distinct ways. Yet scarce attention has been paid to the dimension of sound and its essential role in the construction of image, culture, and identity in the typography of Chinese studies and in the letters of film and media studies in general. In fact, music, and sound in the broad sense, has long taken a secondary seat in film and media studies to the predominant emphasis on visuality, often deemed the greatest importance to cinema; in comparison, a slender number of scholarly works have been devoted to film sound. Even to the extent that the study of film sound has arguably occupied a slippery, if not a marginalized, domain, the conventional theoretical and historiographical model tends to privilege the filmic uses of music and treat a single component of soundtrack separately (e.g., dialogue, voice-over, sound effect, etc.). This has engendered "the soundtrack in crisis," warns Rick Altman in "Inventing the Cinema Soundtrack: Hollywood's Multiplane Sound System."[10] Altman, along with McGraw Jones and Sonia Tatroe, has argued that the epistemology of film sounds should be defined not only through their external, coordinated relationship to image but also equally by "these intercomponent, intra-soundtrack relationships."[11] To extrapolate from this assertion, they propose a notion of *mise-en-bande*—in parallel and correspondence with that of *mise-en-scène*—that foregrounds "the interaction among the various components making up the soundtrack."[12] Whereas Altman's seminal conjecture of a *mise-en-bande*-based approach opened new avenues to understanding cinema's often dimissed auditory properties and the medium's audiovisual totalities, this important proposition has just been applied to Altman's own examination of Hollywood's early sound picture and urges more work to join this new, serious conversation of reframing cinema studies through sound.

In the Chinese context, the traditional stratification of image and sound also prevails. There is a dearth of literature addressing the film's auditory substance. A great deal of writing has been focused on the Fifth Generation, the Sixth Generation, and the underground, independent Chinese films whose visual terminology and political valence often occupy the center stage of the scholarship. There is currently a growing interest in the studies of film sound, as testified by a special issue of *Journal of Chinese Cinemas* in 2013 that yokes together a collection of essays with close attention to the soundscape of Chinese cinema and calls forth "the turn to sound."[13] Inasmuch as research of Chinese film sound has emerged as a new and exciting field, "the turn to sound," as coined by Jean Ma and Matthew Johnson, comprises primarily, besides those appearing in the 2013 issue of *Journal of Chinese Cinemas*, in English, a handful of short articles and book chapters (Yeh 1999, 2002; Tuohy 1999, 2008; Zhang 2005; Pollacchi 2008; Ma 2011), two PhD dissertations (Yeh 1995; Xiao 2010), and Jean Ma's *Sounding the Modern Women: The Songstress in Chinese Cinema* (2015).[14] Ma's book is a significant contribution to the field that offers a compelling and fresh look at the confluence between film and music industries through the lens of the songstress as a ubiquitous and emblematic figure across the varied decades of Chinese film history. Many other works—be they a focused account of popular music in postwar Taiwanese film, or musical discourse in contemporary Hong Kong cinema, or sound practice in metropolitan Shanghai and the golden age of Shanghai cinema of the 1930s and 1940s—represent the bourgeoning sub-field of Chinese film sound studies, but have concentrated predominantly on a single strand of film music in one national and historical setting.

Evoking Michel Chion's notion of "audiovisual contract," these publications examine the symbiotic relationship between image and music and how the two mediums have engaged in the construction of the critical circumstance of national identity, modernity, urban sentiment, gender politics, and so forth. Chion has repeatedly emphasized the direct and immediate relationship between image and sound, whose partnership can lead to a mode of equilibrium and a great "unity."[15] The particular value of Chion's work lies not only in his foundational theoretical framework of music's capacity in engaging image, producing meaning, and functioning as a reflexive sociopolitical marker, but also in his equal consideration to language, dialogue, and other particles of soundtrack that all partake in an egalitarian dialogue with image in a process of what he names "synchresis."

The cinematic aspect of orality—especially language utterance and variation—nonetheless remains largely an uncharted and unpronounced territory, only addressed in an even narrower body of works such as Edward Gunn's *Rendering the Regional: Local Language in Contemporary Chinese Media* (2006) and Jin Liu's *Signifying the Local: Media Productions Rendered in Local Languages in Mainland China in the New Millennium* (2013).[16] Whereas Gunn's and Liu's comprehensive surveys on the appropriations of local languages in contemporary Chinese mass media may have appeared just in time as important icebreakers into this long neglected area, their merits and limitations seem both to stem from their sociolinguist approach that has focused chiefly on the language operations, thus abridging much of their complex connection and interplay with a diversity of formal and aesthetic practices, among which is the visual representational system. The single-handed treatment has preoccupied scholars who, in spite of having shifted attention to sound, are still fixated upon a single thread of singing or language in supporting, complementing, and modifying the film's visual and narrative events.

My research echoes Ma and Johnson's call for "the turn to sound." It addresses this critical lack in the current scholarship with the first book-length study of the soundscape, languagescape, visualscape, mediascape, and culturescape in China in the late twentieth and early twenty-first centuries. Instead, I like to use my term "the critical adoption of sound" in order to highlight the indwelling, conjugative, and formational nature of sound and the very means of acknowledging sound, rather than heedlessly turning away from the visual, extracting sound from image. The phrase "adoption" is employed heuristically to denote first and foremost a sense of unity and integrity that invokes Michel Chion's pioneering conception of "audiovisual contract" and "synchresis"; and secondly, the methodology of recognizing that sound is part of a whole, even if not from the birth of cinema. Like the historical juncture at which sound was introduced to—or rather, I say, resurrected and reunited with cinema after more than three decades of silence up until the late 1920s—the decoding of film sound had to wait for its own threshold that has also taken an uneven road loaded with a similar degree of exhilaration, perplexity, and contradiction. All of these entail a measure of "the critical adoption of sound," specifically an even-handed decryption of the "multiplane sound system" as much as that of the visual enterprise and within the various ramifications of the sonic. I hope that my reflections on the soundscape in its completeness and connection offer a timely intervention and contribute to the *mis-en-bande* study following the lead of Rick Altman.

Drawing upon Claudia Gorbman's insight to "start listening to the cinema's uses to music in order to read films in a literate way,"[17] as is suggested in her book, *Unheard Melodies: Narrative Film Music*, I present here an alternative and "literate" account of contemporary Chinese film, media, and culture by energizing and restoring streams of "unheard melodies," sonorous singing, speaking, narrating, and variants of sound to their filmic, social, economic, and geopolitical tracks. Soundscape remains the central focus of my exploration. It is, however, not the only one. The sociopolitical, cultural, and historical landscape I sketch out parallels the cinematic and auditory trajectory, as the two are inexorably imbricated with one another. On the one hand, cinematic music and language exhibit an inseverable connection to film narrative, structure, plot, character, and *mise-en-scène*; on the other hand, they are symptomatic of mass culture and a wide-ranging economic, political, and social transformation taking place in contemporary China. The sociological and cultural studies' perspectives are necessary in order to track and identify the complex relationship between soundtrack, identity construction, political ideology, and socioeconomic determinants. Simon Frith has proposed a sociological, as opposed to an essentialist musicological, approach to understanding popular music. As he holds: "In analyzing serious music, we have to uncover the social forces concealed in the talk of 'transcendent' values; in analyzing pop, we have to take seriously the values scoffed at in the talk of social functions."[18] Thus, in my analysis, I expand my horizon not only to zoom in on popular music and language inflections within the text and context of film and media, but also zoom out to search for their intertextuality and to "talk" with the social and cultural mechanisms. The book offers a cultural-historical study of sound that has been so closely intertwined with the varied landscape of visual aesthetics, film practices, and historical formations in China in the late twentieth and early twenty-first centuries.

As an interdisciplinary cultural studies project, this book does not simply delineate another narrative of sound, as opposed to the traditional assumptions and approaches to film and media. Rather, staking out popular aesthetics and mass culture in their aural/oral forms in Chinese film and cultural productions, I address terms at the intersection of the distinct domains—cultural studies, film and media studies, and sound studies—and bring them together in a manner not previously attempted. Extending from Arjun Appadurai's famous formulation of the five landscapes that characterize today's global cultural flow—ethnoscape, mediascape, technoscape, financescape, ideoscape[19]—I suggest a similarly parallel and crisscrossed reading of visualscape, soundscape, languagescape, mediascape, and culturescape that conflate to shape the complex and highly volatile Chinascape at a time of drastic change. The soundscape of my particular concentration is a distinct landscape of sound under a postsocialist mass culture condition, a landscape that is multivalent, fluid, and oftentimes socio-historically contingent and contested. To further understand the reconfigurations of popular music and heteroglossic soundtrack under the new conditions, I place a specific emphasis on how they have been conceived and contextualized by the intersecting forces of globalization, nationalism, and indigenization and by the political-economic imperatives that restructure the film and cultural industry at a particular time of transition.

In this book, I engage the notion of postsocialism as a means of structuring and foregrounding my study of the transition. Since the late 1970s, mainland China has undergone a sea change with a decisive turn from socialist governance and centralization to postsocialist marketization and privatization. The market as a new cultural logic and a dynamic integration of transnational capital fostered around the neoliberal axis became the major forces reshaping a wide range of economic, sociopolitical, and cultural lives in contemporary China. Indeed, the term "postsocialism" has been commonly used by critics and scholars as a periodization and a critical category to tackle a new set of paradigms, ideologies, socioeconomic conditions, cultural developments, and aesthetic practices since the market reform of late 1970s. Readily drawing from an a priori model of postmodernism, Zhang Xudong asserts that postsocialism is postmodernism in China, which is "a deliberate signifier (or an ad hoc stand-in) for an unsettled, postponed, living, and reconfiguring collective experience of revolution, modernity, statehood, and the masses."[20] Thus, postsocialism has been quite often interchangeable with such concepts as postmodernism, post-Mao, post-revolution, post-New Era, and post-Tiananmen which attempt to deliver a sense of post-ness, preposterousness, disengagement, reconfiguration, and uncertainty in the vexed, ongoing present. Many studies of contemporary China have indicated that the condition of market-driven productivity and attendant flood of unchecked consumerism have rapidly and mercilessly engulfed the country. However, unlike the West, neoliberal market reform in China has been substantially and consistently associated with state imperatives in that from its inception to implementation to expansion the Chinese state has maintained a dominant and authoritative role.[21]

Chinese neoliberalism and postsocialism, or "socialism with Chinese characteristic" (*you zhongguo tese de shehui zhuyi*), to borrow the presiding official slogan, represent, to a great extent, what Michel Foucault calls "governmentality" in that such expressions justify and identify with the market power and the very social transition in late twentieth century China. With the composite of "government" and "mentality," Foucault posits that his exposition of "governmentality" concerns "the conduct of the conduct,"[22] especially the way in which the practice, tactic, mentality, and rationality of a governable society can be achieved through the processes of neoliberalism and modernization. In a Foucauldian move, Lisa Rofel develops a new understanding of postsocialist Chinese reality from the vantage point of "governmentality" and "biopower." For her, the epoch-making market reform not only introduces a new type of governmental management and political economy to post-revolutionary, contemporary China but also signifies a new psychological and social condition, within which new forms of desires and anxieties, subjectivities and humanities are intricately produced and circulated.[23]

This is particularly true for the last two decades of twentieth century China. In the 1980s, a number of high-profile modernist films of the Fifth Generation, along with various experiments in literature, music, and visual arts, led to a decade of cultural renaissance termed "high cultural fever." This fanatic moment, during which the full scope of Chinese arts, civilizations, and cultures attracted unprecedented popular interest as well as critical investigation, was at once self-reflexive and self-indulgent. Nonetheless, its success was short-lived. Soon after its ascent, Chinese cultural fever and intellectual movement were overthrown by another round of political backlash against "bourgeois liberalization," a cold blast of post-1989 political censorship and ideological control, and a more pervasive flood of materialism and consumer mass culture—all hatched through the trembling postsocialist market reform since the late 1970s.

The decade of 1990s represented a new, second phase of development in the midst of reform. The period followed a dual, tortuous course of economic progress vis-à-vis political backlash and, in summary, the more diversified, "varied landscape," to quote Zhang Yingjin.[24] Zhang goes on to argue that the 1990s indeed suggested a break with the intellectual tradition of the 1980s, bringing to the fore "a new alliance of art, politics, and capital,"[25] the new zeitgeist demarcating the era. Zhang Yingjin is certainly not alone in expounding such a view. It can be argued that *fin de siècle* China was characterized by a bourgeoning mass popular culture, a rampant consumerism, and by contrast a shrinking high culture and enlightenment discourse, all of which strive to negotiate their own spaces amid the omnipresent and increasingly sterile political environment of the moment.²⁶ For Lydia Liu, then, this debate on postsocialism shall not also separate itself from the discourse of transnationalism; both are, in fact, mutually embedded in the contemporary Chinese situation and must be treated as a simultaneous process.²⁷

In this book, I use postsocialism to reassess the concept of transnational capitalism in the Chinese context and to facilitate a methodological move of what I have been calling "global vernacularism." In my endeavor, postsocialism is not only a spatiotemporal structure but also a historical condition and a cultural-aesthetic fashion that defines and builds into my kernel subjects of sound and mass culture. My objective is not to validate or interrogate the concept of postsocialism, but rather to seek an in-depth understanding of soundscape and mass culture across the axes of the postsocialist and the transnational. While it is generally agreed that popular mass culture in contemporary China did not fully thrive until the last decade of twentieth century, it was conceived in the 1980s when the architecture of Chinese society and cultural landscape started to undergo a series of whirlwind deconstructions and reconstructions. Many cinematic and sonic changes took root in this postsocialist threshold, as my historiographical and genealogical reading of Northwest Wind, rock 'n' roll, Leitmotif film, and Chinese hip hop shows in the following chapters. And my treatment of the heterogeneous, unsettled postsocialist-scape hinges upon the key notions of transformation and connection. Associated with a specific historicity and time frame, how has this position of transformation penetrated the textualities, aesthetics, and institutions of Chinese film and a large scale of cultural productions? In particular, how has this historical continuity and rupture been technologically, stylistically, and allegorically embodied through sound practice in contemporary China? Furthermore, how do we talk about and read relationally the various facets of narratives, perspectives, and formations?

To tackle these questions, I arrive with an approach that is both microscopic and macroscopic. By "microscopic," I deal with sound as my central focus and primary point of departure to explore film and other mediums in relation to popular mass culture. With a new emphasis on the importance and equality of soundtrack to visual representation, I closely examine popular music and language articulations that occupy the center of the scene—diegetic music and dialogue played by characters, as well as nondiegetic music and voice-over which often serve as a commentary from the authorial perspective. Delving into the particularity of popular music in Chinese cinema and media, I attempt to break down traditional binaries and rebuild the connections between image and sound, popular and high art, experimental and commercial, global and local. I deploy an open-minded strategy to look at what counts as popular and how popular music is associated with a variety of film genres in contemporary China, such as Chinese Westerns, musicals, rock 'n' roll, youth films, Leitmotif films, and so forth. In my project, popular music soundtracks not only encompass songs which achieve success prior to or after being used on-screen, but also non-vocal music which makes use of musical styles, aesthetics, or metaphors to be massively circulated. Leitmotif film, an extraordinary film form manipulated and streamlined at once by postsocialist cultural industry and state propaganda, derives much of its power from its capacity to produce and circulate a new sense of popular and furthermore what it means to be popular and global. My case study of Leitmotif film, with its national visibility and multinational language track, complicates such understandings of the popular and serves as a prime example to demonstrate my transnational and cross-media approach in this underexplored but increasingly important field of popular culture studies.

This is important not just for the reason that sound is quite often the overlooked aspect in the entirety of audiovisual culture. My extreme close-ups on sound can, at best, draw our attention to this historical moment of shift, in which sound finds a forceful voice and comes to the fore of popular culture and social change. All of these emergent, broader systemic changes are imbricated into film industry and popular music and bring the latter much closer to each other than ever before. The complicated musical turn and historically situated auditory culture under my close analysis consists of a number of dialectical, contentious junctures: 1) state mechanism and Hollywood global capitalism; 2) avant-garde, artistic experiment and commercial interest; 3) Chinese political dogma and the dissenting voice. My thorough assessment of all of these different layers would suggest new ways of approaching and re-evaluating the assumptions introduced by auteur theory and genre studies. Moreover, it corresponds well to my "macroscopic" take by interweaving an organic and polyvalent picture of the cinematic, musical, and linguistic discourses from top to bottom, across the conventional divisions of the high and low culture, the official and the alternative, the West and the East. A plural and "synchresis" form of reading and listening of the cinescape, soundscape and languagescape, I contend, allows us to see cinema as but one of many voices, aesthetic forms, and media channels, evolving concurrently with a wide spectrum of cultural productions, such as literary writing, print culture, popular music, and the newly rising force of digital culture in China.

In juxtaposition with this critical lens of auditory panning, the book also moves vertically along a rough chronology from the 1980s to the early twenty-first century. I set out to examine the manifold visual-acoustic suturing of the Chinese New Wave that reflects upon and allegorizes the paradox of culture, nature, nation, history, ideology, and selfhood in the 1980s (chapter 1 and 2). The book goes forward to scrutinize the aesthetics of *flâneur* (Walter Banjamin) and postsocialist cinema *vérité* in rock 'n' roll film and urban cinema in *fin de siècle* China (chapter 3 and 4). It turns to a variegated sociopolitical and institutionally informed reading of Leitmotif film that reflects and bears witness to the global/local dialectics, an epitome of neoliberalism as exception (Aihwa Ong), and a technology of governmentality (Michel Foucault) in the late socialist era (chapter 5). The last part moves from film culture to an even more diversified exploration of hip hop music, film, and internet video and the manifestations of the glocalization (Roland Robertson) and the carnivalesque and polyphonic (Mikhail Baktin) in the new digital age (chapter 6). The six chapters, delineated as the various embodiments of global vernacularism and underlined by their distinct uses of sound, may be read consecutively, independently, and relationally of each other.

Following Rey Chow's call for "Chinese film in the age of interdisciplinarity," I launch new, different ways of understanding Chinese film in its audiovisual evenness, totality, completeness, and "interdisciplinarity."[28] Chow has suggested how to emancipate film from the grips of a conventionally literary criticism by introducing a new "dialectic of seeing."[29] My operation resonates with and extends Chow's; in addition to "defending" visuality as an essential discourse and as "an opportunity to rethink other modes of discourse,"[30] what is involved in my book is to brew another kind of dialectical thinking—what may be called the dialectic of listening and perception. Like Chow, my objective is to adopt an interdisciplinary and cross-cultural perspective, but my study is a new undertaking exploring Chinese film through the dialectical lens of sound. I choose to begin my reframing with the canonical *Yellow Earth*.

The first chapter revisits the Chinese New Wave cinema of the 1980s and reconsiders Chen Kaige's *Yellow Earth* (1984), *The Big Parade* (1986), and *King of the Children* (1987) from a new acoustic and cross-media angle. I adopt the term "Northwest Wind" broadly in order to reassess, juxtapose, and interlace between the various musical, cinematic, literary, and cultural discourses of the 1980s: the prevalent popular musical form that blends the indigenous folk music of northwest China with the Western style of disco and rock rhythm; the Fifth Generation filmmakers' cinematic modernism often identified as the cinematic version of "Northwest Wind"—the Chinese Western—that showcases the vast, barren, and landlocked northwest China; and the historiographical, self-reflexive impulse of "root-seeking" in literature and popular culture terrains.

Chapter 2 continues to reinterpret Zhang Yimou's *Red Sorghum* (1987) and highlight the film's innovative employment of sound as metaphor and spectacle speaking to the larger issues of gender, sexuality, national identity, and human nature. As a formal analysis of the film and its indigenous songs and musical themes exhibits, Zhang Yimou (the film director) and Zhao Jiping's (the musician) idiosyncratic, legendary collaboration and superlative synthesization of image-music-text have not only created an extraordinary spectacle that few other films could match but have also sparked a new trend of cross-production and cross-fertilization between popular music and film since the late 1980s.

In chapter 3, I take on a specific musical subgenre and delve into the conflation of Chinese rock 'n' roll music and film at the end of the twentieth century. The chapter begins by situating the genesis of this cinematic-musical alliance on the cusp of the late 1980s and early 1990s, a time that bears witness to both the climax of cultural enlightenment and the resurgence of a wave of consumer culture. This is precisely exemplified through Wang Shuo hooligan literature and its popular film adaptions such as Mi Jiashan's *The Troubleshooters* (1988). In the latter part of the chapter, I, then, turn to a systematic navigation of Cui Jian, the godfather of Chinese rock, tracing his voices, images, personas, and iconographies in Chinese films. Close readings of such films as Zhang Yuan's *Beijing Bastards* (1993), Zhang Nuanxin's *Good Morning, Beijing* (1990), Yu Zhong's *Roots and Branches* (2001), and Jiang Wen's *The Sun Also Rises* (2007) suggest that the emergence of Chinese rock 'n' roll film and its development from the late 1980s to the new century shall be seen as a result of widespread and multifaceted transformations in postsocialist China. At the core of this rock imaginary are the politics and poetics of cinema *vérité* and postsocialist realism. The paradigmatic portrayals of rock kids, social outcasts, urban drifters, and postsocialist *flâneur* therefore herald a new wave of what Hamid Naficy has called "an accented cinema"[31] and independent, exilic, and transnational film practice of the Sixth Generation, whose trajectory parallels the rise of youth culture and popular music in contemporary China.

Chapter 4 ensues to chart urban youth cinema in relation to popular music at the turn of the twenty-first century. This chapter branches out to examine the music-film genre in a broader context of the experiments of the Urban Generation, as, for example, in Jia Zhangke's *Xiao Wu* (1997) and *Platform* (2000), Zhang Yang's *Quitting* (2001), and Lu Xuezhang's *How the Steel Was Tempered* (1997). It focuses particularly on aspects of how these films are associated with a historical construction of temporality, spatiality, youthfulness, and an aura of nostalgia and authenticity; all are defined through their signature popular music tracks.

Shifting attention from alternative art cinema to the sector of mainstream commercial production, chapter 5 outlines the so-called Leitmotif film, a heavily state-sponsored film practice shaped by both the market and state mechanisms in the postsocialist reform. The chapter thus complements other chapters with a distinct sociopolitical reading and an institutional analysis of how the Chinese film industry reform, state policy, and a series of political-economic forces play into Chinese cinescape and cultural landscape as a whole. As Chinese film signifies one of the first ventures to incorporate a neoliberal capitalist business model and represents China's *fin de siecle* aspiration and anxiety to "link up with the tracks of the world" (*yu shijie jiegui*), the cinematic display encoded by nationhood, historical reflexivity, transnational imaginary, and multilingual vocal track has become the defining feature of Leitmotif films, as seen in Xie Jin's *The Opium War* (1997) and Feng Xiaoning's trilogy of "China through Foreign Eyes" (e.g., *Lover's Grief over the Yellow River*, 1999). Some of the most expensive pictures made in mainland China, these Leitmotif films are also labeled as Chinese blockbusters, abundantly borrowing ideas and practices from Hollywood hits and transplanting them to local circumstances. The chapter compares these Leitmotif epics to Steven Spielberg's *Saving Private Ryan* (1998) and James Cameron's *Titanic* (1997). Analyzing and comparing their thematic concerns, narrative structures, stylistic forms, audiovisual components, publicity, and distribution, the chapter argues that these streamlined products reproduced by the postsocialist culture industry are in response to, and negotiation with, their Hollywood counterparts and rivals.

The reconciliations of Chinese cinema with Hollywood capitalism, on the one hand, and with its political regime, on the other hand, are the main thrusts of Leitmotif films and public culture in today's China. The second half of chapter 5 calls particular attention to the dualities, multiformities, and foremost the congregations of varied tongues, peoples, and ideologies in the Chinese brand of blockbusters such as Feng Xiaoning's *Red River Valley* (1996) and Zhang Yimou's *The Flowers of War* (2011). Two films I discuss in the last section push the envelope of heteroglossia and of what to sell: Huang Jianxin and Han Sanping's *The Founding of a Republic* (2009) and *The Founding of a Party* (2011). Both are epitomes of Chinawood and of the China Dream that refashion and re-vend national anthem at the restructured concourse of Tiananmen *Guangchang* (Square) in the new twenty-first century.

Chapter 6 concludes the book by scanning the articulations and representations of hip hop in a wide range of domains such as film, popular music, and the newly emerged digital culture in the last decade of the twentieth century and in the new millennium. I argue that Chinese hip hop and rap music are not merely a "knife" but a double-edged "sword" and a prism through which wide-ranging forces and ideologies are reflected. At one end, hip hop is closely associated with the hegemony of leisure, fashion, and consumer culture shaped and exploited by a large network of mass media, ranging from print culture, the music industry, radio, and television to film. At the other end, a group of cinephiles, musicophiles, and young amateur artists have geared their work towards an alternative and subversive ideology that favors the local, polyvocal, and individuality; thus emerges an indigenous and diversified Chinese voice, encompassing vernacular rap, the proliferation of the hip hop network, internet subculture, and cyberactivism on the heels of the digital and social media revolution. Case studies include musicians and artists such as MC Hotdog, Jay Chou, David Tao, the Hidden, Black Head, and Ah Gan and his witty hip hop parody film (e.g., *Happy*, 2009), all of whom have distinctively partaken in hip hop's global dialogue of race, space, and youth subculture, but, in all, are also a symptom of postsocialist reflexivity of the multinational, multiauthored, multicentered, and multimediatized reality. The last part of the chapter proceeds with a critical mapping of the Grass Mud Horse Style that signifies and furthers this new aura of image and sound making in light of technological and social change. Such carnivalesque recreation and defiance of official discourse and the communist orthodoxy can be found in the earlier practices of Northwest Wind, rock 'n' roll film, youth urban cinema, and even Leitmotif films, as I have explored. Challenges are moreover posed against the traditional sense of the cinematic and the centrality of the visual-celluloid.

Hence, *China in the Mix*, my exploration which is mixed with multiple genres, screens, realities, styles, ideologies, ethnographies, nationalities, languages, and possibilities. I take the title from the vital musical concept of "mixing" to develop my musical, acoustic, and cinematic mixing and rethinking. The act of audio mixing, in essence, involves disassembling and reassembling the original before rendering into a multitrack recording and a new palette in which the discrete tracks are made sense of and given new life in relation to each other. This trope makes a lot of sense for the project; my chief objective is to use film and film sound in particular as a lever to probe and obtain a fuller and relational picture of contemporary Chinese society and culture. With the allegorical use of folklore, sound, and silence in the Chinese New Wave, the youth-centered rock 'n' roll, the state-regulated voice of Leitmotif, and the new audiovisual culture of hip hop, contemporary China has undergone one after another and/or concomitantly manifold reforms, modernizations, transformations, and most of all, hybridizations. All of these attempts and changes are by no means a singular, monolithic, homogenous process, but are defined by the complex interplays of China's vernacular selves and the global others.

CHAPTER ONE

Northwest Wind: Folklore, Vernacular, and the Chinese New Waves

> Chen [Kaige]'s work plays a "truly revolutionary music"—"not music which expresses revolution in words, but which speaks of it as a lack."
> —**Rey Chow,** *Primitive Passions: Visuality, Sexuality, Ethnography, and Contemporary Chinese Cinema*[1]

In the last two decades of the twentieth century, a new wave of Chinese cinema emerged, astonishing festival-goers and catching the critical attention of film scholars and critics. Conceived in the heyday of the post-revolutionary market reform, this sweeping "wind" is often acclaimed as a "true" revolution in Chinese film. Its authors are the Fifth Generation, a grouping of eminent Chinese filmmakers synonymous with the Chinese New Wave.[2] The ensemble includes artists such as Zhang Junzhao, Chen Kaige, Zhang Yimou, Wu Ziniu, and Tian Zhuangzhuang, who graduated in the 1982 class of the Beijing Film Academy—the first privileged *coterie* to enter the university after the Cultural Revolution and receive formal training in film in the People's Republic of China (PRC).

Both a distinctive cinematic and a cultural trend, the Fifth Generation changed the roadmap of filmmaking and took Chinese film and culture onto a new path. The bold and creative deployment of lighting, color, and *mise-en-scène*, as well as the minimalist acting and plot, still shots, and jump cuts, fascinated film critics and scholars who quickly hailed the visual novelties of the new wave cinema. This experimentation has been valorized as a cinematic embodiment of modernism and as a return to the ontological film—to a purer sense of aesthetic, a revelation of "its structural depth," and a double act of deconstruction and reconstruction of "the preexisting," in the citation of

Bazin.³ The Fifth Generation filmmaking has therefore been named a movement and an epicenter of Chinese film studies. The topic has been privileged and most exhaustively explored for its high modernism, aesthetic experimentalism, and visual intensity.⁴

Yet what needs to be asked further is: in what ways, then, has the Fifth Generation's cinematic construct of the "truth" appropriated "the preexisting" socialist relations and legacies while engaging the newly fledged notions of popular mass culture to register the intense social, cultural, and ideological changes and conflicts in post-Mao China? My intervention is to treat the realistic, modernist undertakings of the Fifth Generation as by nature a dynamically *intermedial* and *bordercrossing* process. To borrow Miriam Hansen's formulation of "vernacular modernism," the Fifth Generation's "new modes of organizing vision and sensory perception" come into being through a simultaneous identification with and differentiation from international filmic discourses, growing out of the local, colloquial narrative, "of the quotidian, of everyday usage, with connotations of discourse, idiom, and dialect, with circulation, promiscuity, and translatability."⁵

Aiming to free themselves from the spell of the immediate revolutionary past and historical legacy, the Fifth Generation is brazenly radical, subversive, and defiant. Hence, wide-ranging variants of "anti"—anti-narrative, anti-historic, anti-cultural, anti-traditional, and anti-nationalist—are used to underwrite their stylistic strike against "the preexisting." This modernistic and iconoclastic thrust has characterized the early stage of the Fifth Generation's revolution. In conjunction with this high modernist aesthetic and ideology, I want to point out that what cannot be neglected in this cartgography, nonetheless, is a lively attachment to everyday life and a constructive impetus to anchor the newly emerging ideas, symbols, images, and sounds amid the ruins of Mao's establishments as well as in the new realities of market reform.

In my close examination of the Fifth Generation and subsequently the varied film practices in postsocialist China in the following chapters, I argue that a complex and compound picture such as this entails both a synchronic and a diachronic approach. By "synchronic" and "diachronic," I do not seek a comprehensive and exhaustive schematization, nor do I want to repeat a genealogical account along the axis of generations of filmmakers. Rather, I suggest *a vision out of the vision*, a method that looks beyond a central focalization on visual registers and harbors instead a more integrated and multisensory perspective that involves not only viewing but also listening to the music, sound, and linguistic nuances of the work. A parallel reading of the visualscape, soundscape, and languagescape allows us to see the Fifth Generation's cinematic-vernacular modernism as a crystallization of many visions, voices, positions, and tendencies. This multidimensional view of the cultural landscape in general, and audiovisual landscape in particular, is embodied in and facilitated by my broad adoption of the term: Northwest Wind (*Xibei feng*).

Northwest Wind, as broadly defined in my project, refers not only to a distinct narrative that sprang from popular literature and the prevalent ethos of the time—"root-seeking" (*xungen*)—but also to a popular musical form that blends the indigenous folklore of northwest China with the Western rhythms of disco and rock. The same cultural dynamic is imbricated within the films of the Fifth Generation. It is no accident that they were incubated in Xi'an Film Studio, the hub of the northwest region that has effectively become a cradle of New Chinese Cinema. From the mid-to-late 1980s to early 1990s, four of the flagship filmmakers (Chen Kaige, Tian Zhuangzhuang, Zhang Yimou, and Huang Jianxin) intensively worked with Wu Tianming, the then-head of Xi'an Film Studio who was an avid and outspoken patron of experimental films (*tansuo pian*). This period of tutelage was not only vital to the Fifth Generation's swift soar to a nationwide household name as well as a world brand, but was also a decisive influence on forging a characteristic film genre—the Western. As a result, at the turn of the 1980s and 1990s, a large number of excellent productions emerged and caught public attention, e.g., *The Old Well* (*Lao jing*, dir. Wu Tianming, 1986), *The Black Cannon Incident* (*Heipao shijian*, dir. Huang Jianxin, 1986), *The Horse Thief* (*Daomazei*, dir. Tian Zhuangzhuang, 1986), *Dislocation* (*Cuowei*, dir. Huang Jianxin, 1986), *King of the Children* (*Haizi wang*, dir. Chen Kaige, 1987), *Red Sorghum* (*Hong gaoliang*, dir. Zhang Yimou, 1988), and *Ju Dou* (dir. Zhang Yimou, 1990). In the words of Wu Tianming himself, Xi'an Film Studio has specialized in producing Westerns, an alternative, anthropological, and artistic handling of "close-to-home rural subjects," as distinguished from big "studios like those in Shanghai and Beijing [which] were best equipped to deal with urban subjects."[6] Thus, as a film genre, the early Fifth Generation film works have been often identified as cinematic versions of Northwest Wind—the Chinese Western—showcasing the vast, barren, and landlocked landscape of northwest China.

Northwest Wind keenly senses the main ideologies, aesthetics, and spirits at the heart of Chinese culture and society of the 1980s. Northwest Wind is exemplarily synchronic for it is a discursive narrative that encompasses a wide spectrum of discourses and mechanisms of 1980s China, yet it is also diachronic in the sense of being an open, fluid, heterogeneous, and ever-evolving discourse. I interpret Northwest Wind as an interlocking network of trends, phrases, codes, and signifiers of Chinese modernity during the ebb and flow of China's inaugural opening-up. By constantly juxtaposing, interlacing, and moving between the various musical, cinematic, and cultural discourses, this chapter shows that the connections between the enormous popularity of the musical genre known as Northwest Wind and the rise of the Fifth Generation in the mid-to-late 1980s are not merely a coincidence informed by the overlapping temporalities and shared subject matters. Furthermore, the many discourses of Northwest Wind represent both a historical and an aesthetic juncture that unpacks the problematics of "root-seeking" (*xugen*), "experimentation" (*tansuo*), vernacular modernism, the triumph of what Rey Chow terms forbidden and "primitive passions" (concretized and spectacularized by the intertexts of a raw indigenous landscape and a hyperbolic sexuality), and most importantly, a critical reflection on official Chinese rhetoric, individual subjectivity, and China itself at a time of social change.

The Politics and Poetics of Speech, Silence, and Folklore in Chen Kaige's *Yellow Earth*

Wholeheartedly embraced by film scholars and cultural critics as the best film that has ever come out of mainland China in the forty years since the 1949 founding of PRC, *Yellow Earth* is unanimously acknowledged as a milestone in Chinese filmmaking and a breaking point announcing the arrival of the Fifth Generation. Like many of the typical Fifth Generation films that followed it, this cinematic breakthrough is often noted for its catching visual images, experimental film language, bold thematic concerns, and, above all, its rupture from the films of the past as well as for its transnational engagement that took Chinese national cinema to the global screen almost for the first time. Additionally, I want to point out that the film stands out with rich, challenging evocations of Western music and traditional Chinese songs.

Inspired by the prevailing "root-seeking" impulse of the 1980s, *Yellow Earth* is an experiment that draws heavily on Chinese folk music of the northwest. Set in the vast and bleak plateau of northwestern China during the Sino-Japanese War, the film unfolds the difficult journey of a communist cadre, Gu Qing, who is dispatched to collect folk songs with the goal of transforming them into revolutionary propaganda. He stays in a drought- and hunger-stricken village with a poor family: a thirteen-year-old girl named Cuiqiao, her young brother Hanhan who does not speak much, and her widower father. When Gu Qing attempts to talk to the father about the mission of his trip, most of his speeches are met with apathy and silence. But his description of the freedom of marriage and liberation of women unexpectedly strikes a chord with the girl, who desperately looks to flee from her pre-arranged marriage. Gu is not able to take her to Yan'an (the headquarters of the Communist

Party during the Sino-Japanese War) due to the stiff dogma of the party. He leaves the village. In her attempt to escape, Cuiqiao sets out on her own to cross the river by singing the Communist song Gu has taught her.

Yellow Earth has been largely celebrated for its visual novelty and intensity. The technical amateurishness and wavering management of the film's music and sound were, however, deemed as noticeable weaknesses, especially in comparison to its visual style, as is commented in an article in the *Times* on August 8, 1986:

> Chen Kaige's *Yellow Earth* represents a new stage in the Chinese cinema's painful recovery from the depredations of the "Cultural Revolution." It was made in one of the small, newly established provincial studios which have given opportunity for young directors who might otherwise wait years for the chance to direct in the more hierarchical metropolitan studios. It has a refreshness and suppleness new to Chinese cinema, uses remote locations never seen on the screen before, and breaks away from the neatly packaged dogma and obligatory optimism of most precedent Commmunist film-making . . . A second viewing exposes weakness—moments of somewhat self-conscious artistry, shaky post-synchronization of the very taking folk music, and some inappropriate passages of background music quite inconsistent with the skillful manipulation of sound elsewhere in film. They are slight faults in such an encouraging first work.[7]

Paul Clark, a veteran scholar and a compassionate advocate of the Chinese New Wave, has questioned specifically the "clumsy" use of the lush chords of a full Western string orchestra on top of the "powerful" local songs. He goes on to express that this has posed a problem for Western spectators such as himself. This passing remark, nevertheless, does not progress beyond the general charges that the film music is "inappropriate" and "irrelevant,"[8] nor is there an explication of the music and sound system of the work to round out his objections. A thorough consideration of the larger socio-historical framework and of the complications of the auditory, technologized lapse is largely missing in these attempts.

For many, *Yellow Earth* is not simply a harbinger of post-revolutionary change, but a touchstone of filmmaking to come in China in the new reformist era. Its complex, creative visual arts have been well explored, but critics have not paid adequate attention to its sound, which functions similarly as an allegory and a peculiar means of historiography and ethnography. To Clark and many Western scholars, it is the incorporation of the extra-diegetic Western music that belies the film, negating the Chinese folk spirit intrinsic to the production. On the mainland, to the contrary, Chinese critics found the film's use of folklore and rituals rather confounding and problematic. A fierce attack was waged under the pseudonym of White Earth (*Bai tudi,* an obvious parody of the film title) on the reader's page of the August issue of *Contention* (*Zhengming,* an influential journal based on Hong Kong with the primary goals of introducing Western theories and facilitating critical discussions in China).[9] In a rather acerbic tone, White Earth pinpoints that the film's folk song compilation does not actually demonstrate the originality so often attributed to the film, but rather reveals a fabrication as clichéd as the majority of the communist literary works since the 1940s. It is even less rich and sophisticated than the typical folk literature of authors Li Ji, Zhao Shuli, Zhou Libo, and Liu Qing. In response to the mixed view, particularly the prevalent accusation that the scenes of waist-drum dance and rain prayer in *Yellow Earth* conjure up a baleful representation of Chinese peasant life and are two major technical flaws of the film, Shao Mujun, an active critic of the 1980s, holds that they are, in fact, "obviously and purposely constructed errors" with an allegorical, critical thrust.[10]

While the disjunctive points of view on *Yellow Earth* are revealing, few of them really fathom and place the soundtrack within its particular dramatic contexts, nor within the broader socio-historical network. What's more, these remarks barely paid attention to the film's dialogue and narration, another important aspect of sound that works together with music to shape a distinct aesthetic and culture in *Yellow Earth.* In order to better understand the meaning and dramatic function of the film's music, especially in the context of its mixed critical reception, I suggest that we must read both the film's visuality and its sonic performance simultaneously and altogether.

Yellow Earth is an earnest recounting and recitation of the film crew's fieldwork on Chinese folklore. As Esther Yau observes, "their [the filmmakers'] anthropological observations of the local people and their subcultures both enriched and shaped the narrative, cultural and aesthetic elements in the film . . . Obviously, anthropological details have been pretty well attended to."[11] According to Bonnie McDougall, who translated the film script into English and traced the complete course of making the film from its preproduction to reception, director Chen Kaige and his colleagues arranged multiple excursions to north Shaanxi in the early spring of 1984.[12] The film crew set up headquarters in Xi'an and spent a few weeks traveling extensively around the countryside, looking for suitable shooting locations while seeking inspiration to rewrite the script.

The film title and script were continuously revised during the shooting.[13] A considerable amount of revision—as well as significant additions—were made to the film music. The screenplay written by Zhang Ziliang, *Silence on the Ancient Plain* (*Guyuan wusheng*), was based on a short prose piece by Ke Lan titled *Echo in the Valley* (*Shenggu huisheng*), which itself had little to do with music. Chen Kaige himself participated extensively in the script and music design. The folk songs that appear in the film were based upon the materials collected by the film team in northern Shaanxi. Like the fictional protagonist Gu Qing in *Yellow Earth*, the filmmaker set his own *caifeng* excursion (which literally means "scouting around for folklores" in Chinese) to the yellow earth, as documented in the following passage:

> Hearing that there were a lot of peasants in the area who knew many local songs, they invited people to sing for them. One man in his late thirties, He Yutang, first refused, saying that once he started singing he was unable to control himself and would not be able to stop for two to three hours. They heard him out, and it was true that he lost himself entirely in his singing: he would laugh or cry and seemed almost crazy. Asked who taught him the songs, he said that no-one had taught him, but that his grandfather often used to sing. He himself was very poor, only barely able to support his family of four or five children. Chen Kaige was very moved by this man's singing and decided to record his songs. They met another three times and became good friends. The character of the poor singer in the film is based on him.[14]

Moreover, it evokes a kind of reminiscence of the filmmakers' own life experience in the Cultural Revolution. It can be said that the Fifth Generation is a generation of *zhiqing* (educated youth) who were uprooted from their high (or junior high) schools in the city and sent to labor in China's most backward countryside during the Cultural Revolution. Admission to the Beijing Film Academy granted them a ticket to move back to the city after misspending their youth in the countryside. It is not coincidental that many of their early works are structured around a painstaking but fruitless expedition on foot to the faraway marginal areas of China, as in *Yellow Earth*, *King of the Children*, and *The Horse Thief*. In *Yellow Earth*, as the filmmaker exclaims, it is not simply the piercing and painful singing but the awe-inspiring silence that deeply moves them and preoccupies their camera during the trip. *Yellow Earth* starts from this point.

The film begins with a dark screen, against which the opening credits—identifying the film title, literary source, production studio, and major crew members—are highlighted in red and yellow. This informs the film's stylistic color scheme—the juxtaposition and contrast of the monochromatic black, red, and yellow. Running concurrently on the soundtrack is an excerpt of an extremely high-pitched melody played by *suona*,¹⁵ representative of the musical style of northwest China. A caption of yellow small seal-clerical scripts rolls up slowly against the dark screen:

> In September 1937, the establishment of the United Front against Japanese aggression forced Jiang Jieshi to acknowledge the status of the Shaanxi-Gansu-Ningxia Border Area. Because of the persistence of Nationalist local government in parts of central Shaanbei, despite the cooperation between the Nationalists and the Communists, feudalism was still deeply entrenched and the people still suffered under heavy oppression. In this ancient land, the melodies of *xintianyou* (a folk song genre, literally meaning roving around under the sky) drift the year around. Members of the literature and arts troupes of the Eighth Route Army formed into teams and fanned out in different directions. They hoped to find the origins of Shaanbei folk song . . .¹⁶

The music, color design, and Chinese calligraphy, emblematic of ancient Chinese civilization, all work together to give the film a feel of primitiveness and historicity. After the film nails down its diegetic time—early spring 1939—the camera lapses into a set of empty shots of the vast and barren landscape.

The opening shots of *Yellow Earth* introduce a distinct audiovisual rhetoric delivering and defining the important message of the film. The first shot is a nearly ten-second static long shot of the wild, rocky mountain with a sliver of the skyline at the very top of the frame. Sky only takes up a very narrow strip of the frame on the top, whereas the vast, bleak landscape almost overwhelms the rest of the frame. Then the film moves to an overexposed image of the immense, seemingly never-ending land, as the camera slowly pans right until a human figure emerges out of a distant land *tout de suite*. This shot of a human figure is an extreme long shot. In this composition, in reverse, it is the massive sky that dominates the frame with a land now depicted as an even slimmer sliver. In the first two minutes of *Yellow Earth*, what unfolds before us is an extravagant cinematic experience, crafted deliberately through slow pacing, minimalist sound, and special visual effects.

The breathtaking and strongly pictorial images have become a constitutive aspect of the film genre—the Chinese Western. The unusual compositions of the disproportionate frame dominated by the colossal plateau, the Yellow River, and other awe-inspiring natural elements; the exceptional high and low horizon line shots at extreme angles; the small human figure dwarfed by the vast landscape—each of these visual elements can be attributed to the Chinese Taoist philosophy that emphasizes the interdependence and harmony between human beings and nature. Another Chinese aesthetic tradition is also called to mind: When the camera pans horizontally and vertically, the effect resembles the display of a classical scroll painting. Furthermore, the restricted and minimalist color scheme, consisting primarily of yellow, black, and red, recalls the Chinese water-ink landscape paintings (*shuimo shanshui hua*).

Adroitly deploying varied kinds of shots (extreme long shot, medium shot, shot-reverse-shot, point-of-view shot), camera movements (vertical panning and horizontal panning), film angles (extreme low angle and high angle), and special visual effects (washed-out shots, superimposition, and time-lapse photography), the first sequence of *Yellow Earth* is infused with rich visuality. The pleasurably heterogenous and discordant images come together in a remarkably constrained yet penetrating way. The sound aesthetic paired with these shots is also minimalist, ruled by silence. Only the sporadic croaking of a crow (considered an unfavorable omen in traditional Chinese culture, thus foreshadowing the tragic ending of the film) and an almost inaudible whistling of wind sweeping the boundless land disturb what would otherwise be dead silence. As a whole, *Yellow Earth*'s opening sequence uses well-orchestrated audiovisual elements to convey the sense of bleakness and mystery suggested by its original script title, *Silence on the Ancient Plains*. Chen Kaige has therefore summarized the film in Taoist aesthetic terms as "*dayin xisheng, daxiang wuxin*" (the most majestic music would be inaudible; the most magnificent image would be formless).[17] Chen commemorates his pilgrimage to the sublime music, image, and land in a sentimental tone:

> Whenever the Yellow River is mentioned, people think of its rumbling, roaring majesty. But when we stood by the Yellow River, its calm and peacefulness struck us more deeply. Carving open two clifflike banks of stone, it flows confidently and freely, displaying its bold and free form as it quietly flows on. Seen from high up and far away between the hills and mountains, it does not seem to be moving at all and appears to have congealed and set. But it is precisely this quality that shows it is a great river. By its side is the land that has been dry for so long, empty and barren. It made us think of countless thousands of years of historical misfortune.[18]

The film's setting of the yellow earth and Yellow River—the heart of Chinese civilization—along with the exhaustive camera shots and deliberately crafted sound endows the piece an epic quality and an allegorical overtone. Cinematographer Zhang Yimou has also maintained that in comparison to its precursor, *One and Eight* (dir. Zhang Junzhao, 1983), the first work from the Fifth Generation that has stressed dynamic forces, the newer film, *Yellow*

Earth, carries a quiet and still strength.¹⁹ The allegorical meaning of the yellow earth and Yellow River, which have given birth to and nurtured Chinese civilization and the Chinese people, is made abundantly clear throughout the film. The enormous strength and enduring power hidden beneath the quietness and stillness of the land and river then become a touchstone defining the stylistic manner and audiovisual traits of *Yellow Earth*. Images of majestic land and the engrossing and languid river are rendered in extreme long shots and wide angles, captured by a noticeably stationary camera. When the camera moves, it pans slowly. Static shots, long, slow pans, and patient narrative construction are all in compliance with the restrained dialogue, bleak singing, and deliberate silence. Such aesthetic choices are used to depict moments of stasis in Chinese history, to express a longing for gradual change and evolution, and to display the filmmaker's witty criticism of the central tenet of radical change propelled during the communist revolution.

At first sight, *Yellow Earth* appears to be another film adhering to a set of propagandist clichés. It resembles a realistic recounting of a communist campaign during the 1930s and 1940s, when a large number of cultural workers were sent to the remote countryside to collect and record the "vox populi," the voice of the people. More importantly, they were dispatched to the hinterland to educate and transmit communist political views to the peasant class. Traditional folk song became a high stake in this nascent nation-building project. This specific political and socio-historical context has discursively shaped the narrative, especially the characterization of the soldier-protagonist Gu Qing. But on second thought, is this a propagandist film? Or does it suggest a departure from the previous socialist model? When talking about folk music, do peasants and communist soldiers mean the same thing? Do they understand each other? Does Gu Qing accomplish his task? Does his visit bring any change to the village? Are the peasants' good wishes to no longer starve and endure forced marriage fulfilled at the end of *Yellow Earth*?

Following the establishing shots of the raw, seemingly uninhabited landscape, a series of long shots leads to pans in which an army soldier in a grey-blue uniform with a small backpack is introduced. Gu Qing walks alone gradually from the distance to the foreground of the screen. As he comes nearer and his face becomes clearer in a medium shot, Gu is shown turning his head to the right path up the mountain, listening to something intently: "Life is hard for seasonal workers. They are hired in January, dismissed in October." The song is distant but piercing. It is filled with loneliness and suffering. On the screen is a still long shot of the immense, nearly bare hill, with only a solitary, tiny tree perched on the crest in the very far background. The frame lasts six seconds before the camera cuts back to Gu standing on the high cliff alone. Gu listens and takes out his pen, but the song dissipates just as he begins to write down the words in his notebook, an action he will repeat during his stay in this region. This first audiovisual collaboration quite effectively introduces the protagonist as a communist cultural worker and illustrates the initiative of his visit. The crosscutting between the lone soldier and the only tree on the hill reoccurs three times in this short sequence, which cinematically draws an analogy between the two and lays out the essential tone of the film.

This scene is then suddenly cut short as the camera pans and shifts to the march of a traditional Chinese wedding on the yellow plateau in an ethnographic, documentary style. As the film switches back to refocus on Gu Qing a few minutes later, he is seen arriving in a village in the midst of a wedding banquet. The village leader introduces him to men seated at the banquet table as a public officer sent from Yan'an: "Folks, this soldier has come to our village to collect songs." The farmers seem to show little interest in this newcomer and simply reply with "uh" and short interjections of "Eat! Drink!" After joining the group apprehensively, Gu catches a strain of another song. Hurriedly putting down his chopsticks and taking his pen out of his pocket, he starts to take notes. The camera cuts to a close-up of the farmers at the same table looking at him perplexedly. Gu Qing replies as if to himself and with an uneasy smile: "He sings very well!" The man sitting next to him has a final response: "Yes, but in terms of finding a wife, that 'small monk' is worthless. He is already thirty and still hasn't found a wife. All he can do is to sing a *suanqu'er* (sour tune)."

This wedding banquet sequence, following the slow beginning of the film, is one of the most compellingly allegorical scenes signifying some of the central ironies and paradoxes in *Yellow Earth*. Firstly, the freeze-frame shot of the peasant crowd has been repeated six times in this sequence. Squeezing the heads of the peasants to the very bottom of the frame, with sometimes only half of their faces appearing on the screen, recalls the novel landscape cinematography in the opening scene. Despite the unusual ratio of human figures to the wedding house at the background, peasants stand out markedly in the foreground with their expressionless, unidentifiable faces and uniformed, starched outfits (all wearing a dark blue cotton jacket). In addition, a stark contrast between Gu's soliloquy and the peasants' silent response reaffirms and enhances a sense of solitude, repression, and entrapment, which is central to the film.

Secondly, this scene, alongside the wedding march sequence, introduces the film's heroine, Cuiqiao, as an anxious spectator to the wedding (thus foreshadowing her own). The camera highlights her in a medium close-up—alert

Yellow Earth (1984): The opening landscape shot and the first appearance of northwest folklore.

and bewildered—leaning against the door of the wedding house much like a statue. In a form of shot-reverse-shot, the film constantly cuts to the surroundings, presumably motivated by her look, and again moves back to her as she remains motionless throughout the entire sequence. The still image of Cuiqiao has been inserted as many as five times. She looks different because of the red jacket she wears, which distinguishes her from the crowd and establishes an intertextual link between her and the bride; the scene also insinuates doubt and critique of patriarchy, effectively delivered and verbalized through the *mise-en-scène*. In these repeated shots, Cuiqiao takes up the center of the frame in contrast to a Chinese couplet pasted on the door behind her that reads "*sancong sede*" (Three Obedience and Four Merits, a Confucius-derived code that restricts and regulates women's behavior in traditional Chinese society). The inscription is clearly shown in deep focus. It is a cynical commentary and a signifier of Cuiqiao's repressed sexuality, and furthermore a prediction of her tragic future. Cuiqiao does not utter a single word throughout the scene. But the *mise-en-bande*—the playing of *suona*, sputtering of the firecrackers, chattering of the crowd, grievous singing of a poor villager, and plethora of ambient noise in the wedding banquet and Cuiqiao's surroundings—aptly articulates her repression and suggests her fate.

Thirdly, this scene furnishes the first instance of language choice that would become the principal paradox punctuating *Yellow Earth*. To Gu Qing, this kind of song is *shaanbei min'ge* (Shaanbei folk song), whereas the villagers insist on using their own vernacular exclusively, referring to it as *suanqu'er* (sour tune). The film distinguishes these two different denominations and associates them with two distinct groups and ideologies respectively. "Sour

Yellow Earth (1984): Cuiqiao and the wedding sequence.

tune" is a colloquial phrase in a native tongue and a local classification linked with the poor villagers, whereas "Shaanbei folk song" is a new concept formulated by the top administration that addresses the same thing in a more official way. As a whole, *Yellow Earth* has adopted three different designations: *suanqu'er* (sour tune), *shaanbei min'ge* (Shaanbei folk song), and *xintianyou* (roving around under the sky, a formal and scholarly appellation that only appears in the introductory passage of the film), all of which signify the same type of music and a major popular subgenre of folk song in the northern part of Shaanxi province.[20] While these variants may demonstrate the complexity of the music genre, the different interpretations, depending on the agent who classifies the music and for what reasons, foreground the conflict between the party and the people.

The conflict is further echoed and heightened via an auditory, linguistic, and cinematic representation in the following scene. After the young peasant finishes his song, servers bring a dish to the table. It is fish, yet it gives the odd appearance of a wooden simulation. The old man at Gu's table taps the fish with his chopsticks, making a hollow sound: "It is wood. It is just for the meaning." A symbolic device, the pivotal image of fish in an extreme close-up functions to suggest several layers of meaning. Fish, an indispensable dish at Chinese feasts, is homophonous to *yu* (surplus). It denotes a good will for material affluence and prosperity in Chinese culture. At the same time, it alludes to another popular analogy, in which the Communist Party figuratively compares itself to fish, with the masses so described as water essential to fish. Constructed as "*junmin yushui qing*" in communist China, this metaphor suggests the vital relationship and interdependence between the party and the people. In this scene in *Yellow Earth,* fish retains its traditional implication as an auspicious symbol, but it is faked and lifeless in this dry highland. Having thus undermined the socialist mythology that claims to have transformed the fate of Chinese peasants, this imagery, in an ironic way, denounces the long-cherished narrative of the ideology unity between the people and the party.

This key theme finds resonance in another iconic sequence involving both music and food. In one of the few scenes shot in broad daylight, the four main characters are shown sitting in a circle on the ground of the yellow plateau and eating after the hard labor of a full morning. It is a meal between sky and earth, with the Yellow River flowing at the foot of the cliff beneath them. The scene is peaceful and quiet, with the early spring sun at noon lending a warm touch to the human figures. A conversation suddenly erupts: "*Gongjia housheng* (Young officer), what was it you said last night you were collecting?" Gu Qing replies: "To collect our *shaanbei min'ge* (Shaanbei folk songs)." Cuiqiao's father for the first time bursts into laughter: "*Sha min'ge* (What folk songs)!? They are just *suanqu'er* (Sour tunes)!" The disagreement proceeds no further. Gu Qing and the old man never argue explicitly about the discrepancy of the names or the music genre itself in the film.

Later, when Gu Qing asks the old man if he can sing, he responds impassively: "I'm not either happy or sad. Why should I sing now?" Gu Qing continues: "There are hundreds and thousands of our Shaanbei folk songs. Tell me, how can you know them all, and remember them all?" The father remains stoic: "You remember them when times are hard. You collect sour tunes for what use?" Having recorded the full conversation, the scene is comprised of continuous long takes lasting over twenty seconds each. They are stationary medium shots from a slightly low angle, placing Gu and the old man at the two sides of the frame, with the young boy sitting in between, and Cuiqiao captured in the foreground. This visual composition suggests a spatial distance between Gu Qing and Cuiqiao's family, but it also alludes to the disparity of the two musical-political groups they embody: Shaanbei folk song *vis-à-vis* sour tune, the official *vis-à-vis* the vernacular, and the party *vis-à-vis* the people.

In replying to the old man's suspicion, Gu Qing starts to explain his rationale eloquently:

> When we've collected the folk songs and written new words to them, we turn them over to the Eighth Route Army troops, boys and girls of Cuiqiao's age to sing, so everyone can understand why our suffering people are living in fear and wretchedness, why wives and daughters are beaten, why laborers and farmers are carrying out a revolution . . . Our Chairman Mao and

Commander Zhu love listening to folk songs. Our chairman Mao doesn't just get us to sing, he also gets us to read and write. All the girls in Yan'an go around with a stone tablet under their arms, they write, draw . . . Our chairman Mao wants to get all of our suffering people of China to eat millet without husks or weeds.

In a low, affectionate voice, Gu Qing seems to be deeply immersed in his own thoughts. The camera rapidly moves around to zoom in on his audience—Cui Qiao, the old man, the young boy—as if in an attempt to comment on this didactic lengthy speech. They all keep their heads down. Their faces show nothing but stolid indifference. Their eyes confess nothing but emptiness. Once again, the film underscores the irony of ideology through the deliberately designed juxtapositions and interactions between the audio and the visual. The family's stationary position takes up a large part of the screen, as opposed to the lecturer Gu Qing who retreats from the center, shying away from the camera. In particular, the masterful transfusion of abrupt impasse and silence forms a sharp contrast with and satirizes Gu's pompous proclamation.

Gu's superfluous monologues hardly elicit any reaction except for one brief moment. When Gu addresses the suffering of women and moves to a conclusion that ultimately links his action of collecting folk songs to the cause of helping the poor eat properly, the camera cuts to an extreme close-up of Cuiqiao. At this point, she slowly lifts her eyes, looks into Gu Qing with a mixed expression of curiosity and skepticism, and then ducks her head again. This is one of the very rare moments in *Yellow Earth* in which Gu's explanation for communist theory sparks some kind of engagement with his listeners. It soon sinks to an even more prolonged silence, and a crane shot of the four sitting together quietly again on the tableland beside the Yellow River as if nothing had just happened.

The tension between the dueling voices of the party and the masses remains unresolved, reaching a climax when Cuiqiao makes her last, desperate attempt to cross the Yellow River after Gu leaves the village. Similar to the previous sequences in which Cuiqiao is frequently framed in natural or somewhat low-key lighting, her face is almost unidentifiable in the extreme darkness when a long tracking shot follows the protagonist rowing a little boat across the river. One comes to recognize Cuiqiao through her singing of the revolutionary song that Gu Qing has taught her and her younger brother Hanhan:

With sickle, axe, and hoe
We open a road for peasants to go

Yellow Earth (1984): Gu Qing's lecture and his audiences.

Upon the wall the spotted rooster flies
Only the Communist Party can save the people's lives.

Sickle, axe, and hoe are visual symbols representing the social classes of peasant and worker; they give actual form to the emblematization of the Chinese Communist Party. As Cuiqiao rows the boat and disappears in the picture, her song is abruptly cut off and altogether engulfed by the roaring river, which drowns the last syllable of *dang* (party) in *gongchandang* (Communist Party) in her last line. The camera pans up to the misty sky enveloping the dim moon, cuts to a close-up of Hanhan who cries out for his sister, and then fades out to show the turbulent river that overwhelms the soundtrack. The linguistic nuance and carefully crafted audiovisual collaboration work to generate a sense of ambiguity and irony intrinsic to the film. Does Cuiqiao die? If so, is this really a suicide? Or is she actually killed by someone or something? Why is she singing the communist song? What are the implications behind it? I posit this as another exemplary scene in *Yellow Earth*, in which music and sound effects (a sudden halt, followed by a silence) are integrated to problematize and satirize the ambivalent relations between the party and the people. Coupled with rich visual signifiers, these aural puns function to debunk the legitimacy and justification of the official communist ideology, which presumably assumes a unified and homogenous national identity represented by the party.

Synthetically interwoven into the texture of the film, silence is a very powerful device. It enhances ambivalent imageries and creates an open-ended interpretation, as shown above. Silence in *Yellow Earth* voices the reality of daily life, its monotony, contradictions, and innate immutability. This is used to good effect in another scene, where Cuiqiao anxiously waits for her aged groom on her wedding night. A close-up focuses on the big dark hand as it approaches and unveils the bride. Silence prevails except for the girl's fearful gasps, parallel with her frightened eyes on the screen, both of which heighten a sense of terror. Speaking of *Yellow Earth*'s use of silence, Rey Chow cites Geoffrey O'Brien's comments:

> Out of imposed muteness came a film language consisting of splendid images seen in isolation—an empty sky, a river basin, a weather-roughened face, a ceremonial procession—hemmed in by a strained terseness suggesting multiple layers of historical, political, and social meaning that could not be directly stated. Nothing, it appeared, could be more challenging in the wake of the Cultural Revolution than sharply defined pictures devoid of any obvious didactic purpose, surrounded by silence and open to multiple interpretations.[21]

Chow states that it is "actually a way to criticize China's status quo and a form of political resistance."[22] This denotative and allegorical reading of silence seems to be an allusion to Ludwig Wittgenstein's well-known proposition: "What we cannot speak about we must pass over in silence."[23] It also brings to mind another aphorismatic saying by Lu Xun, the best known author in modern Chinese literature. In the foreword to *Wild Grass*, he writes: "When I am silent, I feel replete; as I open my mouth to speak, I am conscious of emptiness."[24] Silence is a potent aesthetic apparatus to express the unspoken and the unspeakable, especially when considering modern Chinese history in general and 1980s Chinese film production in particular, both of which are intricately defined and tangled with the highly centralized state system and censorship.

In his memoir of making *Yellow Earth*, Chen Kaige explains his propensity for silence and nature:

> Northern Shaanxi is peaceful. There are mountains and hillocks, ravines and gullies, and not a sound anywhere. But the scenery is very dramatic and strong. This silent land produced our *xintianyou* folk melodies. Many years ago—there was a high hill, a flock of sheep, and a shepherd. After lingering for a long time, he sang in a high, sonorous voice that could be heard for miles around. Once the song was over, all returned to silence. Standing on that hilltop made me think of many things, including how the earliest adventures of the nation were linked to this grand and majestic natural environment, and how its earliest culture was born out of this silence.[25]

Silence and empty landscape in Chen's film are endowed with rich meanings; they are sophisticated audiovisual signifiers that artfully communicate the filmmaker's historical understanding, cultural awareness, and national identity. Hence, in addition to simplicity and solidity, Chen adopts another term to encapsulate *Yellow Earth*: "*cang*" (hidden), which, to him, is an ideological and aesthetic orientation leading to a distinct system of allegory in the film.²⁶ Many scholars (for instance, Zhang Xudong, Zhang Yingjin, and Rey Chow) also draw on Fredric Jameson's notion of "national allegory" as a frame of reference for reading and interpreting the Fifth Generation films. While allegory becomes an essential and predominant mode in the 1980s Chinese New Wave, the experiment of the Fifth Generation is likewise an allegory of 1980s China itself. Their unwavering effort to pursue cinematic depth and "hidden" truth is mediated through both visual parables and stylistic, often allegorical sound devices.

Yellow Earth captures Gu's eloquent speech and emotional expression in sharp contrast to the aloof and voiceless reaction of his mass audience. Conflict and irony are built not only via audio, through the antithesis of excessive speech and dead silence, but also visually, through the camera that often intentionally positions the soldier in a separate frame from the peasant crowds. In this way, he is rendered as an outsider and an alien, as opposed to an abstraction of revolution and modernity as seen in the conventional socialist texts. Gu is mostly shot in full lighting. The bright color also differentiates him; his light grey uniform appears in stark contrast to his dark surroundings. Throughout the entire film, from the opening until the very last shot, Gu is always portrayed as a solitary, lonely traveler, trekking on the rough yellow plateau.

Perhaps the most disturbing and what might be termed "carnivalesque" Bakhtinian moments of the film occur when attending to the binary between the communist soldier and the peasantry: a traditional wedding that has been repeated twice (the first at the beginning of the film, the second for Cuiqiao's own wedding), the waist-drum dancing cut in just after Cuiqiao's wedding night, and the last scene of rain prayer. All seem to break with this otherwise extremely slow-paced and quiet film and are often criticized as a kind of "self-subalternizing, self-exoticizing visual gestures" to cater to Western voyeurism.²⁷ These seemingly strident, self-Orientalist scenes, however, actually introduce a new dramatic twist, a new optical perspective, and a new aural situation.

In the previous section, I have closely examined the opening wedding sequence that calls attention to the malignity of Confucian patriarchy and the futility of Chinese revolution, intellectual enlightenment, and modernization. A hilarious drum-dancing sequence is later injected halfway through the film.

It gives a new rhythm and transforms *Yellow Earth* from a slow-boiled melodrama to a national saga. Contrasting with the rest of the story are the carnivalesque, celebratory, bright hues seen in this particular scene: a vigorous revolutionized peasantry in Yan'an as opposed to the lethargic, lifeless, static peasantry on the yellow earth; and the flagrant, robust virility as opposed to the dreary wedding and devastating girl in the preceding sequences. What is the most remarkable is not simply the way in which Chen masterly employs various shots (long shot, medium shot, close-up, panning, and tracking) to construct the most (and probably the only) animated scene in *Yellow Earth*, but how a distinct, polyphonic audiovisual space is created. A long take of nearly thirty seconds captures a cohort of young men dancing and vociferating wildly to the clamorous uproar of drum and *suona*. As if dancing with the raucous, deafening din, a low-angle shot looking up tightly from the waist level is mobile, shaky, and raw. Faces of dancing peasants bluntly pop in before the handheld, drifting camera. This evokes a sense of documentary realism and recalls the classic portrayal of collective power and nationalist discourse in many leftist films, including *Street Angel* (*Malu tianshi*, dir. Yuan Muzhi, 1937), *Song at Midnight* (*Yeban gesheng*, dir. Maxu weibang, 1937), and *Children of Troubled Times* (*Fengyun ernv*, dir. Xu Xingzhi, 1935).

Yet the exuberant and bright high spirits in Yan'an are soon replaced and nullified by another carnival—a somber, despondent, and superstitious rain prayer that closes and circles *Yellow Earth* back to its original dryness, darkness, and silence. The last scene shows Hanhan running against a large stream of the afflicted, praying peasants and toward Gu Qing arduously. At last, Gu returns to this small village. He walks from afar as if it were the beginning of the film. This tiny human figure emanating from a sliver of land and immense sky is a re-enactment of the opening shot with only a slightly tilted angle. Is this Hanhan's hallucination? Or does Gu Qing really come back to rescue the "backward," hungry, and thirsty masses? *Yellow Earth* does not provide us with definite answers and the conclusion we are offered is in the form of an empty shot of the enormous, grainy land, when the camera gradually sinks down and the closing credits begin to roll. Resonant on the soundtrack is once again Cuiqiao's shrill singing: "Upon the wall the spotted rooster flies. Only the Communist Party can save the people's lives."

Considered a monumental work that marks "the end of conventional, melodramatic films and the birth of a new genre in Chinese filmmaking,"[28] *Yellow Earth* is groundbreaking not only in terms of its anti-political ideology and spectacular visuality, but also in terms of its sound practice and the dynamic, innovative interactions between sound and image. Music, silence, and speech are carefully aligned, juxtaposed, and sometimes contrasted with the modernist, savory use of *mise-en-scène,* camerawork, lighting, color, and other visual devices in order to build moments of metaphors and symbolism. The deliberate and extensive use of folk songs further hinges upon a dialectic between the filmmaker's attachment to cultural tradition on the one hand and his aspirations to pursue new forms of personal freedom and artistic creativity on the other.

Yellow Earth's film score was composed by Zhao Jiping, a celebrated musician based in Xi'an and a lifelong collaborator with Chen Kaige and many other Fifth Generation filmmakers. The lyrics were reported to be a product of a collective effort, conducted under the meticulous supervision of Chen Kaige. The soundtrack recording for the film was mostly done in Xi'an, with songs rerecorded at Xi'an Film Studio. Notwithstanding that *Yellow Earth*'s sound was critically dismissed as lacking—especially the postdubbing of a professional singer for Cuiqiao's folklore singing accompanied by Western-style orchestration[29]—the film has exploited to the fullest the potential of music to construct story and its prime allegories. Since *Yellow Earth* features little dialogue, the type of folk song, *xintianyou*, is especially constitutive. Its discerning integration into the narrative creates moments of expectation and suspense, in addition to illustrating some of the key dynamics of the film.

For instance, on the night before Gu Qing leaves the village, he gets his first and only opportunity to hear Cuiqiao's father sing. The bleak solo performance goes on as such: "Betrothed at thirteen, becoming a wife at fourteen, a widow at fifteen and for the rest of her life . . . Three low cries, she jumps into the well." The song accompanies the crosscuttings between a close-up of a singing father and a long shot of Cuiqiao's silhouette, alluding to Cuiqiao's own predicament and wretched life. Cuiqiao's melancholic singing is also heard as she sees Gu Qing off in the scene that follows. "I'm afraid that from now on I'll never see you again," Cuiqiao laments, as she cannot see a way out of her poverty and impending marriage. She sings:

Behind the cloud, the sun dips low.
My lips can't speak, my heart is sorrow.
Green grass and cow dung can't put out a fire.
Folk songs can't save me, poor Cui Qiao, poor Cui Qiao . . .

By means of a musical autobiography, this diegetic solo not only literalizes Cuiqiao's innermost feeling almost for the first time but also foretells and sets in motion a series of complications that will lead to the penultimate, ambivalent scene of her crossing the river (discussed earlier). Another song of particular significance in *Yellow Earth* is "Song of the Daughter" (*Nv'er ge*).

Yellow Earth (1984): Cuiqiao, the Yellow River, and "Song of the Daughter."

It becomes a musical metonym and leitmotif for Cuiqiao, recurring throughout the film in scenes where Cui Qiao fetches water from the Yellow River day in and day out. The varied shots of Cuiqiao carrying out her daily chore and enduring her pain quietly are juxtaposed with and complemented by her forlorn singing, speaking explicitly to her distress, sorrow, and the despairing future of impossible change both in the conventional patriarchal order as well as under the new revolutionary conditions.

Yellow Earth's tactical employment of folklore has a historical-cultural root and a particularly vernacular nature, which is inseparably tied to the locale of northwest China, a distinct region with a rich tradition of folk songs. All of these musical numbers and motifs recall "Blue Flower" (*Lan Huahua*), both thematically and aesthetically, a famed *xintianyou* song that laments the disastrous arranged marriages prevalent among peasant girls in rural northern China.[30] Enriched with refined images, *Yellow Earth* extends and enhances the sense of sentimentalism, "sourness," and sarcasm often associated with *xintianyou*. In style, Cuiqiao's songs feature high tessitura, especially an extremely high cry at the outset, and a fairly free rhythm alongside a formulaic narrative that makes constant reference to a season or a time marker. These are characteristic traits of *xintianyou* that have been stylistically carried over and reassembled in the new film context, endowing *Yellow Earth* with a remarkably indigenous voice and sophisticated implications.

The Big Parade, *King of the Children*, and Allegories of Sound

The minimalist yet richly "hidden" (*cang*) audiovisual representation that seeks to underline the uncertainty, ambiguity, and ambivalence of the relationship between human and nature, tradition and reform, nation and individuality has become the defining feature of many Chen's films. Chen's next production, *The Big Parade* (*Da yuebing*, 1986), extends the thematic concerns and artistic vision from his earlier works, but approaches these problematics from a different angle. Set in a contemporary milieu closely linked to the immediate reality, rather than projecting the sociopolitical occurrence from the distance of "root-seeking" (as in *Yellow Earth*), *The Big Parade* is a hyperrealistic account with a documentary feel that records the imminent event referenced in its title, PRC's thirty-fifth anniversary parade in 1984. An intimate investigation of the soldiers of the People's Liberation Army who work devotedly for this grand event, the film displays Chen's signature style in its image and narrative composition, with sound playing a vital role. Paul Clark writes:

> Originally Chen planned to make the film with synchronized sound recording, a considerable innovation in Chinese filmmaking which Wu Ziniu was about to achieve with his banned *Dove Tree*. But the disadvantage of working at a smaller studio became apparent when the equipment necessary for on-location recording was not available and could not be borrowed from one of the larger studios. Sound recording in the finished film, however, retains a complexity and a dialectic with the images that are central to *The Big Parade*'s impact.[31]

So, what complex dialectic between sound and image is specified and harmonized in the film? Throughout *The Big Parade*, powerful and striking visual images are at once complemented and contrasted by voice-overs of the central characters, who have only revealed their true emotions and thoughts to the camera from off-screen. The often perplexing, distressed, and cynical narration lends the film a kind of gritty, raw, quasi-documentary quality—in addition to a sense of uncertainty. As Tony Rayns notes in his observation of *The Big Parade*: "Visual certainties are undermined by aural uncertainties, and this disjunction helps to push the film into a symbolic register."[32] Rayns is right in that, compared to the predominant deployment of darkness, which has almost become a hallmark of the Fifth Generation film, the dazzling brightness and abundant overexposed shots in *The Big Parade* markedly distinguish the film. However, I disagree with his statement of the film's "visual certainities" and the "disjunction" between the visual and the audio handling of the film. In my opinion, the extreme high-key lighting and the different visual treatment do not help clarify the picture any better than darkness does, just as a lengthy speech does not necessarily provide any more meaning than silence does, as is testified earlier in *Yellow Earth*. For me, the visual construction coordinates with the aural and both of them are highly ambivalent in *The Big Parade*.

Superimposed with the film credits, the opening sequence provides an overview of the parading soldiers on the square with a bird's-eye shot and slow panning. Again, what can be heard in this scene is Chen's signature minimalist sound design, comprised of a bugle call, the uniform sound of marching boots, the loading of rifle guns, and an extra-diegetic, low-registered droning, all of which infuse the film with an ominous, military sort of feeling. In the next shot, a bundle of soldiers are introduced into the frame as they go through rigorous medical inspection and outfitting prior to months of training. They step in from the blaze of the noon sun outside the barracks, walk out into the heat, and blur again. The bleary images and close-ups of the various fragments of male bodies render this group of soldiers an almost indistinct, indistinguishable whole. Instead of human beings' voices, the first four minutes of *The Big Parade* has been largely dominated by silence, interspersed with the extremely high-pitched screechy noise. It acoustically alludes to the grim, menacing, and coercive nature of the parade.

The actual footage of the Tiananmen parade appended to the end of *The Big Parade* at the insistence of the censors contains similarly mixed signals. Initially, Chen planned to end the film with an empty shot of Tiananmen Square in full silence, which might have served as a cynical commentary on both the military training and the parade itself. But this idea did not pass the Beijing Film Bureau's rigorous examination. The film was not approved until the alteration of the ending with actual footage of the parade. For the very last minute of the film, Chen manipulates the official footage, replaying it at a slower speed on purpose. The slow motion has again created a fuzzy and ambiguous image of the anonymous ranks of soldiers as they march across Tiananmen Square mechanically, as though they are emotionally blank. Meanwhile, the pensive, melancholic funeral music accompanying the scene serves as another wry comment on the presumably solemn, divine moment of the nation. The last shot of *The Big Parade* is a backlit, twenty-second freeze-frame of a close-up of the shadowy and completely unidentifiable face of a soldier standing in the flaming sun; this is emblematic of a total effacing of oneself for the collective, institutional cause. Reaffirming this idea on the soundtrack, we again hear a bugle call emerge among the presiding silence. The ambivalent, complex visual and auditory registers, to borrow Clark's words, express China's "mixed feelings about service and individual fulfilment" and stand "as a metaphor for the fifth-generation's attitudes to China and their place in the nation."[33]

This intricate audiovisual construction, meant to inform a symbolic reconciliation between formalism and individualism, continues to play a vital role in Chen's third film, *King of the Children* (*Haizi wang*, 1987). Although the

Folklore, Vernacular, and the Chinese New Waves 41

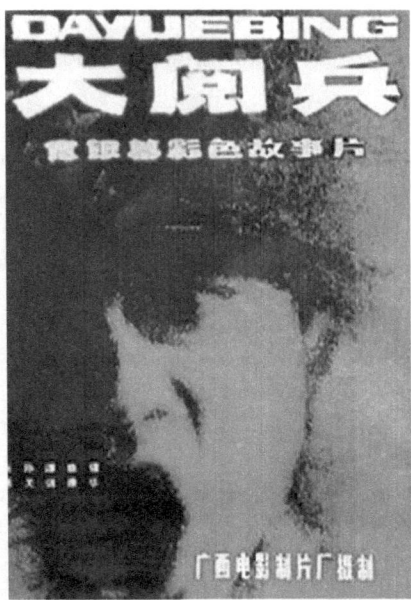

Film poster for *The Big Parade* (1986).

production turned out to be a commercial failure in China, most likely due to its arcane film language, extreme mannerism, and high modernism, this enigmatic work has been favorably scrutinized by many as symptomatic of Chen's elite culturalism, corresponding with a zeitgeist of Chinese cultural fever in the mid-to-late 1980s.[34] I do not intend to repeat an exhaustive reading of the film as a whole, but instead will address one focal point that demonstrates the mode of suturing—what I call the "synthetic visual-acoustic suturing"—in *King of the Children*.

What punctuates *King of the Children*, as many have indicated, is a cluster of images: a lonely, marginalized intellectual, a muted child, the indifferent, taciturn masses, and the open landscape, all of which stylistically conjure up Chen's earlier work, *Yellow Earth*. Similar to *Yellow Earth*, an act of "root-seeking," self-reflexivity, and most of all, the dichotomies between culture and nature, between the collective whole and the individual self in *King of the Children*, are materialized through Chen's idiosyncratic kino-eye and glance/object suturing at the core of the film. As Zhang Xudong explains: "*King of the Children* is first and foremost an autobiographical work and that everything in the film, from subject matter to imagery to thematic content, is fundamentally allegorical."[35] More precisely, the film shows us how contemplative, critical reflections on wounds, traumas, catastrophes, society, political culture, national character, and selfhood[36] can be formalized by cinematic measures, in particular through Chen's filming of mirrors and his discerning adoption of sound and glance-listening/object mechanism.

In *King of the Children*, Lao Gan[37] is the ad hoc "king of the children" who is posted to a remote village to teach reading and writing after spending years as part of a production team during the Cultural Revolution. The film, almost in the same fashion as *Yellow Earth*, dwells on a heroic, self-indulgent journey or exile. At first glance, one may say that *King of the Children* employs various types of suturing: the mechanical look of the camera to stitch together a coherent story, the invested look of the director and audience who are sutured into a position of identification with the character, and the framed look of the character on-screen. However, upon closer scrutiny, one finds a kind of nonsuturable, nonstitchable, and unspeakable divide between Lao Gan and the schoolchildren, between nature and culture, between doctrine and change.

Throughout the film, we see repeated shots of Lao Gan looking into the distance, staring at a broken mirror, gazing in front of the window, and gaping at his caricature on the blackboard upon his arrival at the classroom on the first day of his duty. Quite often, he is placed in a close-up that contains two enlarged images of himself—for instance, he is reflected in the mirror, paralleled with a cartoonish portrait by his students on the blackboard, or standing in front of his window beside his talented student Wang Fu, who is studiously copying the dictionary. This, on the one hand, signifies Lao Gan's double identity and a fractured, fragmented state of his ego, or we may say by extension, the filmmaker's own subjectivity. On the other hand, by conspicuously staging such postures of gazing and meditation and the looked, mediated objects, we look with and through the look of the protagonist. We are constantly reminded of an alert observer, the apparatus of observation, and the film in its own terms. In other words, unlike many conventional fiction films, *King of the Children* does not suture us into the story-world. Instead, we are invited to watch the film from a distance and to consciously reflect upon its "seams," its stylization, and its constructedness. The particular detachment from and critical view on these kinds of means, apparatuses, ideologies, codes, and conventions are what make *King of the Children* both fascinating and "alienating" (in the sense of the Brechtian "defamiliarization effect")[38] to its watchful audience.

Hence, *King of the Children* is much more than a denunciation of the Cultural Revolution and the Maoist indoctrination. In the director's notes appended to the film's English translated script, Chen writes:

> *Repetition is a characteristic of Chinese traditional culture.* The children in the film copied the textbook, then the dictionary, without any comprehension.

Man, in his preservation of himself, has developed culture, but in the end, the culture has become the master of man. *The glory of past cultural accomplishments have left today's men impotent* . . . Thus, what is embedded in the film *King of the Children* is my judgement on traditional culture. The burning of the wasted mountains at the end of the film is *a metaphor of my attitude towards traditional values* . . . I did not directly depict the violent social confrontations that took place during the Cultural Revolution. Instead, I chose to *use the language of film* to create the atmosphere of the era. The forest, the fog and the sound of trees being chopped down are all reflections of China during that period of time. I thought, perhaps, that is enough.[39]

Chen's disparagement of the Cultural Revolution and of the general suppression in Chinese culture is quite telling and forthright in contrast to the "hidden" language he usually uses in his films. In *King of the Children*, Chen patiently and elusively weaves his cutting criticism on Chinese pedagogy, history, and culture through visual metaphors such as "the burning of the wasted mountains," "forest," "fog," and "trees being chopped down." Chen's interrogation of cultural (re)production and symbolic order and his strong desire to bring "copying" and "repetition" to an end are also forcefully captured by an aural metaphor in *King of the Children*: "Once upon a time there was a mountain. On the mountain there was a temple. In the temple there was an old monk telling a story. What was the story he was telling? Once upon a time there was a mountain. On the mountain there was a temple. In the temple there was an old monk telling a story. What was the story he was telling . . ." A piece of Chinese folklore that has been recited for centuries, this popular verse upholds an inherent wisdom linked to Zen's philosophy. In this specific film context, however, the folklore becomes a metaphor of Chinese culture that is at once rich and enduring yet repetitive and stagnant.

In *King of the Children*, when Lao Gan's former friends and co-workers come to visit him at school one day, they flock into the classroom, find themselves a desk, and sit down. Lao Gan begins to give out a lesson as if to his students: "Once upon a time there was a mountain. On the mountain there was a temple. In the temple there was an old monk telling a story. What was the story he was telling . . ." In this scene where Lao Gan recites the popular verse, the camera is placed behind his "students" and observes patiently from the very far end of the classroom. The significant depth of the space gives the scene an uncanny feeling while shadowy, noirish lighting, as well as the extraordinary, nearly two-minute length of the shot, further adds an unsettling, uncertain quality. Lao Gan's class takes a satirical turn when his friends join him in the recitation. Voices grow louder and louder; rhythm goes faster and faster; the group starts shouting and banging the desks as if making percussions. The camera then cuts to another long shot of schoolchildren next door in the foreground; they glare vigilantly at the recitation in the background. Suddenly, the chanting ceases, and this brief silence is immediately followed by a burst of laughter. To one's—and Lao Gan's—surprise, the children quickly pick up the chorus, "Once upon a time there was a mountain . . ." and run into a foggy mountain in the distance. Here again, we see a medium close-up of Lao Gan looking at the children in a daze, it is as if he is lost himself.

In cinematic terms, the previous example is a quintessential illustration of suturing. Rey Chow, in her critical account of *King of the Children*, identifies suturing as a fundamental force and stylistic mode in the construction of the film's narcissist, masculine, and elitist discourse. She poses these questions: "Following his [Lao Gan's] look, we ask: what does he see? If the individual look is a response to a collective gaze, to what does his look respond? What is the larger realm that connects with this look . . . How is Lao Gan's stare sutured? In other words, with what does his look cohere?"[40] It is now not so difficult to unravel this set of questions based on the filmmaker's own commentary and my previous investigation of the film text and its allegorical connotations. What I want to further point out is that both the protagonist's look and listening, as well as the contemplative voice and noise, are suturing devices, which address the core issues of pedagogy, culture, and nation in the film. Extending Rey Chow's intervention, we may also ask: What is Lao Gan reciting? What is he listening to? To what does his listening respond? What is the larger realm that connects with his listening? How is his listening sutured to his look and to the film as a whole?

To unpack these questions, I suggest looking at the beginning and conclusion of the work to examine the specific dynamic of suturing on a sonic level. *King of the Children* opens with a brief empty shot of the foggy sky and a sound which is later revealed to be of a cowbell. Quickly, the frame dissolves into a sequence of panoramic shots looking up to a twisting, muddy path that extends into a secluded school deep in the mountains. The first set of seven shots all fix their gazes on a singular visual image of the village school and natural landscape. Through measured time-lapse photography, a full day in the mountains—from foggy morning, to cloudy noon, and then progressing to sunset and finally dusk—is captured. From off-screen arises an ancient singing that seems to be naturally emanating from the mountains. This, at first, establishes a mysterious and primitive tone of *King of the Children*. As the film proceeds to the opening credit sequence, in which cast and crew members' names are superimposed on a blank page, the initial moment of natural sound is cut off. Cut in are jarring scratches of chalk-writing on a blackboard. The abrupt insertion of the off-screen chalk-writing on the soundtrack—an alien component that seems to breach the tranquillity of the village—introduces a central theme and prefigures the next sequence, in which the "king of children," Lao Gan, is dispatched to the village to teach but is unwelcome and ostracized in this new community.

The simple act of Lao Gan copying the communist texts onto the blackboard, as well as his students mindlessly copying them down onto their notebooks, emerges as the recurrent scene throughout *King of the Children*. This, of course, is a caustic denunciation of pedagogy and furthermore of Chinese culture, which, to Chen, is regrettably characterized by this kind of repetition. The unbearable burden of history and tradition is then expressed not only through the wearying, unusually long takes but also through the uncanny silence and noise that would disquiet even the most patient and composed audience. Sound thus becomes a way of suturing, in and with the visible form, to convey Chen's radical and the Wittgensteinian "unspeakable" castigation of Chinese culture and ideology. Many scenes in the film are submerged in silence, including Lao Gan noiselessly copying the texts, and in his daydreams, the quiet students, Wang Fu's reticent father, and the mute cowherd. These moments of nearly complete silence are often abruptly interrupted by sequences featuring a textural cacophony of ambient sounds: reverberations of nature, oracular echoing and chanting of ancient texts, grinding scratches of chalk on the blackboard, rustling of pencils on notebooks, and by contrast, the female teacher's stentorian voice reciting propagandist texts next door.

As Tony Ryans has indicated, it was not until *King of the Children* that Chen Kaige was finally able to experiment with synchronized sound recording.[41] The film deploys the technological advancement of sound to create a special air for the story in which the enigmatic sound of nature and prayer are aptly recorded. The primitive nature of the film, coupled with naturalistic sound and lighting, as well as the minimalist documentation of folklore reciting and chanting, endows it with a philosophical, allegorical aura.

King of the Children contrasts the mute cowherd and his natural knowledge with the communist, dogmatic education the schoolchildren are subjected to in the classroom. In the last part of the film, Lao Gan is discharged for his later heretic "non-copying" teaching method and he leaves the village in the midst of the burning of mountains. We once again encounter the ghostly cowherd and a dreamlike scene of the hazy mountain and phantasmal field of black stumps. Following Lao Gan's wary listening and look, we hear the sound of the cowbells and of someone pissing before being shown a full shot of the cowherd relieving himself. The camera moves closer to the face of the cowherd and his eyes under a broken straw hat as he vigilantly looks back at Lao Gan and thus the camera. The next shot is a reverse shot that shows the perplexed

King of the Children (1987): Lao Gan's gaze in front of school and echoes of the nature.

Lao Gan; following this, the cowherd disappears. Standing in front of our eyes are black stumps and the cowherd's hat on one of them. The film then alternates swiftly between quick, phantasmagoric shots of the anthropomorphous stumps and those of the stunned, stump-like Lao Gan, finally revealing a clear image of the cowherd without his hat as he turns and looks into the camera.

With the amplification of the cowbells and explosions of the burning mountains, the film comes full circle to the opening shots of the landscape: red earth, school hut, the winding path, and immense mountains all dyed orange and enveloped in a thick smoke. Resonant in the soundtrack is a mix of hallucinatory sounds: cowbells, echoes of nature, explosions of fire, trees cracking, children playing, and Lao Gan and *zhiqing* reciting the circular story that gets louder and louder. The burning mountain and circular folklore, as illustrated earlier, are all symbols that crystallize Chen's cultural criticism. With a diminishing sound, a freeze-frame of the Chinese character "cow water" written on the blackboard conspicuously appears and takes up the entire screen. In our understanding of the film, this is a nonexistent Chinese character invented by Lao Gan, drawing from his and the cowherd's experience, which again derides the official, political, and cultural orthodoxy. The household cyclical folklore deeply embedded in Chinese collective consciousness is juxtaposed and contrasted with Lao Gan's heroic, Sisyphean attempts at change and invention, encapsulated herewith in the creation of "cow water." The camera stares at the enlarged character "cow water," tinged with a ray of sunshine. At the conclusion, we see brief shots of a hazy sunset and of an empty classroom, and we hear the original silence. Through the deliberate parallel and suturing between visuality and aurality, *King of the Children* subtly builds a set of encounters and contradictions between the linguistic and the anti-linguistic, between the expressible and the ineffable, between collectivity and subjectivity, between nature and humans, between human nature and ideology, all of which lie at the heart of many early Chen projects.

"Hills of Yellow Earth" and Music of Northwest Wind

The mid-to-late 1980s saw an explosion of a new musical style known as Northwest Wind (*xibei feng*), derived from and nurtured by the soundtracks of Fifth Generation films, many of which are cinematic adaptations of "root-seeking" literature. While *xibei* is a geographic term used to trace the root of this musical genre back to its native locale, northwest China, the word *feng* has a complex set of meanings in Chinese. It could literally mean "wind" on the first level; and is largely used figuratively on the second level to signify a social and cultural "trend," "fad," or "craze" characterized by mutability, new directions, and quick dissemination. Moreover, when used in reference to folklore or folk song, it is often associated with the kind of ethnographic-oriented fieldwork depicted in *Yellow Earth*.

Yellow earth, with its rich and nuanced significations, has become not only the quintessentially Chinese national emblem, but also an allegorical image of China at the crossroads of the revolutionary past and the reformed present. Claimed as the mythical cradle of Chinese civilization and birthplace of the Chinese socialist revolution, it is seen as at once the most backward and most free-spirited area and as the place to excavate and recuperate a deeper, inner form of national roots. This trope has been fanatically embraced by and is given another resounding articulation in "Hills of Yellow Earth" (*Huangtu gaopo*), a musical hit that quickly swept the entire country like a "wind" in 1988:

> My home is on high hills of yellow earth
> Strong wind blows down from the slopes
> It doesn't matter if it is the northwest wind or the southeast wind
> It's all my song, my song . . .

The symbolism of the yellow earth and the Yellow River has persisted in both the Fifth Generation films and Northwest Wind music: "Generations of ancestors handed it down to me / Left me a boundless song to sing with this Yellow River still by my side." It was not merely a cinematic and musical invention but the product of a larger movement of "cultural fever" and "root-seeking" that has made its ubiquitous presence felt in literature, film, television, popular music, and a vast range of cultural and media sectors in 1980s China.

A widespread movement, the "root-seeking" craze is characterized by a comprehensive and intensive discussion about Chinese culture and Western civilization, which can only be matched by the May Fourth Movement some sixty years ago. The critical discourse revolves around two thematic axes. The first axis is temporal. Adopting a dictum of Nietzsche (a cult figure in Chinese cultural discussion of the 1980s) that states, "Man today, stripped of myths, stands famished among all his pasts and must dig frantically for roots,"[42] root-seekers resorted to the remote past which they believe to be comparatively free of both Western influences and Chinese communist totalitarianism. The second axis, then, is spatial. Caught between the residue of revolutionary dogma and the sudden barrage of Western culture, root-seekers sought to excavate and reinvigorate a sense of national identity by returning to the historical past and peripheral sites of Chinese civilization as sources of inspiration. Like the May Fourth period in the early twentieth century, the 1980s was also a time to witness an influx of concepts and ideas from the West that inspired a re-examination of traditional Chinese culture. Paradoxically, the course of "embracing the old" conflates with an eclectic approach to "absorbing the new," while the quest for the nation's past consequently converges with the search for a modern future. Nurturing from both repertoires, root-seekers shifted between China's traditional past and the West's contemporary present.

In Northwest Wind, a humanist and self-reflexive handling of China's legendary past in connection with contemporary moment forms an underlying thrust that fundamentally distinguishes this musical genre from others, especially the imported popular music from Hong Kong and Taiwan (*gangtai yinyue*), which features instead a softer and more romantic tone.[43] Praised by many as the very first indigenous popular music to emerge on the mainland since the beginning of the post-Mao reform, Northwest Wind is regarded as a strong reassertion of mainland cultural independence after nearly a decade in which China was flooded by foreign cultural products from Hong Kong, Taiwan, and the West. Triggered by the debut of "Xintianyou," a 1986 song named after its regional folk song classification, the genre's popularity soon led to a nationwide "wind." It reached its peak in 1988, dubbed as "The Year of Northwest Wind." Northwest Wind's blowout was seen in the Third CCTV National Youth Singing Competition of 1988, the largest and most influential event of its kind. The contest of that year became exclusively a concert for the style of Northwest Wind. Six finalists all presented the same Northwest Wind song, "Hills of Yellow Earth," unprecedented in Chinese popular music history.[44] Although the Northwest Wind fad did not last long and began to decline the following year, it nevertheless cultivated a constellation of young music stars. The first generation of professional popular singers on the mainland, such as Tian Zhen, Na Ying, Sun Guoqing, and Liu Huan, were all "discovered" and elevated to stardom during this Northwest Wind fever and they continue to wield a significant influence in the current pop music world.

In explaining Northwest Wind's exuberant growth and massive appeal, Mercedes M. Dujunco, one of the first music scholars who has directed attention to this phenomenon, writes:

> At a time when the Chinese nation was plagued by self-doubt and a crisis of faith in its own culture and in socialism, *xibeifeng*, along with the so-called "root-seeking" literature of the mid-1980s, and the films of the Fifth Generation directors, helped to meet an overwhelming need for symbols that would raise the morale of the population and put them back in touch with their "roots," thereby helping to maintain political stability. Moreover, the commercial success of *xibeifeng* recordings was itself a source of nationalistic pride, signalling for many Chinese the ability of native pop music to compete with that imported from Hong Kong or Taiwan.[45]

On the one hand, it may be appropriate to say that folk elements intrinsic to Northwest Wind offer a positive view of Chinese history and culture and arouse the kind of nationalistic sentiments often exploited by the government. The song titled "The Virile Spirit of Asia" (*Yazhou xiongfeng*) reflects such an endeavor to package and disseminate patriotic propaganda through the channel of popular music. It is a widely known song in Northwest Wind style which was drafted and sanctioned by the Chinese state, thereby engineered to mobilize public support for the 11th Asian Games hosted in Beijing in 1990.

On the other hand, besides being a vernacular instrument of the top-down dissemination of power and knowledge (in the Foucaudian sense),[46] what shall not be dismissed in the larger picture of Northwest Wind is the ambivalent and mixed messages it carries, as well as its inherent vernacularity as an indigenous tongue and originally an entity of *suanqu'er* (sour tune). In his book, *China's New Voices*, Nimrod Baranovitch points out that "despite the nationalistic sense of pride and love for the homeland, *xibeifeng* songs were also filled with tragic overtones and articulated a sense of dissatisfaction and a strong desire to change things."[47] He compares "Nanniwan," a classic revolutionary song in Mao's China, to "My Beloved Homeland" (*Wo relian de guxiang*), a 1987 hit that features the same geography and demography. The lyrics of the latter, on the contrary, project a somewhat dystopian and cynical view of the northwest countryside:

Popular music cassette in the style of North Wind: *Shaanbei 1988* (Beijing: Zhongguo dianying chubanshe, 1988).

Popular music cassette in the style of North Wind: *Shaanbei 1989* (Beijing: Zhongguo dianying chubanshe, 1989).

> My homeland is not beautiful at all
> Low straw huts, bitter well water . . .
> On a barren soil harvesting a meager hope
> Staying year after year

The work, like many of the sour tunes found in *Yellow Earth*, is at once nostalgic and biting: "My homeland is not beautiful at all." It was one of the first times popular artists voiced discontent, disclosed the crudeness and hardship of rural life, interrogated its status quo, and raised the question of who should be responsible for the country's unchanged poverty and backwardness. Meanwhile, Northwest Wind songs also pronounce a strong urge to escape from and transform the homeland, and a modernist yearning for economic advancement and opening-up in post-revolutionary China.

According to Jin Zhaojun, a leading music critic on the mainland, the elusiveness, poignancy, and critical edge of Northwest Wind are precisely the qualities that propelled it to both quickly spawn and to decline almost overnight in late 1980s China. In other words, the "heavy-heartedness" of Northwest Wind has gradually become an unfit character incongruous with the new, increasingly voluptuary, commodified market conditions. And Jin provides an instructive commentary on the popular music scene in reformed China:

> The aesthetic ideas that Northwest Wind attempts to convey are very clear. Its lyrics carry a very strong tone of cultural critique. In terms of melody, it greatly draws from the vast musical repertoire of northern music, whereas on the aspect of compiling and performance, it adopts the techniques and formats of rock music in order to create a striking impression and a striking power. To some extent, Northwest Wind is a spontaneous incorporation of

rock music culture under a specific historical circumstance. It also reflects the longings, aspirations, anxieties, and doubts that prevailed among the masses in the Reform era.[48]

For him and many Chinese, Northwest Wind caught their ears as a "sinicized indigenous form of rock music" (*zhongguo minzuhua yaogun*), namely, a hybrid form combining the folksy characteristics of northwest Chinese music with a strong, fast Western beat derived from disco and rock. The appeal of this music genre stems from this synthesis. Furthermore, the pleasure of this music, I argue, is often attributed to the singer's rough, powerful, and virile vocal delivery and the song's strong rhythms that could readily stimulate dancing and body movement. In this regard, the crude, exotic, and erotic property of Northwest Wind evokes Roland Barthes's famous notion of "the grain of the voice" that references music not only as an artistic, cultural practice and a listening experience but also as a visual and physical engagement.[49] Drawing from this concept, I see that the distinct musical and visual discourse of Northwest Wind can ultimately tie back to the basic instinct and core of physicality and sexuality. And this is best illustrated in Zhang Yimou's directorial debut, *Red Sorghum*, which blasts the corporeality and diversification of Northwest Wind, and in the real sense, the conglomeration of popular music and cinema, a subject to be examined in the next chapter.

CHAPTER TWO

The Convergence of Popular Music-Film: Zhang Yimou-Zhao Jiping and Spectacles of Sound

> In *Red Sorghum* I did not deliberately try to combat or contradict the traditional way of making film . . . [However] that was indeed the purpose when we made *One and Eight* [*Yi ge he ba ge*] and *Yellow Earth,* and especially when we made *One and Eight*. At that time I was filled with anger whenever I set up the camera. All of us were basically fed up with the unchanging, inflexible way of Chinese film-making, so we were ready to fight it at all costs in our first film. I would set down the camera and take a look, and [say to myself], Oh, god, the composition is still the same as the old stuff! No! Turn the lens around—just turn it around, raise it, just for the sake of raising it. Actually *if you ask me whether there was any concept in this kind of incomplete composition, the answer is no, but the point was simply and deliberately to be different.*
> — **Zhang Yimou**[1]

Arguably the last film of the cinematic new wave and the first effort at hatching a new transnational commercial genre, *Red Sorghum* has been hailed as a landmark that signifies the Fifth Generation's paradigmatic shift from modernist avant-garde experiment to a new form of capital-driven practice backed by international funds and institutions from Taiwan, Hong Kong, and the West.[2] In Dai Jianhua's words, "As *Yellow Earth* and *King of the Children* may be termed failures of salvation, *Red Sorghum* certainly represents the salvation of failure."[3] Dai's brilliant formula of "salvation" and "failure" in defining the Fifth Generation denotes the ways in which this cinemanic cohort represents not only a collective mode of reconciliation with official discourses, modulated by intellectual and artistic reflections upon history and conventions, but also a school of experimentation with internal diversity, negotiation, and ramifications in reformist China. In Chen Kaige's films, discussed earlier, the kind of Sisyphean struggle to rescue nation and film from the burden of history has been lonely, heroic, and futile. Under the pressure of a new market economy and changing social circumstances, *Red Sorghum*'s coming of age in 1987 signals a decisive turn within the Fifth Generation movement from a self-indulgent heroism and elitism toward a secular and pedestrian life. Although the film similarly undertakes a "root-seeking" approach to reinvigorate national tradition and spirit, Zhang Yimou adopts a "mischievous attitude toward this extraordinarily heavy material"[4] and explores the idioms in a quite different manner.

Both *King of the Children* and *Red Sorghum* came out in 1987. *King of the Children* lost at the Cannes Film Festival and turned out to be an even more dismal fiasco in the domestic market. In contrast, *Red Sorghum* was the Golden Bear winner in Berlin, the first Chinese film ever to achieve the highest honor at one of the leading international film festivals. Zhang Yimou was also the first among his generation to turn a cinematic experiment into a box office hit. *Film Review* (*Dianying pinjie*), one of the leading film criticism journals in mainland China, published an article in September 1988 which meticulously analyzed the thrilling triumph of *Red Sorghum* in contrast to *King of the Children*, which was mockingly bestowed a "Golden Alarm Prize" (*jin naozhong jiang*) in another review on the same page.[5] To critics, *King of the Children* was "a wake-up slap" (*yiji erguang*) to Chen and other Fifth Generation filmmakers who were still intoxicated with their self-styled narcissism and elitist experiments. *Red Sorghum* was, then, at once a timely alarm and a harbinger, convincing filmgoers and critics that the "matured" Fifth Generation was capable of honing both aesthetically competent and commercially viable works. *Red Sorghum*'s deliberate coordination of artistic pursuits, commercial mechanism, and popular mass culture was successful on all counts.

Set against a vast, mythical land in north China before and during the Sino-Japanese War, the film tells the story of a young girl bethrothed to a rich old leper who later engages in an "illicit" affair with the sedan carrier for her wedding. After her "legal" husband is mysteriously murdered, the girl Jiu'er becomes the winery owner and leads the war against Japanese invasion. Investigating the factors behind the film's appeal, which is similar to *Yellow Earth*, critics have first and foremost addressed *Red Sorghum*'s eye-opening and breathtaking visual components: the hilarious, outlandish wedding ceremony on the yellow earth plateau; the defiant, sacramental lovemaking between the bride and sedan carrier in an enigmatic, exuberant sorghum field; and the visually beautiful, preindustrial, and communal labor of winemaking at Eighteen Miles Slope.⁶ Equally important, I want to stress, is the film's mesmerizing soundtrack impregnated with rough, natural, and indigenous voices and songs. This singular auditory montage resonates with and enhances the visual spectacle and the unique style of *Red Sorghum*, announcing the merger of popular music and film at its finest.

"Four Songs and One Color": Music and Picture in *Red Sorghum*

What comprises *Red Sorghum*, in a nutshell, are several concentrated scenes deliberately organized around what can be termed "four songs and one color" (*sige yise*).⁷ The four principal chapters (wedding, love affair, wine-making, and anti-Japanese war) are each embodied by one of four diegetic songs ("Jolting Sedan," "Sister, March Forward Bravely," "Ode to the Wine God," and a children's ballad at the end). All of these revolve around a central code—red—that encompasses rich and sometimes antithetic meanings: revolution, desire, passion, birth *vis-à-vis* death, destruction of the old order *vis-à-vis* construction of a new world.

The film begins with a male voice-over on a completely dark screen for nearly thirty seconds: "Let me tell you a story about my grandpa and grandma. Where I come from, they still talk about it to this day. It has been a long time, so some believe it, some don't." A cacophony of noises and wedding music then snaps in and the frame dissolves into a close-up introducing a beautiful young bride: "This is my grandma." The introductory sequence therefore economically establishes a number of features key to the characterization and theme of the film. The dark screen at the opening of *Red Sorghum* discursively posits the narrative in a misty past—the undefined, prehistoric, and premodern era prior to either the Japanese invasion or the communist occupation (herein insinuated as being an example of sociopolitical turbulence leading to the destruction of the sorghum field). Underscored by the calm, retrospective narration, the opening carries a nostalgic and mythical tone. Likewise, the very first frontal shot of "my grandma" resembles a static oil portrait and is endowed with a sense of historicity and mythology. A succession of extreme close-ups that fragment and display the female protagonist's body from various angles—her face, hair, eyes, lips, hand, neck, and ears—present "my grandma" as the object of desire from the outset, establishing her as a source of "visual pleasure," to quote Laura Mulvey's famous concept.⁸ This barefaced sexuality and subjectivity proves pivotal to the aesthetic appeal of the film. But what I really want to emphasize in the following study is that the "pleasure" generated in *Red Sorghum* is not only visual but also conspicuously aural, geared toward the audience both in and beyond the theater.

The opening wedding sequence showcases the grandmother's stunning feminine beauty. It displays her distinctive personal traits through a refined audiovisual plot of her first confrontation with her clamorous and chaotic surroundings; she is composed, determined, and self-contained. This double-edged presentation of femininity or complex female sexuality—the passive, erotic, and fetishized woman versus the active, aggressive, and self-aware woman—is fused, transfigured, and further problematized in the ensuing tossing-the-bridal-sedan sequence. As the scene exclusively places "my grandma" in a group of young men and confines her in a traditional red sedan, it could easily be taken as a scene of a vulnerable woman at the mercy of lustful men. The five-minute sequence probes, in what Rey Chow terms an "ethnographic" way,[9] the very first prominent rite of *Red Sorghum* featuring a gang of sedan carriers tossing the bridal sedan and singing an outrageous flirtatious song, "Jolting Sedan," on the way to the wedding ceremony:

> Look closely, pockmarked face
> Flat nose, cleft mouth, and piggy eyes . . .
> Oh, my little darling throws into my arms . . .
> Erdan [a metonym for the groom] sleeps in the pigpen tonight

The blaring, brassy tune associated with the sexually suggestive lyrics ostentatiously speaks to the sedan carriers' own sexual fantasies, whereas Big Head Li, to whom "my grandma" is betrothed, is explicitly ridiculed in the song. At first glance, the film portends the victimization of the heroine by Big Head Li, whose only boast is his wealth as a winery owner. Big Head Li "generously" trades a big mule for a beautiful young bride. But he is narratively and symbolically a leper, representing both impotence and lack on a more general level, while also being actually absent from the screen for the duration of the film. By contrast, the image of the sweating, semi-naked, and muscular males yelling and dancing in the dust, in a half-drunken way, loudly pronounces and glorifies libidinal power, masculine potency, or a sort of sadomasochistic desire.

The sensuous visual imagery, coupled with a raucous auditory register, may seem quite rough and grating, and could easily be simplified as a foolhardy male chauvinistic act. But upon a closer examination, this hyperbolic, campy utterance not only introduces a new form of sexual relationship related to material production and social order (which I will explore later) but also functions as an essential critique of the oppression and repression of passion, sexuality, and human nature in Chinese culture. A typical shot-reverse-shot

Red Sorghum (1987): "Jolting Sedan" and the wedding ceremony sequence.

structure depicts both the interior and exterior space of the bridal sedan. However, almost in a reversal of the classical Hollywood mode of the male voyeuristic gaze, the camera identifies instead with the female protagonist's point of view: her dizzy, desirous look, as she tries to stabilize herself in a jolting sedan while curiously peeking through the slightly raised curtain. In this glance/object suturing construction, it is the shirtless, respiratory, and perspiratory males who are objectified and fetishized by the titillated camera, becoming the body of desire. On the contrary, the bride's gaze is autonomous and self-contained. Not only is she placed and tossed inside the womb-like red sedan, a powerful symbol of maternity, human beings, and roots of life, but also her radiant, red, and seemingly drunken face, accompanied by heavy breathing, panting, and gasping, suggests an undertone of sexual ecstasy.

Red Sorghum can be read as another spectacle of "root-seeking" that discloses and extols lifeness—the origin, truthfulness, and artistry of life. It is also a film equally and dialectically oriented by the discourses of femininity and masculinity. From the beginning, it is "my grandma" who initiates the gaze, setting in motion a game of sexual seduction and progression of the film's narrative. She is, in every sense, a classic example of a rebel against the name of father—her biological father, her legal husband (Big Head Li), and other paternal and authoritative figures and forces (for instance, the Japanese). Even when she throws herself into the arms of "my grandpa," she brings passion through her body, but she also brings her tact, composure, and defiance, which in fact save her from the first abduction incident. On the way to the wedding, a daunting kidnapping interrupts the sedan procession in Qingsha Kou, the haunted sorghum field. As an interloper approaches the sedan and unveils the bride, the point-of-view shot from the outlaw's perspective reveals a calm, fearless bride who even stares and smiles back at the bandit. Totally enthralled, the robber orders her to step out of the sedan and walk into the thick sorghum field. As the camera tracks her walking lingeringly into the field, "grandma" pauses, turns around, and looks provocatively at the head sedan carrier—"my grandpa"—to rescue her. The distinct glance/object mechanism again plays a prominent role and is another prime example of suturing: the confident, powerful look of the female in linkage with the masculine, sexualized male body, which has been casted under her—and the camera's—eyes; and ultimately, the suturing and union of the two sexes.

This motif of sexuality and subjectivity is further enhanced and reaches climax in the second abduction scene. "My grandpa" kills the robber and falls for the bride. A few days later, when the bride rides home after the wedding, she runs into another kidnapper only to discover that he is instead "my grandpa" this time. They have sex in the sorghum field, a daring scene hitherto rarely depicted in Chinese cinema. The exuding exoticism and eroticism are not only vividly visualized but also foregrounded in a diegetic song following the sex scene. "Grandpa" shouts out a song, "Sister, March Forward Bravely," to "grandma" as she heads back home at sunset after their date:

Hey! Sister, you march forward bravely, *ah!* . . .
Tossing a *red* bridal ball, *ah!* . . .
Hitting me right on the head, *ah!*
I'll drink a pot with you, *ah!*

The enigmatic, highly stylized sex scene ambivalently shifts the boundaries between rape and what Zhang Yingjin calls "a moment of desperate triumph of the 'primitive' body, with all its undaunted violence and vitality, over the repressive tradition of the Chinese (patriarchal society)."[10] Not only is the rape—or rather, lovemaking—poeticized and passionately celebrated through the carnivalesque color of red ("From now on, you'll be building a *red* bridal tower, *ah!* / Tossing a *red* bridal ball, *ah!* / *Red red* sorghum wine, *ah!*") but also through melody and vocality that are formulated around a series of husky shouts and earthy, voluptuous singing (the italicized lyrics I will discuss in more detail shortly). Furthermore, this transgressive love affair and adultery is endowed with a sacred connotation through creative audiovisual means.

In the midst of the chase, the kidnapper pulls off his mask and is revealed as the head sedan carrier. The crosscuttings between the man and woman as they exchange gazes silently, and the extreme close-ups of their longing faces, enunciate their strong attractions toward each other. Without saying a word, "grandpa" hurriedly tramples out a space in the thick sorghum field, a round circle which is like a sacrificial altar. Close-up, medium, and bird's-eye shots

Red Sorghum (1987): "Sister, March Forward Bravely" after the sex scene.

with a mobile camera create a sense of thrill and urgency. Silence dominates the soundtrack, save for "grandpa's" heavy breathing and gasping, which adds another layer of sexual tension. Taking "grandma" under his arm in a boorish manner, as if carrying a sorghum plant, the clandestine lover walks resolutely through the thick, wild sorghum field into a cleared center. "Grandma," in an extreme close-up, closes her eyes and slowly lies down onto this love bed. The camera then cuts to a crane shot with a full image of the bride lying on the ground and facing the sky, representing the Chinese character, *da* (meaning "big"), while the man kneels down. Resembling a form of goddess worship, it is a divine moment, one of deification which resurrects the bonds between a potent matriarchal order and acts of "primitive passion." The *mise-en-scène* and editing justify this illicit love affair, for the marriage ritual and oath are often referenced as "bowing to heaven and earth" (*baitiandi*) or "heaven and earth as our witness, moon and sun as our agent" (*tiandiweizheng, riyueweimei*) in classical Chinese texts.

On the soundtrack, a drumbeat arises, growing louder and louder. Just moments later, a special wedding symphony in the style of Northwest Wind joins in. It begins with a series of sustained major tones in the highest register, which contributes to a festive mood; next, the thickening of the music's texture, accompanied by a crescendo at an agitato tempo, further reinforces the climactic moment of this sexual encounter. On the screen, the camera shifts from the ceremonial depiction to a montage of the sorghum swinging in the wind as if choreographed to the symphony. Writing the music primarily for a dramatic rather than commercial context (as the music never appeared on any kind of soundtrack album or music record), musician Zhao Jiping is

Red Sorghum (1987): Wedding symphony and the highly stylized sex scene/love affair.

very proud of this novel experiment and often cites it as his most satisfying endeavor. A journal article indicates:

> To glorify the life, Zhao Jiping had thirty *suona* (double-reed aerophone), four *sheng* (mouth organ), and one *dajiangu* (dajian drum) all play clamorously together. When recording this music passage in the studio, the recordist told him, "You'd better take off some *suona*, since the volume was so loud that it went beyond the red line already." But Zhao Jiping stayed on his ideas of these seemingly "dissonant" musical notes, which helped him cultivate a "wild" feeling for the film.[11]

One of the few nondiegetic atmospheric cues in the film, this musical stanza involves a dramatic rising line. And the traditional Chinese musical instruments make a striking appearance in this overly dramatic and fervent representation of the return of the repressed ritual, desire, and subjectivity.

Set in the heart of the wine distillery, the third festive, ceremonial episode focuses on wine-making. While the camera fully displays a wonder of this pristine labor through its highly stylized and fetishized view of the half-naked male body, the rustic simplicity and artistry associated with the Dionysian spirit are even more explicitly emphasized in their chorus of "Ode to the Wine God":

> On September the Ninth, we make new wine . . .
> Drink our wine, it will nourish *yin* and strengthen *yang*, your breath won't smell . . .
> Drink our wine, you won't kowtow to an emperor . . .
> Good wine, good wine, good wine!

Drinking, as a leitmotif, not only pervades this particular song but also recurs throughout the entire film. First, wine (*jiu*) is homophonous to the number nine in Chinese, which is also the name of "my grandma"—*jiu'er*. Thus, drinking in *Red Sorghum* serves as an analogy for sexual drive as well as femininity. By equating drinking with both virile masculinity and female sexuality, the song and the film set up drinking-qua-sexuality as an antithesis to disease: "Drink our wine, you'll breathe well and free from coughing." At the second level, drinking is valorized as a positive way to resuscitate the balance between *yin* and *yang* (a set of Chinese philosophical concepts which presume the duality of substance and hold that opposite forces are actually interconnected to make up a whole—for instance, man and woman) and to retrieve long-lost masculinity and femininity, as opposed to the socialist realist productions that had arguably erased gender differences in Mao's China. Third, as suggested in the lyrics, "Drink our wine, you'll dare to cross Qinshakou by yourself," drinking is symbolically celebrated as a route that frees one from constraints and leads to transcendence and ecstasy. It is a way to achieve prowess and freedom, and most of all, a means of defying dictatorship.

This poetic glorification of individuality and independence is reiterated in the final scene of *Red Sorghum*. Before they set out for revenge against the Japanese after the horrifying slaying of Luohan (the winery manager who disappears mysteriously and is later alleged to have been sent back by the communists to organize local resistance), male workers line up in a row in front of a portrayal of the wine god, led by "grandpa." As usual, they perform their ritual prayers. "Drink our wine," they chant, "you won't kowtow to the emperor." The second appearance of this wine ceremony, along with the final combat episode (which is also represented in a ritualistic manner), is another pronounced expression of self-assurance, extolling the vigor and vitality of life rather than a hackneyed "anti-imperialist" or "nationalist" narrative.

Red Sorghum's inclusion of an anti-Japanese episode in the last third of the film led many reviewers to conceive of it as a nationalist text.[12] Debates were also leveled about the coherence of the final section in relation to the work as a whole. In an article entitled "Sing a Paean to Life," director Zhang Yimou expresses his intention to "demonstrate a joyful and boundless view of life." He writes: "I was not interested in imposing a lot of significations on *Red Sorghum*, nor did I intend to endow it with various sociopolitical ideologies. We worked together to make it simple, interesting, and visually attractive. The other goal of ours is to convey the quintessential characteristics of Mo Yan's novels—a restless and hilarious life."[13] According to Zhang Yimou, what attracted him to Mo Yan's stories "Red Sorghum" and "Sorghum Wine," upon which the film is based, was "the wild sorghum field, its miraculous

Red Sorghum (1987): "Ode to the Wine God" and the wine-making scene.

characters, men and women so reckless and unconstrained, so generous and at ease."[14] All of these paradigms may easily conjure up a number of critical frameworks, such as the return of the repressed (Freud), the liberation of desire (Lacan), a celebration of the Dionysian spirit (Nietzshe), and most of all, a cinematic evocation of the carnivalesque (Bakhtin).

Having no intention to reiterate or repudiate the above interpretions, my focus is rather on how the film is motivated by the dynamic of popular songs, in conjunction with its cinematography and choreography, to build Zhang's cinematic signature—a hymn to life and a jollification of natural being and human nature. I argue that, although often placed under the rubric of nationalism, *Red Sorghum* is a dramatic rewriting of a nationalist discourse and a main departure from the socialist ideology. Instead, it espouses the disparate approach of "Sing a Paean to Life," as opposed to "Sing a Folk Song to the Party" (*Chang zhi shange gei dang ting*), a well-known propaganda song that elicited absolute allegiance to the party during Mao's era.

Underneath this nationalist façade, a principal focus on the sorghum field and red sorghum wine still dominates the last segment of *Red Sorghum* and articulates a Dionysian spirit and canivalesque air accordant with earlier sections. The ending is similarly allegorical and can be aptly described with Nietzsche's words from his famed *Birth of Tragedy*: "Not only does the bond between man and man come to be forged once more by the magic of the Dionysian rite, but nature itself, long alienated or subjugated, rises again to celebrate the reconciliation with her prodigal son, man."[15] The sorghum field that has nurtured numerous lives and galvanized bountiful productivities now turns into a battlefield in the face of the crush of modernization and Japanese imperialism. However, by linking the Japanese military troops, patrol trucks, and machine guns with savageness and totalitarian forces that destroy harmonious nature and a peaceful, egalitarian utopian society, the film evinces a keen interest in the primitive, cultured China and a scathing skepticism toward authoritarian modernity, similar to *Yellow Earth*. During this deadly battle, the sorghum landscape is still a mythic, sacred place casting a spell on everyone. Both its raw, handmade products and natural, indigenous sources, such as red sorghum wine, folk music, and even human urine, are invested with magic power. They have prevailed over modern military machinery in a poetic and surrealist way. For instance, the sorghum wine mixed with "my father's" urine (who is a child in the story)—reminiscent of a previous scene in which "grandpa's" mischievous urination into the wine barrels miraculously produces the best wine in local oral history—is diegetically deployed as dynamite used to destroy a truckload of Japanese soldiers. Of particular interest is the "Jolting Sedan" song that makes its second and final appearance in this climactic moment. Believing the Japanese have a natural fear of music and sound, winery workers resort to the tune as another fantastic measure to countervail modern technology.

In *Red Sorghum*, the final battle begins with the heroine's unexpected encounter with Japanese soldiers while on her way to deliver food and wine to her people. A narrative twist featuring the dreadful death of "grandma," associated with the previous brutal death of Luohan, serves to legitimize the final revenge of the film. A fierce battle is dramatized through deliberate slow motion and prevailing red hues. It again projects a clash of two opposing forces—the premodern, maternal, natural, and canivalesque on the one side, and modern, industrial life, articulated as masculine, destructive, and inhuman, on the other. The presence and resurgence of musical cues at this point are also highly allegorical. It is through this aural presentation that libidinal fantasies vis-à-vis modernization are affectively verbalized and materialized. It is also through this musical point of view that the past is mediated, reconstructed, and totalized. "Jolting Sedan" accompanies and portrays the last fight and death of "grandma" in the diegetic space, whereas the tune is presented herein without its original lyrics and textual elements. Slow-motion sequences of "grandma" falling down in the sorghum field, and of male workers dashing onto the battlefield, are coupled with the deafening music working together to invest the scene with a surreal and metaphorical quality.

As a freeze-frame foregrounds "grandpa" and "father," the only survivors of the battle who stand still in the bloody sun at the end of the war, the theme song "Sister, March Forward Bravely" is heard again off-screen and swells to a nostalgic, romantic climax. The reprised musical number plays through and interweaves with the crosscuttings between a close-up of the petrified "grandpa," a long shot of the thriving sorghum field, and a circular moving shot of the battlefield at the end of *Red Sorghum*. This recalls another important scene where the song is re-enacted for the second time in the middle of the film. "Grandpa," being driven out of the winery for his uncouth acts, returns during a wine-making ceremony. This time, he is sober and looks more determined. Instead of directly referring to their love affairs in the sorghum field, as he did previously, he hums the tune while mischievously urinating into the wine. Aligned with the return of "grandpa," the melody of "Sister, March Forward Bravely" briefly re-emerges. This musical recitation recapitulates the theme of libido and sexual ecstasy established earlier, but the different sonic quality of the singer's voice—"grandpa's" crooning—yields a distinctly sentimental and hypnotic tone. Such a blasphemous affront leaves all of the workers in a daze. "Grandpa" then shovels distiller's grain out of the boiler. The grain pours down onto "grandma," who remains still and astounded, as if in a shower. This shot carries a strong sexual overtone alluding to sexual intercourse, which has been often euphemistically referred to as "cloud and rain" (*yunyu*) in Chinese texts. Indeed, the next tracking shot shows "grandpa" carrying "grandma" under his arms, exactly as he has done in the sorghum field, and stoutly walking into her bedroom.

In its third and last appearance toward the end of *Red Sorghum*, "Sister, March Forward Bravely" is associated with other distinguished musical themes, such as the sedan song and a child's incantation, epitomizing the polysemic nature of Zhang Yimou's film music as a whole. On the one hand, the convergence of various musical themes serves as an auditory summary of the thematic threads of the work. On the other hand, this climatic *denouement* can be seen as an extension and externalization of "grandpa's" subjective envisioning during, and in the aftermath of, the war. Zhang Yimou uses a red filter to create stunning visual effects. A flashback from a musical perspective recounts the critical moments of "grandpa's" past life, underscoring the connections between the past and the present. It is also through this musical replay that the film's representation of various pairs of opposites—masculinity and femininity, self and other, war and peace, life and death, destruction and reconstruction, and day and night (which is foregrounded in an illusory shot of a fleeting solar eclipse that signifies the conclusion of an old era and the beginning of a new era)—are fused together, leaving the film open to multiple interpretations.

The last scene cuts back to a wide shot of the wild sorghum, so strong and strapping. It swings again under the blood-red sky which declares the final victory of "primitive passion." As if echoing this iconic imagery of the vital,

Film poster for *Red Sorghum* (1987); it is a still from the final battle sequence.

thriving sorghum, the music shifts from a child's haunting incantation of a prayer for the mother's soul (resembling an ancient Chinese rite of the evocation of death and ancestral souls) to a full restatement of the lovemaking theme by the entire orchestra which ushers in the closing credits. The climactic readoption of the lovemaking theme played by a full orchestra during the film's conclusion not only recuperates the central romance through music, but also exalts the triumph of a passionate, persevering, and free-spirited life, the most resounding note of *Red Sorghum*.

Zhang Yimou-Zhao Jiping: Contemporary Trends in Film and Music Cross-production

Three theme songs from *Red Sorghum*—"Jolting Sedan" (*Dianjiao qu*), "Sister, March Forward Bravely" (*Meimei, ni dadan de wang qian zou*), and "Ode to the Wine God" (*Jiushen qu*)—have become among the most popular songs in Northwest Wind style, embarking on a new trend of collaboration and cross-promotion between film and music in late 1980s China. In an interview, Zhao Jiping discusses the genesis and his scoring for *Red Sorghum*: "We had a great team and it was a perfect match. We incorporated *unconventional* ideas, *unconventional* languages, and *unconventional* musical ensembles into the film, which achieved an *unconventional* effect. All of these were never taught in the textbook."[16] Zhao Jiping's candid and daring declaration is in fact a manifesto of the film's approach as a whole. Both *Red Sorghum* and its music showcase a spectacular landscape, the spectacle of nation, culture, history, and ultimately that of the sex being, the individual being, and the living being. Like other cinematic apparatuses, film music is by no means autonomous. Not only is Zhao's music, I shall point out, "conventionally" predicated upon the internal diegesis of the film, it is also a cultural commodity intricately entangled in the political-economic network of 1980s China. Given the unique standing of *Red Sorghum* in Chinese cinema history, I am particularly interested in examining how Zhang Yimou's film and Zhao Jiping's music collaborate and reconcile themselves with China's nascent popular mass culture of the post-revolutionary era while breaking new ground aesthetically and ideologically. This complex and careful modulation between convention and invention, between commercial and artistic aims, I show, has become a pivotal theme that runs through all of *Red Sorghum* and its soundtrack.

Unlike many film composers, especially his predecessors in Shanghai during the 1930s and 1940s who were trained in the Western musical tradition, Zhao Jiping completed his formal training in Chinese folk music and opera. He enrolled in the department of folk music at Xi'an Music Conservatory with a particular focus on *erhu* performance (one of the most popular traditional Chinese string instruments). After graduating in 1970, he was assigned to the Shaanxi Opera and Drama Research Institute, where he worked for nearly twenty years. Throughout his career, Zhao was always engaged in the research and practice of folk music and regional opera. This experience allowed him to develop important skills that would later serve him well in writing film music, including a broad knowledge of folk idioms, a profound firsthand grasp of various indigenous musical forms, and most of all, a knack for expressing the essence of images in musical form. In 1988, Zhao got his big break in *Red Sorghum*. His ascension to center stage in film scoring parallels to a great extent the upsurge of Northwest Wind in music circles in the late 1980s.

In fact, Zhao's long-term collaboration with the Fifth Generation filmmakers had been well established by this point. It could date back to the production of *Yellow Earth* when Chen Kaige and Zhang Yimou came to Xi'an to look for a composer for their recently finished film. Zhao was a natural choice both because of his intensive experience with northwest folk music and his preeminent work for large-scale orchestra performances of similar works. Despite the meager budget, Zhao proved himself adept at creating both a commercially and artistically appealing piece. Through *Yellow Earth*, a constellation of musical talents, including He Yutang who played himself as "the best folk music singer" in the opening wedding sequence and Feng Jianxue who dubbed Cuiqiao's songs, were discovered and subsequently signed to contracts for an array of music albums. He Yutang was even pronounced the "King of Folklore" (*min'ge dawang*) by the Ministry of Propaganda in 1986. The theme song "Song of the Daughter" also generated a keen interest in northwest music and spearheaded a Northwest Wind craze to come in the following years.

After *Yellow Earth*, Zhao Jiping's music became an indispensable supplement to the Fifth Generation films. His music has been continuously featured in the two leading Fifth Generation filmmakers' works to this day. Among them are *The Big Parade* (*Da yubing*, 1986), *Farewell, My Concubine* (*Bawa bieji*, 1993), *Together with You* (*He ni zai yiqi*, 2002), *Forever Enthralled* (*Mei Lanfang*, 2008), *Red Sorghum* (*Hong gaoliang*, 1988), *Ju Dou* (*Ju dou*, 1990), *Raise the Red Lantern* (*Dahong denglong gaogao gua*, 1991), *The Story of Qiu Ju* (*Qiu ju da guansi*, 1992), and *To Live* (*Huo zhe*, 1994). When Zhao Jiping's score for *Red Sorghum* received the Best Original Music Award at the Chinese Golden Rooster Film Festival, the laurels were surely a signal which reaffirmed the Northwest Wind fad in 1980s China.

Unlike many other big productions, Zhao's music for *Red Sorghum* was not created for a full, conventional orchestra but rather composed for small ensembles of a few instruments at a time. This was in part owing to economic constraints. But its limitation also prompted Zhao to work in a manner more appropriate in the film context, particularly with Northwest Wind idioms. For a great number of films, Zhao relied chiefly on traditional Chinese musical instruments such as drum, *suona*, *sheng*, *xun* (a vessel flute, known as one of the oldest Chinese musical instruments that has been brilliantly incorporated into Zhang Yimou's *Judou*), *sanxian*, and *erhu* (a three-stringed banjo and a two-stringed bowed lute that form a prominent presence in Chen Kaige's *Life on a String* and Zhang Yimou's *To Live* respectively).

The indigenous, distinctly Chinese sounds occupy a central role in underpinning and imparting a unique flavor to his scores. While his instrumental repertory is comparatively small, Zhao is often able to achieve remarkable dramatic effects. For instance, in the wedding night episode in *Red Sorghum*, when the female protagonist is sent into the bridal chamber for Big Head Li, Zhao's almost exclusive use of a *suona* solo in a minor key with fairly slow pacing contributes to the dark and menacing quality of this sequence. The

Music album *Electric Shadow: Film Music by Zhao Jiping* (*Zhao Jiping dianying peiyue jingxuan*, Beijing: Teldec Record, 2000).

musical configuration complements and auralizes visual images that capture the communication and exchange of glances between "grandpa" and "grandma" in silence. Grandpa's hesitant glance while standing alone under an arch on top of a hill in a long shot is intercut with grandma's several backward glances, a help-seeking signal that resembles the first abduction scene in the sorghum field. The next shot depicts "grandpa" disappearing in an enveloping darkness, followed by an empty wide shot of the moon hanging on the sky.

This musical cue is repeated with certain variations in a succeeding scene that details the winery's significant restructuring after the mysterious murder of its original leprous owner. A major key is employed here to create the musical equivalent of a celebratory mood suggesting the revival and transfer of winery to the new, nurturing hand of the motherhood. Just as a crescendo reaches its peak, the musical theme is abruptly cut off. The brusque ending, nonetheless, signals a narrative transition when "grandpa" is seen suddenly breaking in with his drunken revelation of their secret lovemaking in the sorghum field. Feeling insulted by his vulgar and obscene words, "grandma" throws him out of her house, which also prefigures "grandpa's" dauntless return in the ensuing celebratory scene of wine-making (as mentioned earlier).

Unlike many film soundtracks, as Zhao Jiping notes in his brief memoir, the scores and lyrics of *Red Sorghum* were drafted before the actual film shooting.[17] The prominence of music in *Red Sorghum* is, in the first place, an indication of the acute grasp of the musician and filmmaker of the film's core and their audience's proclivity. The director Zhang Yimou explains his point of view of the film market:

> We wanted to reveal our thoughts and ideas in a natural and relaxed manner. There are many truths in this world. And actually, film is an artistic process. I've always felt that there is no need to use the screen to display profound truths—let philosophers deal with that. The most profound truths of the world are perhaps the simplest ones finished in a sentence. *Red Sorghum* of course wants to discuss some truths and ideas but hopes that they will be accepted easily and more appealing . . . When *Red Sorghum* was filmed, I also gave Wu Tianming [head of Xi'an Film Studio] three guarantees—no trouble from the government, artistic quality, and commercial box-office success.[18]

It has become almost inevitable that when addressing the Fifth Generation, many tend to pull together a comparison between Zhang Yimou and Chen Kaige, the two best-known Chinese filmmmakers. Both directors themselves also consciously make references to each other. For instance, the preceding account by Zhang Yimou has suggested the distinct paths the two filmmakers undertake. Different from Chen Kaige, whose oblique film language and cynical, elitist attitude are often at odds with a mass audience, Zhang Yimou seems more accessible and has earnestly tried to address popular desires and represent the zeitgeist of the time. In this light, *Red Sorghum* was conscientiously designed to appeal to a mass audience in order to boost its box-office returns. The incorporation of popular music into the film demonstrates this pragmatic approach.

Like other aspects of the film, its use of popular music represents a carefully managed enterprise. Zhang Yimou began to involve himself in the creation of music at a very early stage, thus facilitating a well-crafted synergy of image and music from the film's inception. Not only did he regularly meet with Zhao Jiping to discuss the overall sound of the musical score, but he was also directly involved in the composition of lyrics. For two of the four principal songs, he wrote the lyrics on his own, coupled these new songs with lavish folk traditions, and elaborately exhibited them on the screen.[19] Moreover, Zhang himself is a popular music enthusiast and singer, who has performed his own material. In his book *Like a Knife: Ideology and Genre in Contemporary Chinese Popular*

Music, Andrew Jones, one of the first Western scholars to study Chinese popular music, writes of his astonishing personal experience in 1988 when Beijing and the nation were flooded by fans yelling "Sister, March Forward Bravely" and the extravagant film musical wave of *Red Sorghum*.[20] Their phenomenal popularity reached a peak in July 1988, when the Beijing Worker's Stadium was inundated by more than 10,000 feverish fans for a concert of Northwest Wind hits. Most of the singers at the concert were professional pop stars. The atmosphere in the stadium reached a frenetic apex when Zhang Yimou, joined by Wu Tianming, filmmaker and the principal of Xi'an Film Studio, roared out his Red Sorghum songs to a fanatical audience.

Second of all, the reversed order of film shooting and musical composition in the case of *Red Sorghum* helps foster an unprecedented and cultish appreciation of film music insofar as it alters the conventions of spotting (the process by which the composer, director, and music editor determine the placement of music in relation to visual sequences after shooting). This is novel in that it invokes a new mode of audiovisual relations different from that of classical film scoring. In *Red Sorghum*, music plays a privileged rather than a subordinate role in constructing the diegesis. If we say that the "sour tunes" in *Yellow Earth* are to challenge the institutions and conventions of history, culture, and national identity in socialist and patriarchal Chinese society, the folk songs of *Red Sorghum* then unpack the exotic rural landscape and hyperbolic sexuality, repackaging them into visual and audible commodities. Andrew Jones goes on to illustrate the appeal of *Red Sorghum*'s music from a cultural standpoint and a perspective of spectatorship:

> "Sister, Go Bravely Forward" is a song to be shouted, and its popularity lays the fact that listeners were gratified by shouting along with the song . . . Complex issues of gender are also at work here, for this kind of shouting is, both in the film and in everyday usage, an expression of the "primitive" virility of male sexual desire. At the same time, the discursive context of the song—i.e. its links to a public debate over the organic, subjective, and liberating nature of the primitive culture from which China ostensibly arose—add an implicit ideological dimension to the song's pleasure.[21]

For Jones, it is the rough, powerful, masculine, and sexy quality of the vocal song that accounts for its unfailing popularity among Chinese youth and urbanites. Thus, my question is: how and by what means exactly? If one reads and listens to the song closely again, one may find that the vocal lines of "Sister, March Forward Bravely" are essentially structured around a sequence of yells and loud cries. Each stanza begins with a "hey" that takes up the entire measure. Each line of verse ends with a shouted "ah" that conspicuously lasts a full beat.

The sound the voice makes, as Kaja Silverman contends in *The Acoustic Mirror: The Female Voice in Psychoanalysis and Cinema*, is perhaps the purest of all that is "closely identified with the infantile scene."[22] What Silverman implies is that, as opposed to language (which is the site of the symbolic and law of the father), the voice represents a pre-Oedipal phase outside of language and patriarchal dominance—in other words, a powerful, "*vraisemblable*" and "sexually differentiated" domain. "The voice is never completely standardized, forever retaining an individual flavor or texture—what Barthes calls its 'grain.'"[23] To be sure, the husky, earthy singing—uttered naturally without any musical accompaniment and voluptuously acted out by the musically untrained but well-shaped, virile character in *Red Sorghum*—is again a classic example of Barthes's conception of "the grain of the voice." The basic thrust of music, as Barthes states, lies in its sensuality and capacity to connect to the audience through the language and sound of the body. Hence, it is ultimately "the return of prosodic and metrical work of the language," "the body in the voice as it sings," "the hand as it writes," "the limb as it performs."[24] In this light, I argue that some of the key musical moments in *Red Sorghum*, such as the boisterous sedan jolting, the enigmatic lovemaking in the sorghum field, and the sacrificial offering to the wine god, achieve their special auras because of their inscription on the body and indeed their close linkage to physical corporeality and impetus. The body and the moving image responding to music become part of music. Zhang Yimou's accentuation and use of sound and body in such an integral way offers a model for a specifically experimental yet popular film practice in postsocialist China. Simply put, *Red Sorghum* is a cinematic and musical ode to life and is, in itself, a song-and-dance ritual in awe of nature, human nature, and the human body.

Derived from a mixture of regional operas and folk songs, and deeply rooted in everyday life, this breathy and hearty singing, on the one hand, sets itself apart from the officially recognized bel canto and artistic folk/national style. On the other hand, the singing cannot be read as simply a challenge to cultural hegemony and to what Chinese authorities deem appropriate aesthetically and ideologically. It is a cultural negotiation with "Southeast Wind" (*dongnan feng*), the prevalent popular songs from Hong Kong and Taiwan often marked by a sense of intimacy and sentimentalism. In contrast to the polished crooning of the imported pop songs from Hong Kong and Taiwan, the loud, coarse cries in *Red Sorghum* appear somewhat raw and harsh. But it is through this unique vocal catharsis that the performers, filmmakers, and audiences vent their repressed desire and reassert their subjectivities. It helps the first popular music current on the mainland—Northwest Wind—regain some of the mainland's esteem and cultural privileges which had been lost since the founding of PRC. As Jones further points out, *Red Sorghum*'s popular songs significantly resonate with and evoke a particularly nationalist sentiment in 1980s China. To extend this point, I argue that *Red Sorghum*'s image and music dynamics, and their virtuoso infusion, create a space for political intervention and social dialogue at a particular juncture of transformation. This, then, is the third important factor contributing to the film's record-breaking success both at the box office and on the music charts.

To summarize, the fact that *Red Sorghum*'s well-crafted music is intricately related to the film's visual narrative is what largely allowed it to achieve a unique and distinctive cult status in film and cultural history. It accomplishes "root-seeking" through cinematic-musical breakthroughs with a modernist, post-revolutionary goal to unleash repressed desire, subjective consciousness, and a "primitive passion" for love and human life. The literary source of Mo Yan, winner of the Nobel Prize in Literature in 2012, paved the groundwork for the film. Yet a considerable part of the film, especially the traditional customs and music in film, was nonetheless of Zhang Yimou's own design.[25] As a close, semiotic analysis of *Red Sorghum* has just shown, the cinematic imaginary of folklore and vernacular customs is not only integral to narrative construction, but is also a vital means to win the identification of a mass audience within the larger context of the Northwest Wind craze during the late 1980s. Zhang Yimou and Zhao Jiping's idiosyncratic creation and collaboration, as well as the exquisite integration of image-music-text (in the code of Barthes), is a pragmatic posture that grapples with contemporary concerns and possibilities and in turn shapes the shifting popular landscape in China's sea change.

Breaking Silence, Vernacular Artifacts, and the Son's Generation

In the wake of *Red Sorghum* becoming a sensational hit, Zhang Yimou became a household name, as did the generation he represented. In the mid-to-late 1980s, when the historically old was giving way to an oncoming socio-economically and culturally new, the Fifth Generation's critical and aesthetic exploration of selfhood through audiovisual experimentation was grounded in and synthetically linked to high cultural fever and elitist discourse of the 1980s.[26] By virtue of the post-revolutionary sharp turn, the Fifth Generation enjoyed unprecedented freedom to craft and infused their films with artistic vitality and intellectual insights. Their works in many ways signify an ideological-historical-cultural break with socialist doctrines, Confucian tradition, patriarchy, and by extension, the symbolic order. Yet what should be taken into account is that their productions in the early phase were still by and large cultivated and spawned within the socialist state studio system. Most filmmakers were contracted to the state-owned studios.

In this regard, the Fifth Generation's revolution is not completely separated from but is instead vitally connected to the cinematic, musical, artistic, and cultural traditions of China (such as Chinese landscape painting, Taoist philosophy, folk music, and so forth). Their stylistic audiovisual innovations operate through a new lens and a new language, but they are nevertheless inscribed on the body of older customs and rites, as is evident in their ethnographic, lavish depictions of wedding ceremonies, preindustrial labor, prayers for rain, chants for ancestors, and sacred funerals. The linkage is also noticeable in their appropriation and negotiation with predominantly socialist genres, including the revolutionary epic and ethnographic minority film, as well as in their recyling of the formulaic spatio-temporal symbols, such as the Yellow River, Northwest Plateau, Mongolian grassland, mountain village in southwest China, and historical backdrops of the Sino-Japanese War and the Cultural Revolution. As Rey Chow writes perceptively:

> Regardless of their personal intentions, Chen Kaige, Tian Zhuangzhuang, Zhang Yimou, and their contemporaries become their culture's anthropologists and ethnographers, capturing the remnants of a history that has undergone major disasters while at the same time imparting information about "China" to the rest of the world. In their hands, filmmaking itself becomes a space that is bifurcated between the art museum and the ethnological museum, a space that inevitably fetishizes and commodifies "China" even while it performs the solemn task of establishing records of China's cultural violence.[27]

In another incisive portrayal of the Fifth Generation, Dai Jinhua, an eminent feminist scholar and film critic from mainland China, to a great extent agrees with Chow's claim of the Fifth Generation's pragmatic "packaging" of landscape, oppressive women, and local culture for a new kind of filmmaking, namely, filmmaking as a mode of ethnography, autoethnography, and most of all, cultural consumption and translation. Dai moves on to draw a conclusion that the Fifth Generation is "the generation of the son" which is paradoxically preoccupied while wrestling with the historical past; hence, "the son" who rebels "in the name of the father." She comments:

> Like all cultural movements after May Fourth, it [the Fifth Generation's movement] is built on a dilemma. On the one hand, it conducts a "root-searching movement" in order to revive national culture, national tradition,

and national spirit. On the other hand, it issues a call for enlightenment, a call to critique and negate national culture and tradition, to excavate "the ills of national character," and to portray the silent spirit of the citizenry.[28]

Such remarks invoke a famous quote by Lu Xun, one of the greatest writers in modern China, who pities Chinese culture and traditional ideology. In the essay "Silent China," he writes: "We have men but no voices, and how lonely that is! Can men be silent? No, not unless they are dead, or—to put it more politely—when they are dumb. To restore speech to this China which has been silent for centuries is not an easy matter. It is like ordering a dead man to live again."[29] In this essay and many other writings he published—for example, "A Madman's Diary," "The True Story of Ah Q," and "My Old Home"—Lu Xun penetratingly portrays a prototype of the apathetic Chinese and lambasts Chinese culture as being inarticulate, impassive, and therefore cannibalistic. Silence—the dumb, unnerving silence—becomes, alas, a feature that defines Chineseness, or what Lu Xun terms "national character" (*guomin xing*). At the end of this piece, Lu Xun calls for a reform, a change, and the future of a new China: "First our young people must turn China into an articulate country. Speak out boldly, advance fearlessly, with no thought of personal gain, brushing aside the ancients, and expressing your true thoughts . . . And only then shall we be able to move the people of China and the world. Only then shall we be able to live in the world with all the other nations."[30] These passages, although written over half a century ago, are, in my judgment, a fitting description of and prophecy for the new wave cinema and the overall cultural atmosphere in 1980s China.

It can be argued that the Fifth Generation movement of the 1980s is a critical reflection on silence and a reconfiguration of the familiar scenario of silence in cinematic terms. Their films deliberately and dramatically deploy the language of silence and the ineffable to reflect their doubts, predicaments, and subject positions as "the son" in post-revolutionary China. The status and stance of the son for the Fifth Generation is profoundly allegorical. In an interesting way, the son-child figure from their films—for example, Hanhan in *Yellow Earth* and the cowherd boy in *King of the Children*—is often inarticulate or mute. This serves as a sarcastic and cartoonish self-portrait of the filmmakers themselves or what Dai Jinhua calls "the allegorical icon of the non-linguistic reality."[31] In other words, the son's films have become both an allegorical and linguistic space, in which fictional characters as well as filmmakers themselves are caught between historical circularity, the inexplicable experience of the nation, and their personal, individualist endeavors. Reflecting on the "non-linguistic reality," the Fifth Generation distinguish themselves in their unusual use of minimalist dialogue, elliptical speech, and evocative silence. The aural ambiguity, opacity, and symbolism, in sync with visual intensity and density, have underscored the cinematic allegory of the Fifth Generation.

Through the alliance of the filmmaker and musician, *Yellow Earth* and *Red Sorghum* aptly tapped into the popular trends and fed the late 1980s' craze for Northwest Wind. An array of customs and iconographies from *Red Sorghum*, such as the wedding parade and the hilarious sedan bouncing, were extensively reproduced in the marketplace and became a symbol of indigenousness or "Chineseness" in festival celebrations and in performances for tourists— what I would call vernacular artifacts in that sense.[32] The same applied to the trademark waist-drum dancing from *Yellow Earth*, which made recurrent appearances during some of the nation's most important moments, such as the opening ceremony at the 11th Asian Games in 1990 and Hong Kong's handover ceremony in 1997. In much the same way, a stock of imageries and musical patterns from the Fifth Generation films are disassembled and reassembled into Northwest Wind music videos, serving effectively both as narrative devices and commercial attractions. For instance, capitalizing on the Northwest Wind craze, a refurnished drum-dancing sequence and wedding ritual derived from *Yellow Earth* and *Red Sorghum* feature prominently in the music video of "Hills of Yellow Earth," a big hit performed by the popular star Li Na and one of the first music videos produced in China.

In conclusion, the Fifth Generation's new wave cinema stands markedly in the typography of Chinese film history as *the* watershed or a "severed bridge," to borrow Dai Jinhua's formula, which is allegorically situated at the crossroads of a revolutionary past, the reformed present, and an unwritten future. The metaphorical description of "severed bridge" also explains and epitomizes the Fifth Generation's modernist and vernacular treatment of film music and sound and their conceptualization of sound in the form of allegory-cum-spectacle. With the staple of "Northwest Wind," the son's generation creates a prototype of popular film music and cinematic modernism-vernacularism that would come to penetrate Chinese life throughout the late 1980s, 1990s, and into the twenty-first century. Furthermore, it inaugurated a postsocialist zeitgeist whose aesthetic metaphor, folksy style, modernist pursuit, and indigenous impulse would continue to exert a fundamental influence upon youth subculture and rock 'n' roll film in the next decade.

CHAPTER THREE

"Rock 'n' Roll on the New Long March": Cui Jian and the Voices and Moving Images of Chinese Rock Kids

> [You] have heard about, but never seen twenty-five thousand miles...
> Keep my head down, and march forward in search of my true self...
> —**Cui Jian**, "Rock 'n' Roll on the New Long March" (1989)[1]

As Northwest Wind—a popular musical style that distinctively draws from indigenous culture, especially folklore tradition of the yellow earth—began to decline, another musical trend overtook it. This new style, which incubated almost concurrently with Northwest Wind and a larger movement of cultural fever, sprang up before the outbreak of the Tiananmen Square protest of 1989, made its transition to the 1990s, and continues to exert a profound impact on Chinese music and cultural life to this day. I am referring to the phenomenon of Chinese rock 'n' roll (*yaogun yinyue*). Historians and critics trace the roots of Chinese rock 'n' roll to the summer of 1986, when an angry young musician named Cui Jian stirred up the country with "Nothing to My Name" (*Yi wu suo you*), an innovative fusion of Western rock rhythm and Northwest Wind melody. The song debuted as part of the 100 Pop Stars Concert at the Beijing Worker's Stadium. Not only is this song acknowledged to be a milestone in Chinese rock history, but it also made Cui Jian's name synonymous with Chinese rock music.

Charged with a subcultural sensibility, rock music was enthusiastically embraced by a cohort of Chinese youth and scholars alike, who came to valorize its unique status as politically subversive and artistically authentic. "Since its release, the wide availability of this music of anger and frustration has continued to empower opposition to the regime. *Yaogun yinyue*'s role as an objectification of anti-government feeling—as a resource for use in political opposition—has intensified."[2] Brace and Friedlander's forceful characterization here invokes a conventional paradigm of how popular culture is predicated on its political valence and social relevance. In this regard, Chinese rock is "politicized pop" *par excellence.* The intensely celebrated and romanticized "rock mythology,"[3] as Jeroen de Kloet puts it, rests on two distinct yet interdependent thrusts; while the definition of Chinese rock as a music genre manifestly draws back to its Western heritage, it also derives its particular meaning from its opposition to the hegemony of both the state and the commercial mainstream. Put another way, although Chinese rock has been identified by its innate Western (transnational) character, it is still largely evaluated by its political (or rather oppositional) values. Cold War discourses tend to dominate discussions of Chinese rock and a wide spectrum of cultural forms and artistic expressions (including the Sixth Generation's filmmaking) in academic circles. However, to reduce Chinese rock simply to a symbolic act of rebellion and classify it under a monolithic label of "alternative" and "subversive" prioritizes a constricted ideological reading and neglects the nuances and different dimensions at work within the genre. My book takes a different approach.

In this chapter, I argue that the Sixth Generation, or a new generation of urban young filmmakers in a broader sense, has fostered a more direct relationship with popular music. This draws on (but fundamentally differs from) the cinematic and musical vocabularies of Northwest Wind. Commonly regarded as a new batch of independent vanguard artists, the Sixth Generation filmmakers earned a good deal of cultural and symbolic capital through their brazen efforts to evade the state studio system and other mainstream institutions. For the most part born in the 1960s, they were the first generation to grow up in the city in PRC; their personal "coming of age" narratives therefore overlapped historically with the course of socialist revolution and postsocialist reform. As a cluster of young urbanites who found creative ways to document the ever-changing cityscape they have experienced, this new group of film auteurs are as marked by the turbulent events that structured their youth as by their hyperbolic positioning as dissidents. The films produced by this group of talented firebrands were made for, and mainly circulated among, a limited number of underground cineclubs, festivals, and Western art-house theaters. Unlike their renowned Fifth Generation predecessors, they are also the first group of directors to be caught up in a maelstrom of institutional film reform. The transformation of film studios from state-monopolized entities into market-driven enterprises has pushed them to the forefront of the market with fewer attachments to—as well as protection from—the state.

These artists' relative freedom to make personal pieces, as well as their newly gained economic power enabled through transnational capitalism, allowed them to hone films in entirely new ways; hence the rise of a new generation and the second Chinese New Wave. Taken together, the Sixth Generation films are at once "political" and "anti-political" in the sense that they vigorously bypass the official channels overseen by the state from financing to production to distribution and herald a new wave of transnational cinema and independent artistic practice. This unique film trajectory, in a significant way, parallels the growth and development of youth culture and popular music in the 1990s and the new twenty-first century.

Popular music, rock in particular, penetrated the cinematic space of everydayness beginning in the late 1980s and provoked the formation of a specific film genre: Chinese rock 'n' roll. The alliances between the Sixth Generation and rock music have attracted considerable scholarly attention in recent years,[4] but many of these analyses are still limited by traditional classifications of film genres and conventional historiographies of Chinese filmmakers, the dominant discourses and methodological frameworks in Chinese film studies. My intent, in this chapter, is by no means to challenge the important link between the Sixth Generation and rock culture, as their films were openly concerned with youthful characters, subcultural sensibilities, and a peculiar visual-vocal style that was soundly integrated with Chinese rock culture. This is clearly evident in many films including *Beijing Bastards* (*Beijing zazhong*, dir. Zhang Yuan, 1993), *Dirt* (*Toufa luanle*, dir. Guan Hu, 1994), *Age of Sensitivity* (*Ganguang shidai*, dir. Ah Nian, 1994), *Weekend Lover* (*Zhoumo qingren*, dir. Lou Ye, 1995), *How the Steel Was Tempered* (*Gangtie shi zenyang liancheng de*, aka *Zhangda chengren*, dir. Lu Xuezhang, 1997), and *Quitting* (*Zuotian*, dir. Zhang Yang, 2001). Yet rock has also found its way into a vast array of works across different generations, ranging from Zhang Nuanxin's *Good Morning, Beijing* (*Beijing, nizao*, 1990), Xie Fei's *Black Snow* (*Ben Mingnian*, 1990), both with directors from the elite background of the earlier Fourth Generation; to works by the eminent Fifth Generation group, including Tian Zhuangzhuang's *Rock Kids* (*Yaogun qingnian*, 1988), Zhang Yimou's *Keep Cool* (*Youhua haohao shuo*, 1997); to films from the more commercially oriented "newcomers," such as Mi Jiashan's *The Troubleshooters* (*Wanzhu*, 1988) and Xia Gang's *Half Is Water, Half Is Flame* (*Yiban shi haisui, yiban shi huoyan*, 1988).

Deliberately crafted to assert a specific cultural identity and reflect social change at the turn of the twentieth century, rock became a platform upon which diverse generations of filmmakers, ideologies, styles, and artistic practices converged. The complex character and intricate intersections of rock 'n' roll and urban cinema thus call for a more nuanced deliberation, as rock in some of these films is neither merely a dissenting outcry nor a simple matter of "generation," but rather a polyphonic voice and aesthetic regime, representing a specific zeitgeist for a new period of globalization and postsocialist reform.

Everyday man-woman and urban subjects resurfaced and were reinvigorated in films and other popular media in the late twentieth century after nearly four decades of obliteration since the founding of PRC. This is demonstrated by Wang Shuo Fever, a fad named after an extremely popular writer whose works were zealously adapted into films and TV plays in the late 1980s and 1990s. Popular music—specifically, rock songs—were widely used in these films to supplement and underline their characterizations and dramatic actions; and moreover, to endow a strong sense of contemporaneity, social urgency, and irony characteristic of Wang Shuo's realistic, sardonic works. The nervy limning, questioning, and conflicting sentiments of the current status quo in the cutthroat transformation of postsocialist China are not only present in adapted works from Wang Shuo—for example, *The Troubleshooters* (to be analyzed in the following section)—but are also what make *Beijing Bastards* arresting and pleasantly disturbing in the playlists of Chinese classics, arguably the first Chinese rock 'n' roll film featuring Cui Jian in the multiple roles of protagonist, scriptwriter, and co-producer.

By examining how Cui Jian's rock star persona and his film persona coalesce in various films, I argue that Chinese rock 'n' roll movies are not just symptomatic texts of youth rebellion or another privileged example of orchestrating sight and sound, but are also a lens focused on the traumatic and confounded postsocialist experience and the "lost" generation in search of identity against the backdrop of urbanization and globalization. In sync with the kaleidoscopic manifestation of the cityscape and the long tracking shots of protagonists roaming the metropolis, rock music, alongside the handheld mobile camera, seeks to document a reality of postmodern life and capture a feeling of postsocialist anxiety—a concern for realism also articulated through quotidian dialogue and ambient sound recorded live on the spot (*xianchang*).

Troubleshooters or Troublemakers: Noise, Hooligans, and the Rise of New Urban Youth Culture

The late 1980s was a period of fundamental transition in Chinese cinema and culture. Zhang Yimou's *Red Sorghum* astutely encapsulates the changing currents in which it does more than simply register the elitist discourse of high modernism and new wave cinema. It provides an idiosyncratic portrait of the raw, unfettered world of nature and human beings. What's more, on the threshold of 1987, the film exhibits the critical ways in which the Fifth Generation, in the face of a slump in film attendance, strived to adapt their works to the everyday, secular world, readdressing a mass audience stylistically, visually, and musically. The same year saw a steady rise of popular films in which the urban reoccupied the center stage. Except for a few films, such as *Red Sorghum* and *King of the Children*, in which the camera still lingered on rural and historical landscapes, a large number of filmmakers shifted their lenses to the new terrain of the city—to contemporaneous and everyday life. This move mirrored a significant turn in post-revolutionary reform from initial agricultural experiments to an in-depth modernization in all realms, especially of the major cities and urban areas.

Zhou Xiaowen's *Desperation* (*Zuihou de fengkuang*, 1987), Huang Jianxin's *Dislocation* (*Cuowei*, 1986), Zhang Zeming's *Sun Showers* (*Taiyangyu*, 1987), and Sun Zhou's *Put Some Sugar in the Coffee* (*Gei kafei jia dianr tang*, 1987) are paradigmatic examples of this new social, cultural, and cinematic shift. These filmmakers became active at the same time as Zhang Yimou, Chen Kaige, and Tian Zhuangzhuang, yet they worked in a mode quite unlike their internationally acclaimed colleagues who had conspicuously adopted a "root-seeking" and "Northwest Wind" formula of film languages and genres. Instead, this faction of urban filmmakers moved their cameras closer to everyday scenes and plebeian figures to create a new spatiotemporality and a novel aesthetic of urban realism. The vast constellation of urban personae created or recuperated by market reform and urbanization—including police officers, criminals, engineers, party cadre members, small vendors, young entrepreneurs, and delinquent youth—now came to dominate the screen. These films range widely, from lighthearted, cheerful comedies to serious social dramas with a humanist tone to sarcastic, cynical sketches of the present society.

In 1988, immediately following the overwhelming success of *Desperation*, Zhou Xiaowen went on to make a sequel in his "Frenzy" (*fengkuang*) series, *Obsession* (*Fengkuang de daijia*, 1988)—a well-crafted blend of crime noir and detective thriller that again proved to be both artistically and commercially viable. At almost the same time, under the auspices of Xi'an Film Studio, Huang Jianxin, a Fifth Generation maverick, finished the third piece, *Samsara* (*Lunhui*, 1988), of his urban trilogy. The work extends Huang's trademark social satire and absurdist approach, into which he often weaves a deft critique of the socialist (and postsocialist) status quo. The narrative features an adventurous young entrepreneur whose professional identity (*daoye*, an unemployed smuggler who lives through illicit deals using goods from the black market) and personal traits pose great challenges to the existing social norms and moral boundaries. Based upon Wang Shuo's popular novel, the film pays homage to hooligan literature (*pizi wenxue*) and the hooligan craze Wang Shuo polemically provoked at the end of the 1980s.

Wang Shuo's extremely intimate, *outré* depictions of antiheroes in contemporary urban milieus have been popular but also enormously controversial. As disclosed by the numerous accounts of Wang Shuo's life, as well as his own autobiography, *I Am Wang Shuo* (1992), when the economic reform took off, Wang Shuo quit the navy and a job in a medical company to pursue a career as a freelancer and a full-time writer. No longer contracted to the state with a fixed wage, Wang Shuo made a living from his own writing and enjoyed the new degree of freedom offered by self-employment, a phenomenon *du jour* only made possible after the market reform. In another sense, Wang Shuo's popular writing, addressing common people and everyday life, suggests a significant break from the elite, culturist movement of the 1980s. Identified as "the most conspicuous and articulate epochal marker for the transition of the 1980s into the 1990s," Wang Shuo and Wang Shuo Phenomenon have been quite often singled out as signals for the final advent of the "plebeian stratum" (*shimin jieceng*) and civil society in contemporary China.[5] Such a turn evidenced and propelled by Wang Shuo indeed anticipated the explosion of mass consumer culture in the post-1989 era.

Wang Shuo rose to prominence as a bestselling author in the mid-to-late 1980s. Many of his works were then quickly adapted into films: Ling Qiwei's *Angels and Demons* (*Tianshi yu mogui*, 1987), Huang Jianxin's *Samsara* (*Lunhui*, 1988), Mi Jiashan's *The Troubleshooters* (*Wanzhu*, 1988), Ye Daying's *Big Breath* (*Dachuanqi*, 1988), Xia Gang's *Half Is Water, Half Is Flame* (*Yiban shi haishui, yiban shi huoyan*, 1988), Li Ziyu's *A Mysterious Couple* (*Shenmi fuqi*, 1991), Xia Gang's *No One Cheers* (*Wuren hecai*, 1993), Feng Xiaogang's *Gone Forever with My Love* (*Yongshi wo ai*, 1994), Jiang Wen's *In the Heat of the Sun* (*Yangguang canlan de rizi*, 1995), and many more.[6] 1988 was even dubbed the "Wang Shuo Year of Chinese Cinema," after four of the above films were adapted from his popular novels within the span of just twelve months. They all became big hits in theaters, and this joint venture between novel and film turned Wang Shuo into a household name.

Among them, *The Troubleshooters* offers a faithful cinematic adaptation of its original literary source; it pays tribute to Wang Shuo's unique social satire, signature hooliganism, and "hedonistic view of life." Riding on the coattails of the so-called Wang Shuo Fever (*Wang Shuo re*) and the new vogue that Wang Shuo's popular stories provoked, *The Troubleshooters* is "the first specimen" of a "marketized" cinema[7] and a prelude to the proliferation of urban youth film that would follow in the next decades. The film opens with a dark screen, against which the name of the production company—Emei Film Studio—conspicuously occupies the center of the frame in a striking white tint. The camera then fades into a completely blacked-out screen, from which three highly stylized modernist sculptures emerge, superimposed with the film title and a freeze-frame lasting over twenty seconds. In tandem with this peculiar cinematic setting and *mise-en-scène*, music and sound effects are distinctively incorporated hereby to evince a similar interest in modernist irony and (sur)realist aesthetics within postsocialist city life. A slice of music emanating from "Hills on Yellow Earth" (*Huangtu gaopo*), a popular Northwest Wind song that virtually became the national anthem for the year of 1988, reveals the diegetic and production time of *The Troubleshooters*. Blended together is a creative appropriation and amplification of various ambient sounds. Hence, we hear an aural collage consisting of the wailing sirens of a passing ambulance, a male voice brazenly hawking movie tickets for Jet Li's martial arts flicks that seems to compete with the public announcement from the Chairman Mao Memorial Hall at the Tiananmen Square, among other acoustic tropes. All of these effectively anchor the film in a post-revolutionary urban milieu, Beijing specifically. This uncanny opening shot with a tangible, evocative auditory design is pivotal in that it introduces a seemingly conflicting postsocialist realistic and surrealistic undertone essential to the film.

The Troubleshooters then lapses into a visual assemblage of varied snapshots of the urbanscape of late 1980s China: panoramic shots of a sprawling city penetrated by cranes, scaffolds, and rapidly erected skyscrapers; long shots of traffic moving through streets and busy intersections; close-ups of breakdancers, tattooed youngsters, rockers with spiky hair, and a Chinese national flag; wide shots of a milling crowd filling the job fair and flea market; colossal throngs with puzzled looks; and, finally, a blond woman who walks around the square with taglines of "Foreign Devil" (*yang guizi*) and "No Foreign Exchange" (*meiyou waihuijuan*) scratched on her T-shirt. The establishing shots of rare footage and flashcards of an urban landscape in a quasi-documentary manner are reminiscent of the classic opening of *Street Angel* (*Malu tianshi*, dir. Yuan Muzhi, 1937), an exemplary piece in Chinese film history noted for its realistic portrayal of 1930s thriving Shanghai, a Chinese city of great importance for its role in negotiating reconciliations between East and West, between traditional and modern, and between different epochs.

In his post-production interview, director Mi Jiashan peruses the particular opening scene to explicate his creative goal. To him, it was intentionally "designed as though it were a naturally occurring moment in real life. The moment was further emphasized by the time, background, and live

The Troubleshooters (1987): The first auditory and visual cues generate an uncannily realistic/surrealistic feel.

atmosphere. Modern buildings were shot reflected in a window, which distorted their appearance and matched the group of distorted, disturbed characters in the film."⁸ Mi concludes that what he attempted in *The Troubleshooters* was a deliberate departure from the Fifth Generation's extravagant historical epics and instead aimed for "the merger of absurdity (*huangmiu*) with an on-the-spot (*xianchang*) recording style."⁹

On the one hand, the film is tinged with a hyperrealistic tone through audiovisual techniques and inherent social concerns and criticism. Many of the street scenes, for example, were shot secretly by a hidden camera and a telephoto lens deployed from a car.¹⁰ In addition, *The Troubleshooters* thoughtfully incorporates synchronized sounds and noises of urban life, such as sirens, crowd chatter, and public broadcast over loudspeakers, adding a documentary feel and a sense of raw reality to the film. Crosscuttings between long shots and close-ups, and the creative coordination between slow-motion and fast-action photography, are rendered as such to evoke and mimic the speed, pace, and atmosphere of the city, as well as the rhythm of the theme song of the film, "I am the Troubleshooter" (*Wo shi wanzhu*). Accompanying the opening sequence, we hear the first bit of the song:

> I dreamed of modern city life . . .
> The number of skyscrapers is increasing everyday here . . .
> Everyone puts on an artificial mask
> Ah, ya, ah, ya, how could I possibly put into words?

The cityscape, cultural T-shirt, and rock song "I am the Troubleshooter" in the opening sequence of *The Troubleshooters*.

The extra-diegetic insertion of a rock song over the opening scene not only provides a fitting commentary on the visual mélange of modern city life as previously depicted, but also identifies and highlights a distinctly youthful point of view. The stammering and puzzled idlers referenced in the song represent an archetype of the new young urbanite in reformist China. "Finding a friend to kill time in the pub," drinking, wandering about, and listening to "popular songs from the recorder"—all youth-oriented activities described in the song—fill up large sections of screen time in *The Troubleshooters*. Most importantly, the song's implied "I"—a daydreamer, cynic, and irreverent observer who has been complexly entwined in a multi-layered, mixed reality of "on-the-spot" and "absurdity"—becomes a central character on film for the first time in the real sense.

On the other hand, *The Troubleshooters* sketches out the unusual services of the Three T Company (*santi gongsi*, literally meaning "the three substitutes") in a surrealist, comic style, whose aim is chimerically to "get people out of difficulty, help people amuse themselves, and take the place of people in trouble" (*tiren paiyou, tiren jienan, tiren shouguo*). Loosely structured around a sequence of bizarre occurrences that the Three T Company is involved in, the film chronicles the struggles of the special company formed by three unemployed, disaffected youths (Yu Guan, Yang Zhong, and Ma Qing). One is hired by a doctor as a stand-in to date his girlfriend; the other is to take the blame from a furious wife; and another to stage a fake literary award for a distressed author who cannot sell his books but desperately aspires to fame. Like Wang Shuo's novel, the film features a new breed of insignificant "little characters," or antiheroes, who are tauntingly anti-parent, anti-society, anti-intellectual, anti-state, and, above all, anti-authority.

In the first part of *The Troubleshooters*, Yang Zhong is sent to fill in for a doctor who is not able to show up for a date. Yang tickles the girl and kills time by babbling about the meaning of life, constantly referring to Western theories from Nietzsche to Freud to existentialism, all of which acutely serve as parodies to the social-cultural trends of the day. This is a scene that astutely seizes the cultural fever of 1980s China, a moment when the West and critical discourses of Western high modernism were feverishly and indiscreetly embraced by intellectuals as well as the ordinary masses. The hackneyed Western concept, for instance, of Freud's Oedipus complex, is tactfully recycled here to augment the playful and ironic tone of the film. And the captivated girl, whom the film calls "a modernist" (*xiandai pai*), comes up with a quip in typical Wang Shuo-esque humor:

"Hey, according to Freud, all sons want to marry their mothers. Don't you?"

"The one who married my mother is my dad. It is impossible for me to marry my mother before my father," Yang Zhong retorts.

"What I'm saying is not you are married to your mother but you cannot because of ethical considerations. No one can marry his mother. What I mean is that you only want to marry your mother but you cannot because of your father; you can't fall for anyone else because of your father. Huh, how come I'm talking in circles?" The girl pauses, touching her cheek for a second thought.

This scene nicely captures Wang Shuo's tongue-in-cheek satire, particularly his denunciation of high culture and high theory as totally hollow and meaningless. In the same fashion, the film ridicules the presiding elite culture and intellectuals in the reform era. Often disparaged by cultural authorities and self-proclaimed serious artists of the 1980s as representative of *pizi* ("riff-raff" or "scum"), the petty characters in Wang Shuo's films, however, stand out as a unique group of youth who relentlessly lampoon Chinese intellectuals and their notions of morality and integrity. Moreover, they seek pleasure and profit contrastingly and talk about fame and money with open bravado. Hence, a newly coined term by Wang Shuo, *wanzhu* ("master of mischief"), which lends its name to the original title of the film in Chinese.

Wanzhu's peculiar appeal to urban youth stems firstly from this open, materialistic pursuit—what Wang Shuo calls the "hedonistic view of life"—and the characters' courage to interrogate the pre-established "truth" and stay true to their own feelings. The second dimension of its appeal, then, resides in the oral-aural—the film's snappy dialogue and humorous urban slang with Beijing inflection. It has amusingly invented a new kind of urban vernacular such as *wan'r* ("to play"), *kan* ("fast-talking" or "babbling"), and *xiahai* ("plunging into the business ocean").[11] These seemingly frivolous but truly vibrant idioms had such a mesmerizing hold on the young generation that they were quickly absorbed and became almost the standard sayings amongst youngsters of northern cities in late 1980s China.[12]

Another trend derived from *The Troubleshooters* was the loose, crew neck T-shirts with prints of humorous, ironic catchwords, as shown in the first scene of the film. Referred to as "cultural T-shirts" (*wenhua shan*), Geremie Barme observes that these special shirts were not merely fashionable commodities but also sociopolitical commentaries and satires that erupted prior to and in the aftermath of the 1989 Tiananmen incident.[13] Extending Barme's inference, I would add that the cultural T-shirt has become a unique outlet for unofficial popular culture and individual expressions, which can otherwise hardly be heard on official mainstream channels. It goes without saying that its primary source of inspiration was Wang Shuo's novels and films. Then the questions to be asked are: why at this particular time? And in what ways are "cultural T-shirts" and Wang Shuo's works peculiar embodiments of commercial culture and powerful critiques of postsocialist China? In the previous section, I have discursively mapped out the complications and contradictions of cultural productions of late 1980s China. To further unravel the problems, I wish to return to Wang Shuo's singular creation: the voice, body, and personalities of "troubleshooters," or hooligans (referred to *pizi* in Chinese), actualized and personalized at this critical juncture of postsocialist change.

So *pizi*!? Masters of mischief? Or to put it in another way, masters of playing? Are they "troubleshooters" or "troublemakers"? To a great extent, the archetypal *pizi* or hooligan in Wang Shuo's novels and film adaptations is a Chinese variation of the French *flâneur*, distinctly shaped by postsocialist consumerism and mass culture. The *flâneur* is the central figure of Charles Baudelaire's and Walter Benjamin's in-depth investigations of modernity and urban culture in nineteenth-century and twenty-century Paris. In *Charles Baudelaire: A Lyric Poet in the Era of High Capitalism*, Benjamin examines the concept and asserts forcefully:

> The crowd was the veil from behind which the familiar city as phantasmagoria beckoned to the *flâneur*. In it, the city was now landscape, now a room. And both of these went into the construction of the department store, which made use of *flânerie* itself in order to sell goods. The department store was the *flâneur*'s final coup. As *flâneurs*, the intelligentsia came into the market

place. As they thought, to observe it—but in reality it was already to find a buyer. In this intermediary stage ... they took the form of the *bohème*. To the uncertainty of their economic position corresponded the uncertainty of their political function.[14]

Benjamin's intricate deliberations of the *flâneur* and urban commercial culture provide an instructive way of understanding the metaphors, aesthetics, ideologies, "economic positions," "political functions," and "uncertainties" of urban youth film on the historical threshold of reformist China. The "troubleshooters" on-screen are in essence the Chinese counterpart of the *flâneur* who materialized at *fin de siècle* Europe. *Flâneur* arises because of the specific, concrete changes in the city's physical space—in Paris known as Haussmanization—which has rebuilt the neighborhoods, opened up new boulevards and parks, and modernized the city. In late twentieth-century China, a parallel situation of market change and demolition-and-reconstruction also produced sudden reorganizations of class structure and urban space. The "urban contract,"[15] in the words of Yomi Braester, figures actively into cinema and new visual forms, facilitating the practice of *flanerie*, which has been resolutely about vision and visuality and the relationship between capitalism and consumers. Thus, the appearance of the *flâneur*, or the equivalent figure of *pizi* in Wang Shuo's popular works, can be construed as a direct outcome of marketization, urbanization, and the particular sociopolitical changes in China since the 1980s.

In a similar vein, *pizi* is a city dweller who submits to the shock and intoxication of the commodity. He is a window shopper who goes by the *flâneur*'s gospel of loitering and is implicated in this privileged male-looking relationship. This youthful character is at once a consumer and a seller, a troublemaker and a troubleshooter, who derives sheer pleasure (*wan'r*) from urban spectacles, scopophilic pursuits, and gratifications to be found in the act of roaming through urban spaces without a specific purpose. Like Wang Shuo himself, who is quite often a descendant of the political officials from a well-off family, *pizi* is an upper-middle class figure who is able to move conspicuously about the city and who first adapts to the market event and engages in commerce (*xiahai*) owing to his advantageous gender and class status. All in all, he is a bourgeois-bohème and a member of the whole new batch of city amblers and observers who are "itinerant metaphors that register the city as a text to be inscribed, read, rewritten and reread."[16] He is, therefore, an allegorical figure closely associated with the experience of modernity, the phantasmagoria of the city, and its commodities and material culture.

The core idleness is not only embodied in *pizi*'s discursive, ambivalent gaze, but also in his mercurial dialogues and characteristic *kan* ("fast-talking" or "babbling"), which can be deemed in this light as an oral-aural form of *flanerie*. *The Troubleshooters* seems to suggest that, despite their motiveless strolling and senseless babbling, what the Chinese society lacks the most—authenticity—can only be found in these *flâneur/pizi* characters, even though they have almost become extinct. Susan Buck-Morss has expressed the same deploration in an even more compelling way:

> On the boulevards, the flaneur, now jostled by crowds and in full view of the urban poverty which inhabited public streets, could maintain a rhapsodic view of modern existence only with the aid of illusion, which is just what the literature of flanerie—physiognomies, novels of the crowd—was produced to provide. If at the beginning, the flaneur as private subject dreamed himself out into the world, at the end, flanerie was an ideological attempt to reprivatize social space, and to give assurance that the individual's passive observation was adequate for knowledge of social reality. In Benjamin's time, even this ideological form of flanerie was at the brink of decline: The flaneur had become a "suspicious" character . . . If the flaneur has disappeared as a specific figure, it is because the perceptive attitude which he embodied saturates modern existence, specifically, the society of mass consumption (and is the source of its illusions). The same can be argued for all of Benjamin's historical figures. In commodity society all of us are prostitutes, selling ourselves to strangers; all of us are collectors of things.[17]

"The combination of distracted observation and dream-like reverie,"[18] the specific urban experience, and the observational-aural-perceptive mode of the *flâneur/pizi* are projected onto *The Troubleshooters* and are especially invested into the film sequence of the fashion show.

The film rolls on to the second story in which Bao Kang, a young man without literary talent but with an insatiable greed for fame and power, approaches the Three-T company in the hope of being awarded a prize for literature. The Three-T company then has to contrive a fake award ceremony for him, which turns out to be a totally absurd, indeed dreamlike game of the *flâneur*. No trophies, certificates, or any conventional type of prizes are bestowed. Rather, a jar of Chinese pickles is capriciously awarded to each recipient who saunters to the stage and recites a "famous" line from the topical high literature. The farce of *flanerie* culminates when Bao Kang, a *pizi*-turned-writer, presents a keynote speech at the conclusion of the award ceremony, which is endowed to the same extent with hyperbolic performativity and eccentric looks. Bao Kang chatters and is even moved to tears:

> It was at that moment that I remembered my mother, my childhood, the little river that ran along the edge of the village, the squeaking noise made by the elementary school teacher as her chalk moved along the blackboard. I also remembered my aunt, and the policeman in my town; they both treated me well, not as a bad guy. When I was unsuccessful I didn't feel sad for myself but rather for them. I'd rather jump to my death than disappoint them. From that moment on, I poured all my energy into my work.

This is instantly reminiscent of the dry, clichéd speech that communist leaders and socialist heroes often delivered on important occasions similar to this, now being parodied in a postsocialist context to generate a strong comic effect.

Rightly cut into the Three-T literature award is a fashion show, the film's craziest moment that accentuates a feel of distraction, illusion, and *flanerie* as just discussed. In a substantial exegesis of the Wang Shuo phenomenon, Geremie Barme makes a reference to a journal article describing the scene as follows:

> Various pairs of opposites from throughout Chinese history are thrown together: an imperial plenipotentiary with a near-naked female weightlifter; a landlord and a poor peasant; the Red and White Armies; the PLA and Chiang Kai-shek bandits; a Red Guard and a Capitalist Roader . . . all disco dancing on the same stage. It is a historically important text, for it is a miniaturization of the text of contemporary Chinese society itself in which numerous ideologies are discoing together . . . [19]

Deliberately constructed as a performance within a performance, this fashion-show-cum-dance-party — or put differently, the circus sequence — engages critically a degree of self-reflexivity. The "historically important text" serves as a microcosm of contemporary Chinese society that penetratingly encapsulates China's new status quo—a profit-obsessed, morally corrupt, politically disillusioned, and socially restless nation—on the cusp of its metamorphosis from socialist revolution to postsocialist commodification.

Therefore, the prime targets of Mi's "inverse caricature," in the formulation of Baudelaire, are those political and cultural elites in the historical past (for instance, landlords, soldiers, party cadres, and intellectuals in the show) as well as elite high culture, which took predominance but was dwindling at the end of the 1980s and into the 1990s. "By its mania for dressing the trivia of modern life in antique clothing, it constantly commits to what I would call an inverse caricature."[20] Baudelaire endorses the value of caricature and conceives it as the most daring yet sophisticated mode of expression with critical power and revolutionary potential. Caricature's empowering force thus lies in replicating and redressing with a critical intent the medley of the old and the new, and the dialectical tension of modernity vis-à-vis antiquity. This modern/antique contradiction of the caricature could apply to *The Troubleshooters*, as we, in this doubly diegeticized moment of a comedy within a comedy, come to a "historically important" crossroads and conundrum of 1980s China: all the preexisting chronological, ideological, and logical institutions and hierarchies are dismantled and consequently inverted, and "various pairs of opposites" of times, spaces, classes, parties, races, and genders are converged and "all disco dancing on the same stage."[21]

How, then, is this cinematic invention and diversion formulated and positioned vis-à-vis the other main elements of the film, particularly the transparent opening scene of the urbanscape, which stands in stark contrast? In what ways does this fabricated scene re-register, reclaim, and redress the reality, or postsocialist realism, which forms the dominant concern of *The Troubleshooters*? How are Wang Shuo's "hooligan" attitude, his *flâneur*-inspired impulses, and his relish for Chinese urban youth culture mediated in the scene through various audiovisual means? The director's account may lend important insights to the questions above:

> The energy of the street scene I used with that music [the thematic rock song] was totally linked to that musical rhythm; we actually tried to match the beats, which helped create the atmosphere ... Nonetheless, I still believed the street scene was not strong enough to convey my feelings about confused modern urban life, so I continued to search for a stronger, more concrete way to express the idea. In the novel, the 3-T literature award ceremony ended with a dance party. By itself it would be an ordinary event, a common event, so I arranged a fashion show with a circus atmosphere. This idea was based on Eisenstein, who postulated that circus idea was to stimulate the audience's vision, which is the foundation of entertainment ... The fashion show and circus was my favourite, although it was a shift from the general tenor of the film; however, its absurdity resonates with the absurdity of the whole movie. It was also accepted by the audience for its rational sense.[22]

On top of his own interpretation and comparison of the two important scenes in the film, what is most remarkable in this elaborate annotation is Mi's underlining of "confused modern life" and "a circus atmosphere" as the main thematic motifs of *The Troubleshooters*. An intimate link between these two,

The fashion show/dance party in *The Troubleshooters*.

as he explicitly declares, is illuminated and influenced by Eisenstein's famous notion of "circus" and "montage." One can, then, argue that this luscious and ludicrous music-performance-dancing sequence is, in Eisenstein's definition, a "montage of attractions" *par excellence*: "a purposeful 'fusion' of compositional elements together with a generalized 'contour' of the image."[23] In *The Troubleshooters*, discrete images, details, and shots are juxtaposed, contrasted, disassembled, and reconstructed to create new meanings that reflect upon a distinctly mutable China and the new historical era. This "montage of attractions" is "an aggressive moment in theatre, i.e., any element of it that subjects the audience to emotional or psychological influence, verified by experience and mathematically calculated to produce specific emotional shocks in the spectator in their proper order within the whole."[24] Eisenstein goes on to conclude that "these shocks provide the only opportunity of perceiving the ideological aspect of what is being shown, the final ideological conclusion."[25] Eisenstein's view that visuality occupies a central place in the film's representation is well taken. Yet would it be "the only opportunity"?

If the aforementioned sequence in *The Troubleshooters* fancifully and playfully visualizes social chaos and ideological turmoil within 1980s China, which instantaneously delivers a series of visual shocks rather than a coherent narrative, the sense of carnivalesque and "dreamlike reverie," as I will show, is further communicated through its soundtrack and music design. The signification of the show and dance party is and has always been aligned with the "attractions" of the aural rather than merely a visual carnival. In this scene, the prominent use of electronic music, especially the incorporation of theremin sounds, helps to evoke a bizarre and whimsical tone that perfectly corresponds to the eccentric, cynical mood of the sequence and the film as a whole. Synthesized sounds saturated with drones, burps, whirs, whines, throbs, hums, screeches, as well as the audience's laughter and applause, is elicited almost in the same manner as montage, resulting in a deep sense of ironic pastiche. A strong disco rhythm—a sonic signifier of the 1980s—then notably chimes in and mingles with the various noises. Both the film's visual style and acoustic design work together to break down such familiar demarcations of binaries between profane and sublime, truth and simulation, the West and the East, local and global, elites and hooligans, inviting the audience to experience the atonal, arrhythmic, frenetic world to its fullest. When this postmodern, postsocialist fashion show evolves into a fanatic dancing party on and off the stage, the disco music is precisely the cue that opens the floodgates for all, pushing the ironic play to its extreme.

In explaining his stylistic choice, the director recalls this creative scene and discusses how elements of disco music and rock 'n' roll fit into his film on the basis of mood, melody, and rhythm. Although rock music is not arranged as an overarching schema that structures the entire film, it is used for "emotional expression," specifically to "match the uneasy mood and aesthetic psychology of the youthful audience."[26] This is also exemplified in the conclusion of the film, when the finale of the rock song "I Am the Troubleshooter" is carefully interwoven to allude to the imminent demise of the Three-T Company. A live concert of this rock song by its original artist has been added to *The Troubleshooters* as a form of authorial, auditory commentary on this seemingly absurd, fruitless youth experiment. Wang Di, the rock singer, in his extra-diegetic, live performance is analogous to the fictional, vagrant "troubleshooters," who all appear disoriented, sweaty, greasy-haired, and expressly maddened on film. The music clip has been intercut with long shots of the three protagonists furiously walking along the street and the documentary-style footage of everyday Beijing and its spontaneous occurrences "on the spot" to make some kind of intertextual referentiality.

The ending of *The Troubleshooters*, to a great extent, recalls the opening cityscape. It makes identical use of frame composition, jump cuts, collage, repeated musical patterns, and sound effects, all of which reiterate the postsocialist reality with a sarcastic twist. The Three-T Company is ordered to close down, despite their "goodwill" and their "earnest" effort to help people out of "trouble," and the company is shut down even before it fully opens. The very cramped, messy office they temporarily rent forms a symbolic space, epitomizing the bustling city in a state of extreme and constant flux. A seedy shack crammed into the even more jampacked city, the company's office appears on-screen so crude, poorly equipped, dimly lit, and is often punctuated by various noises off-screen—for instance, sounds of construction like hammering, nailing, shoveling, scraping, and traffic moving along in the street. The urban-characteristic image and sound again conjure up a sense of transition, mobility, and postmodern absurdity, which are intrinsic to the film. All of these come to inform an unforgettable ending of *The Troubleshooters*, which is an extraordinary display of people lining up outside the company's office the next morning, regardless of the government dismissal order.

A dramatic pan of the large crowd standing in a queue establishes itself as yet another carnivalesque moment in the film—comparable to the waggish, dreamlike fashion show, which I just discussed. The final long shots, filmed on location to produce a realistic effect, are incorporated to amplify the cynical tone of the film's *denouement*. A slice of lighthearted tango music is heard, in Mi's own words, "to heighten the film's humor."[27] Its fast, jovial tempo corresponds to the camera movement and the flow of the crowd, conveying a contemporary, urban spirit and underscoring the film's unresolved, open ending. The cessation of the Three-T company is problematized. The motivations of the lined-up crowd are also ambiguous. Are they waiting to acquire "troubleshooting" services, or are the gathered onlookers here to appeal against the "troubles" the three delinquent youths have caused? The film leaves this judgment to the audience, again presenting uncertainties and contradictions as fundamental to the film. Caught between actuality and illusion, everyday life and high culture, socialist tradition and postsocialist reality, *The Troubleshooters* crystallizes many of these paradoxes and demonstrates a singular audiovisual means of breaking down these binaries and re-blending them together. In addition to being an evocation of Wang Shuo's sardonic popular fictions of the late 1980s, it is a transitional film and a harbinger of a new wave of urban youth film to come in the post-1989 era. In it, rock 'n' roll becomes the aural signature of this new cinematic form.

The Sixth Generation and Cui Jian: Bastards to the Beat of the City

Following the last two decades of the twentieth century, China has witnessed a veritable explosion of films directed toward youth, inscribed with the aesthetic and ethic of rock 'n' roll. This musical device has been explored by a group of newly emergent young filmmakers who became preoccupied with an introspective probing of the transfiguration of the self through the figure of the Wang Shuo-like *flâneur* or the disaffected youth in films such as *Dirt* (*Toufa luanle*, 1993), *Weekend Lover* (*Zhoumo qingren*, 1995), and *How the Steel Was Tempered* (*Zhangda chengren*, 1995), among others. Rock becomes paramount not only for its narrative functions, but also for its effectiveness in maximizing the film's cinematic reach, yielding a youth-tinged cinematography to match the ascendancy of rock 'n' roll in postsocialist China. Of particular importance is *Beijing Bastards* (*Beijing zazhong*, dir. Zhang Yuan, 1993), which audaciously heralded the coming of age of the Sixth Generation. Moreover, this film engaged the audiovisual confluence of Chinese rock and urban youth cinema, from its financing, production, and distribution to its content and style.

Acclaimed as one of the first films to be made entirely outside the state studio system, this refreshing and daring work was funded in large part through the aid of investors from Hong Kong and the West (including support from the Hubert Bals Fund of the International Film Festival Rotterdam; Shu Kei, a Hong Kong director and producer; and Christopher Doyle, the award-winning cinematographer who had worked in Hong Kong with Wong Kar-Wai on *Days of Being Wild* two years earlier). In addition, Zhang Yuan himself helped finance the film with earnings from directing music videos, the style of which carries over into *Bejing Bastards*, as I will examine later. The film was officially banned in mainland China and has never been released there. Provocatively adopting the name "Beijing Bastards" for both the film's title and for the production group—instead of giving credit to any of the state studios, as had been the predominant practice on the socialist screen—Zhang Yuan poignantly parodied himself as well as his cinematic experiment as the illegitimate offspring of the nation.

Many critics observe an important link between rock music and the *vérité* style that underpins *Beijing Bastards*, as well as a large number of other Sixth Generation films. Both the music and film dynamics are closely intertwined with a high level of romanticism and symbolism, in which rock and Sixth Generation films have been constructed as an imagined, idealized site of authenticity as well as a marketable commodity for alternative culture. As Geremie Barme astutely points out: "Zhang was one of many mainland artists who over the years discovered a successful formula for the production of marketable alternative cultural material."[28] While I agree that, in the context of *Beijing Bastards*, a similar approach of mythmaking, or the "theatricalization" of the Chinese "bastards,"[29] as Berenice Reynaud puts it, plays a pivotal role in the rock texts and subtexts and the characterizations of rock artists, the integration of image and music, however, is more complex and multifaceted than the dual frame of "cinema *vérité* plus rock documentary" and "theatricalization" can account for. Instead, I ask: should we—and how do we—"de-mythologize" and "de-theatricalize" the so-called Chinese "bastards" and the associated rock imaginary? To appraise this, I focus closely on the representation of Cui Jian to explore how his joint undertaking of music and film taps into varied yet entwined discourses of authenticity, art, politics, and commerce, all central concerns of rock culture and the Sixth Generation filmmaking.

Bejing Bastards opens with a close-up of a shirtless young man playing a Chinese bass drum (*dagu*). The low, solid beat of the drum and the tight framing of the drummer silhouetted against a foggy background evoke the hypersexuality, narcissism, and mystery often associated with rock 'n' roll performance, while at the same time unveiling this formerly clandestine music to the gaze of the ordinary viewer. The next shot shows a tableau of the band; the camera slowly tracks around it before cutting to a close-up of Cui Jian's face, singling him out as the star vocalist. At first glance, this opening resembles the montage sequence in many music videos; the image and the music are glossy, meticulously crafted, and perfectly synchronized. Later, after providing this first striking glimpse into Chinese rock, the choreographed music video-style shots of the band performing begin to crosscut with a second, dramatic scene while the song plays underneath. In a rainy, cosmopolitan city, against the noirish backdrop of traffic, a young couple (Karzi and his girlfriend) stand under a highway bridge and urgently discuss what to do about the girl's pregnancy. They argue about the possibility of an abortion until the confrontation is more than the girl can take. She runs away into the night.

Like many other rock films, *Beijing Bastards* makes extensive use of musical cues to reflect the characters' emotions and comment on dramatic situations. But what matters is not merely how rock music serves such narrative functions, but more importantly how it informs the film's visual style and creates affect and meanings. As a new kind of docudrama, *Beijing Bastards* defies traditional narrative structure and shifts constantly between oppositions of onstage and offstage, fantasy and reality, fiction and documentary. Following Karzi's strolling through the city to look for his runaway girlfriend, the film is loosely structured around an array of incidents and visual collages that unfold in a highly stylized fashion reminiscent of MTV.

Zhang Yuan's camera meanders like the *flâneur* protagonist. It pans and drifts around streets, boulevards, apartments, eateries, construction sites, dark back alleys, the dilapidated compound house, and a boisterous marketplace to record a fast-changing urbanscape of contemporary Beijing. It is also through this filmic *flânerie* that the camera roundly excavates a hidden network of urban drifters, social outcasts, and marginalized artists in a quasi-documentary mode, a radical departure from the predominant socialist realist tradition of Chinese cinema. By having most of these characters play themselves and sometimes talk to the camera spontaneously, Zhang Yuan reveals to us the rough reality of the underground scene that is a trademark of his work. A gang of cynical painters, writers, rock artists, and unemployed young people dominating the screen all happen to be Zhang's real-life friends and personal acquaintances.

From an insider's vantage point, Zhang probes a secret lifestyle in the mystifying underworld, endowing *Beijing Bastards* with a quality of liveliness and transparency that recalls the Western aesthetic mode of a rock documentary (or "rockumentary"). The film's fairly loose organization and erratically flowing narrative are also reminiscent of the structure of rock music. Ingredients of rock 'n' roll have inspired many aspects of the film's *mise-en-scène*. Cinematic devices such as rapid zoom, as well as editing that coordinates with musical rhythms, indicate the influence of two important genres: the concert film and rock documentary, both of which focus particularly on live performance and star power. A foggy ambience and neon color scheme evocative of the onstage rock performance have characterized many musical scenes and furthermore penetrated the world behind the curtain, the space of postsocialist reality. Thus, it can be argued that, as a whole, *Beijing Bastards* seeks a kind of rock-and-documentary spirit—that is, audacious, authentic, vernacular, and revolutionary.

The film's appeal, to be sure, centers on its remarkable soundtrack and its live, archival footage of Chinese rock 'n' roll documenting Cui Jian as well as several other rising rock stars of the time, including Zang Tianshuo, Dou Wei, and He Yong. Cui Jian, the godfather of Chinese rock 'n' roll, not only played a pivotal leading role in the film, but also participated extensively in filmmaking, sharing credits with Zhang Yuan as a producer and screenwriter. This was certainly a marketing strategy designed to attract a young local audience in addition to his Western music fans and cinephiles. *Beijing Bastards* successfully capitalized on Cui Jian's cult status as a rock legend and an icon of Chinese youth subculture.

Cui Jian's screen persona was carefully managed to enhance his public persona as a rock star. From the first sequence, the film always places him in live performances and foregrounds him as the rock star. Even when the camera shifts to the other narrative thread concerning the quarreling young couple, Cui Jian's singing voice remains on the soundtrack, serving as an authorial commentary:

> I don't love you anymore, but I don't hate you either
> Although you are still you, I have no energy
> And I don't think it is really necessary
> That I must fight you . . .

"Tolerance" (*Kuanrong*), the song over the opening scene, sketches a picture of a suffering youth, whose pain and frustration permeate the entire film: "Let's see, let's really see who can / Stick it out right to the very end." Alienated and frenetic, the protagonist Karzi is a prototypical "Beijing bastard"—a

Cui Jian and his leading role and music in *Beijing Bastards* (1993).

flâneur who is shocked, lost, and lingering in the liminal space of the postsocialist city. The film appears to causally track his directionless but watchful cruising across the city, showing him engaging in drinking, random sex, and senseless brawls. These occurrences are represented in a seemingly unmediated manner. It is also from Karzi's point of view that we get a grasp of the city of Beijing and its underground milieus.

To a great extent, Karzi is a mirror image of Cui Jian in the nonmusical, secular world. Although these two characters are cast in the same frame in just one scene (which is also one of the very few scenes where Cui Jian is seen talking), *Beijing Bastards* deliberately uses the central theme of *flânerie* and *searching* to link them together. Parallel to Karzi's despairing journey in search of his missing girlfriend, Cui Jian's band has lost its rehearsal space and must race against a deadline to find a new venue. To take it further, the *flâneur* means of wandering, or sometimes purposefully searching, functions as an overriding structure that binds the film's discrete strands together in a meaningful signifying way. In the film, a college student is hunting for a job that she may count on to keep her in Beijing after graduation; Liu Xiaodong, a painter who plays himself and played a similar role in Wang Xiaoshuai's directorial debut *The Days* (*Dongchun de rizi*, 1993), is seen pursuing patrons for his work; and Zang Tianshuo, a rock singer himself, plays a hoodlum, who alongside another bummer rummages throughout the city to get the money back. The various roamings are a key signifier that bespeaks the edge of authenticity and cultural opposition, two important attributes of rock 'n' roll.

In many ways, *Beijing Bastards* achieves an interesting tension between stage and backstage, reality and imagination, diegetic and nondiegetic, fiction and documentary. Its experimental innovation derives not just from such shifting boundaries, but also from a kind of musical dynamic. Rock songs and performance occupy much of the screen time, including Cui Jian's "Beijing Story" (*Beijing gushi*), "The Last Complaints" (*Zuihou de baoyuan*), "Like a Knife" (*Xiang yiba daozi*), and "Tolerance" (*Kuanrong*), Dou Wei's "Dark Dreams" (*Hei meng*), and He Yong's "Bell and Drum Towers" (*Zhong gu lou*). Central to this rock festival is the symbolic, powerful presence of Cui Jian that has accentuated the rock flavor and youth subculture undertone of the film.

For many Chinese, rock music is inseparably linked to the name of Cui Jian. Tremendously influential among Chinese adolescents and urban residents of the 1980s and 1990s, he became an icon for youth rebellion. Cui Jian came to prominence with "Nothing to My Name" (*Yi wu suo you*, 1986), considered the first Chinese rock song, which has been vitally noted as "an emotional catharsis" and "an allegorical jab at the dominance of the CCP."[30] His first album, *Rock 'n' Roll on the New Long March* (*Xin changzheng lu shang de yaogun*), released in 1989, was a commercial hit and helped to elevate rock music from its underground arena to the spotlight of the mass public sphere. More importantly, Cui Jian's rise to fame coincided with the Tiananmen Square event of 1989, a formidable social uprising in which students played and sang his songs in the demonstrations "as a means for affective empowerment, cultural critique, and as a conduit for explicitly political protest."[31] Although he was subsequently banned from performing on television and in other public venues, Cui Jian, like Zhang Yuan and many of his vanguard contemporaries, has built his career in close association with Chinese underground youth culture targeting international awards and its own niche market.

This context is key to understanding *Beijing Bastards*, for Zhang Yuan critically drew on the symbolic power of Cui Jian to formulate his version of cinematic authenticity, resistance, and soundscape. The film substantially relies upon popular memory and the viewer's awareness of its intertextual references to Cui Jian's rock star persona as part of its promotional efforts. A number of his early songs—for example, "Like a Knife" from the album *Solution* (*Jiejue*)—constitute a large part of the soundtrack whereas newer songs, such as "Beijing Story," "Tolerance," and "The Last Complaints," were successfully premiered in the film and significantly benefitted from this savvy act of cross-promotion. In this light, it is certainly no stretch to see this independent, low-budget film as a feature-length music video,

China's first rock album by Cui Jian, *Rock 'n' Roll on the New Long March* (Beijing: Zhongguo lvyou shengxiang chubanshe, 1989).

exploiting Cui Jian's cultural capital to sell a notion of Chinese subculture to its film and music audience.

In the spirit of a rock documentary, *Beijing Bastards* admits us into a private, seemingly unscripted world. Improvised elements of the quotidian are exposed to the kino-eye as much as the spectacular onstage performances. The flip side of these raw, realistic depictions, however, is the film's rigorous control of Cui Jian's image and voice. From beginning to end, the film constructs Cui Jian wholly as a singer; the role closely matches his image in popular consciousness. Even within the diegesis, he still lives up fully to his public persona: he plays music, sings in his signature growl, organizes his band, plans performances, and looks for a rehearsal space. We hear his singing voice much more than his speaking voice. He speaks only sporadically and in a constrained manner, in stark contrast to other characters' cascades of speech in heavily accented Beijing vernacular. By playing himself, Cui Jian endows the role with an iconographic significance and a ritualistic property. In this sense, Zhang Yuan demystifies the rock mythology while reconstructing it at the same time.

A review of the film text and music lyrics, especially in the last scene, will help further illustrate my points. At the end of *Beijing Bastards*, Karzi eventually succeeds in finding his girlfriend, but he is utterly shocked to learn that she has had the baby. The film dissolves to a close-up of his bewildered face, followed by several shots of him walking aimlessly again on the street, to the beat of Cui Jian's "Beijing Story":

> Sang for quite a while but still didn't sing completely about
> The pain of this city
> But the more pain, the more we are able to imagine
> The happiness of tomorrow

This scene immediately recalls the enigmatic ending of *The Troubleshooters*. Both films present an idiosyncratic juxtaposition and superimposition of the rock singer and *flâneur* along with their singing voice, and by contrast, their plight of aphasia. In *Beijing Bastards*, the closing theme song is also particularly important. On the one hand, it literally rearticulates Karzi's inner world, afflicted as he is with pain, rage, and disillusion: "I wear a smile on my face like everybody else / Still living on this earth / I'm prepared to speak / The fucking truth, lies, and nonsense." On the other, it concludes the film with an open, ambivalent reading and injects a metaphor of (re)birth and *bildung* ("formation") into the story of a child's birth, an event that marks Karzi's growth out of adolescence and into adulthood.

Karzi's sudden realization that he is a father at the end reverse-mirrors the opening scene, in which the fatherless Karzi rejects the idea of becoming a father himself. Film scholars, including Dai Jinhua and Cui Shuqin, have identified a dominant pattern of fatherlessness or the absent father in the Sixth Generation films.[32] While the motif of the denunciation of the father (and patriarchal authority) finds its greatest resonance in *Beijing Bastards*, the film also works to rebuild the father figure from a different angle. In contrast to the biological father who has been totally erased from Karzi's story, *Beijing Bastards* provides a symbolic father as compensation; the primacy of Cui Jian and his penetrating voice clearly serve to fill this vacuum. The film foregrounds Cui Jian as a rock star and most of all, a spiritual leader and symbolic father. Cui Jian's exiguous yet deliberately constructed "ordinariness," portrayed in a *vérité* rockumentary fashion, only reinforces him as the godfather of Chinese rock and the new leader of the young generation.

Acousmatic Presence of Cui Jian across Time, Space, and Screen

To a large degree, Cui Jian's singing voice is a self-sufficient entity that could flow freely as a pure, transcendental, and timeless experience. On top of the prevalent synchronized sound and ambient noise that characterizes the soundtrack of *Beijing Bastards*, the rock songs happen to be the chief nondiegetic acoustic element inserted into many dramatic scenes. As Cui Jian's voice remains external to the events on-screen, his singing connotes a position of absolute knowledge, endued with a capacity to travel across temporal and spatial boundaries. To borrow Michel Chion's concept, Cui Jian is often the *acousmêtre* (and sometimes the visible *acousmêtre*), who has "the power of seeing all," "the power of omniscience," and "the gift of ubiquity."[33] His disembodied voice and spectral presence are markers of the supreme power of rock, reflecting the autonomy of such music and sound to not only live independently of the image but also have the ability to expand the montage and visual reach of the film.

Cui Jian's acousmatic presence and godfatherly persona are further fleshed out in *Roots and Branches* (*Wo de xiongdi jiemei*, dir. Yu Zhong, 2001), a popular tearjerker in which Cui Jian plays an actual father. An insipid remodeling of Zhang Yimou's *The Road Home* (*Wode fuqin muqin*, literally translated "My Father and Mother," 1999), the original title of *Roots and Branches*— "My Brothers and Sisters"—may have been a deliberate attempt to attract a larger audience. The film fared well at the domestic box office but failed critically. In response to the harsh criticism leveled against the film and Cui Jian's role specifically,[34] the director Yu Zhong explains that the association of Cui Jian with a father figure is not accidental, but rather "a look back to the past, a return to an innocent, idealist age that Cui Jian symbolizes."[35] Here, Cui Jian played a role other than himself for the first time, but the film was nonetheless designed and scored in reference to his musical persona and iconography. In defense of this part, Cui Jian remarks that "if the role had not been specified as a music teacher, I wouldn't have participated in the project."[36] It is also through this cinematic role that two key components of rock youth culture—rebellion and nostalgia—are merged and sutured.

Although Cui Jian has a secondary part in *Roots and Branches*, it occupies a privileged space. He plays a father who only exists in flashbacks, emblematic of the "good old days." He is a source of enlightenment and is the most intriguing figure in the film, always associated with truth, wisdom, the highest moral standards, and, above all, the empowerment of song. In the climactic scene where the "father" teaches his final class and bids farewell to his students, the camera slowly pans across the entire class as they rehearse "Dream" (*Meng*, a song composed by Cui Jian specifically for *Roots and Branches*). The camera fixates on Cui Jian, gradually zooming in until his face almost fills the entire screen. Michel Chion's concept of the "auditory closeup"[37] is evoked here; in juxtaposition to the heroic visual close-up we hear Cui Jian's stentorian, epigrammatic remark: "Wherever music exists, our soul will never feel alone," amplified until a melodic and empathetic music cue joins in.

Cui Jian plays a father and a music teacher in *Roots and Branches* (2001).

And the aphorism about music feeding the soul immediately recalls a famous line from Cui Jian during his performance of "A Piece of Red Cloth" (*Yikuai hongbu*) from a 1990 tour: "If you feel that some things in life are not reliable, I hope you will make music your one exception. Music will never deceive you."[38] Cui Jian went on to blindfold himself with a piece of red cloth as he performed the song:

That day you used a piece of red cloth
to blindfold my eyes and cover up the sky . . .
I couldn't see you, and I couldn't see the road
You grabbed both of my hands and wouldn't let go . . .

Through this symbolic act and through the song itself, Cui Jian boldly confronts the party-state, which, in his view, has manipulated and smothered the people's true feelings for nearly half a century. On the contrary, he celebrates the essence of innocence, sincerity, and purity that can be found squarely in rock 'n' roll. Zhang Yuan directed the music video for "A Piece of Red Cloth" and for several other rock songs around the same time when he made *Beijing Bastards*.[39] It is, then, no surprise that "A Piece of Red Cloth" coincides with the chromatic red tinge and overflowing "red cloth" in a scene of *Beijing Bastards* where Cui Jian performs "The Last Complaints": "I want to look for the source of my grievances / I can but face the wind and move forward . . . I want to end this last complaint / I can but face the wind and move forward." Although "The Last Complaints" does not have an independently released music video, the exceptional eight-minute scene from *Beijing Bastards* contains rich audiovisual manifestations and could serve as a full-length music video literally and figuratively.

Whereas rock mythology and its aesthetic of authenticity have fundamentally shaped *Roots and Branches*, what this dreary melodrama stresses is ultimately music's pragmatic and pedagogic function. The ideology by and large resonates with the traditional Confucian notion of music as a kind of safety valve, an educational tool, and an instrument to pacify anger. Cui Jian's shaggy, bristly look and his hard, rough voice were thus greatly tamed and softened to serve the dramatic and commercial interests at work in *Roots and Branches*. Cui Jian's first above-ground appearance drew a large audience, but it also raised the eyebrows of many reviewers who maintained that Cui Jian's stardom cannot yet adequately compensate for his insufficient dramatic experience.[40] Cui Jian replied, aware of the gap between his musical charisma and his screen persona: "I am above all a musician. I still identified myself as a musician even when I was involved in the film."[41] He recalled his performance in *Beijing Bastards*, which to him was more of a documentary experience: "I was still myself in front of the camera. I never acted intentionally and I didn't know how to act at all."[42]

Cui Jian's venture into cinema poses an interesting case, for he is not so much a film star as a rock artist but in a double role that both de-iconizes and re-iconizes his status. His film persona is predicated on a discourse of authenticity, stemming from the underlying ideology of rock music and the rock culture that he embodies. We can say that the most "authentic" moments in Cui Jian's film roles are when he is most himself—namely, when he gets close to his iconic rock stardom and engages in his signature singing. Furthermore, Cui Jian's idiosyncratic voice constitutes an important signifier, a sonic manifestation of what Dick Hebdige describes as the oppositional style of subculture.[43] At the vanguard of Chinese rock culture, Cui Jian gives voice to the political and poetic complexity of the underground scene at the end of the twentieth century.

Cui Jian's most direct, daring challenge to the current regime lies in, first and foremost, his metrical, highly expressive, and metaphorical song lyrics. Many of his songs adopt a similar narrative that conspicuously stages and foregrounds a confrontation between "you" and "me," a man and his lover, a son and his father, a human being and the exterior social-cultural milieu, and by extension, the conflicted relationship between the people and the party-state. Such a conundrum also characterizes Sixth Generation films and many other contemporary Chinese artistic practices.

Wang Shuo salutes Cui Jian in his essay of contemporary Chinese society: "I really like Cui Jian's songs. When I heard 'A Piece of Red Cloth,' I almost cried. He is really sharp. I felt what we have done with thousands of words cannot at all match with these very few lines of his. He precisely portrays the entangled, inseparable relationship between us and our extrinsic conditions, the very contradictions, and complex emotions they induce . . . I think Cui Jian is the greatest troubadour of our nation."[44] In his comparative study of Cui Jian and the Fabulous Troubadours, a famed southern French band, Gregory B. Lee also claims that, regardless of all the cultural-historical differences, both are at heart "the voices of subversive, trouble-making troubadours" against the center. He goes on to assert: "Chinese rock star Cui Jian turns the tropes and signs of remembrance back on the state, to recall what he wants to forget, but he also redeploys them in his own patriotic project which aims to save China from the new materialism through the consumerist culture of popular music that he calls the 'Long March of Rock 'n' Roll.'"[45] The most important point Lee raises in this article, I think, is that in spite of Cui Jian's clearly expressed pose as an antagonist and his conscious adoption of Western popular music idioms, his "Long March of Rock 'n' Roll" is *au fond* a "patriotic project," part and parcel of the larger project of nation-building, shared by Chinese writers and intellectuals throughout the entire twentieth century. This is evident in Cui Jian's recuperation of national symbols and particularly his appropriation of nationalist visual signifiers, for instance, the Long March, the red blindfold in "A Piece of Red Cloth," the red star in Cui Jian's hat, and the green jacket of the People's Liberation Army Cui Jian often wears in his films and music videos, all of which would have a deep resonance in the Chinese collective imaginary.

Cui Jian's dual deployment of nationalist sentiment and rhetoric for the construction of the nation on one end and for the deconstruction of authority on the other end is noteworthy. He becomes the most widely known musician, idolized and canonized in writings and textbooks of contemporary China—for example, in *A Guide to the History of Contemporary Chinese Literature* (*Zhongguo dangdai wenxueshi jiaocheng*), which devotes a chapter exclusively to the discussion of popular music and Cui Jian.[46] The beautiful rhyme, refined parallelism, and poetic prose in Cui Jian's songs, redolent of Chinese poetry, have thus attracted serious attention and his "Nothing to My Name" and "Space Here" (*Zhe er de kongjian*, 1991) were even selected for inclusion in *The Centennial Chinese Literature Classics* (*Bainian zhongguo wenxue jingdian*).[47]

Cui Jian's aesthetic and ideological significance is also deeply implicated in the soundscape of his music. His songs are slow and melodic, yet punctuated by strong beats. His singing is loud, husky, low, throaty, and sometimes even unintelligible, complementing the sense of ambiguity that his lyrics often convey. His voice is macho and powerful, but also lonely and tormented. His

Cui Jian's performance of "A Piece of Red Cloth." Source: bbs.clzg.cn.

performance style is unique and unconventional as he fuses sonorous shouts and murmuring narration with his maverick pattern of accentuation and intonation. In addition to the sounds of electric guitar and drumbeat, Cui Jian deliberately incorporates traditional Chinese instruments such as *erhu* (a two-stringed fiddle), *pipa* (a four-stringed lute), *guzheng* (a seven-stringed zither), and *xiaohao* (trumpet). Cui Jian played trumpet in a state-run orchestra before he went independent to form an underground band and embarked on his "Long March of Rock 'n' Roll." He also incorporates the folk music style of northwest China, so as to sinicize rock and produce a hybrid, fluid, and multifarious soundscape.

Cui Jian's celebrated iconoclastic pose, idiosyncratic singing style, nationalist sentiment, and border-crossing music have thus struck many filmmakers as a new means for registering the emerging ethos of a youthful urban identity in contemporary China. *Age of Sensitivity* (*Ganguang shidai*, dir. Ah Nian, 1994) features Cui Jian's song "Greenhouse Girl" (*Huafang guniang*) as a poignant commentary on a young photographer's painstaking, solitary struggle within a commodified society and his yearnings for artistic and personal freedom. In another cinematic representation of contemporary life, *Good Morning, Beijing* (*Beijing, nizao*, dir. Zhang Nuanxin, 1990), Cui Jian's personality and voice are also appropriated to pronounce the decisive arrival and revival of self-consciousness, individuality, and cosmopolitanism in the new market-driven society. *Good Morning, Beijing* includes a vital scene in which the film's two protagonists, Ai Hong (played by Ma Xiaoqing, who portrays the Freudian modernist in *The Troubleshooter*) and Keke (played by Jia Hongsheng), visit a bar. Keke joins the band, dedicating a popular song to Ai Hong. It is Cui Jian's "Fake Monk" (*Jiaxingseng*):

> I want to go from south to north
> I want to go from white to black
> I want everybody to watch me
> But not to know who I am . . .

The lively performance fully charged with youthful energy and passion dazzles Ai Hong, who has a monotonous day job as a bus conductor. This rock song crying out for pure love without restraint strikes a deep chord in her. Although she is confused upon hearing it for the first time, Ai Hong starts to use the Walkman that Keke gives her and learns the song by heart. It is the Walkman with a rock 'n' roll tape inside—itself an emblem of cosmopolitanism and youth culture—that captivates her and helps Keke win her heart. In contrast, her other admirer, the bus driver Zhou Yongqiang (played by Wang Quan'an, an award-winning Sixth Generation filmmaker who turned to directing in *Lunar Eclipse* from 1999), lives with his parents in a cramped traditional courtyard and dutifully takes care of his family. His only hobby and means of self-expression, playing Chinese *erhu* and later Western guitar, are nonetheless constantly silenced by his mother. Ai Hong's choice between the two suitors, between Walkman and *erhu*, is symbolic. Her decision to favor the individualist, adventurous, and open life over the conformist, secure, and traditional life provides an allegorical snapshot of the prismatic, head-spinning yet determined turn in late twentieth-century China from the stagnant, state-controlled life to a new marketized, "free" era.

As Tang Xiaobing has perceptively pointed out: "Her [Ai Hong's] narrative therefore presupposes the possibility of becoming, and it is this conviction that supports a *profound optimism* about social change and self-transformation, personal as well as collective."[48] While many scholars have likewise suggested that *Good Morning, Beijing* is a film demonstrating a fascination with the new prospect of market reform and urban modernity, it does not express its "optimism" without reservation. A critical deliberation of the seemingly utopian future that modernization and market economy may bring forth is embodied in Cui Jian's revered rock song and its venerated appearance in *Good Morning, Beijing*, as is a sense of embedded ambivalence. At first glance, Keke comes off as a likable character—good-looking, energetic, and romantic. His preliminary identification as a returned Chinese *émigré*, as well as his *soigné* appearance, markedly sets him apart from the plain-spoken and inhibited bus driver Zhou Yongqiang. Yet beneath Keke's "polished" façade lies his "truer" identity. As the story unrolls, he is subsequently unmasked to be a flamboyant idler, an unemployed (and self-employed) huckster, and paradigmatically a *flâneur* of contemporary China. This resonates well with Wang Shuo's famous portrait of the "troubleshooter," as previously analyzed, who is both a product and a trailblazer of the market.

The use of Cui Jian's rock song "Fake Monk" helps establish these important interpretations of a postsocialist urban life. Marked by a sense of romanticism, dynamism, and libidinal energy, the song is first associated with Keke's sunny outlook and his youthful vitality. Yet the performance, though live, is merely an act of mimicry; Keke works hard to imitate Cui Jian, who does not appear in the film. Keke's conscientious imitation of a cosmopolitan, international citizen and of Cui Jian points to what Fredric Jameson has identified as a symptomatic postmodern feature of "depthlessness."[49] The loss of aura in this aural reproduction in the Benjaminian sense[50] also calls to mind another basic principle of rock culture's "authenticity" and reflects another view of modern urban life as pathologically superficial, fabricated, fluid, and at times conflicting. In *Good Morning, Beijing*, this young man's wholehearted performance paradoxically conveys his craving for freedom and self-empowerment (the other constitutive aspects of rock culture) and his wish to be transformed, synthesized, and integrated into the new socioeconomic system.

The ambivalent feeling toward the prevailing zeitgeist of market reform and commercialization is further amplified and manifested at the end of *Good Morning, Beijing*. Ai Hong, a young woman who aspires to live a fashionable, modern life, leaves Zhou Yongqiang and her original post. She marries Keke eventually and starts a private business to sell fashion goods. The end of the film depicts her as an individual broker (*getihu*) and a new species of entrepreneur who now gets onto the bus as a passenger, where she encounters Zhou and other former co-workers. The climactic reunion represents the last confrontation and a new (and renewed) relationship between the present and the past, modernity and tradition, the new and the old, and open market and previous forms of political economy. All of these tensions are intricately woven into this last part of the film, where Ai Hong's return to the bus has been pointedly interpreted by Tang Xiaobing as a "rhetoric of compromise." To critics like Tang Xiaobing, the conclusion of the film, smacking of the "affirmation of a certain value system or accepted ideology," has evidenced a "comforting moment of rapprochement."[51] Rather, I would call it a momentum of *ineluctable rendezvous*, a recurring motif in 1980s and 1990s literature and films, which resolutely declares China's break with the historical past and its hearty embrace of the new market ideology.

Director Zhang Nuanxin spoke of the film's motives and major themes with zest before the film was put into production: "I entitled the film *Good Morning, Beijing* because it is a crystallization of the living of millions of Beijing citizens, a depiction of those ordinary people who work quietly in the lowest strata of our society. We dedicate this film to these common people who make up today's China."⁵² Zhang relished the thought of making the piece into "a nondramatic, essayist kind" in "expressive, documentary" style, utilizing location shooting, natural lighting, mobile camera, and a coloring of "refreshing harmonious grey." The soundtrack, as she conceived it, would be fairly simple and natural, incorporating for the most part live and synchronized recording: "The opening and ending of the film use a passage of music, and no music for most part of the film in the middle. The music design is peaceful, blithe, and inherently affectionate."⁵³

Bearing this decisive "neorealist" rubric and cinematic vision, *Good Morning, Beijing* brings closure to the romantic triangle—or, as I see it, China's romance with cosmopolitanism—and results in a "happy" ending. The camera pulls back to exhibit a panoramic picture of all the protagonists and different people aboard the same bus as it placidly moves forward along the streets of Beijing; it is an allegorical coda signifying the totality and historicity of China's invariable progression to market reform and modern urban life in present time. The film then cuts to an empty shot of a serene city embellished and awakened by the first rays of sunshine at dawn. At this point, the last and "rarely used" musical cue seeps in—soothing and contemplating music by a Chinese bamboo flute and chime bells. This lyrical, redemptive, yet somewhat unsettled ending is endowed with symbolic significance, evoking a sense of freedom, promise, and open possibilities, all reminiscent of the motif of youth and transformation that forms the core of Zhang Nuanxin's earlier features, such as *Drive to Win* (*Sha ou*, 1981) and *Sacrifice of Youth* (*Qingchun ji*, 1985).

In conclusion, Cui Jian's venture into film is exemplary in the evolvement of rock 'n' roll film. His iconic status in Chinese rock history made him a natural to appear in rock 'n' roll movies. His screen roles have been carefully crafted in accord with his rock star identity. Cui Jian's intimate collaboration with the new urban filmmakers who share a common interest in Chinese youth subculture contributed to the burgeoning of Chinese rock 'n' roll film, a unique brand of audiovisual synergy initiated in *Beijing Bastard*. By the time this film had garnered important awards at international film festivals in 1993, Cui Jian was at the height of his fame. His two albums, *Rock 'n' Roll on the Long March* (*Xin changzheng lu shang de yaogun*) and *Solution* (*Jiejue*), both became bestsellers as well as sensational hits that topped the national music charts.⁵⁴ Cui Jian continued to produce albums in the following years: *Balls under the Red Flag* (*Hongqi xia de dan*, 1994), *The Power of Powerless* (*Wuneng de liliang*, 1998), and *Show Your Color* (*Gei ni yidian yanse*, 2005), none of which achieved the same success. While his prestige and Chinese rock music in general suffered a substantial decline at the turn of the new century, Cui Jian appeared in his second film during this period. His role as a virtuous father in *Roots and Branches* in 2001 signaled a nostalgic return to his musical roots and was a tribute to the golden age of Chinese rock in the last two decades of the twentieth century.

In 2007, Cui Jian played a cameo part in *The Sun Also Rises* (*Taiyang zhaochang shengqi*, dir. Jiang Wen, 2007). Ostensibly invoking Ernest Hemingway's highly esteemed novel of the same title, the film is nonetheless not a *roman à clef* but an overly surrealistic fantasy. In director Jiang Wen's own words, it is "a poetic rhapsody of memory, madness, serendipity and an ode to pleasure and fantasy."⁵⁵ Set in the most "un-magical," dismal time of modern Chinese history, the Cultural Revolution, the film ingeniously dissects and satirizes the rhetoric and history of insanity and absurdity through Jiang's most daring cinematic experiments, including his expressionist cinematography, lavish visuality, rich symbolism, elliptical narrative, blatant defiance against the realist tradition of Chinese cinema, and all in all what the critics have hailed as Jiang Wen's spellbinding "magical realism."⁵⁶

In the third episode of this "magical" quadruplet, Cui Jian appears momentarily in the role of Old Tang's close friend and virtually of his mentor. In real life, Cui Jian is one of Jiang Wen's best friends and has scored the music for Jiang Wen's 2000 film *Devils on the Doorstep* (*Guizi lai le*). Played by the Sixth Generation director Jiang Wen himself, Old Tang is identified in *The Sun Also Rises* as a *zhiqing* (educated youth), which instantly calls to mind the protagonist in Chen Kaige's *King of the Children* (discussed in my first chapter). In the company of his wife, Old Tang relocates to the countryside to perform physical labor while going hunting at leisure. He seems to enjoy a peaceful life in the village and makes friends with local children until one day when he learns that his lonely wife has slept with a village teen. His determination to kill the juvenile is, however, impeded by a question from the young boy, who compares his wife's belly to velvet and asks, "What is exactly velvet?" Tang makes an expedition to the capital of Beijing to look for the mythical "velvet" and is herein advised by Cui Jian. Cui Jian is inserted into the sequence only for a few minutes, but this segment again testifies to and consolidates the key aspects of his rock star personality. Learning about Tang's story, Cui Jian scribbles out the notes with indecipherable scripts and symbols. But, as before, he is invariably persuasive, imbued with magical power. The *mise-en-scène* of

Cui Jian's cameo appearance in Jiang Wen's *The Sun Also Rises* (2007).

the ancient Chinese courtyard and imperial palace heightens the mysteriousness and mightiness of Cui Jian, again a paragon of the visible *acousmêtre*. Never visibly presented in the film is how Tang's request is then satisfied or how the "real" velvet looks.

Left in the riddle of a perplexing ending, one ponders: Why velvet? What exactly is velvet? Are there any perceptible links between the clandestine "velvet" in the film's domain and what is known as "velvet prison," as Miklós Haraszti has conceptualized? Haraszti, in his scathing and saddening account of late socialist culture, holds that the totalitarian and authoritarian culture of post-Stalinist state socialism in the nuanced, civilian guise is even more ubiquitous, effective, and deeply implanted than the crude militant socialism of the Stalinist and Maoist era. As such, he names this "the velvet prison culture" and claims: "Post-Stalinist art shares a similar objective with Stalinist art: to strengthen social integration. The difference is that civilian or soft aesthetics are designed not for an audience newly incorporated into the socialist state but for a populace born into it. Socialization, not conquest, is the underlying assumption of the new aesthetic."[57] Haraszti's pointed observation of the artists under the post-Stalinist regime in Eastern Europe may shed some light on the Chinese situation.

Geremie Barme follows this logic and speaks about the condition of post-socialist China in an almost identical manner:

> As mainland China enters the phase of "soft" technocratic socialism, the parameters of the cultural Velvet Prison are being measured out in everyday practice. But this does not mean that there is no resistance to a new, higher level of co-option, conformity within the deep structure of the State.

> Individual artists struggle to maintain or achieve their independence . . . they are faced with a choice of suffering complete cultural ostracism or accepting the State's efforts to incorporate them in a new social contract, one in which consensus replaces coercion, and complicity subverts criticism.[58]

Barme sums up the nature of the velvet prison as "a realm in which the crude, military style of Stalinist (for which we can also read Maoist) rule with its attendant purges, denunciations, and struggles has finally given way to a new dawn of 'soft,' civilian government . . . It is a prison with an aesthetic all of its own; even (self-)repression has become a form of high art."[59] First published in 1989 and later rewritten into his book in 1999, in the shock and dreadful shadow of the Tiananmen massacre, Barme's assessment and prognosis of postsocialist China is largely pessimistic. He adheres to Haraszti's framework of the velvet prison insofar as he concentrates chiefly on the confrontations and wrestlings of the artists as opposed to the political regime. What he failed to see, or was not able to see by that time, is the vast and tremendous transmogrification of Chinese society in the post-Tiananmen era. That is how artists and cultural practitioners, on the one hand, come to grips with official mandates, and, on the other, how they come through in the clutch of global capitalism, enacting a similar process of co-option, self-censorship, and self-renewal. When speaking of arts and cultural activities in postsocialist China, the ever-present fist of the state shall be not underestimated, but the increasingly pressing command of the market and profit should be equally taken into account. Hence, I think Chinese postsocialist culture cannot be merely limned in the phrase of "velvet prison under state socialism."[60] It becomes now a more complex network, a double-layered velvet prison under the imperatives of both the state and the market, and a remolding process that may be called the capitalization of socialism. How the twofold velvet prison—or, in other words, the double stake of state control and capitalistic rhetoric—shapes and plays a crucial role in contemporary Chinese filmmaking and public popular culture is what I seek to investigate in my fifth chapter.

The soft, plushy, imaginary "velvet," only palpable within the auditory realm of *The Sun Also Rises*, therefore signals the material lack in Maoist China, but it can also be read as a discursive symbol that addresses and uncovers another lack and fatal flaw of Chinese society—the prevalent violence, censorship, and repression (be it hard or soft) upon sexuality, individuality, and self-expression. In this light, Cui Jian's brief appearance proves tenable, as he has always been, through various representational works, configured as an icon of rebellion and resistance, whose break from the velvet prison has quintessentially "become a form of high art."[61]

Cui Jian's film adventures have taken another turn in recent years, as he has gradually retreated from the music stage and developed a greater interest in film. In 2006, he produced and directed a seven-minute internet film, *The Age of Repairing Virginity* (*Xiufu chunvmo shidai*). Centering on the subjects of gender politics and women's liberation in contemporary China, the video won the 2007 Best Mobile Movie awarded by Sina.com, one of the most popular web portals in China today. Then, teaming up with veteran filmmakers Fruit Chan and Jin-ho Hur, Cui Jian directed the sequel to *Chengdu, I Love You* (*Chengdu, wo ai ni*), which was chosen as the closing film at the 2009 Venice Film Festival. His most recent project is a feature-length, eponymous drama sharing the title with and loosely based upon his previous hit song, "Blue Sky Bones" (*Lanse gutou*, 2005). The cinematized version was released in 2014 after much anticipation from his music and film fans. Cui Jian assumed the multiple roles of screenwriter, producer, and director. Asked how he relates to filmmaking as a musician, Cui Jian has said: "I believe film and music are essentially the same. It is the common desire for self-expression and showing concern that motivates me to delve into the domain of cinema. It is also the spirit and energy of rock that drive me to continue traveling the path of film and creativity."[62] While Cui Jian's rock stardom might have brought him offers of screen roles and film contracts, his latest directorial works show a critical departure, which have less and less to do with his music iconography. Accordingly, they enrich and diversify the image of Chinese rock 'n' roll and urban youth cinema, which have continued their Long March into the new era.

CHAPTER FOUR

"At the Intersection of Film and Music": Jia Zhangke and Urban Youth Cinema

> If we compare the basic traits of film with those of music, we will find they are so similar. Film is an art about and a product of temporality and spatiality.
> —**Jia Zhangke**, "At the Intersection of Film and Music"[1]

Like Cui Jian, Jia Zhangke shows a strong interest in the long-standing and multifarious relationship between film and music, starting from the time when he studied scriptwriting and film theory at the Beijing Film Academy in 1993 to 1997. He wrote his bachelor's thesis on the connections between the two mediums, particularly on the aspects of how they work to build the aesthetic of temporality. A young and talented director, Jia Zhangke emerged in the late 1990s and has since become one of the most prominent Chinese filmmakers in the international film circuit. Many of his films and aesthetic innovations have been meticulously studied and underpinned as emblematic of "a bold new style of urban realism in contemporary Chinese cinema."[2] For example, Jia's earlier works, such as *Xian Shan Going Home* (*Xiao Shan huijia*, 1995) and *Xiao Wu* (1997), are said to demonstrate a register of postsocialist critical realism with a *vérité* stylization inspired by the so-called underground, independent film movement of the 1990s. His third, more ambitious production, *Platform* (*Zhantai*, 2000), then, extends the indigenous, *vérité* path Zhang Yuan and other pioneers have paved, yet provides a subtle variation within the movement, as it is suffused with the more aestheticized, transnational trend of long takes.

While considerable research has surveyed his cinematography, stylistic form, and social meanings, previous studies have not yet adequately examined Jia's use of a singular music track and distinctive soundscape.[3] Liu Jin and Sheldon Lu are among the few scholars who have paid attention to Jia's soundtrack. Their particular emphasis is on how Jia's maverick use of local dialects contributes to a sense of regionalism, an atmosphere of realism, and an undercurrent of marginality.[4] In my own discussion of Jia Zhangke, I continue to investigate Jia's postsocialist-realist aesthetic mode, but reconsider this enactment from a musical vantage point. My objective in this chapter is to examine the ways in which music has worked with visuality to form an integral part of Jia's *vérité* style and also how it serves as a metadiegetic vehicle for his construction of time, space, and the very concept of authenticity.

Vérité and Acoustic Empathy in *Xiao Wu*

Jia Zhangke has extensively used existing popular songs as spatio-temporal markers to build a tone of *vérité* in his films. Reproduced, repackaged, and circulated amongst his works, these musical elements and symbols dovetail cohesively to enhance emotions and to assert a distinctive youth or local identity in the context of social change. In *Xiao Wu* (aka *Pickpocket*, 1997), the central conflict lies between the rapidly shifting social milieu and the protagonist Xiao Wu, who is left behind as a dignified "artisan" (*shougong yiren*)—a title he ironically bestows upon himself—while many of his former colleagues and delinquent brothers have now been "rehabilitated" and achieved a higher social standing of businessmen, whether illegal or semilegal. Xiao Wu, the hapless pickpocket, thus becomes a signifier that is less outwardly negative than acerbically associated with the past—the "lost art" of pickpocketing and the paradigm of a "superfluous man" who is dismissed and marginalized by the dominant political economy (the "orthodox" ideology of market reform and the downfall of business culture in postsocialist China). The contradictions are not only framed by the film's narrative and visual composition, but are also more explicitly articulated through the music track when Xiao Wu strolls the market, drifts around the streets, and ventures in and out of karaoke bars.

The reticent, eccentric Xiao Wu and his eerie silence are often unexpectedly and disconcertingly juxtaposed with the hubbub of the marketplace, his previous time-served territory, and his new haunt, a dimly lit, clamorous karaoke bar. During the middle of the film, the focus turns toward Xiao Wu's courtship of Mei Mei, a hostess who works in the karaoke bar he frequently patronizes. In a remarkable long take, Xiao Wu comes to find Mei Mei in her dormitory when she is absent from the bar. Here, the two are seen nestling together on Mei Mei's bed for comfort almost for the first time in the film. An enclosed space with a shimmering sense of privacy and security is deftly built through the audiovisual device. At first, an unobtrusive camera pulls back from its subjects of gaze at a great distance, producing what Bertolt Brecht termed an alienating and defamilarizing effect. The lighting employed is natural but unusually bright and soft if we compare it with most other scenes in *Xiao Wu*, which are largely handled with low-key lighting similar to the noir fashion. A drop of broad light gushes from a nearby window they lean upon, creating a romantic and poetic feeling. The deliberate use of the static camera, as well as a long shot and a long take, and the strident ambient noises from the bustling street oozing in through the window, help impart a contemporaneous, realistic feel to the scene. And the particular spatial construction of the lovers lying side by side provides a heretofore rare glimpse of intimacy. In no way built to arouse an erotic response, the spatial *mise-en-scène* instead subverts and closes the emotional distance generated in the previous design of the narrative.

Faye Wong's song "Sky" (*Tiankong*, 1994) fittingly comes in at this double de(alienating) moment, eliciting a degree of empathy and identification with Mei Mei. Asked to sing a song, she picks Faye Wong's "Sky" and performs it devotedly:

> Why is my sky always wetted by tears . . .
> Drifting to the edge of the world
> Afflicted by solitude again and again
> With a desperate yearning in my sky

This melancholic, unaccompanied solo subtly delivers sentiments of sadness, solitude, and aspiration, underscoring Mei Mei's and Xiao Wu's unique but complementary characterizations. Beneath the pensive lyrics is an additional layer of implication that would be apprehended by Chinese audiences as well as international cult fans familiar with the song's original context. The original singer, Faye Wong, who is perhaps most recognized around the world as the wistful, alienated, and capricious sandwich-girl-turned-stewardess in Wong Kar-wai's *Chungking Express* (*Chung Hing sam lam*, 1994), is China's Madonna, the queen of Chinese popular music. As Anthony Fung and Michael Curtin have shown, Faye Wong's hallmark popularity in the Sinophone world is undergirded and paradoxically built upon the controversial values and strong, "anomalous" personalities she embodies in her films and popular songs, as well as in her off-screen personal life.[5] Wong's offbeat personality, obstinate attitude, outspoken desire for independence—not to mention her status as a youthful female icon—have all been projected onto Mei Mei. In a similar vein, constructed in *Xiao Wu* as an adventurous, longing, and wistful girl, Mei Mei appears as Faye Wong's double in this metadiegetic moment of singing—or, we may say, as Xiao Wu's alter ego.

Mei Mei, in the middle of singing, is unable to continue and bursts into tears. An interlude of awkward silence dominates the filmic space. To break the silence, Mei Mei urges the habitually reserved, taciturn Xiao Wu to sing as well. Xiao Wu, after a brief hesitation, responds by opening a cigarette lighter that emanates a cover version of the world-famous "Für Elise." The remix of Beethoven's classic tune through this shoddy piece of merchandise is by no means random; it gives a sense of disparity and contradiction between the aesthetic object and its mimetic commodity, encapsulating the very realities of a postsocialist, postmodern era in which mass reproduction and commodity fetishism dominate. This moment also poignantly alludes to the humble origins of the protagonists, who, at the bottom of the social ladder, are not well assimilated into the mainstream (the consumerist, capitalist order) and are becoming consigned further to the margins (pickpocket, convict, and karaoke mistress). The "Für Elise" lighter is ironically a material emblem of Xiao Wu's ego: a souvenir Xiao Wu takes from his estranged friend Xiao Yong when he goes to visit him uninvited before his wedding. It is a keepsake of their lost friendship.

In his elaborate discussion of *Xiao Wu*, Jason McGrath scrutinizes almost every visual detail of the extraordinarily long take depicting the delivery of a wedding gift, a shot which, to him, reveals "an intractable Chinese reality."[6] What I want to add is that the particular karaoke duet "Choice" (*Xuanze*, 1992), playing at the background of the scene, also effectively engages the realistic mode, speaking for the image and for the incommunicative characters. In a static, long-shot composition, the two former childhood friends are seen sitting face to face at a desk, with a karaoke player placed in the background of the frame. In the foreground, the two characters are seated, smoking nervously, and located at opposite sides of the composition. This deliberate placement visualizes the widening gap between the characters in terms of social standing. Xiao Wu reproaches Xiao Yong for "have fucking forgotten [their old days]" and not inviting him to the wedding. Xiao Yong replies in a halting voice, failing to give a good reason. This long take of four minutes is filled with prolonged stretches of silence, eerie mumbling and stammering of the characters, and uncannily, a popular song "Choice" performed almost in a similarly staccato manner. The crescendo of the song is accompanied by ardently romantic lyrics: "This kind of feeling, this kind of path, we have been going through together. I wish you could love forever. I wish you could keep me company wherever I go. I choose you and you choose me, oh . . ." Synchronized to the images and rhythms of other sonic

Xiao Wu (1997): Mei Mei sings Faye Wong's popular song "Sky" (1994).

elements within the scene, the carefully chosen song accentuates the *vérité* look of the film. Further, it offers a lyrical summary of the thematic narrative that, as McGrath has asserted, "dramatizes the central relationship of Xiao Wu and Xiaoyong and by extension interrogates the relationship between the new classes they represent."[7]

It is evident that Jia Zhangke wishes to cast empathy on Xiao Wu and Mei Mei, the two petty characters who are the "residuals" of the postsocialist project yet are the last vestige of dignity and morals. This sympathetic portrayal continues throughout the film and is specifically injected into a scene where the couple, in the dimly lit, red-tinged karaoke bar, embraces each other and dances to a plaintive torch song, "The Bold and the Beautiful" (*Ai jiangshan geng ai meiren*, 1994): "Live with honor, live in love. No heroes want to be alone. Good men are bold. Voyage through the world with spirit and gusto." The stark contrast between ideal and reality, aspiration and despair, mainstream and marginal, fabricated and authentic is also conveyed in the preceding sequence, in which Xiao Wu, all of a sudden, bursts into an a cappella version of the popular song "Heart Rain" (*Xinyu*, 1993) during the bath. It is a song he had not sung successfully before, no matter how hard he had tried to sing it, including at the karaoke bar and when it was garishly played at the wedding of Xiao Yong, his sworn brother and now "successful personage." In the diegetic events, the song, then, becomes a wry parody of Xiao Wu's own unrequited romance with Mei Mei, who "will become someone else's bride tomorrow," just as the song laments. Notwithstanding Xiao Wu's attempts to sing the song in public and at the karaoke bar (a space contradictorily endowed with both a sense of intimacy and performativity), he is not able to do it until he has been stripped fully naked and left alone in an old-style public bathhouse.

This is a scene with a minimalist *vérité* poetry that beautifully echoes Mei Mei's recent a cappella performance. The remarkable, intrusive shot invokes, as Tony Rayns calls it, "an almost Bressonian path to the core of Xiao Wu's psyche, stripping away layer after layer of his loser's armour until he's left as 'naked' as a person can be."[8] Parallels have been frequently drawn between Robert Bresson's *Pickpocket* (1959) and Jia Zhangke's *Xiao Wu*. A kind of homage to Bresson's neorealist masterpiece, *Xiao Wu* shares a similar critical and sympathetic view of modern society and its victims—the aberrant, quixotic heroes who "claim special privileges above and beyond common morality"[9] and are largely portrayed by amateur, common actors (*qunzhong yanyuan*). This "almost Bressonian path to the core of Xiao Wu's psyche"[10] and to the culpability and social ills of a postmodern, reformed life leads to the chilly ending of *Xiao Wu*, as described by Zhang Zhen, "where the gawking crowd during the shooting, refusing to be dispersed, came to 'play' the diegetic witnesses 'on the scene' of the crime, as it were, of a pickpocket's utter humiliation and exposed marginality when he has been caught and chained to a telephone pole on the sidewalk of a booming town street."[11] "The gawking crowd," so to speak, can be readily identified as but another re-enactment of one of the most famous tropes in modern Chinese history: the numb and apathetic onlookers who gaze indifferently at circumstances of crime, victim, humiliation, and violence—the shocking, paramount stock image in Lu Xun's fiction and modern Chinese literature generally.

A chauvinist song with a pounding beat and a towering male voice, "Farewell, My Concubine" (*Bawang bieji*, 1996) saliently reappears just before the dismal ending. The song is first played at the beginning of the film during a scene in which Xiao Wu furiously strides into Xiao Yong's house upon the news that he is not invited to his sworn brother's wedding. A point-of-view shot through his eyes captures the date of 1982 and names of Xiao Wu and Xiao Yong once carved on the brick wall of the house in an extreme close-up and a freeze-frame, all of which symbolize their bygone era and the bleak reality of the present. Reciting an ancient story about the valiant king Xiang Yu, his mournful fiasco and heart-rending romance, "Farewell, My Concubine" implores:

> I stand in the blowing wind
> Heart-wrenched and full of sorrow . . .
> With sword in my hand
> I ask the world, who is the hero?

In the final twist of *Xiao Wu*, against a highly affective musical backdrop, Jia's camera stands still to observe emotionlessly the busy street, pedestrians and bikers passing by, and last, the cuffed pickpocket footslogging the swarming town center. This calls to mind the hyperrealist recording of the opening cityscape in *Beijing Bastards*. Xiao Wu's misfitted self-value, vain struggle against the postsocialist onrush, and heroic Bressonian tragedy all seem to be parodied in the last humiliating scene, as well as in this final musical cue. As Liu Jin has rightly pointed out, in *Xiao Wu*, "popular songs, as an integral part of the soundtrack, function empathetically for the silent protagonist."[12] In addition, I argue that the use of popular musical numbers in *Xiao Wu*, primarily diegetic and all from 1990s China, which is attuned to the diegetic time of the work, gives the film an added sense of cinema *vérité* while at the same time imbuing it with an urgent contemporaneity.

Platform: A Meta-Music-Film

If popular songs in *Xiao Wu* serve largely as a conduit for emotional catharsis, laying bare the character's innermost feelings and speaking to one's hidden desires that cannot be otherwise expressed, music in *Platform* is employed in a more allegorical way to reference and encapsulate a particular period of history in postsocialist, reformed China. The title of the film, as Jia himself remarks, draws directly from a Chinese rock hit of the 1980s, "Platform" (*Zhantai*, 1987):

> Long long platform, long long waiting
> Long long train, taking my transient love away
> An uproarious platform, a lonely waiting . . .
> Our whole hearts are waiting, waiting forever

Explaining his choice of the title song, Jia states: "Platform was a hit rock song throughout China during the 1980s. It is a song about expectation. I choose this as my film title as a tribute to people's innocent hope. A platform can be a starting point as well as a finishing one. We are always expecting, searching, always on the road to somewhere."[13] A rock song such as this is arranged to capture feelings of anticipation, trivial moments of waiting, and a spate of final disappointment, all of which have, in fact, set the major tone for this highly aestheticized and allegorical film.

The train (and platform) thus underlined becomes a central image of the film that perpetuates a nostalgic past as well as a particular narrative of *Bildungsroman* (coming of age):

Fenyang, where I was born, is a country town in Shanxi province. It's deep inland. When I was young, we had no television. The little we knew of the outside world came from the public loudspeakers installed on the main streets. I remember once hearing a distant train whistle, the railroad was more than 30 miles away, and the sound was carried by a freak wind. I'd never heard about trains before. I began riding [a] bicycle at the age of 14, and the first long ride I took [with] my friends was to see the railroad. We saw a freight train carrying coal, and [an] intimation of the wider world.[14]

This very personal and affectionate memory has been translated to and recast in *Platform* as one of the film's most compelling trademark moments, described by Jason McGrath: "Indeed, at the time depicted in the film no railroad even ran through Fenyang, and thus during their travels in one key scene the performance troupe members dash across a dry riverbed and up to a bridge just to get a glimpse of a passing train. The train is thus both a literal industrial emblem of modernization and a more abstract symbol of a modernity actually experienced largely as an absence and a longing."[15] In McGrath's reading, the imaginary train and consequently the pivotal scene of the first, close encounter of this kind is important in *Platform* for its semiotic functions. My view of the symbolism of the train is pretty much in line with McGrath's notion. At first, the train is endorsed as an emblem of the longed-for modernity and liberal world values, a window to the vast outside expanse, and a vehicle loaded with youthful yearnings and desires to escape from the geographical imprisonment of the isolated inland. Second, the train is one of those vital metaphors embodying an inductive set of contradictions between rural and urban, hinterland and coastline, the East and the West, the past and the present, and, above all, "anticipation and disappointment."[16] It really speaks to the bewildering experience of third world's (China) date with modernity. In *Platform*, the train suggests a journey, a movement, and a state of development and progression. It provides a metaphorical and cinematic setting for the romance, encounter, and evolution of postsocialist modernization that unfolds throughout the story. Therefore, the train is configured not only as an empathetic code pronouncing the feeling of the scene but also as a broader reference to the spatiotemporal deterritorialization and reterritorialization—the dramatic historical change that China has undergone in the late twentieth century.

In a nutshell, *Platform* is an epic of post-revolutionary China. Or, to borrow Fredric Jameson's famous concept, it is a national allegory that projects the public political situation of postsocialist China onto the private individual domain of Chinese youth.[17] The historical time of the 1980s and lived

Platform (2000): The young performers from a small provincial town and their thrilling, first encounter with the train during their travels.

experience of a young generation interweave and are concretized through the lens of a performance troupe and its marked transmutation over the course of the reform era. *Platform* opens with Jia's masterful tableau framing and an extreme long shot of a trite musical performance, *A Train Heading for Shaoshan* (*Huoche xiangzhe shaoshan pao*), which explicitly sets the beginning of the narrative at a crossroads between the downfall of Maoist period and the advent of a new epoch of reform. Shaoshan is the birthplace of Chairman Mao and has been unanimously cited as the revolutionary cradle in socialist films and various performances. Just as this revolutionary play fades out, the film shifts to a post-performance scene where young actors and musicians are seen gathering onto a bus. In response to the troupe leader's skepticism about authenticity in his performance, Cui Mingliang, the film's main protagonist, takes the initiative of imitating the train's horn, thereby ushering in a chorus by the whole group of young people.

The echoes of train whistles on the soundtrack, leading into the opening credits, instantaneously establish a set of stylistic and thematic "anticipations," which are intrinsic to *Platform*. As if bringing the anticipations to a complete close, the film concludes with another one of Jia's signature immobile long shots. Cui Mingliang is seen lolling his head and napping on a couch during a lazy afternoon in the far background; at the center of the frame, his wife, Yin Ruijuan, teases their son in front of a stove while the kettle comes to boil. The kettle's boiling whistle interestingly mimics the iconic sound of the train's horn at the beginning, bringing the story full circle. Ergo, a sonic return to *Platform*'s starting point, exemplifying, in Jason McGrath's words, Jia's realist approach to "life time" and his aestheticized conception of "ellipses."[18]

What McGrath means is that the postsocialist time depicted cannot be simply read as a shared memory tinged with nostalgia. The gritty portrayal of this bygone era is not only chronological but also appears almost motionless and prosaic by means of the prevalent static long takes used in the film. In *Platform*, the slow, barely moving temporality corresponds to the film's geographical and spatial particularity, which attests to and accentuates the "actual inertia" and "frustration"[19] of a small, remote town that is left behind by the frantic rush for marketization and opening-up in the reform era. Such tensions between the crushing transformation (the new postsocialist official discourse) and pedestrian life (which is instead immersed with idleness and futility), between nouveau riche (arising to be the new model citizen) and the residual (being left out of sync with the new pace of modernization) have become the defining feature of *Platform*, as well as *Xiao Wu* and Jia's many other works.

My emphasis, nonetheless, is on the distinct ways in which a continuous stream of popular music and popular culture have been seamlessly inserted and woven into *Platform* as an attempt to document social change, while creating such dialectics of temporal-spatial (in)motions. My reading aligns with Jia's own attitude toward the crossover between film and music cited at the beginning of this chapter. To use Michel Chion's formula, it is "the audiovisual contract." Chion explicates two forms of using music in film:

> In my book *Le Son au cinema* I developed the idea that there are two ways for music in film to create a specific emotion in relation to the situation depicted on the screen. On one hand, music can directly express its participation in the feeling of the scene, by taking on the scene's rhythm, tone, and phrasing; obviously such music participates in cultural codes for things like sadness, happiness, and movement. In this case we can speak of *empathetic music*, from the word empathy, the ability to feel the feelings of others.
>
> On the other hand, music can also exhibit conspicuous indifference to the situation, by progressing in a steady, undaunted, and ineluctable manner: the scene takes place against this very backdrop of "indifference." This juxtaposition of scene with indifferent music has the effect not of freezing emotion but rather of intensifying it, by inscribing it on a cosmic background. I call this second kind of music *anempathetic* (with the privative *a*-).[20]

Chion's theoretical proposition of empathetic and anempathetic music is illuminating for my audiovisual exploration of Jia's film. As I have demonstrated in the previous study of *Xiao Wu*, popular songs are synthesized in an *empathetic* fashion to speak for the character, to convey feeling, and to match the pace, mood, and theme of the action on the screen. This still holds true in *Platform*. Likewise, music serves as a dramatic device in storytelling and is ascribed with emotional property to evoke an empathetic response in the viewer. Yet, in *Platform*, popular music also mediates in a somewhat different manner from that of *Xiao Wu*, which, one may say, is palpably anthropocentric and character-driven. Instead, the soundscape in *Platform* is superimposed onto a "cosmic background"[21] to make up a grand and abstract story of a nation, history, and culture. How, then, does sound exactly function in *Platform*? Is it empathetic or anempathetic? What is its relation to the visual track of the film if speaking of the "audiovisual contract"?

Compared to *Xiao Wu*, which is an intimate, anthropocentric short story about a pickpocket, *Platform* works on a larger and more ambitious canvas. It chronicles the change of a performance troupe from Fenyang (Jia's native town) that, trekking through the yellow earth, has been transmogrified from a state-run, propagandist cultural group into an overtly commercial, privatized enterprise in the midst of postsocialist reform, renamed the Shenzhen All-Stars Rock and Breakdance Electronic Band. The film centers on two pairs of young performers who are also lovers: Cui Mingliang (Wang Hongwei, Jia's best friend in the Beijing Film Academy who plays Xiao Wu and many important roles in Jia's works) and Yin Ruijuan (Zhao Tao, Jia's second wife who has since become Jia's muse and "forever" protagonist in all of his works); Zhang Jun (Liang Jingdong, Jia's classmate in the Beijing Film Academy who is the art designer for *Xiao Wu* and *Unknown Pleasures*) and Zhong Ping (Yang Lina, an award-winning documentary filmmaker herself, which again demonstrates Jia's close affinity with the indigenous new documentary movement). In addition, other important roles include the leader of the troupe played by Xi Chuan (one of the most influential poets in 1990s China), a peasant worker for the coal mine sweat factory played by Sanmin (Jia Zhangke's cousin in real life), and many other extras who happen to be Jia's friends and hometown acquaintances, all of whom are veritably playing themselves in the film. All of these factors suggest that *Platform* can be read as a semi-autobiography, a realist product, a nostalgia work, an homage to bygone youthfulness, and a discourse of *Bildungsroman*. However, such a reading is not yet complete without considering the vibrant role popular music and culture play in this benchmark piece.

In an interview with film critic Tony Rayns, Jia Zhangke elaborates on the distinctive roles that popular music plays in the social and cultural life of contemporary China. He professes the popular music-culture appeal in the following words:

For many years Chinese have found their identity in groups; we were brought up to think of ourselves as cogs in the huge machine that is the nation. Until quite recently, individual identity was barely acknowledged, spiritual life was very limited, and entertainment was minimal. This was true not only in Shanxi, but all over China. When the "door" finally opened, the first thing to make a real impact was popular music from Hong Kong and Taiwan. Love songs reminded us that we had a right to love; the pop music sub-culture stimulated a wider awakening of individual consciousness . . . It's no real surprise, then, that pop music liberated people from a rigid idealism. Pop music was followed by television, which brought us American sci-fi, soap operas from Japan and martial-arts serials from Hong Kong. The sub-culture destroyed the spiritual prison we'd been in, but at the same time it overturned moral norms. I try to reflect that duality in *Platform*. I have to say that I am sometimes very touched by those old pop songs.[22]

Set in Jia's hometown of Fenyang on the threshold of market reform, the opening sequence of *Platform* quickly switches from the local cultural troupe that is performing a revolutionary play to a mother who is altering Maoist blue pants into contemporary-look "bell-bottom trousers" for her "fashion-awoken" son—the first hint of the arrival of Western popular culture. In the following sequences, a flux of Western modernity and influence, springing from foreign films and TV series such as *Awara* (India, 1951) and *Garrison's Gorillas* (US, 1967–68), introduces new values and lifestyles to the young generation in this small town. Like a previous sequence in which Cui Mingliang is chastised by his "traditional" father (who is ironically revealed to be the real "wanton," abandoning his wife and children for a younger mistress in the second half of the film) for his bizarre Western fashion, his romantic interest, Yin Ruijuan, is forced to leave the theater by her worried father who considers the foreign film being played too "liberal" and "corruptive." This touches upon a core set of issues in the film: the thematic tensions and conflicts between the East and the West, traditional and modern, the old generation and the young generation. The camera then moves to a dimly lit shot of the young protagonists surreptitiously gathering together to listen to an "illegal" radio broadcast from Taiwan of Teresa Teng's ballad "Wine and Coffee" (*Meijiu jia kafei*, 1972). The immense popularity of the Taiwanese singer Teresa Teng among Chinese adolescents in the 1980s is representative of the early influx of popular music, which offered an alternative space for individuality and self-expression outside of the official, political channel, as Jia just noted.

It is no coincidence that popular music, as a key source of inspiration for Jia's cinematic exploration, comes to dominate the soundtrack. While we may surmise from the above evidence that *Platform* appears to be a very personal work infused with a deeply melancholic, nostalgic feeling, popular music and culture have truly become a major constituent of Jia's poetic construction of postsocialist realism. Almost every single song (and even snippets of sonic elements) are intricately associated with particular temporalities and locales. *A Train Heading for Shaoshan*, for instance, is a tribute to the socialist past. Meanwhile, Teresa Teng's "Wine and Coffee" and Su Rui's "Whether or Not" (*Shifou*, 1989) came from Taiwan; "Genghis Khan" (*Chengjisihan*, 1987) poured in from Hong Kong; and "Young Friends Come Together" (*Nianqing de pengyou lai xianghui*, 1980), "Platform" (*Zhantai*, 1987), and "Little Girls under the Street Lamp" (*Ludeng xia de xiao nvhai*, 1987) were embedded in the domestic mainland. These popular songs become messengers, introducing a postsocialist reality and bearing witness to the dramatic change postsocialist China has undergone. Finally, the soundtrack of *Garrison's Gorillas* played off-screen, and *Awara*, an Indian film captured within the diegetic frame, is used to signify the advent of a new, open era in which China becomes increasingly implicated in global currents and networks of Western modernity. These distinct songs and sounds are, in large measure, diegetic and turned into a storytelling device themselves. Appearing mostly as either live performances or synchronized diegetic sound, they are restored and integrated into the diegesis to generate a quality of authenticity. In addition, the preexisting, well-known tunes open up an imaginary space to engage the film's audience in a process of personal reminiscence.

Platform stands out for its distinctive *vérité* approach and its artfully realistic style. Jia's verisimilitudinous, nostalgic portrayal of his hometown Fenyang in the 1980s, a stand-in for a broader China during the era of reform, is masterfully executed through his trademark observational long takes, distant long shots, static camera, minimalist, and natural setting and *mise-en-scène*, which appear to register the mood, tone, and rhythm of the scene "indifferently" and purport to convey such feelings of estrangement in the maelstrom of reform "objectively." To borrow from Michel Chion, I call this type of vision "anempathetic." On the screen, we get glimpses of actions and happenings piecemeal, but part and parcel of the events are often wholly recorded under the watch of an omniscient, surveillant camera, as if nothing had really happened or changed. This anempathetic effect is thus essentially produced by Jia's immobile long-take and long-shot cinematography, the aesthetic vision that film critics often identify in *Platform*. The unmediated documentation of time in a quotidian life as simply passing and endured—and the studious control of "sentimentality even in the most dramatic scenes"[23]—rightly uncover an intractable reality and predicament of China's reform: the resulting distance and uncompromised rift between the public and the private, rich and poor, city and countryside, inland and coastline, and most of all, the ideal and the reality.

On the other hand, *Platform* is also fused with a very strong personal sentiment and a feeling of "reflective nostalgia."[24] It is, then, the music and sound, I argue, that perform an "empathetic" role and register the actions and thoughts of the characters "emotionally." Jia gives the soundtrack an exceptionally prominent place; there are a total of twenty popular songs tagged into *Platform*, as my study in the auxiliary chart evidently shows. Popular songs inundate the screen time and effectively support visuality. Moreover, the musical commentary and sound effects add a degree of depth to the film's narrative by expressing one's innermost and sometimes hidden feelings explicitly and allowing us glimpses into the character's mental state. Hence, I conclude that an art film like *Platform* displays a formalist concoction of audiovisual elements and such a relationship in-between can be seen as contrapuntal. This "audiovisual contract," I extend, can be described as a synthesis of anempathetic camera vis-à-vis empathetic sound.

In order to see how music and sound constitute the major elements in *Platform* and elicit affect in the audience, I devise a table (see the appendix) that seeks to understand when and how sound occurs, as well as the multiplicities and contingencies of sonic experience in relation to the action and vision of the film. A close reading of a specific sequence of five consecutive shots will cast additional light on this fascinating audiovisual aesthetic in *Platform*. The first shot of the sequence occurs nearly two hours into the film, right after the sudden break-up of Zhong Ping and Zhang Jun, the most outspoken and modernized couple who seem to have the most stable relationship in *Platform*. The film then shifts to an extended medium shot that fixates on the revamped performance troupe rehearsing Su Rui's popular hit "Whether or Not" in a small, dark flat. As if tracing the man's singing, the camera begins to move and slowly pans right to display the source of the voice; Cui Mingliang stands in an empty courtyard, smoking and crooning this romantic song to music produced by an electronic keyboard. This is a conspicuous audiovisual marker of the critical change; the traditional instruments of *erhu* and accordion are replaced by electronic keyboard, guitar, and Western-style drum as the performance troupe completes its capitalist transmogrification. Most remarkable in this single shot is not only the fact that it lasts a little over one minute but also the way in which the unique camera movement and sound are forcefully linked together. Jia's camera circles

The "Whether or Not" sequence in *Platform* (2000): Shot 1.

around and scans the locus and exterior surrounding the sound happening using 360-degee panoramic cinematography. The former meeting room of the troupe with the buzzing crowd, symbolic of an authoritarian socialist space, is now unsheathed as a dilapidated and deadly desert in the present time of postsocialist reform.

The second shot then begins with a medium view of a road being constructed at the town center. Bulldozers and construction workers are framed in the extreme foreground. In the background, we see Yin Ruijuan trekking through the ramshackle street alongside her bicycle. The camera captures her as she approaches and pans to follow her until she walks far away in an extreme long shot. During the bulk of the shot, the clamor of ongoing construction penetrates the soundscape. This adds an edge of raw realism to the scene, the kind of aesthetic style and sound design favored in *Xiao Wu*. In a similarly realist manner, this scene and by extension *Platform* can therefore be deemed a prelude to *Xiao Wu*. Spanning more than a decade of the 1980s, *Platform* foretells the increasingly alienated reality of the mid-1990s in *Xiao Wu*. On the other hand, this scene is also a sensible continuation and elaboration of the pivotal theme of postsocialist reform and modernization in the throes of demolition and reconstruction, resonating with the prior scene just discussed.

The following shot is, perhaps, one of the most exquisite long takes and serves as an aesthetic climax in *Platform*. In one extraordinary shot lasting about two-and-a-half minutes, Yin Ruijuan is seen loafing in an empty tax office in the middle of the night. She has taken off the demure black coat depicted in the preceding scene and now wears a sleek yellow sweater and a white bandanna bow in her hair, all of which adds a touch of warmth and

The "Whether or Not" sequence in *Platform* (2000): Shot 2.

feminine sentimentality to the scene. Beginning in an extreme long shot, Yin lolls around the office in the far background and listens languidly to a radio station airing a song request program. As one particular song begins to fill the diegetic space, she moves bit by bit toward the camera and affectively improvises a beautiful freestyle dance to Su Rui's "Whether or Not":

Whether or not this time I am really going to leave you
Whether or not this time I am not going to cry anymore
Whether or not this time I am going to be gone and never come back
Walk to that long forever endless road

Originally composed and written by Luo Dayou, the highly esteemed godfather of music (*yinyue jiaofu*) from Taiwan, the song is a tribute to a nearly ideal romance he had with Sylvia Chang, a unique woman who has an unprecedented profile in all aspects of acting, singing, scriptwriting, producing, and directing in the Sinophone world. The original song, among others, becomes an important musical number in *Papa, Can You Hear Me Sing* (*Dacuoche*, dir. Yu Kanping, 1983), a musical melodrama that details the tearful story of a mute veteran and his adopted daughter in postwar Taiwan. In its reappearance in *Platform*, "Whether or Not" not only functions as a kind of narrative device that explicitly articulates and explains the character's subtlest actions and innermost feelings, but also summarizes and reinforces the film's youthful, nostalgic themes (as I explored earlier).

In contrast to the quite open, effervescent couple, Zhong Ping and Zhang Jun, the relationship between Cui Mingliang and Yin Ruijuan seems dubious

The "Whether or Not" sequence in *Platform* (2000): Shot 3.

and nebulous—mostly due to the fierce objection of Yin's father, a local policeman. While the troupe goes through the postsocialist privatization and continues on its capitalist adventure, Yin has to stay home to care for her ill father and subsequently takes a job as a tax officer. Yin remains cold, unapproachable, and emotionally distant in the scene, but the loud outcry of the song betrays the true feelings she tries so hard to hide even from herself. The explication of the lyrics and the high, intensified timbre of the singing, which coordinates perfectly with Yin's beautiful dancing, reveal the character's innermost desires and romantic yearnings—for instance, her broken dreams of going to see the train and the "glamourous" outside world—and the frustrations of being imprisoned in a small provincial town while endlessly waiting and idling. This is one of the most touching moments in *Platform* created through a highly aestheticized "audiovisual contract." It also conjures up another highly stylized musical scene in cinema history, where the lavish cigarette smoke swirls and sensually dances in close-ups to the ravishing violin and cello of "Yumeji's Theme" in Wong Kar-wai's *In the Mood for Love* (2000), when Tony Leung sits and smokes alone under the warm light of a lamp in an empty office.

In this carefully polished sequence in *Platform*, the fourth shot continues with a reverse tracking move that captures the now uniformed Yin driving a scooter along a street and passing the city gate. In the next shot, the camera cuts to a wider frame that follows a moving truck through the vast countryside. In a long shot, we see an almost invisible Cui Mingliang on the bed of the truck as he gazes back, suggesting another departure from his hometown as he leaves for a remote and perhaps unattainable destination (and goal), which is attested in the following sequence of his live performance of

The "Whether or Not" sequence in *Platform* (2000): Shot 4.

"Platform" at the renamed Rock and Breakdance band. These two dynamic scenes featuring a hastily retreating landscape are distinguished from the rest of the film, where the stationary camera and slow pans are more pervasive. They are among the very few instances of subjective shots and nondiegetic music in *Platform*. What does Cui Mingliang see, as he stares back from the truck? And what does he hear? The answers are readily hinted at in the preceding shot: Cui's gaze and hearing are indeed tied to his love interest, Yin Ruijuan, and to his secluded hometown, Fenyang. Thus, the fourth shot can be read backwards and interpreted as a point-of-view shot of Cui, in which he sadly bids farewell to Yin and his hometown for a new journey.

In addition to this innovative reverse object/glance mechanism, the popular song also operates as an important suturing device that stitches together the object and the look, coheres the two shots, and conflates two lonely hearts. Su Rui's "Whether or Not" continues to play sonorously until the song retreats tenderly to the last line and to the end of the sequence. The specific song, heard over the succession of the five shots, is, on the one hand, associated with Cui and Yin. It functions as a kind of intimate and poetic expression of their relationship. On the other hand, it can also be broadly perceived as a musical motif that recounts and reflects upon the romantic fantasy and youthful aspirations of Zhong Ping and Zhang Jun, as well as the other troupe members, yielding a particular affect of nostalgic sorrow that characterizes the film.

As my analysis of the film indicates, popular music in *Platform* not only provides significant commentary to onscreen actions and the broader social changes, but also becomes a persistent narrative in its own right—a driving

The "Whether or Not" sequence in *Platform* (2000): Shot 5.

force that structures the film as a whole and connects various spatial and temporal segments together. As a film pursuing a realist aesthetic, what is remarkable about *Platform* is not only Jia's inventive ways of selecting and arranging popular songs aligned with particular visual images and themes, but also his careful maneuverings of the setting and ambience of the sound. Popular music and sound exude from a wide variety of sources and social-cultural-geopolitical contexts, such as the stage proscenium, film theater, domestic space, restaurant, cafe, bar, street, courtyard, dance hall, public loudspeaker, television, radio broadcast, and even the stereo of an old broken truck that plays the cassette tape of Zhang Xing's "Platform," reverberating over the desolate, vast yellow plateau and inspiring the title of the film. Working with a large repertoire of popular songs, ambient noises, and other sources of sound that have been seamlessly infused into the everyday scenarios of the film, the extraordinary soundtrack of *Platform* can be considered authentic, reflectively realistic, and moreover, postmodern.

Fredric Jameson's articulation of a postmodern reality that is saturated with images and sounds from many kinds of media implacably encroaching upon forms of representation is relevant here. In the postmodern condition, the role of music lies, first, in remaining a marker of "taste" and "social distinction"; second, "it mediates our historical past along with our private and existential one and can scarcely be woven out of the memory any longer"; and furthermore, "the most crucial relationship of music to the postmodern, however, surely passes through space itself."[25] Thus, critical reading of music and sound requires attention to its current socioeconomic and geopolitical functions. Also needed is an investigation of its formal and historical interest in the past, the irrevocable and incommensurable bygone era. In short, music and sound retrieve and mobilize an ambience of nostalgia. Jameson asserts that contemporary nostalgia culture or postmodern nostalgia film does not represent the "real" past, but merely offers false realism in the mode of "nostalgia for the present" that is so fully subsumed by capitalist forces now.[26] It represents the utter reification and commodification of history. Film scholar Dai Jinhua, when discussing the rhetoric of contemporary Chinese film, argues in a similar vein that

> if, during the conquest of the 1980s and 1990s, one of Chinese culture's ongoing internal efforts is to consciously construct and strengthen a mesmerizing mirror of the West while at the same time relentlessly fabricating Oriental mythology in front of this magical mirror, then the "fashion" of nostalgia sentiment becomes one application of such a construction, as well as a necessary misleading and explication of the construction. No nostalgic writing can be considered a "re-creation of the original scene." Different from a written record that calls up memories of yesterday, nostalgia, as the fashion of contemporary China, uses the construction and embellishment of remembrance to assuage the present.[27]

In this light, *Platform* can be inevitably read as a nostalgia film. It is also a recreation of yesterday for the present; staples of postmodernism, like pastiche, hybridity, and ambiguity between the real and the fictional, abound in the film. How do we, then, reconcile the sort of Jamesonian critical discourse of the ascendency of nostalgia culture that arose solely for commercial appeal with the characterization of *Platform*, a film that carries a melodic and critical thrust about a major historical and cultural transformation in reformist, postsocialist (postmodernist) China?

One instance that immediately comes to mind is the *mise-en-scène* of the old city walls that acts as a singular backdrop for many beautiful shots of *Platform*. McGrath points out that these mesmerizing scenes were "filmed in Fenyang's neighboring, much more picturesque, city of Pingyao, where the city wall dates to the Ming dynasty and where enough traditional architecture survives to have made the town a major domestic tourist destination starting in the late 1990s."[28] Such a historical and mythical space, on the one hand, serves a representational function as it highlights and illuminates the ambiguous and estranged relationship of Cui and Yin, an aspect of the film that is closely examined by both McGrath and Michael Berry.[29] The ancient wall thus becomes a metaphor for tradition and stasis, and it also represents the barrier between Cui and Yin and by extension their youthful longings vis-à-vis the immobile reality, all of which stands in direct opposition to the train motif of *Platform*. On the other hand, in a manner reminiscent of *Spring in a Small Town* (*Xiaocheng zhichun*, dir. Fei Mu, 1948), an early Chinese classic, Jia's cinematography of the city remnants expresses a sense of melancholy, loss, "cultural schizophrenia" (identified by Jameson as another defining feature of postmodern nostalgia film),[30] and moreover, a quintessentially Chinese style and "Oriental mythology."

Another example of using false realism to create a nostalgic effect (and ironically an aura of authenticity) is the film's oral dimension in terms of its dialogue. In *Platform*, only the leaders of the troupe and Zhong Ping speak Mandarin, while all other characters speak local dialects. Jia cast Wang Hongwei in the lead role of Cui Mingliang, but Wang actually doesn't speak Fenyang dialect as presumed; all of his lines are instead delivered in Wang's own Henan dialect. Yet most audiences, especially international audiences, will hardly notice the nuanced distinctions between the varieties of the dialects and the extent of cinematic fidelity to the linguistic "reality." Rather, attention is ostensibly drawn to this daring, full-length use of local dialects on the big screen for almost the first time, a distinction which brings *Platform* the accolade of "cinema with an accent."[31] All of these aspects have reaffirmed Jia's uniqueness and his status as an artist and intellectual filmmaker. His output attempts to deconstruct the official narrative monopolized by standard Mandarin, and thus his cinematic experiment rescues and reconstructs history from the most fundamental grassroots level and the local perspective. While the dialects and many-tongued soundscapes in *Platform* reach a new level of aestheticized realism, the film displays a form of self-Orientalism like many of his Fifth Generation predecessors and Sixth Generation contemporaries, whose independent, transnational films were in large part funded by international investors and allegedly almost exclusively geared toward the international art-house audience.

I wish to conclude this discussion of *Platform*'s auditory particularity with a quote from Michael Berry:

> In *Platform*, another such example occurs when the thirty-fifth anniversary of the founding of the PRC (1984) is announced over a radio broadcast as Zhong Ping slaps Zhang Jun and stamps into the clinic operating room to have her abortion. Here the birthday of the nation is sarcastically matched with the death of Zhong's unborn child. Towards the end of the film a loudspeaker announcement issues a list of criminals wanted by the government (a cryptic reference to the crackdown in the wake of the 1989 student demonstrations) which coincides with the end of Cui Mingliang's idealistic

wanderings and his settling down into a stable family . . . In a tone typical of official state announcements, a female voice reads off the list of suspects: "Yu Lik Wai, twenty-four, male, born in Guangdong province, a native of Zhongshan county, 5.58 feet. He has strong Cantonese accent and is fluent in French." Yu is, of course, not a student activist, but Jia's Hong Kong cinematographer. In a comic self-referential move, Jia has also touched on the very real predicament that he and fellow independent film-makers faced as "illegal" or "underground" artists.[32]

Berry convincingly demonstrates how noise or ambient sound is tightly knitted into *Platform*, carrying out Jia's idiosyncratic postmodern nostalgia and self-reflexive irony. I will add that in *Platform* a time of historical, postmodern change is pronounced not only through the direct reference over the soundtrack to a chronology of historical incidents, including CCP's issuing of the "Resolution on the Rehabilitation of Comrade Liu Shaoqi" (1980), the promulgation of the one-child policy (early 1980s), the Sino-British Joint Declaration (1984), and the Tiananmen Square student protest (1989), but also through the audible progression of popular youth culture in broadcast (Teresa Teng's "Wine and Coffee"), film (*Awara*), television (*Garrison's Gorillas, River Elegy*), and, especially, popular music. On the one hand, the popular music soundtrack in *Platform* is a commodity—a product of the burgeoning market economy and mass consumer culture in postsocialist China. On the other hand, the exuberant manifestation of music and sound serves to represent a key concept of motion and change, a sense of historiography and temporal movement, and furthermore to assert a distinct youth identity and a touch of self-reflexivity at this particular juncture of social and cultural transformation. In this regard, although *Platform* itself might not be readily classified as a musical, it nevertheless functions as a musical montage, a pastiche, and a tribute to the greatest decade of Chinese popular music of the 1980s. Ultimately, it would be completely appropriate to read the film in the context of popular music history. All in all, I would call *Platform* a meta-music-film.

The Rock 'n' Roll Generation, *Yesterday*, and How the Bastard Is Tempered

The emergence and development of Chinese urban youth cinema from the late 1980s through the early twenty-first century can be seen as the result of a widespread and multifaceted transformation taking place in postsocialist China, in particular in the private, everyday domain. Examining films ranging from independent, experimental works such as *Beijing Bastards*,

Xiao Wu, and *Platform* to more commercial, mainstream pieces such as *The Troubleshooters*, *Roots and Branches*, and *Good Morning, Beijing*, I offer a lineage of urban youth cinema and Chinese rock from an audiovisual perspective. "Urban youth" as a trope has been represented in contemporary Chinese filmmaking through the singular use of rock and popular music on cinematic soundtracks. Rock 'n' roll functions in this context not just as a specific film genre or as a kind of formal practice, but more broadly as a conceptual, analytical, and aesthetic framework that allows us to investigate how discourses of politics, subculture, youth rebellion, individualism, marginality, and authenticity surrounding various aspects of rock culture play into the formation of a new urban cinema in the maelstrom of a drastic, relentless social change.

The Fifth Generation's breakthrough, as I have claimed, was to overthrow the shackles of socialist indoctrination, patriarchal Confucian ideology, and the repression of the father's order as the son's generation. The new urban generation, in turn, becomes the generation of the bastard, of those living in the shadow of their glorious Fifth Generation "father." This generation of bastards struggles to challenge and surpass their fathers—their cultural, ideological, and cinematic forebearers. They achieve this with a more radical rendering of the absent father, the unknown father, the incorporeal father, and the father who is nowhere. A signifier of postsocialist contradiction, such a fatherly figure haunts and is thrust into the filmmakers' memory and youthful imaginary as a representation of lack (*Beijing Bastards*, *Dirt*, *Black Snow*, and *The Sun Also Rises*), quite often as a nightmare (*The Troubleshooters*, *Xiao Wu*, and *Platform*), and sometimes, rarely, as an incarnation of utopia (*Roots and Branches*).

Another work exhibiting a complex ambivalence toward the father, rock culture, and postsocialist urban transformation is Zhang Yang's *Quitting* (aka *Yesterday*, *Zuotian*, 2001, a referenced image on the cover of this book). The film is but one of a handful of independent art-house experiments by the young Sixth Generation, released by Sony Pictures in the United States and produced by Imar Film Company (the first independent film company that had formed a joint venture with Rock Records, the Chinese pop music giant; this allowed for Imar's ample use of Rock Records' music library, as exemplified in *Quitting*). Hallmarks of the Sixth Generation are present in *Quitting*'s convoluted production and exhibition history (the enthusiastic applause of the international art film circuit vis-à-vis the as-yet restricted access to the domestic market), its bold, pathological anatomization of sensitive subjects (drug addiction, mental illness, rock music, and the underworld of Chinese art), and most of all, its innovative film language that shows a consistent fascination with *vérité*, urban realism, and the dynamic of audiovisual synergy.

In an alternative audiovisual fashion resonating with that of *Beijing Bastards*, *Quitting* examines the torn-apart life world of an actor and rock performer, Jia Hongsheng, who was actually made popular through his roles in *Good Morning, Beijing* and a batch of internationally acclaimed Sixth Generation works, including *Weekend Lover* (*Zhoumo qingren*, dir. Lou Ye, 1995), *Frozen* (*Jidu hanleng*, dir. Wang Xiaoshuai, 1996), and *Suzhou River* (*Suzhou he*, dir. Lou Ye, 2000). As a youthful meditation on, and acute observation of, a chaotic liminal era, *Quitting* is no less an intimate (auto)biography that documents in minute detail Jia Hongsheng's descent into drugs and his painstaking trajectory of rehabilitation and "quitting" drugs, daydreaming, and rock music in 1990s China.

Three key components that often combine to create the typical example of urban youth cinema—rock music, *flânerie* amidst the quotidian everyday life against the vast changing cityscape, and self-projection of film and artistic experiment in an increasingly commercialized yet politically stringent social structure—weave a poignant story of quitting yesterday. In *Quitting*, there are copious audiovisual references that allude to the plight of urban youth in a changing society, conjuring up special feelings of entrapment, alienation, repression, and the loss of innocence. Such aspects are notably found in the film poster and clip from Martin Scorsese's *Taxi Driver* (1976) and a very rich rock music track consisting of Cui Jian's "A Piece of Red Cloth" and "Fake Monk," Tang Dynasty's "The Sun" (*Taiyang*, 1991) and "The Moon High" (*Yuemeng*, 1991), Zhang Chu's "Shameful Being Left Alone" (*Gudu de ren shi kechi de*, 1994), He Yong's "Garbage Dump" (*Lajichang*, 1994), Dou Wei's "The Higher Being" (*Gaoji dongwu*, 1994), "Black Dream" (*Heimeng*, 1994), and "God Bless Me" (*Shangdi baoyou*, 1994), and most of all, the Beatles' "Let it Be" (1970). The original Chinese title of the film, *Zuotian* ("Yesterday"), also conspicuously recalls Lennon's canonical song and a bygone age of youth and innocence.

Zhang Yang, like his Sixth Generation peers, explores new forms of expression and constantly challenges the limits of cinematic representation. *Quitting* purports to be a cinematic reinterpretation of a true story, in which all of the characters play themselves during the interview, on the stage, and throughout the story. The film's daring structure works synchronically on three crisscrossing planes of reality between diegetic space, theatrical stage, and documentary interview. The entangled spatio-temporal framing—and the practice of cutting back and forth between fiction and reality, between the representational and the representable, where boundaries are purposely blurred—is not something completely new to the Sixth Generation experiments, as often seen in their realist and documentary-influenced works. Yet it is the figure of the father—the recentralization and resurrection of a father—that *Quitting* employs to distinguish itself from the breed of bastard-like

Quitting (2001): Jia Hongsheng in juxtaposition with his spiritual father—John Lennon—and his own father.

films. Put differently, this film is not so much about a "postmodernist deviant" (*houxiandai de liguizhe*)³³ but about the continuing moral and social valence of the family in postsocialist China, which has witnessed a massive disintegration of faith, moral value, and social fabric during the last two decades of the twentieth century and into the present.

Quitting confronts, in a most candid and clinical manner, the nearly "hopeless" struggle of Jia Hongsheng in a postmodernist abyss of drug obsession, neurosis, and nihilism. It is obvious from the second sequence, which introduces Jia's parents, both theater actors in northeastern China who retire early and move to Beijing to help their "perverted" son. Therefore, the film appears to be a story about the deterritorialization of the family in posthumanist condition. The son constantly breaches Chinese family codes by offending, accusing, even slapping his father and claiming instead John Lennon as his "real" father. Such a dramatization of the Oedipus complex is pervasive in a wide range of Fifth Generation and Sixth Generation patricidal narratives. Upon closer inspection, however, *Quitting* is one of the many reinterpretations of the century-long hackneyed narrative of salvation; it is also a piece about the reterritorialization and regeneration of family, steering away from the muddled "yesterday." Jia Hongsheng is sent to a mental hospital for rehabilitation, and once fully recovered, is welcomed back home at the film's end. Like *Shower* (*Xizao*, 1999), a commercially appealing production Zhang Yang shot only one year earlier, Zhang's focalization is inherently on the conflict between father and son, modernity and tradition, and ultimately between the redemptive power of the father (and tradition) in the face of postmodern urban decay (and postsocialist reform).

I want to conclude the chapter with a brief discussion of one final Sixth Generation film, not least because rock is core to this work and also because of its intricate relationship with both the canonized Fifth Generation and another aspect of the state and the mainstream, which will be the focus of my next chapter. *How the Steel Was Tempered* (*Gangtie shi zenyang liancheng de*, aka *Zhangda chengren*, dir. Lu Xuezhang, 1997) provides an epic view of a "lost" generation of Chinese youth in search of selfhood and subjectivity amidst postsocialist change, struggling against the alienation caused by relentless urbanization and globalization. Chronicling the transformation of its protagonist, Zhou Qing—from the trivial moments of his adolescence in the last year of Cultural Revolution to his dull, lackluster days in the railway station as a boiler stoker in the early 1980s to the *viva voce*, visually absent period of self-exile in Europe and finally to his return to an even more disenchanted life as a rock guitarist in late 1980s and early 1990s Beijing—*How the Steel Was Tempered* can be understood as a stylistic adaptation and a sequel to *Beijing Bastards*, as well as an unwitting prelude to *Quitting* and *Platform*.

Rock and popular music are incorporated into the film to cast light on everyday reality in juxtaposition with vast historical changes. For instance, it deploys the soft music of "Night at the Naval Port" (*Jungang zhiye*, 1980), Teresa Teng's love ballads, Luo Dayou's "Master of the Future" (*Weilai de zhurenweng*, 1983), Faye Wong's "Vulnerable Woman" (*Rongyi shoushang de nvren*, 1992), and Pink Floyd's "Hey You" (1979) in this manner. The guitar and bits of the string music become a paramount dramatic and symbolic device associated with Zhou Qing (played by Zhu Hongmao, who is in fact a notable rock musician in Beijing and appears as Jia Hongsheng's best friend in *Quitting*), which sets a nostalgic tone and injects a youthful sensibility into this melancholic *Bildungsroman*. Again, rock occupies a pivotal place as a flamboyant marker of youth, freedom, individualism, creativity, and liberation in *How the Steel Was Tempered*, even though it could lead to a different direction (as the film demonstrates). Upon his return, Zhou Qing finds himself in an unfamiliar world, where he comments on the circle of artists and musicians: "These people have healthy bodies, but already lost their healthy minds." The film, in a gritty, realistic style, probes the seedy underground of "Beijing Bastards," where drug deals, "postmodernist deviance," and ostensibly corrupted social mores prevail.

It is only when he thinks again of the Russian revolutionary classic *How the Steel Was Tempered* and "Zhoukhrai" (the character's real name and identity are not explicitly revealed until the end, so the film adopts this nickname, which is Zhou Qing's special way of addressing him) that Zhou Qing finds a modicum of comfort. "One of the red canons and 'signposts' (*rensheng lubiao*) for Chinese youths from the 1950s to the 1970s," *How the Steel Was Tempered* has enjoyed a very long life and enormous popularity in socialist China.[34] In the new age of market reform, the revolutionary canon continues to serve social and ethical causes as an emblem of enlightenment, inspiration, and idealism, which indeed sparked the title of this particular film. In Nicolas Ostrovski's orginal text, Zhoukhrai is a sailor who guides Pawel Korchagin, the hero of the novel, to endure all the harsh challenges and become a real revolutionist. In Lu Xuezhang's film, "Zhoukhrai" is a righteous locomotive engineer and the mentor of Zhou Qing, whom he first meets while working in the railway station. Lu Xuezhang's prudent appropriation of the literary classic as a narrative thread and a metaphor turns Zhou Qing's story into a prototypical revolutionary *Bildungsroman*, like its original novel. As Mikhail Bakhtin defines the important qualities of *Bildungsroman*:

> Along with this predominant, mass type, there is another incomparably rarer type of novel that provides an image of man in the process of becoming. As opposed to a static unity, here one finds a dynamic unity in the hero's image. The hero himself, his character, becomes a variable in the formula of this type of novel . . . He emerges *along with the world* and he reflects the historical emergence of the world itself. He is no longer within an epoch, but on the border between two epochs, at the transition point from one to the other. The transition is accomplished in him and through him. He is forced to become a new, unprecedented type of human being. What is happening here is precisely the emergence of a new man.[35]

How can we relate Lu Xuezhang's rewriting of *How the Steel Was Tempered* to Bakhtin's concept of *Bildungsroman*? Is the protagonist Zhou Qing similarly engaged in a moving process of emergence? Has he ultimately become "a new, unprecedented type of human being"? How does he embody Bakhtin's notion of "transition in him and through him"? It is hard not to recognize that "Zhoukhrai" is, in fact, the true hero in *How the Steel Was Tempered*. He is the "unprecedented type of human being" who looks after and protects Zhou Qing all along, bravely fighting the evils of society, while blinded and paralyzed like the contemporary Chinese Pawel Korchagin. In the second half of the story, "Zhoukhrai" disappears from Zhou Qing's life after he donates his bone to Zhou in an accident; a sheer metaphor of incarnation. Zhou Qing strives hard to copy and emulate "Zhoukhrai." Zhou becomes alive and sensible chiefly through the film's voice-over narration. This happens through an exhaustive search for, recollection of, and (re)imagination of "Zhoukhrai";

and is dramatically depicted in a final daydream sequence of revenge and "emergence." Although Zhou Qing's resistance against materialist society and its alienation is quite revealing over the course of the film, it is the larger-than-life iconography of "Zhoukhrai" and the spirit of *How the Steel Was Tempered* that have been foregrounded as an exemplary antidote to social ills (including the disillusioned rock experience). "Zhoukhrai" thus becomes what Michel Chion has termed *acousmêtre*, the highest being and the ideal father, which uncannily evokes the iconic "time-image" (Gilles Deleuze)[36] of Cui Jian on Chinese screen.

Tian Zhuangzhuang, a preeminent Fifth Generation filmmaker, was the film's producer. He played "Zhoukhrai" and personified this mythical and imaginary hero/father in *How the Steel Was Tempered*, a landmark work that signals the "coming of age" of the young Sixth Generation. Besides the extensive recuts and reedits, the film also had to change its title to *Zhangda Chengren*, which literally means "becoming a man" in Chinese, when it finally landed in Chinese theaters. *How the Steel Was Tempered*, then, is an (auto)biographical type of cinematic *Bildungsroman* for the young filmmakers themselves that works as a saliently postmodern form of nostalgia in its tortuous journey to self-discovery, while also paying homage to the father's generation (arguably the Fifth Generation forerunners) and the revolutionary past.

In *How the Steel Was Tempered*, Zhou Qing's only action is not enacted until the very end where he finds the criminal who maimed "Zhoukhrai" and steps up at last to avenge the crime by stabbing him with a butcher knife. The individualist, heroic climax, however, is belied by the starkly disparate color scheme of washed-out gray and further by the subsequent voice-over that confesses this is just his fabricated dream; the criminal is "in reality" found by the police and legally punished. Such a collision of the real and the imaginary when "indiscernibility constitutes an objective illusion"[37] manifests again what Deleuze has called the "time-image." And a different sense of compromise and consolation clumsily draws the film to a dreary happy ending where the authority of the state apparatus and family are restored and continue to dominate. The last scene affixes a postscript that the shattered relationship between Zhou Qing's parents is "magically" cured. This "self-corrective" dual ending is, according to the filmmaker himself, the result of the forced "correction" of the film.[38] But it also bespeaks the politics of Chinese filmmaking and the dilemma of the "emergence" of a new moviemaker who is unavoidably caught in the very confines of sociopolitical restrictions and commercial imperatives in a postsocialist era.

How the Steel Was Tempered stands out as an allegory marking the "coming of age" of the Sixth Generation in that it is literally the first work of this young generation to be issued an official stamp of approval and to be publically

The Fifth Generation filmmaker Tian Zhuangzhuang plays the hero "Zhoukhrai" and represents the highest form of morality in *How the Steel Was Tempered* (1997).

released in state-owned theaters and television media on the mainland. The hefty price it paid, however, as Lu Xuezhang later bitterly recalled in various interviews, is three years of arduous reediting, eleven revised versions, the dropping of its original title, and the adding of a new self-negating coda. Lu Xuezheng was probably reluctant to close the film as such and he tried his best to provide an ambiguous, open ending within the boundary of the system; we hear the familiar voice-over and the recurrent string music that tells us Zhou Qing has set out to leave Beijing and will congregate with the girl from Lanzhou at the place where there is "Zhoukhrai." The film attempts to extend a sense of hope, anticipation, and *Bildung*, as suggested in the last long shot of the soon-to-depart train, a pivotal image that has a deep resonance in *Platform*. This wrenched, ambivalent feeling about becoming "a new, unprecedented type of human being" and being "normative" in the current sociopolitical environment is what makes *How the Steel Was Tempered* a strikingly fragmented but "recognized" work, as is also the case in *Quitting*.

In *Quitting* (aka *Yesterday*), Jia Hongsheng returns home after he returns to "normal." He has been "tempered" in the mental institution to finally acknowledge a debt to his "biological" father while forsaking his "spiritual" father, John Lennon. Everything at home has been changed upon his return: furniture rearranged, rooms refurnished and remodeled, and his old rock paraphernalia sealed off. Jia Hongsheng walks back into his room and looks around with his gaze laid on the formerly cherished portrait of John Lennon.

He puts the portrait upright over the music player and finds a cassette tape from the sealed box. What emanates from the tape is no longer Lennon's rock music but the crying of a baby, a timeworn metaphor of (re)birth that could reference back to the end of *Beijing Bastards*. Jia Hongsheng's mom walks in and asks anxiously if he has taken his medicine "today." With a cooperative "yes," she walks out. Everything is back in its place. The camera pulls back and up in a crane shot to present a portrait of the entire family (and the full stage). Lights dim out. After a final silence, that's the end.

At this point, it is not too difficult to discern that the overall trajectory of both films is to lead eventually to a criticism of the "Beat Generation" and corrosive capitalist individualism, and most importantly, to a longing for a return to the "premarket" past and social normative order. It is only when the son submits himself utterly to authority and the "velvet prison" that "a piece of good steel can be forged." In consequence, the father serves as the locus of both departure and return. While these young directors worked so hard to vivify their *Bildungsromans* with personal touches, they could not help but infuse an ironic twist to their own stories of nirvana. Jia Hongsheng jumped to his death from the apartment that he shared with his parents in 2010, as sardonically alluded to and already envisaged in *Quitting* and *Frozen* (Wang Xiaoshuai's second film documenting an avant-garde artist seeking the meaning of life and art by performing and displaying death to its real core). Zhu Hongmao vanished without a trace (just like the end of *How the Steel Was Tempered*, where his character leaves Beijing to look for "Zhoukhrai," or he simply disappears from our sight). Zhu Jie, the female star in *How the Steel Was Tempered* and Zhu Hongmao's girlfriend in real life, died from a drug overdose even before the film passed the censorship of the Film Bureau and was officially released in 1997 (a fact that is conveyed by Zhu Hongmao himself in *Quitting*). Director Lu Xuezhang died suddenly at the age of forty-nine in 2014. The true stories are at all times rockier and more cinematic than the film, reflecting Deleuze's most cited postulation: "It is doubtful if cinema is sufficient for this; but, if the world has become a bad cinema, in which we no longer believe, surely a true cinema can contribute to giving us back reasons to believe in the world and in vanished bodies? The price to be paid, in cinema as elsewhere, was always a confrontation with madness."[39] In contemporary China, what world/cinema, then, are we building? What vanished bodies and memories? What confrontations? Simply stated, would this be a confrontation with concurrently the deeply entrenched "paternal" madness and the now inundating "market" frenzy?

CHAPTER FIVE

National Anthem at *Guangchang*: Languagescape, Ideoscape, and Mediascape in the Time of Global Picture

> Although it is still difficult for scholars like us to grasp the significance and intricacy of a changing China in the nineties, perhaps we can get an approximation of its complexity by way of analyzing the meaning of the term *guangchang* (a Chinese translation of the word *plaza*). In the term *guangchang* we see *a new marketplace rhetoric intermingled with memories of the revolution* . . . Tiananmen Guangchang had figured in the sinocentric imagination as the "red heart" of world revolution throughout the history of socialist China. Now the superhighways, chain stores, skyscrapers, giant shopping malls, and the flow of happy consumers form a picture of the generic, homogeneous world metropolis, a spectacle of globalization, featuring the "landscape of fast-food restaurants along the highway."
> —**Dai Jinhua,** "Invisible Writing: The Politics of Mass Culture in the 1990s"[1]

At the climax of *The Big Parade*, instead of showcasing the grandeur and majesty of the 1984 procession, Chen Kaige had pictured something else in his mind—an empty shot of the Tiananmen Square (*Guangchang*). The Beijing office, of course, did not consent to this ambiguous ending and insisted on the inclusion of the actual parade and official celebration—in other words, a standardized tribute to the nation as a legitimate, absolute closure to the story. Nevertheless, Chen diplomatically complied with the official command and spliced state footage of the parade with his own exceptional editing and audiovisual re-enactment, as I detailed in my first chapter. Thus, *The Big Parade* can be seen as an incisive anatomy of both the parade and the official concept of nationhood through Chen's hallmark elusive language and metaphorical lens. It embodies the Fifth Generation's anti-climactic struggles and becomes what Paul Clark has called an "anti-nationalistic nationalist"[2] film. The production simultaneously plays with and against the logic of the "movement-image" and rhetoric of the state, the latter invariably aligned with occasions of Tiananmen Square in the collective imagination. This profound current of skepticism and apostatical "time-image" continues to grow in other post-Mao works, most conspicuously in *The Square* (*Guangchang*, 1994), co-directed by documentarian Duan Jinchuan and Zhang Yuan, a leading figure of the alternative Sixth Generation, whom I considered in chapter three. A documentary shot nearly a decade later, *The Square* probes into and juxtaposes the mundane life of ordinary Chinese citizens and grand political forces through the allegorical platform of Tiananmen Square. In the film, a central dialectic between the rising lighthearted city life and awareness of inviduality and dwindling political influences culminates in a final shot of the empty, silent square that eventually concretizes Chen's original ideas for *The Big Parade*.

Unlike propaganda productions, these cinematic reinterpretations of Tiananmen Square suggest a vital break with the normative, sacred practice of *Guangchang*. Many of them are formed to undercut the homogeneity of the site and the "chronotype of perpetual revolution," in the phrase of Yomi Braester. As Yomi Braester has defined, Tiananmen "supported what may be called a *chronotype of perpetual revolution,* which stressed the perpetuity of Party ideology through the square's unchanging spatial practices."[3] The square is an epitome of the "chronotype of perpetual revolution." It *is* the revolution itself, a site that represents both the continuity and discontinuity of the revolution and its ability to engage in the contentions of history, national identity, selfhood, globalization, and ideology through artistic and cultural practices. Filmmakers such as Chen Kaige and Zhang Yuan do not necessarily equate to political heretics, but they "have turned the rich tradition against itself, making informed use of the symbolic iconology to challenge state ideology."[4] Moreover, in post-revolutionary China, Tiananmen Square, or *Guangchang* (square or plaza) in a broader sense, has acquired new significations to become "a new marketplace rhetoric intermingled with memories of the revolution,"[5] as Dai Jinhua has pinpointed in the opening epigraph of this chapter. Many of these competing narratives, highlighting various aspects of "perpetual revolution," are to be found in Leitmotif films, a state-endorsed (albeit mercurial and still-evolving) genre I take up in this chapter.

Leitmotif film (*zhuxuanlv dianying*), a characteristic Chinese formation with a musical reference in its name, is a newly formulated state-subsidized film project that has experienced unprecedented growth and popularity at the turn of the new century. Yet little research has been done in historicizing and theorizing this peculiar film genre, which has been marginalized in the festival-oriented scholarship of Chinese film studies in the last few decades. A privileged and highly figurative term that is often linked with state sponsorship and political intervention, the category of Leitmotif poses complex questions for cultural critics, film historians, and theorists of mass media. Generally seen as conformist and didactic, one may ask: What is the value in studying such blatantly propagandist films? While China has officially adopted an open door policy, market reform, and a series of structural adjustments, the state is still reluctant to let loose its ideological and political controls. As a cultural product of these nuanced, often contradictory principles and rationales, how does Leitmotif film reflect this economically liberal but politically conservative climate with "Chinese characteristic" in the late socialist era? How does a critical study of this genre enable us to rediscover the continuing significance of ideology criticism to cinescape and to re-evaluate the positioning of propaganda in the current neoliberal milieu?

My specific interest in this chapter is what Attali has called "the game of music" that "resembles the game of power,"[6] the game of filmmaking, and the complex network and interrelationship in-between in the intricate cartography of contemporary, global China. Hence, shifting focus from experimental art cinema to mainstream commercial production, from the stakes of music to the rhetorics of language and ideology and the metaphor/irony of music, this chapter complements my previous discussions. It offers a large picture of postsocialist public culture and audiovisual dynamics through a sociopolitical, historical niche reading of Leitmotif film, a state-subsized genre shaped by both the market and state mechanisms in postsocialist reform.

Performing the national anthem at the square—a grandiose center of political power that has intricately become a fluid center stage for various forces intermingling and wrestling with one another in the new era—allows filmmakers to employ the largest crews and best equipment, benefiting from immense economic and ideological support, although it also subjects them to extreme surveillance and microscopic inspection. These Leitmotif films are often called Chinese blockbusters because they were churned out of the postsocialist film industry with "Chinese characteristic" with robust sponsorship from the state, be it capital support or autocratic sellout. At the same time, the genre abundantly borrows and deliberately appropriates the images and neoliberal practices from Hollywood hits to boost its sales at the box office. Hence, a cinematic display invested with nationhood, historical reflexivity, and transnational imaginary has also become the defining feature of Leitmotif film, as seen in *Bethune: The Making of a Hero* (*Baiqiu'en: yige yingxiong de chengzhang*, dir. Phillip Borsos and Wang Xingang, 1990), *Red Cherry* (*Hong Yingtao*, dir. Ye Daying, 1995), *Red River Valley* (*Honghegu*, dir. Feng Xiaoning, 1996), *The Opium War* (*Yapian zhanzheng*, dir. Xie Jin, 1997), *My 1919* (*Wode 1919*, dir. Huang Jianzhong, 1999), *Lover's Grief over the Yellow River* (*Huanghe juelian*, dir. Feng Xiaoning, 1999), *Shadow Magic* (*Xiyangjing*, dir. Hu An, 2000), *Purple Sunset* (*Ziri*, dir. Feng Xiaoning, 2001), *Charging out Amazon* (*Chongchu yamaxun*, dir. Song Yaming, 2002), among many others. On one side is the ever-present "totalitarian" state, on the other side is the "liberal" world and dream of Hollywood; the two seemingly opposing factors conflate interestingly to form an uncanny *mélange* of commercial propagandist film in the volatile *fin de siècle* China.

The peculiar cinescape of fused ideological-mercenary mechanisms and audiovisual registers entails careful deliberation, especially in light of the pervasive and contentious debates on transnationalism, global capital, and the avowed China Dream (*zhongguo meng*) vis-à-vis the American Dream.[7] How do the essential concepts of the American Dream, such as individualism, universal humanity, globalization, and the free market, find thematic resonance in Chinese mainstream film? In what ways, then, does the China Dream, often referenced as an emulation of its American counterpart as well as a remaking of China's image, manage to refashion and resell a sense of nation-state in the post-Tiananmen epoch, while the party-state is confronted with an aggravating challenge of social unrest, political tension, and a credibility crisis? Particularly, what role does the narrative paradigm of East-meets-West play in the construction and circulation of the official view and in the cultural imaginary in general? How, and to what extent, do language hybridity and multinational inflections in Leitmotif official films encapsulate post-Tiananmen sentiment—for instance, in their dialectics of nostalgia and amnesia and of Chinese nationalism and American neoliberalism? While the term "leitmotif" connotes an explicit musical reference, how is this cinematic trope based upon, and related to, its musical roots and sound practice?

Through close analyses of some of the most popular and recognized pictures in the Chinese public arena, including Xie Jin's *The Opium War*, Feng Xiaoning's "China through Foreign Eyes" trilogy (e.g., *Red River Valley* and *Lover's Grief over the Yellow River*), and Zhang Yimou's *The Flowers of War*, this chapter attempts to address these concerns. I argue that this hybrid and fractured cinematic configuration represents a specific, often sophisticated way of reconstructing China as a postsocialist, postnational entity institutionally, visually, and acoustically. It has become a plural and fraught site in which both a more complex and ambivalent picture of the neoliberal world order and China's self-reflexive image are projected onto the screen and heard over the soundtrack.

"Leitmotif and Diversity": State, Market, and Chinese Film Industry in an Age of Reform

A coinage growing out of the Western Romantic tradition, "leitmotif" as a specific music idiom can be traced back to Richard Wagner's idea of "motifs of reminiscence." It is by definition a central, characteristic, and recurring musical theme associated with certain characters, times, settings, and scenes. The classical Romantic convention that emphasizes leitmotivic structure, theme writing, and symphonic orchestration had a decisive impact in classical Hollywood cinema and film music.[8] In Chinese circumstances, "leitmotif" is a borrowed term figuratively referring to a national film practice characteristic of postsocialist China, with the goal of satisfying both the political interest of "depicting the major trends of the reforms and the historical era" and the economic demand for "market" and "diversity."[9] In other words, this Chinese subgenre of musical metonymy is a metaphoric adoption that intends to resurrect and anchor the continuing significance of state ideology in the neoliberal cinematic context.

The concept was initially suggested during a meeting of the principals of national film studios in March 1987. Proposed as one of the two important components that make up the slogan, "Foregrounding Leitmotif, Persisting in Diversity" (*tuchu zhuxuanlv, jianchi duoyanghua*, abbreviated as "leitmotif and diversity" hereafter), leitmotif is essentially another top-down act of governmentality (Michel Foucault, see my discussion in the introduction) to totalize and neutralize the wide-ranging artistic practices in post-revolutionary China. Three factors contribute to the emergence and evolution of "leitmotif and diversity," which embodies a film discourse, an ideology, a scheme of governmentality, a regime of moods and sentiments, and the general sociopolitical landscape in late twentieth century China. First, the agenda provides a set of two parallel and integrated dynamics that are anticipated to unify into a whole. The emphasis on "leitmotif," on the first ground, was made after the previous socialist filmmaking model, which privileged cinema's political obligation and pedagogical function. An open, present call for "diversity," on the second ground, explicitly promoted creativity and contentions in the film-cultural circle, reflecting a new climate of cultural liberalization in the post-Mao period. In explaining its nature and objective, the dialectic and interdependent relationship between the two imperatives was stressed by film officials and cultural leaders from the Propaganda Department:

> To highlight leitmotif in the film production is to enforce the socialist themes and orientations; while the persistence of diversity is to promote the competitions among various genres, forms, and styles, which will ultimately contribute to the prosperity of Chinese cinema. Leitmotif and diversity are two interrelated concepts: leitmotif determines the direction of diversity, which in turn undergirds and reinforces the development of Leitmotif as a whole.[10]

In this regard, what is aimed at is a rhetorical middle ground that could sustain an aesthetic enterprise of intermediation between leitmotif and diversity, between the historical heritage and social present, and moreover, between the Chinese (post)socialist film industry and global capitalist system.

Second, this formula can be understood as a byproduct of, and is intrinsically linked to, the lasting, unsettling debate on the function of cinema and art throughout Chinese film history; should it be considered a propaganda tool to serve political causes, an autonomous regime, or is it a commercial industry tied to market principles? A hopeful undertaking to carry the double duty of cinematic medium as both ideological apparatus and entertaining instrument, the proclamation of "leitmotif and diversity" conjures up the two guidelines in socialist China's artistic and cultural realm—"Two Servings" ("Serving the People, Serving the Socialism") and "Two Hundreds" ("Let a Hundred Flowers Bloom, Let a Hundred Schools Contend").

This polemic dates back to Mao's *Talks at the Yan'an Forum on Literature and Art* of 1942. Mao compels intellectuals and artists to forsake their bourgeois affections and suppress their personal individual needs, outlining their duties in terms of glorifying the "new" world and the mass. And in his definition, the masses equate to a label of social class, referring discriminately to such revolutionary forces as workers, peasants, and soldiers.[11] Mao's instructions set up fundamental tenets and boundaries for today's "leitmotif and diversity" as well as a wide array of official popular cultures in contemporary China, for instance, the market cult of Mao and a new fashion of "rewriting the red classics," both of which erupted and caught people's attention in the aftermath of the 1989 Tiananmen protest.[12] By contrast, the other set of the *two*—"Two Hundred Flowers"—points to two national campaigns, in which a relatively open and liberal change in the artistic field took place in 1956–57 and 1978–81, respectively. The two movements, infused with a more democratic cultural climate, pushed forward a critical reflection on the current regime and government policies, and most important, offered some breathing room for different ideas and diversified artistic practices in the still highly politicized environment of socialist China.[13]

In this dual context, the so-called "leitmotif" move, in a reformist vein, appears to be a conscious, pragmatic political strategy in the face of an eroding sociopolitical structure and a swelling of incoming capitalist commerce. When the call for "leitmotif and diversity" was applied to the sector of filmmaking beginning in the spring of 1987, a new period of liberalization and market reform was unfolding in full swing, which is the third factor I will emphasize. On October 12, 1984, "Decisions on the Reforms of Economic System" (*guanyu jingji tizhi gaige de jueding*) was passed by the Central Committee of the Chinese Communist Party at the Twelfth Party Congress.[14] Following the mandate that attempted to establish a "planned market economic system" (*youjihua de shangpin jingji*), in the mid-1980s some studios began to demand more autonomy from the Film Bureau, the primary government entity overseeing all activities of filmmaking (it was a section under the umbrella of the Ministry of Culture until 1986, when it was handed to the rule of the Ministry of Radio, Film and Television, renamed as State Administration of Radio, Film and Television in 1998). In the first three decades of the PRC, relying completely on government administrative guidance and financial support, the film circuit was forced to abide by the unanimous form of state monopoly for film purchase and sales. This situation was profoundly changed in the wake of market reform of the 1980s. Block booking and blanket sales were the first things to be removed. In 1987, MRFT made a bigger stride and issued "Document No. 975." This allowed local film distributors to purchase films and forced film studios to share box-office profits with the distributors conditionally. For the first time, the triple functions of cinema—pedagogical, aesthetic, and commercial—and the tripartite relationship between the filmmakers, the party, and the audience were at last unified in the PRC.[15]

Originating in the heyday of market reform, "leitmotif" is symptomatic of the conflation and negotiation between socialist conventions and neoliberal spirits of market fever and cultural fever in the 1980s. The narrative also significantly encapsulates a range of ruptures, tensions, and contradictions within the reform itself. In particular, it was formulated to correspond to a public campaign against "bourgeois liberalism" (*zichan jieji ziyouhua*) in early 1987. Writing an article that was collected by *the 1990 China Film Yearbook*, Liu Cheng, who later produced a Leitmotif film entitled *Kong Fansen* (1995) himself, indicates that "bourgeois liberalization" was one of the most harmful tendencies in films of the late 1980s, as "we found more representations of hooligans, enemies, spies, and prostitutes on the screen . . . but less class analysis of characters and ... fewer positive depictions of workers and peasants."[16] Liu argued that in order to purify the film market and save films from the "spiritual pollutions of bourgeois liberalization" (*zichanjieji ziyouhua de jingshen wuran*), the political directions of cinema needed to be redressed and its pedagogical function reinforced. Many articles from that year shared a similar point of view, apparently targeting the Wang Shuo hooligan literature and popular fad and, alternatively, the future direction of Chinese cinema.

Under such circumstances, a notion of "leitmotif" was propagated from top-down as a regulative device. Films were forced to conform to positive party images such as the depiction of great achievements of the reform and revolution and glorious events in history, as stipulated:

> At first stage, we are interested in using the definition of "Leitmotif" as a classifier of genre to explore and promote the realistic themes of agriculture and industry reforms and images of new leaders. But after practice, we found that it is far from enough to underwrite the significance of "Leitmotif" in terms of genres and subject matters. It should be elevated to the spiritual level, namely, an overriding spirit and voluntary consciousness in the artistic practice to embody and advocate the reformist, socialist and patriotic ethos of the time.[17]

Accordingly, film officials showed strong support for Leitmotif not only by establishing its leading roles among film genres but furthermore through the sanctifying process. It has been iconized as a spirit of creation determining the form and content of mainstream filmmaking in the new era. The category of Leitmotif can thus be expanded to include "any films that have positive and healthy content and are exquisite in quality."[18]

Since the end of the twentieth century, Leitmotif film has experienced enormous popularity and unprecedented growth. Several anniversaries related to the key events of Chinese revolution in 1991 (the seventieth birthday of the Chinese Communist Party), 1993 (the 100th anniversary of Mao Zedong's birth), 1995 (the fiftieth anniversary of the victory of Sino-Japanese War), and 1999 (the fiftieth anniversary of the PRC's founding) largely explain why the genre flourished at this juncture, along with the increasing instutional change and a further marketization of Chinese cinema. The Chinese film industry reform significantly parallels the trajectory of Leitmotif film. A bold effort to substitute the capitalist mode for the state-planned economy first took place in the distribution-exhibition sector. By specifying that studios should take care of distribution themselves and insuring that the market determined ticket prices (instead of having the China Film Corporation set prices as previously), the 1993–94 reform was a decisive turn, which effectively emancipated studios from the CFC's distribution monopoly. Moreover, as the reform pushed film institutions toward greater economic independence, governmental financial support was greatly reduced. As a result, capital investments from private avenues, both domestic and foreign, were involved, which opened the floodgates to a new wave of co-productions. Film companies established with private funding and independent film producers that have overstepped the party's stringent control mushroomed across the land. Most notable are Imar Film Company, which successfully recruited the young Sixth Generation filmmakers to produce urban youth attractions, Beijing Forbidden City Film Company, and Shanghai Yongle Film Company. These last two entities, conveniently located in the political and economic hubs of China, quickly rose to become the two chief "dream factories" of China, known specifically for their sheer streamlined Leitmotif products.

While the overall institutional reform was geared toward greater autonomy and diversity, the state, with an economically liberal but politically conservative stance, was still reluctant to completely unleash the film system into the market. By the mid-1990s, the increasingly conservative environment induced a succession of restrictive policies from the panoptic "Five Ones Project" (*wuge yi gongcheng*) to the "9550 Project" imposed on the film sector specifically. Launched by the Ministry of Propaganda in 1992, the "Five Ones Project" was implemented to place a number of new regulations on censorship, the installation of awards, and the quota of domestic productions which ordered every local province to create one extraordinary work in the categories of film, television, literature, stage drama, and song every year (which has been later expanded to include radio play, critical essay, etc.) Likewise, the reinforcement of an official film policy was advocated at a conference of Chinese filmmakers in March 1996 in Changsha. During the conference, a project named "9550" was intended to further reinvigorate Chinese national cinema by allegedly enhancing film quality. The goal was to produce fifty "quality films" (*jingpin*) within the government's Ninth Five-Year-Plan, an average of ten per year.[19]

When it came to the question of what amounts to "quality," Ding Guangen, minister of the Ministry of Propaganda, declared in his talk: "Films should have the function of making audiences love the Party and their socialist country, rather than arousing their concern and dissatisfaction; film should advocate justice prevailing over evil rather than pessimistic sentiments, and should bring happiness and beauty to the audiences rather than wasting their time on absurdity and fabricated plots."[20] Four major categories of "quality films" were listed and supported by the state—history, children, peasants, and the communist army, in contrast to those that did not fit into Ding's standard—for example, Wang Shuo's one and only directorial piece, *I Am Your Dad* (*Woshi ni baba*, 1996), and Feng Xiaogang's *Living a Miserable Life* (*Guozhe langbei bukan de shenghuo*, 1996). They were either banned after production or abandoned during shooting. Primarily aimed at reasserting pedagogical and ideological functions and regaining top-down control of film and media production, the decrees of the 1990s were a conspicuous move to overtly privilege Leitmotif film, thereby propelling its immense popularization at the end of the twentieth century.

Meanwhile, several important neoliberal measures continued to exert their influence on the film circle, especially on the production sector at this point in time. In 1995, MRFT released "Policies and Regulations on Reforming the Production and Administration of Feature Films" (*guanyu gaige gushipian shezhi guanli gongzuo de guiding*) that dismantled the monopoly of sixteen state-owned film studios over film production and licensed local institutions from the major thirteen provinces to produce films. In 1997, another MRFT document, "Announcement of Issuing License for Single Feature Film Production" (*guanyu shixing "gushi dianying danpian shezhi xukezheng" de tongzhi*), further opened the sector of film production to all the qualified institutions including private companies. Overall, the film institution reform in the 1990s was a crucial attempt to revitalize Chinese motion picture business, marked by a greater extent of marketization and decentralization. However, simultaneous state interventions and the tightening of censorship and state control created an ambivalent cinescape fraught with anxieties and contradictions, which significantly affected the content and structure of Leitmotif film and many other cultural phenomena.

Starting in the early 1990s, Chinese filmmakers began to undergo a tortuous divorce battle with the state, and gradually assumed the entrepreneur role, more closely responding to market forces rather than to government mandates. This change can be seen in a body of the Fifth Generation filmmakers who, after building their fame in the 1980s with artistic films produced largely within the state-run studio system, now turned to a broader audience and the popular market. The new co-productions and semi-independent films of the Fifth Generation, made with the absorption of private investment and Western capital and still drawing heavily from creative personnel and resources of the previous structure, had to punctiliously seek a balance between market and state. Chen Kaige's *Temptress Moon* (*Fengyue*, 1996) and *The Emperor and the Assassin* (*Ciqin*, 1998), and Zhang Yimou's *The Road Home* (*Wo de fuqin muqin*, 1999), *No One Less* (*Yige dou buneng shao*, 1999), and *Hero* (*Yingxiong*, 2002) are good examples that testify to the evolution and adjustment of the Fifth Generation in itself and the broader atmosphere of co-option that prevailed in the post-New Wave Chinese cinema at the turn of the twenty-first century. The Fifth Generation auteurs, after going through a bumpy path of confrontation and censure by the Chinese state in the early 1990s, at last returned to a liberal yet politically cooperative market stance that enabled them to move closer to the mainstream or even up to the center of the sociopolitical stage.

By contrast, another tale was told by the young Sixth Generation, whose films were mostly made outside the official system, barely accessible to the general mass on the mainland. The process of a film being banned, attracting the attention of a "liberal" Western world, and returning home with international accolades (hence the lift of the official ban) may illustrate an alternative mode of market rationality in the non-Western contexts or a form of "neoliberalism as exception," to borrow Aihwa Ong's formulation.[21] As Ong forcefully argues, neoliberal interventions in postcolonial, postsocialist situations articulate a distinct relationship between market mechanism and state sovereignty from the Western "liberal democracies." When the self-governing and self-enterprising values of neoliberalism are translated into a specific milieu, the new arrangements and reterritorializations of capital, labor, and knowledge are quickly merged into the local-global market to form a new cycle of neoliberal movement. Neoliberalism that promotes individualism and entrepreneurialism can be repositioned, reterritorialized, and reconfigured in the sites of transformation and become part of the feature of "governmentality." This neoliberal exception logic explains the preceding phenomenon and the increasingly varied, contingent, and ambiguous landscape of contemporary Chinese cinema and culture. In the post-1989 period, when a neoliberal ethos takes root and penetrates deeply into a large scale of socioeconomic and cultural domains, many independent artists surfaced from the underground to join the market. In an ironic way, making a domestically banned but internationally recognizable work has become a shortcut to entry into the mainstream. Such films with an edge targeting international film festivals and small audiences in arthouse cinemas are a testimony to the exceptional logic of neoliberalism.

In response, a notion of "New Mainstream Cinema" (*xin zhuliu dianying*) was formed among a group of young filmmakers in Shanghai around the period. Keen on the market power and fast-changing environment neoliberalism has engendered, they began to advance a new form of cinematic practice that embraces at once self-enterprise and market-driven modes of governing. In "New Mainstream Cinema: A Suggestion on Domestic Filmmaking," Ma Ning, an official of Shanghai Film Studio, begins with the premise that, unlike the Sixth Generation's alternative film that places too much emphasis on stylistic and aesthetic experiment, "New Mainstream Cinema," being a mediator between the marginal and the mainstream, is intended to build and develop "the innovative low-budget commercial film." Future directions are suggested in this enthusiastic manifesto. Firstly, as a discursive strategy to save the national film industry from crisis, accelerated and exacerbated by globalization and Hollywood's market penetration, independent filmmakers are encouraged to move out from the periphery toward the center and possibly align with the official apparatus. Secondly, it requests state sponsorship with the budget of 1.5 million–3 million yuan (approximately $200,000 to $400,000), whereas filmmakers as individuals should take other matters into their hands with greater autonomy and less restrictions. Thirdly, this model, neither preoccupied with political and ideological orientations nor containing an avant-garde and polemical edge, is rather committed to commercial appeals, clinging closely to the interests of the masses.[22]

"New Mainstream Cinema," forged under the rubrics of neoliberalism, is a call for a middle ground where film-as-business and filmmaker-as-entrepreneur are to be securely anchored in the postsocialist fabric, mutually defined by the market and the state. In a sense, it is a rewriting of "leitmotif and diversity," a possible solution when facing the bleak reality of a shrinking national film industry vis-à-vis the invasion of Hollywood globalization at the turn of the new century. However, problems did not fade away in this new leitmotif model. It is hard to know, first of all, whether or not the proposition that attempts to win over both official acknowledgement and market profit is feasible in the long run. As a matter of fact, the plan was aborted soon afterwards and most of the films in the blueprint were never completed. Secondly, it was unclear, and little was explained about, how this solution operates in relation to, and in negotiation with, the two opposites—Leitmotif and experimental, independent films. It should be noted that, however, Ma Ning and Shanghai Film Studio, who had pushed forward this concept of "New Mainstream Cinema," have been involved in the productions of Jia Zhangke's films since 2004, when *The World* (*Shijie*) was his first piece admitted to Chinese theaters. The director, through their facilitation, has completed his transition from covert to legitimate and toward the mainstream.

Big Hollywood, Blockbusters with Chinese Characteristic, and *The Opium War*

Given its vast output, Leitmotif film has occupied a preeminent place in the landscape of contemporary Chinese culture industry. According to Li Yiming's estimation, in the mid-1990s, the genre reached 20 percent of the domestic annual production, whereas other kinds of entertainment films totaled 75 percent and art films 5 percent.[23] The Leitmotif portion continued to grow in the second half of the 1990s and reached its peak at the dawn of the new century, when the PRC was to celebrate its fiftieth anniversary. Not only were these films labeled as "A Tribute to the Nation" (*xianli pian*), but they were also seen as a milestone signifying the resurgence of mainstream, political film in the post-revolutionary cartography.

Attributing the bourgeoning Leitmotif film mainly to the revival of a specific genre—revolutionary war epics—Hong Junhao applauds this new trend as a signal of "the maturity of China's film." In spite of his reservation that films are "once again functioning chiefly as an ideological or political instrument," he argues that, for the most part, the "phenomenal change" tends to be "more entertaining" and, at the same time, "much more objective, bold, and open when reflecting history."[24] Hong's general account of war pictures and the mainstream sphere in PRC points out new directions of study, yet it is far from complete. Certain questions need to be asked and answered. Why and to what extent does this new film culture—and the resuscitation of war epics specifically—in the 1990s represent the "maturity" of filmmaking in contemporary China? In what ways, then, do they appear "entertaining," "objective," "bold," and "open" in their new ways of retelling national and revolutionary history?

On the contrary, Chris Berry is much more critical of the popularization of Leitmotif film. He points out that the putative high yield and high box-office return shall not elude some of the Leitmotif's reactionary dispositions—that is, "denying difference and blocking changes."[25] He laments: "This return to revolutionary history is an attempt to reunite precisely those fragments."[26] While I agree with the two scholars that this new film paradigm may represent both a setback from the diversified, liberal discourses of the preceding decade and a retreat from the authoritarian revolutionary epoch, the rise of Leitmotif product in the post-Tiananmen regime showcases a fundamental turn in the larger cultural cartography of contemporary China.

The development or progress is visible, as the genre incorporates market forces and neoliberal sensibilities into a new formula on both aesthetic and economic terms. First, as Chinese society has become more diverse and interactive with other parts of the world, an important hue has been added to a large canvas of rewriting national history, namely, a growing fashion in the Chinese film industry to make films with subjects of East-West cultural clashes and reconciliation. In other words, it is a trend in Leitmotif film to offer a new, alternative view of modern Chinese history by foregrounding the dynamics between nation-building and transnational-imaginary construction in ways not previously attempted. Second, although the ideological-propagandist function of such films continues to be prioritized over their entertainment value, studios and film companies' interest in box-office returns has pushed Leitmotif films toward adopting a market-driven formula, a solution that purports to emulate, and is specifically inspired by, Hollywood pictures.

The socioeconomic impact of Hollywood imports is another crucial aspect in shaping Leitmotif films. A large corpus of this genre is often, if not exclusively, discussed in comparison to its Hollywood counterparts, marked as "Chinese blockbusters" or "big pictures" (*dapian*). This coinage, by implication, suggests a business pattern that is attributive or similar to Hollywood as much as it is attuned to local sensibilities. Two factors contribute to this singular synthesis: the recession of the Chinese domestic film industry and the simultaneous erosion of Hollywood blockbusters. Starting in the mid-1980s, the Chinese domestic film market continued to decline, while in 1994, Hollywood began its re-entry into China under a revenue-sharing arrangement. The annual output of domestic films in 1995 was around 100 films, which received only 30 percent of the box-office revenues; the other 70 percent went to ten big imports (six of which were from Hollywood). The shadow of Hollywood loomed larger over the Chinese film industry in 1997 and 1998, when *Titanic* and *Saving Private Ryan* accounted for about one third of the total box office in big cities such as Beijing and Shanghai.

To prevent a further collapse of the domestic market, the Ministry of Radio, Film and Television and the Ministry of Culture issued a joint circular in the spring of 1997 to mandate the allocation of two thirds of screen time to domestic films, especially "quality films"—namely, the quintessential national films in the mold of leitmotif. The China Theater Chain, in an effort to consolidate 300 theaters in large urban areas, was built to guarantee quality domestic films with the best and most screen time. Moreover, a succession of ad hoc measures were taken to relieve the tax burdens for these film exhibitions and to increase the average budget of a domestic feature from 1.3 million yuan (approximately $150,000) in 1991 to 3.5 million (approximately $400,000) in 1997.[27] It should be noted that if the major objective of these new directives was to rescue domestic film from its devastating slump, apparently, it was the state-sponsored Leitmotif films, or the so-called "Chinese blockbusters," that benefitted most of all from these protective methods.

The widespread, crushing influence that Hollywood hits had on the Chinese film industry is a double-edged sword. On the one hand, it led to a cinematic space loaded with tensions and anxieties, yet, on the other, it simultaneously provoked the rise of Chinese blockbusters and opened up the domestic industry to both the perils and benefits of Hollywood and global capitalism. In "'What's Big About the Big Film?': 'De-westernizing' the Blockbuster in Korea and China," Chris Berry suggests that "the idea of the 'blockbuster' has been appropriated into local critical discourse, to refer not only to American blockbusters but also to local productions considered blockbusters."[28] What Berry means here is that in today's new world order, "blockbuster" or "big feature" is no longer a fixed designation exclusively tagged to Hollywood or America. The notion of "blockbuster" is also relevant if speaking about a group of Chinese major productions, which were largely "spurred by a desire to emulate Hollywood blockbusters following their Chinese success."[29] Yet this self-styled big picture and localized form—the "blockbuster with Chinese characteristic," so to speak—is by no means a mega picture by American standards, as Berry and other critics have pointed out. Although there has been "a tenfold increase on the most expensive 1990s film," "at the moment, a thirty million *reminbi* budget [under $4 million] counts as a 'big film' in China. Actually, in America that would be a 'little film.'"[30] By what standards, then, can these Leitmotif films be defined as blockbusters, if inevitably different from the American originals?

The Opium War (*Yapian zhanzheng*, dir. Xie Jin, 1997) represents Berry's concept of the Chinese blockbuster and is an epitome of the Leitmotif films that came to fruition by the end of the twentieth century. First and foremost, the film's extremely extravagant budget was unlike any other production made that year or even in the entire history of Chinese film. The project was carried out with an investment of over 100 million yuan (approximately $13 million), a record in Chinese filmmaking. Director Xie Jin, moreover, broke the record by founding a new company, the Opium War Ltd. Film Company, solely dedicated to the production and distribution of this particular film. All of the financing was acquired through individual, unofficial, and public channels instead of the previous mode of state sponsorship, a fact stressed by the director.[31] It is perhaps worth noting from the outset that this valiant effort was realized in large part due to the cultural and symbolic capital Xie Jin had already accumulated in his longstanding, committed, and eminent filmmaking career (1957–2001). It is no exaggeration to say that Xie Jin is one of the country's most prestigious, prolific, and popular filmmakers; he has carved out the Xie Jin Model, which has been emulated by numerous filmmakers, particularly during the 1980s.[32] The distinctive features of his films are his realistic approach and humanist touch, resulting in genuine and exquisitely crafted melodramas that elicit tears and identification within the masses. He has earned the crown of the people's filmmaker.[33]

Xie Jin is a Leitmotif filmmaker who has keenly responded to sociopolitical changes through his unique command of the film medium within the state studio system. Many of his popular melodramas have rich political implications, in which he embraces party policies, empathizes with the suffering of good, innocent people, celebrates the restoration and reinforcement of moral values and state governance, and more importantly, projects a bright political future. All of these qualities can be located in, for example, his effervescent portrait of communist New China and a group of vivacious young basketball players in *Women Basketball Player No. 5* (*Nvnan wu hao*, 1957), his adroit blending of the Hollywood melodramatic tradition, the realistic mode of the 1930s and 1940s leftist filmmaking of Shanghai, and revolutionary ideology and aesthetics in *The Red Detachment of Women* (*Hongse niangzijun*, 1961) and *Stage Sisters* (*Wutai jiemei*, 1965), and his good-willed criticism of political errors yet unfaltering faith in the party in *Legend of Tianyun Mountain* (*Tianyun shan chuanqi*, 1980) and *Hibiscus Town* (*Furong zhen*, 1986). In sum, what makes Xie Jin a "model" in the cultural and cinematic life of PRC is precisely his social awareness, political sensitivity, and astute handling of cinema as both educational and entertaining.

Indeed, this is what the Chinese state is in need of when it vigorously seeks out new and old measures to reproduce and replenish itself under the new conditions of modernization, neoliberalization, and globalization. And this is also the second aspect that justifies Xie Jin's *The Opium War* as a quintessential Chinese blockbuster and Leitmotif film in postsocialist China. Speaking of his motives for making the film, Xie Jin pronounced with candor, his trademark "revolutionary fervor," as well as a strong sense of social responsibility and historical reflexivity:

> I shoot this film not merely to extol Lin Zexu [the Qing Governor and hero who launched a campaign to suppress opium, which led to the outbreak of the First Opium War of 1839–42], but rather to display a full picture of that particular historical moment, its grandness and solemness. The film is suffused with grandiose scenes and a vast range of characters from the autocrats and ruling class of the Qing court and the British Empire to the ordinary people. The Qing court was forced to cede Hong Kong after the Opium War, which is a calamitous humiliation in Chinese history. One hundred years later, today's China rises and stands in the rank of powerful countries. All the Chinese people across the world view July 1, 1997 as one elating moment of ridding of humiliation and proving ourselves. *The Opium War* is to demonstrate such a reasoning that the country will suffer if it lags behind and it cannot be defeated only if it is strong. I wish our audience will re-examine the history from the contemporary perspective. I believe this film will inspire our future audience as well.[34]

It is clear that what distinguishes *The Opium War* from the previous version, *Lin Zexu* (dir. Zheng Junli, 1959, which has already been canonized as a "model" for historical films in revolutionary China), is Xie Jin's historiographical deliberation and genealogical charting of nineteenth century China, Hong Kong, and global system from a historical distance and in a contemporary vein. In many ways, the film serves as a timely reflection on the impending return of Hong Kong's sovereignty to the Chinese government and China's accession to WTO at the turn of the new century. Both are significant signs of China's recent miraculous elevation to new economic and political power and the restructuring of a new world order.

On the one hand, *The Opium War* secures the state stamp of approval and its own theatrical attendance through its political correctness, timeliness, as well as its status as a historical epic. On the other hand, the film effectively grips the viewer with its uncompromising blockbuster spirit—its *bigness*—in nearly every aspect of its production: big screenplay (the original script was written by a group of four acclaimed writers together and underwent eleven meticulous revisions in about a year); big equipment and sets (the film was shot with the most advanced technology and lavish equipment of the day; spectacular scenery was built in a colossal land of fifty-three acres at Hengdian Film City in Zhejiang province; more than 200 film sets, 20,000 sets of costumes, 20,000 pieces of props, and forty-seven ships were made to evoke the distinct ambience of nineteenth-century Guangzhou city as depicted); a big cast and crew (the film's cast amounted to 50,000 people; most intriguingly, it employed a massive cast of 3,000 foreign actors, which can be said as utterly transnational); as well as big cinematography (the film was shot on eight different locations, ranging from Guangdong and Zhejiang to as far away as England).[35]

The result of this full spectrum of "making big" is a big effect in terms of visuality and socioeconomic, political impact. Although hailed as a new-era "autonomous" film by critics and the filmmaker himself, the work was still closely affiliated with dwindling state power and the new thriving force of marketization and commercialization. A wide range of administrations, government entities, and political organs were involved—for instance, the Shanghai Municipal Committee, Sichuan Municipal Committee, Guangdong Municipal Committee, MRFT, and even the People's Liberation Army, which consigned thousands of soldiers as extras and stuntmen for the extravagant war scenes of the film. *The Opium War* was also endorsed by President Jiang Zeming, who interviewed Xie Jin before production and urged him to cultivate a high-quality, nationalist picture for the "big" historical moment of the incoming 1997 return of Hong Kong. In consequence, the finished product was premiered in the People's Great Hall in Beijing, organized by MRFT and the Hong Kong and Macao Affairs Office of the State Council. The film's economic return was propitious, if not optimal (the ticket sales almost met its production costs). With a harvest of 72 million yuan (approximately $9 million), *The Opium War* became one of the top-grossing national films in 1997.

Berry, in his poststructuralist "de-Westernization" of the "Oriental" blockbuster, goes on to indicate that *The Opium War* rightly testifies to the localized blockbuster with Chinese characteristic and that it, moreover, signifies a conflation of two subgenres, the "giant film" (*jupian*, epic, or Leitmotif film) and "big film" (*dapian*, blockbuster). He maintains that "blockbusters are, by implication, less serious and lacking in pedagogical purpose."[36] What, then, is big about the big film? What is giant about the giant film? Who is bigger, larger, or greater, or more giant? In what terms and by what criteria? Berry's dinstinction between the two is rather ambiguous. I believe it is not necessary to split them because both may contain similar patterns, generic styles, and draw on the resources of national history and social conventions for political-commercial purposes. In doubt are Berry's definition of blockbusters and his point that "seriousness of purpose" is the essential element distinguishing the "giant film" from the "big film," and Chinese blockbusters from American blockbusters. In today's increasingly globalized world and post-socialist-captalist atmosphere, do such clear-cut divisions still hold true? It should also be noted that the Chinese blockbuster is not exclusively confined within the Leitmotif genre, as Berry starts to touch upon. A good number of light-hearted New Year Celebration Comedies (*hesui pian*), urban thrillers, and action films fit into such categories of "bigness" on the basis of their similarly gigantic thematic concerns, production costs, and box-office revenues. For example, Feng Xiaogang's amusing New Year Celebration Comedies have entered into a rivalry with and quite often overtaken Leitmotif products in the domestic box office since the late 1990s. To quote Jason McGrath's precise summary: "They [Feng Xiaogang's films] thus constitute an alternative vision of a Chinese national cinema, namely an emerging domestic entertainment cinema that serves as an alternative to Hollywood in the context of a globalized market."[37] Would the recent "giant films," or Leitmotif epics, go by the same description then?

"Leitmotif films should not be misunderstood as shallow, vulgar works merely extolling and illustrating government policies,"[38] stated Wu Ziniu, a lesser-known Fifth Generation filmmaker who, despite being ostracized for years because of his abstract, ambivalent, and avant-garde war pictures, returned to mainstream "normalcy" in his artistic endeavors. Commenting on his new project, *National Anthem* (*Guoge*, 1999), a grand epic about the birth of the PRC's national anthem, under the aegis of Xiaoxiang Film Studio at Hunan with a hefty investment of 20 million yuan (approximately $2.5 million), Wu identified "patriotism" as the leitmotif and main motive behind his creation. Dedicated as a hymn to "the nationalist spirit, to the Chinese nation, and to outstanding Chinese people like Tian Han [a playwright and the songwriter for PRC's national anthem, 'The March of the Volunteers'],"[39] *National Anthem* was heedfully designed with Wu's learned cinematic vocabulary and aesthetic taste, and most of all, his ardent (and ironically self-denunciative) embrace of nationalism and the state order—the main thrust of many outstanding mega pictures of Hollywood, in his view. "Some of the excellent Western blockbusters (*xifang dapian*) in recent years are inherently a prototype of Leitmotif film. Whatever styles they cling to, the core of these films is to promote nationalism and national spirit with strong visual attractions. This has truly enlightened me."[40]

In this light, it is no surprise that the optimal model many Chinese filmmakers and critics frequently refer to is in fact a mode of Hollywood neoliberal pictures where market rationalities, political needs, and artistic values are proficiently melded and seamlessly sutured together. In the next section, I engage the concept of the "Chinese blockbuster" by examining the politics of this cinematic pattern and observing the contradictions and reconciliations between depoliticization and repoliticization, Westernization and de-Westernization in Leitmotif films. While critical emphasis has been placed on the prominent role that political economy plays in characterizing blockbusters—a useful key to distinguish the Chinese blockbuster from its Hollywood equivalent—attention should be given to the ways in which this market-oriented practice gets translated, rearticulated, and appropriated in the postsocialist context, in particular the transcultural and translingual journeys it often undergoes. A close look at Feng Xiaoning's *Lover's Grief over the Yellow River* in his "China through Foreign Eyes" trilogy will help illustrate my points. Considered one of the most important Leitmotif films, as well as a representative of the Chinese blockbuster, it was second highest-grossing film among domestic productions in 1999. The film was also selected by the Chinese government to compete in the Oscars in the category of Best Foreign Language Film, although this effort failed and it remains scarcely known in the international market. I will compare this China-made war epic to *Saving Private Ryan* and *Titanic*, two of the most lucrative films in motion picture history, in the aspects of visual representations, narrative structures, publicity strategies, and cultural impacts. I argue that *Lover's Grief over the Yellow River* is a Chinese neoliberal variation with rich intertextual references to its Hollywood counterparts.

The Global/National/Local Negotiations in Feng Xiaoning's Vision of "China through Foreign Eyes"

"Aimed at repackaging (or fetishizing) the founding myth of the Communist Party and socialist legacy in an age riddled with ideological and moral uncertainty,"[41] Leitmotif films constitute a new and integrated paradigm to both address Hollywood neoliberalism and mediate socialist discourse in an alternative and revisionist manner. Even though doubts were expressed as to whether or not such a state-monopolized circuit of manufacturing, wholesaling, and distribution is feasible in the long run, Leitmotif films, forged under the blockbuster hallmark, have made progress that allows studios to earn profits and approach the mass audience in a more accessible way. Another noteworthy development is that, in addition to its firsthand subscription to ideology and market, this film genre pursues new viable and artistic ways of revisiting the national past and defining selfhood under new sociopolitical circumstances. The direct or indirect intervention from state organs and agencies, however, cannot be underestimated. Leitmotif film as a propaganda machine is highly monopolized by the state in almost every aspect of its operation. Primarily dealing with party leaders, historical events, and critical moments of socialist triumph over foreign interests, these films were venerated as a special version of blockbuster which foregrounded Chinese nationalism and collective consciousness via three forms of support.

First, the government provided an abundant supply of finance, labor, and production equipment, and the genre is produced, packaged, advertised, and promoted by official apparatuses. The second method was to elevate their artistic or aesthetic worth by bestowing a series of film awards on them. Since the early 1990s, Leitmotif films have become the major recipients of Chinese film awards, such as the Golden Rooster Awards (*jinji jiang*) and Hundred Flowers Awards (*baihua jiang*), the most prominent film prizes in mainland China, equivalent to the Academy Awards and Golden Globes in the US. The Huabiao Awards, an important government award overseen by MRFT and the Ministry of Culture, has showed an even stronger preference for Leitmotif films. Almost every year, the Best Picture winners have been invariably awarded to Leitmotif pictures. Third, in the distribution-exhibition sector, a great deal of the box office is ensured by unions, work units, and public schools that are collectively and systematically organized to fill up theater seats. Documents were often red-tagged from top administrations with such titles as "Notice on Organizing the Viewing of Film XXX." Not surprisingly, even though tickets were sold out, theatrical attendance was still low.[42] Many with free tickets were uninterested in going to the theater to receive political lessons or enjoy the sort of "social welfare." In this regard, Leitmotif's "big," record-breaking box office is more of a political plot than an economic fact.

An essential propagandist medium in the post-Mao era, Leitmotif film has moved simultaneously toward market liberalism and the transnational circuit while maintaining its political edge. The struggles and negotiations between postsocialism and transnational neoliberalism are well demonstrated in Feng Xiaoning's trilogy of "China through Foreign Eyes" (*Yangren Yanzhong de Zhongguo*)—*Red River Valley* (*Honghegu*, 1996), *Lover's Grief over the Yellow River* (*Huanghe juelian*, 1999), and *Purple Sunset* (*Ziri*, 2001). I suggest that "China through Foreign Eyes" is symptomatic of a resurgent Chinese nationalism on the axis of postsocialist China. It further presents the fluid and multifarious reality of neoliberal globalization conceptualized by Appadurai as the intensified interactions between the various discourses of languagescape, ideoscape, and ethnoscape under the new structure of turn-of-century.[43]

Following the sensational reception of *Red River Valley*, *Lover's Grief over the Yellow River* is the second sequel in Feng Xiaoning's trilogy. It draws on similar resources of the so-called revolutionary war pictures and rewrites historical memory and East-West cultural clash through a well-designed blockbuster tool. The story is set during the closing days of World War II in the Chinese hinterland, where an American pilot's plane is hit by the Japanese but is rescued by a Chinese shepherd boy and a unit of the communist-led Eighth Route Army. The central storyline revolves around how to save the American pilot Irving and escort him to Yan'an, the Chinese revolutionary cradle and symbolic home in the national cultural imaginary. At the end, a team comprised of three communist soldiers—including a beautiful Chinese army nurse, An Jie, with whom Irving falls in love—all sacrifice their lives in this "grand" mission.

The film starts and concludes with Irving, who is now a grandfather, returning to the Yellow River and the Great Wall to memorialize the Chinese heroes and heroines. This, to a great extent, resembles the thematic and stylistic strategies of *Saving Private Ryan*, where an elderly Ryan returns to Normandy and stands before the captain's grave marker in a testament to truth and humanity. In a similar manner, *Lover's Grief over the Yellow River* is a refurbished version that nostalgically represents the war and transforms public history into private memory. Through the deliberate deployment of subjective flashbacks and voice-over narrations, a question of great significance that runs throughout *Saving Private Ryan* finds its peculiar resonance in this Chinese epic. What is the value of human life amidst all of these secular, material, political, ideological, and cultural choices and pursuits?

Lover's Grief over the Yellow River explores a number of possible answers, particularly through a detailed delineation of the marked convergence and divergence of Eastern and Western ethics with regard to life value and the related notions of "sacrifice" and "surrender." An intriguing sequence is exquisitely designed to present the East-West cultural clash by showing Irving's involvement of a fierce quarrel with Heizi, the group leader and communist protagonist in the film. Upon Irving's request to surrender to the Japanese enemy in order to prevent the maiming of innocent, ordinary people, Heizi retorts: "We would like to die rather than surrender." The deep focus on Heizi in the background and the crosscutting between these two figures in juxtaposition with their verbal arguments on the soundtrack effectively displays their differing standpoints and cultural backgrounds. In contrast to Chinese cultural tradition, and communist ideology in particular, which champions and glorifies collective, national interests, Western society and culture are distinctly represented in the film, and Chinese popular media in general, as incarnations of the highest ideals of liberty and freedom, a credo which gives the most credit to individuals. When the battle between these two factions almost reaches a deadlock, An Jie moderates the dispute, putting an end to the fight. Balance is reinstated through her elaborate explanation and rationalization of the seemingly intractable cultural gap.

If this particular scene invokes a neoliberal call to free human subjects from socialist universality, as well as a search for individual and private humanity, the whole narrative of *Lover's Grief over the Yellow River*, then, echoes a predominant postsocialist allegory of modernity in which people's sexual, economic, and political self-interests are both embraced and channeled on the national level and reproduced across borders to become cosmopolitan in a globalized world. Apparently, *Lover's Grief over the Yellow River* is a cinematic text in response to the provocative debates and heated discussions in the wake of *Saving Private Ryan*'s release in mainland China in 1998 (the second highest-grossing box-office earner of the year, the film earned around 82.03 million yuan—approximately $13 million).[44] Moreover, as a war epic loaded with heterosexual and transnational romance, it is an exemplary piece that borrows ideas from another big Hollywood hit and efficiently transplants them to local circumstances.

An unparalleled commercial miracle in the mainland film market, *Titanic* set the all-time box-office record with 306.5 million yuan (approximately $44 million). Aside from its integrated neoliberal market ethics, a number of external factors contributed to *Titanic*'s box-office triumph and smashing success in China. Upon his return from a visit to the United States, President Jiang Zemin urged Chinese filmmakers to study and follow the example of *Titanic*. The film was interpreted as a highly efficacious mix of romance and social reality (including class conflict). In Jiang's view, it provided a prime model of the integration of entertainment and pedagogical

Film poster 1 for *Titanic* (1997).

goals in contemporary filmmaking. The Chinese highest official's enthusiastic endorsement stimulated an even more aggressive promotion of *Titanic* in all sectors and consequently turned the film into an unprecedented national cultural phenonmenon whose influence went far beyond movie theaters.[45]

Riding on this *Titanic* fever, it is no surprise that *Lover's Grief over the Yellow River* deliberately borrowed many features from *Titanic*. Most spectacularly, the film appropriated the iconic image of Kate Winslet at the bow of the ill-fated ocean liner. In *Lover's Grief over the Yellow River*, a female protagonist is framed by a full-circle panorama and positioned within the breathtaking *mise-en-scène* of a surging river, posing between flying over and embracing the water—a studious reworking of the signature shot of *Titanic*. This iconographic image of the female protagonist—as well as a close-up of the romantic, transnational couple—was extensively featured on posters, DVD covers, and other promotional material that brought the film to the spotlight of contemporary popular life. The Chinese title, meaning "a desperate love on the Yellow River," would, on the one hand, readily assist those who followed Hollywood to effortlessly identify the main narrative and establish a link between the two versions. On the other, the underlying text of the Yellow River, an embodiment of Chinese civilization, with its sharp contrast to the blue ocean, a unique symbol of the Western culture in the Chinese imaginary,

Film poster 2 for *Titanic* (1997).

would allow spectators to recognize the film as a Chinese translation of *Titanic* that accommodates at once the rhetorics of Hollywood global flow and the localized, vernacular flavor.

In this regard, *Lover's Grief over the Yellow River* seems to be a visual comment on how Hollywood mega-productions penetrate the Chinese cinematic and popular consciousness and reappear as a hybrid, cohesive entity in the postsocialist context. After PRC reopened the floodgates and its marketplace to the Hollywood giants in 1994, the portentous, overflowing specter from the West turned out to be a threatening yet productive discourse, often acknowledged as both a high concept and a soft power to be emulated by the Chinese film industry. Jiang's successor, President Hu Jintao, reiterated the same admonition in the early 2010s: He said that while "international hostile forces" are "Westernizing" and "infiltrating" China through the soft power of popular culture, the international influence of Chinese culture and arts is, by contrast, apologetically feeble.[46] He summoned Chinese artists and cultural workers to hone popular products similar to America's in order to propagate the Chinese point of view; hence, there was an urgent need for a "big-handed" investment in China's own brand of soft power. The Leitmotif genre is, then, framed as a quintessential constituent of this soft power venture in reformed Hollywood fashion. In other

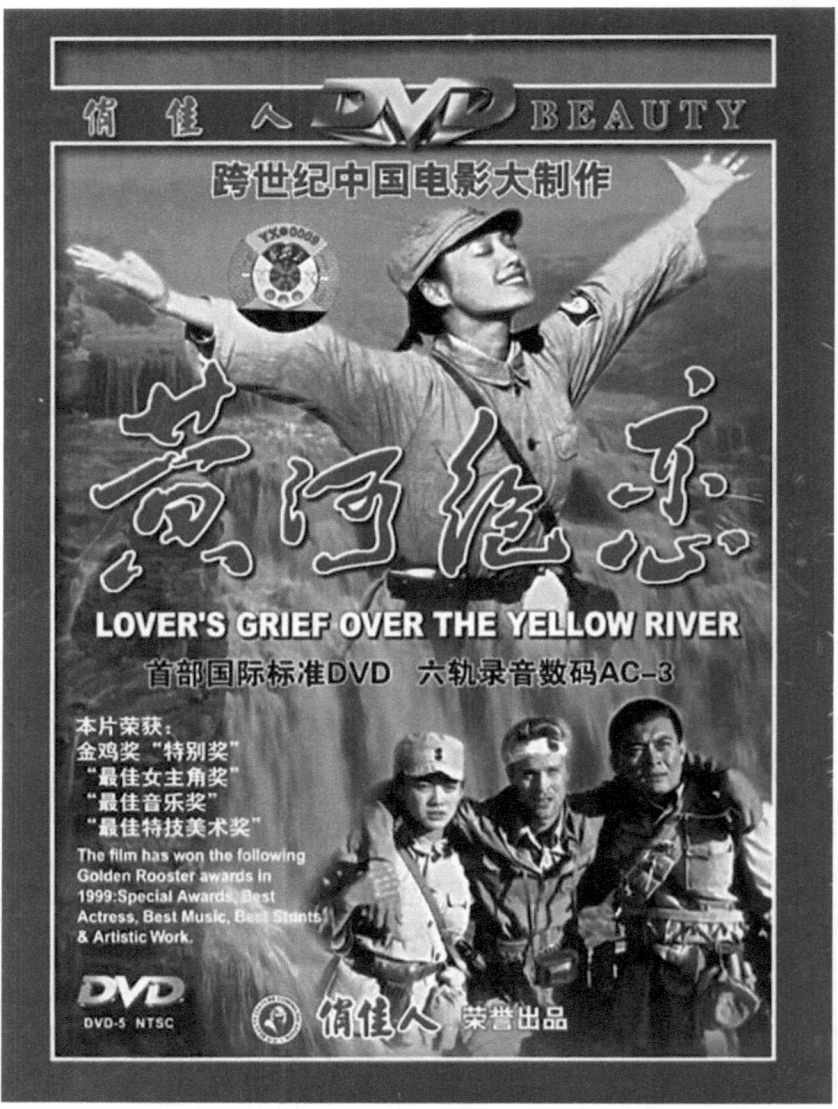

DVD cover for *Lover's Grief over the Yellow River* (1999).

words, a popular cultural form at once nurtured by the state and spurred by Hollywood encroachment, Leitmotif film cannot be simply understood as a nativist reaction and resistance against American domination and capitalism. Rather, it exhibits China's fervent aspirations to a fuller integration into the world system by submitting itself so willingly and tirelessly to the velvet

Film poster for *Lover's Grief over the Yellow River* (1999).

prison of Hollywood hegemony as well as of the Chinese authorities in the post–Cold War era.

In the following section, I continue to examine the political economy of this popular mainstream cinema with particular concentration on the key notion of soft power and the artist's contract with revolution and the state. What aims does China's soft power seek? How and in what ways? Has the soft power achieved or can it ever achieve its principal goals as plotted? I tackle these issues by returning to Feng Xiaoning's first installment of his "China through Foreign Eyes" trilogy, *Red River Valley*, and by opening up a new dialogue on the variegated, intertwined transnational languagescape, ideoscape, ethnoscape, memoryscape, and imaginary that form the core of this peculiar piece. Before I begin a close textual analysis of *Red River Valley*, I want to offer some observations on the context of the work, which will also serve as a compact survey and summary of the overall sociocultural and critical landscape of post-Tiananmen China.

During the last decade of the twentieth century, mainland China experienced a dramatic turn of events that influenced its standing in international politics. Occidentalist longings for Western modernity, which reached an apex during the elitist, liberal-minded era of the 1980s, grew in tandem with, and were quickly outpaced by, an eruption of Chinese nationalist sentiment in the 1990s. This is evident in *China Can Say No* (*Zhongguo keyi shuo bu*, Song Qiang et al.), a bestseller that caused a nationwide stir in 1996. In a pompous tone, this pamphlet lambasts the popular tendency of "kowtowing to the foreign"; as the authors argue, this is akin to a virus that has infected the well-being of the Chinese nation for nearly a century. Consequently, it calls for a hard-line move to bring Western colonization and domination to an end, thereby restoring China's stature as a strong, independent country and the so-called "central kingdom" (China, *zhongguo*, stands for "central kingdom" in Chinese literally).

The perennial view of Chinese selfhood in negotiation with Western forms of identity and the broader globalscape has been in a state of flux. In *Occidentalism: A Theory of Counter-Discourse in Post-Mao China*, Chen Xiaomei chronicles the reception and reconfiguration of Western images and culture in modern Chinese history and stresses how highly imaginary perceptions of the West inform and shape cultural trends and identities in the Chinese sociopolitical landscape. Orientalism, in Said's account, is in large part a Western strategy for domination,[47] whereas Chen's work shows that Chinese Occidentalism becomes a discourse invoked by various and competing social groups for a variety of ends. She argues that there are two different modes of deployment: the official Occidentalism with a patriotic and Sinocentric bent that disciplines and regulates the Chinese self; and the anti-official Occidentalism that also uses the imaginary Western Others as a political tool but nevertheless subverts dominant ruling ideologies. Chen's original, dialogic thinking, "marked by a combination of the Western construction of China with the Chinese construction of the West,"[48] is instructive and of particular relevance to the phenomena I discuss in this chapter because images of the West in juxtaposition with multiple forms of Chinese self-portraiture have conspicuously registered the dimensions and intensities of a hefty number of Leitmotif films today.

In the shadow of the Tiananmen incident, the Western media's assessment of the party and political environment of China was predominantly depreciatory and belligerent. Then, in 1993, Beijing lost the bid for the 2000 Olympics. The controversies of the Tiananmen crackdown and China's human rights issues were thought to be the chief reasons that Western delegates blocked China's further stride into the global arenas. Several other events around the millennium—for instance, the massive student demonstrations against the North Atlantic Treaty Organization's bombing of the Chinese Embassy in Belgrade, which targeted American embassies in the cities of Beijing, Shanghai, Guangzhou, and Chengdu in 1999, and the collision between US Navy aircraft and a Chinese jet at the Hainan island in 2001—reflected antagonism and further exacerbated *fin de siècle* tensions between China and the West, particularly the United States.

On the one hand, as the 2000 Olympics bid reveals, in today's global map, China is still quite a victim of the deeply ingrained logic of Orientalism and Eurocentrism. This duo of forces "sanitizes Western history while patronizing and even demonizing the non-West; it thinks of itself in terms of its noblest achievements—science, progress, humanism—but of the non-West in terms of its deficiencies, real or imagined,"[49] as Ella Shohat and Robert Stam note in *Unthinking Eurocentrism: Multiculturalism and the Media*. On the other hand, in the fuzzy, strained political climate of post-Tiananmen China, when confronting Western imperialists, China thinks of itself as both victim and empire ("central kingdom"). An upsurge of extreme nationalism or the revival of Sinocentrism at the turn of the century is evident in the plethora of jingoist moments just mentioned. Instigated by this bout of "China Can Say No" fever, television stations and movie theaters immediately joined in the popular mass resistance by halting screenings of Hollywood imports and replacing them with classic anti-American revolutionary pictures or politically correct Leitmotif films. At the critical level, blockbusters from Hollywood such as *Saving Private Ryan*, *Titanic*, and *Star Wars* were debunked and reexamined as vehicles of propaganda, which, it is argued, have exported the high concept of American-centrism in order to "re-colonize" China. For example, an article entitled "Reunderstanding American Blockbusters" published by *Beijing Youth Daily* in May 1999 provides an overview of the recent successful Hollywood blockbusters. Drawing from a wide range of comments by intellectuals and popular audiences, the article uncovers Hollywood's underlying ideological, didactic goals underneath its peaceful, romantic veneer as indicated from the keywords and subheadings of the essay, including "Tailored for the Mainstream Society," "Culture of the Mass or of the Politicians?" and "Cultural Imperialism in the Heat of Blockbuster."[50]

Produced in this specific context, Feng Xiaoning's trilogy carries a double thrust. Presented as Chinese Westerns, featuring the vast, wild nature of the yellow earth and Tibetan plateau, these Leitmotif attractions invoke the acclaimed "root-seeking," national-allegory aesthetic modes of the Fifth Generation and contemporary Hollywood neoliberal stylization. An epithet such as "China through Foreign Eyes," on the one hand, is marketing hyperbole that complies with and capitalizes on a burgeoning tide of chauvinist nationalism to make a quick sale. On the other, it is a backhanded configuration that, in Rey Chow's formulation, self-Orientalizes China, subscribing to the voyeuristic-fetishist gaze of the West once more.[51] On top of envisioning China as spectacle—as is implied in Feng's gaudy self-branding—which rightly exposes its Hollywoodish ambitions, I suggest, another perspective is also at play in this cross-cultural game: namely, the West as an object of the Chinese gaze and a channel through which Chinese identity is reflexively projected, mediated, and heard. To quote Rey Chow, "'the East,' too, is a spectator who is equally caught up in the dialectic of seeing."[52]

It should be noted that a third dynamic—the representation of Tibet—is added to and convolutedly entangled with this Orientalism/Occidentalism dialogue. Among an exiguous body of Chinese films about Tibet,[53] *Red River Valley* is the first work recounting an important event in modern history, the British-Tibetan War in 1904. Although created by a crew and a cast who are predominantly urban Han Chinese, this film draws heavily on Tibet and Tibetan culture from subject matter to thematic consideration and visual representation. It is symptomatic of another fever, the so-called "Tibet fad," that swept China at the end of the twentieth century. In this seemingly new fashion, the image and word of Tibet became a paragon of the sublime and divine. It shook Chinese literary circles when the fiction of a half-Tibetan, half-Han writer named Tashi Dawa, among other Han authors (e.g., Ma Lihua), welled up on bestseller lists. Exhibitions of paintings and photographs based upon journeys to Tibet also seized the spotlight of the 1990s mainland art world.

In popular music, Tibet has been similarly appropriated as an antidote to corrupt social mores and destructive capitalistic desires in contemporary Chinese society. Zheng Jun's rock song "Return to Lhasa" (*Huidao Lasa*) and Zhu Zheqin's popular folk tune "Sister Drum" (*Ajiegu*), the top hits in the music charts of 1994 and 1995, respectively, both appeal to Tibetan motifs. The lyrics of "Return to Lhasa" are as follows:

Return to Lhasa, return to Potala Palace
Wash my heart clean at The Yarlung Tsangpo River
Awaken my soul on top of the Snow Mountain . . .
Return to the home we have been separated from for so long

"Return to Lhasa" was the most popular hit of Zheng Jun's 1994 debut album, *Naked* (*Chiluoluo*). As Baranovich has pointed out, the album was intended to be a truly candid, bold critique of "the materialism, commercialization, and fakery that he believes . . . has taken over China in recent years."[54] In contrast to mainstream culture mired in a swarm of materialism, consumerism, and socialist residues, Tibet stands for absolute pureness, authenticity, spirituality, and the highest ideals of beauty, which pair well with the characteristics of rock. The intrinsic link between the emblematic Tibet and rock music was further articulated and reinforced in the music video of "Return to Lhasa," in which a rush of idyllic, awe-inspiring scenery of Tibet is set against and brilliantly fuses with a sultry live rock performance. The music video was directed by Lu Xuezhang, a Sixth Generation filmmaker who made *How the Steel Was Tempered*, an extraordinary 1990s rock 'n' roll film previously discussed. Zhu Hongmao, the leading actor in *How the Steel Was Tempered*, also partook in this music video project as the chief guitarist and musical arranger, another manifestation of such vital connections between music and visual discourses. It comes as no surprise that the symbolic significance of Tibet as the venerable, sacrosanct spiritual home was also aptly captured and sanctified by a Leitmotif production, *Kong Fansen* (dir. Chen Guoxing and Wang Ping, 1995). A biopicture that documents a communist party cadre who dedicated himself wholly to his Tibetan charge, the film can be best described in Zheng Zun's line: "In the pure sky flies a pure heart." This provides another example of how the state apparatus interacts with the alternative, unofficial, popular voices of minorities, neutralizes them and effectively transforms them into an agitprop-cum-commodity—an important feature that defines *Red River Valley* (to be examined shortly).

The Tibet fad emerged in the particular postsocialist, consumerist climate of 1990s China. Although a considerable number of literary and audiovisual products presented a revisionist view of the flattened, totalized history and helped to raise public awareness about the distinctive identity of Tibet, predominant political conceptions about Tibet still affected the ways in which the region was approached and re-imagined. Debates revolved around the unique status of Tibet vis-à-vis the mainland and other countries and, above all, the question of who has the right to represent a true Tibet and in what ways. Janet Upton studies "Sister Drum," a 1995 hit by the Chinese singer Zhu Zeqin (aka Dadawa), which she regards as a transnational musical product involving disparate parties of interest. Contrary to its high-profile success in mainland markets, the song was boycotted by the expatriate Tibetan community and their Western supporters in international circles, deemed as yet another inaccurate representation and ruthless propagation of the state order to assimilate Tibet into the hegemonic nation-state of the PRC.[55] Such tensions between the nation-state, ethnic-local identity, global discourse, and artistic innovations are framed and grappled with in *Red River Valley*, which aimed at constructing a modified, moderate—if not radically novel—image of Tibet and China. Negotiations between these mechanisms are often formally and stylistically embodied by a set of parallel and intertwined narratives and visualities, which are in coordination with and furthermore animated by a fluid, hybrid multilingual soundtrack in the film.

Transcultural Imaginary and the Voice of Self-Others at the Crossroads of *Red River Valley*

Enjoying a wide release and garnering critical accolades across the nation,[56] *Red River Valley*, alongside Feng Xiaoning's second hit, *Lover's Grief over the*

Yellow River, shall be considered as "big pictures made in China." They are given this designation not only by virtue of their "bigness"—big budgets,[57] big stars,[58] big effects,[59] big publicity, and big box-office return[60]—but also because they are made in response to Hollywood films with similar themes, as I just discussed. *Red River Valley* is a state-sponsored Leitmotif project that appropriated the Tibet craze as subject matter and served as China's soft power response to a pair of Hollywood productions on the same topic, *Seven Years in Tibet* (dir. Jean-Jacques Annaud, 1997) and *Kundun* (dir. Martin Scorsese, 1997). In an interview with *Popular Cinema*, Feng Xiaoning, a 1982 graduate in Art Design from the renowned Beijing Film Academy, explains:

> At the end of 1995 when Chinese film industry suffered from a great depression, the major concerns of officials in Shanghai Film Studio were not only constrained by profit-seeking, but more importantly the experiments that purported to stimulate film market through big investments with prime artistic qualities have ushered in a new model of blockbuster of our own. All these factors have considerably contributed to the success of *Red River Valley*.[61]

Interestingly, Feng Xiaoning is one of the few vaguely labeled—if not unclassified—filmmakers with a BFA genesis. He is strangely filtered out from the generational pedigree probably because he is not making the same kind of artistically potent films as his internationally acclaimed colleagues. Produced by Shanghai Film Studio in 1997, *Red River Valley* was the first blockbuster in Feng's trilogy depicting socio-historical and cultural clashes between China, Tibet, and the West through the lens of transcultural journey. The subsequent sequels, *Lover's Grief over the Yellow River* and *Purple Sunset*, both follow the same travel paradigm and draw on the genre of revolutionary war picture. A multitude of spatio-temporal and language encounters are employed to probe national history and re-envision conflicts and memories of war, which are paramount in the historiographical and cinematic formulation of "China through Foreign Eyes."

Red River Valley is an allegorical reconstruction of a historical past through the double visions and voices of the self and others during the war. The film begins in an ethnographic fashion with an elaborate sequence of the primitive rain praying rite over the Yellow River in early twentieth-century China, whose *mise-en-scène* instantly recalls *Yellow Earth*. Two Han women, unfortunately, become the human sacrifices for the calamity of massive drought. One of them manages to escape along the river to a remote village in Tibet. The next scene lapses into a close-up of a spinning prayer wheel, introducing the audience to the enigmatic, exotic world of Tibet. As the camera pans slowly across the vast

Tibetan plateau, an elderly woman in traditional dress is discerned in medium close-up with the spinning wheel at hand. At this point, a voice of a Tibetan boy, Gaga, chimes in, revealing his perspective: "The coming of that Han girl was a miracle created by the Goddess. From then on, she became one of us, my sister." *Red River Valley* appears to be the story of a native Tibetan unfolding in flashbacks with a voice-over. Yet it is ironically and contradictorily delivered in Mandarin Chinese, the official, standard language in mainland China that dubs and substitutes for Tibetan, the native tongue of the depicted territory. Here, the opening visual clue and voice-over establish a central theme and an allegorical overtone of the film, which are particularly concerned with the imaginarily harmonious, intricate relationship between Tibetans and the Han Chinese. The banished Han girl, Xue'er (meaning "snow" in Chinese, which has instantly established a link to the Tibet theme), is renamed as Xue'er Dawa (a metaphor of rebirth), adopted and dearly loved by a Tibetan family, and swiftly acculturated into the Tibetan lifestyle.

In the ensuing moments, *Red River Valley* shifts to another arrival scene and announces the second narrative strand, which is organized through another first-person narration of a British journalist-translator. In a letter, Jones exclaims to his father:

> Father, you're absolutely right. I have indeed entered the dream land, one would almost expect no white appeared. Is this Tibet!? It is so fresh, so enticing, and an area of mystery. Where is the Sacred Mountain you mentioned? They say every snow-capped mountain here is a God. I haven't seen one person yet. Perhaps Major Rockland knows what he is doing. So I needn't worry. Well, he did fight his ways with the Allied Forces into Beijing not long ago . . .

The ectastic interjection and poetic recital conspicuously invoke the stylization of a Western travelogue and frontier narrative upon the discovery of a new, mythical land. *Red River Valley*, at a second glance/hearing, then shifts to another tale described with an English viewpoint and tongue, as it progresses, by contrast, in a linear, chronological order. From Jones's perspective, often initated through his binoculars and camera, the film cuts to extended long shots of exotic rituals and other ethnographical details, as well as the vast spectacular wilderness. Interspersed with these moments, it is revealed that the Englishman is an enemy combatant. In comparison to the first narrative of the Tibetan boy, which is invested with a warm hue of mutual understanding, trust, and sympathy, the second thread of the Englishman is outwardly thrilling but associated with an atmosphere of distance, ambivalence, and antagonism.

Red River Valley is a revolutionary war epic consisting of two parallel and intertwined visual images and soundtracks. The Tibetan boy, Gaga, is the first witness and narrator who follows the progression of the entire incident. Juxtaposed and accompanied by the deep, resolute voice of a grown-up, seen on-screen Gaga is a small, quiet, and inexpressive child. This consistently conjures up the prototype of the mute children in such Fifth Generation films as *Yellow Earth*, *King of the Children*, and *Red Sorghum*. Conversations are barely heard in the first portion of the story centering on the Han-Tibetan relationship. It is the plenteous lighting, vibrant color scheme of crystal-clear blue, pristine white, lush green and enlivening cherry red, and an abundance of jubilant laughter that punctuate the Tibetan boy's nostalgic voice-over, conveying a sense of joy, intimacy, and human harmony. To a great extent, Gaga stands almost outside of the events. He is barely characterized, nor included in the main actions of the film. He exists largely in his commentaries—an *acousmêtre* in the Chionian sense (see my discussion in chapter three). The nondiegetic voice-over, in which the original Tibetan is deliberately eliminated with the substitute of Mandarin Chinese, attests to the official ideology of nation-building and points to the irony of Han chauvinism.

As it mimics a certain style of travel writing, the second metanarrative focuses on a third component—the Westerners who breach the established balance between the Han Chinese and Tibetans. In this part, the Englishman Jones dominates the tale both by his actions and his subjective point of view in voice-over. Jones's voice is distant and poignant as he writes and recounts the incidents to his father, his principal confidant who is visibly absent yet audibly accessible through the soundtrack. His utterances inaugurate, accompany, and conclude discrete visual components in the film. The complex feelings of perplexity, dis/replacement, and dis/reintegration as a consequence of his close exposure to the clash of two (or three) cultures and civilizations pervade this bittersweet transnational journey. Interestingly, there is no dubbing here; Jones's original English inflection (English with a southern American accent) remains intact on the soundtrack and is translated to Chinese subtitles. The foreignness of his tongue creates and reinforces a sense of estrangement, uncertainty, and conflict.

Red River Valley is loosely based upon *Bayonets to Lhasa: The First Full Account of the British Invasion of Tibet in 1904* by Peter Fleming, a British travel writer and special correspondent of the *Times* who published extensively on his colonial adventures through Brazil, Russia, Manchuria, China, and Tibet in the early twentieth century. The film successfully translated this particular form of travel writing to convey the kind of reconciliation and transculturation that followed in the wake of China's confrontation with

The Tibetan boy Gaga as a witness and narrator in *Red River Valley* (1997).

simultaneously primitive, ethnic others, as well as modern, Western others in the nineteenth and twentieth century. Why, then, is the story told distinctively through the viewpoints and voices of the others?

The last decade of the twentieth century witnessed a rewriting, refabrication, and consumption of modern Chinese history and the Chinese revolution by the mass culture industry through the prism of the outsider and "foreigner." Commenting on this prepossessing picture of what she calls "a tide of Red nostalgia," Dai Jinhua asserts that the stylistic "chromatic juxtaposition of olive-green and revolutionary red" is bound up with the postmodern commodification and the familiar postcolonial thinking that still privileges the West over the East in a stereotypical spectator/spectacle split. She argues: "This kind of fashion, or unfashionable fashion, has once again come to form a mottled and listless tide, once again using transnational cultural representations to reveal the process of remapping the contemporary Chinese cultural cartography."[62] Zhang Huiyu, in his lengthy study of the market cult of historical tales and revolutionary narratives in late twentieth-century China, expresses the same criticism. He adds that the sort of deliberate alienation (*yizhihua*), de-revolutionization (*qugeminghua*), and de-politicization of revolutionary works, moreover, reaffirms the prevalent New Historicist approach of the 1980s that deconstructs the work of art as part of "cultural effect" and "cultural poetics."[63]

Dai Jinhua and Zhang Huiyu's sharp observations shed light on the films addressed in this chapter. The internalized perspective of the West has introduced a new alternative, possibly "objective" point of view, injected a "humanist" spirit, and most of all, has enabled the neoliberal promise of individuality, modernity, multiculturalism, and the globalization of postsocialist life to be fulfilled on-screen and in the marketplace. But it should be noted that *Red River Valley* is not a serious, "objective" historical film in the strict sense because it creates bias more insidiously, effectively, and artfully. The translatability of Tibetan and untranslatability of English to Mandarin Chinese, as rendered intentionally on the dialogue track, is one of the signs of this bias. The cultural imagination of postsocialist China strives to incorporate difference into a total self and synthesize the undivided, unified, and homogenous Tibetan and Chinese "us" vis-à-vis the heterogeneous, emulable Western others. Such an internationalist and universalist practice is commonplace in many Leitmotif films, including Feng Xiaoning's second hit, *Lover's Grief over the Yellow River*, in which an American soldier is the sole witness, narrator, and survivor of the war and collision of the worlds.

These two very different voice-overs and the linked double imageries are pivotal to the organization of *Red River Valley*. Voice and language variety, however, is not the only allegorical tool in the film. If we say that Jones's first-person travelogue infuses the film with a fresh air of subjectivity and intimacy, then it is through the apparatus of the camera we find a technocratic and thereby "objective" view. In analyzing the complex functions of the camera in modern society, Jonathan Crary contends that the camera "was not simply an inert and neutral piece of equipment or a set of technical premises to be tinkered with and improved over the years; rather, it was embedded in a much larger and denser organization of knowledge and of the observing subject."[64] It is not a coincidence that in *Red River Valley*, Jones is the central figure who literally possesses a camera (besides other modern goods, such as the lighter and binoculars)—the power and knowledge of kino-eye—to follow and document the occurrences. The seemingly rational and modernist construction of knowledge in the cinematic world is integrated with a deeply entrenched logic of cultural imagination, characterized by Shohat and Stam as a "Eurocentric" mode of writing that privileges the position of a knowing subject over its perceived, primitive others.[65]

If we follow this mode of "unthinking" that the camera is a metaphysical eye more than a mechanical eye, we better understand why and how landscape and sex are always the two fundamental motifs that engage the camera in *Red River Valley*. Tibet, in Jones's writing and through his narration and photographic perspective, is a pure and magnificent wonderland, which is by no means intellectually, spiritually, and morally inferior to Western culture, in spite of its "crudeness." The film uses a number of cinematic tropes and audiovisual instruments to delineate a bright and optimistic picture of Tibet/ China. The well-lit panoramic shots caress the fantastic landscape and iconic landmarks, including the Sacred Mountain, the Goddess Lake, and the Yellow River, which appear materially raw but cinematically rich. These images become a symbol of the Chinese/Tibetan spirit that can never be excluded from the camera nor extinguished by the Western cannons/canons. Clearly, this is more of a political imagination approved, sponsored, and formulated by the state propaganda in today's China than a prevision of a Western imperialist in the early twentieth century. Put differently, *Red River Valley* is a Leitmotif work imbricated within the populist politics and aesthetic of late 1990s Tibet fever evident in Zheng Jun's rock hit "Return to Lhasa," which was characterized as "the saccharine ode to the beauties of an exoticized Tibet."[66] By the same token, the film not only "harmonizes" with but, furthermore, saliently trumpets the government agenda to "downplay ethnic conflict by celebrating ethnic exoticism."[67]

Red River Valley can be understood as an ethnography of contemporary Chinese culture. Moreover, it illustrates a mode of what Mary Pratt has termed "autoethnography." In a pioneering and critical diagnosis of travel writing in Western literature, Pratt defines "autoethniography" in this way: "Autoethnograhic texts are not, then, what are usually thought of as 'authentic' or 'autochthonous' forms of self-representation . . . Rather autoethnography involves partial collaboration with and appropriation of the idioms of the conqueror."[68] Teemed with copious, extravagant location shots of Tibet, *Red River Valley* has a strong ethnographic character. However, for the most part produced with a Chinese cast and crew and addressed to the majority Han audience in the urban theaters, the film readily assumes and identifies with the dominant Han's standpoint as well as the Orientalist, autoethnographic approach that often sees East-as-spectacle and East-as-woman.

Whereas representations of nationalism and national identity in Leitmotif films rely heavily on one specific genre—historical epic—the second strategy dwells on gender politics, particularly through the delicate (re)construction of sexuality and subjectivity in the new postsocialist, transnational context. The two sacrifice rites in *Red River Valley* exhibit the ways in which woman is built as both a historical form of victim/goddess and a new globalized form of commodity, containing the double desire of the "conquerors" from both inside the nation and the outside Western world. The first sacrifice appears during the opening rain prayer of the Han Chinese in the yellow earth and the second during the Tibetan-British War at the Tibetan plateau. The two female sacrifices in blazing red (in allusion to marriage, life, and war), or in immaculate white in the second scene (a cultural denotation of chastity and death), serve as a source of visual pleasure (Laura Mulvey) and as the focal point of the unfolding drama. Female bodies are offered literally and figuratively as objects, prizes, and tributes to the symbolic nation. Furthermore, they represent the nexus between East and West, primitive and modern, past and present, collective and individual, and the national and global.

Although the war has been, in a historicist sense, construed as inevitably resulting from clashes of different civilizations, *Red River Valley* proposes and advocates ideals of cultural harmony through mutual understanding and respect, and more provocatively, through transcultural affection and romance. This type of intercultural relationship and transnational practice is theorized in Pratt's term as the "contact zone." It is "the space in which peoples geographically and historically separated come into contact with each other and establish ongoing relations, usually involving conditions of coercion, radical inequality, and intractable conflict."[69] Pratt further examines how a quintessential Eurocentric and Orientalist scenario comes to shape and underpin the often contentious and nebulous formulation of an intercultural amour-liaison: "It is easy to see transracial love plots as imaginings in which European supremacy is guaranteed by affective and social bonding; in which sex replaces slavery as the way others are seen to belong to the white man; in which romantic love rather than filial servitude or force guarantee the willful submission of the colonized."[70]

In *Red River Valley*, both Gaga's and Jones's grave and melancholic narrations, burdened with history, are smoothed out and embellished with two transitory, blithe romantic renditions. Gaga is the barefaced witness to a fairytale romance between his brother, Geshang, a Tibetan hero, and the exiled, adopted Han girl, Xue'er. Jones (un)expectedly falls for Danzhu, the daughter of the Tibetan governor, who later dies during the war he is unwittingly involved with. Danzhu is played by a popular actress, Ning Jing, who became famous for Jiang Wen's 1994 film, *In the Heat of the Sun*; she is not a Tibetan but a member of the Naxi minority from Yunnan province. In *Red River Valley*, she is stereotypically an exotic and erotic object of the male-imperialist gaze of Jones—beautiful, innocent but wild and unruly. Most indicative of the ethnographic and autoethnographic orientation is a scene where Jones takes a photograph for Danzhu and her family. He cuts her father and fiancé out of the developed picture. In a metaphorical manner, Danzhu in a separate close-up becomes a "free" woman who is detached and emancipated from the traditional patriarchy that has previously owned her or is soon to claim her. Yet it is the "free" capital and new global order that victoriously occupy and engulf her (and the virgin land of Tibet/China) at last.

Spectacular, exotic scenery and transracial, erotic love become the focus of *Red River Valley* (1997): the romance between the Tibetan hero Geshang and the Han girl Xue'er.

Toward the end of *Red River Valley*, Danzhu is seized and held hostage by British soldiers, which constitutes the second sacrifice act of the film. It is, then, the humiliation and violation of the body of the virgin by foreign invaders that provoke the natives to rush to "her" defense (another trope of woman-as-nation). In this national-allegory sequence, the West appears as the absolute, atrocious other in contradistinction to the imagined united front between "us"—the Han Chinese and ethnic minorities such as Tibetans—when facing the juggernaut of Western modernity. The seemingly harmonious and mellifluous fusion of the Han majority and its ethnic minority others perfectly embodies the state rhetoric in simplifying the far more complex reality of ethnic conflict by underlining instead external distinctions and stark oppositions between the Western other and China-Tibet self, which is deemed to be an inseparable, unitary whole.

A similar pattern of what Pratt considers the "contact zone" and sexual-cultural linkage with the Western order can be found in a large body of Chinese Leitmotif films, especially in Feng Xiaoning's trilogy. In *Lover's Grief over the Yellow River*, this formulaic relationship takes place on the yellow earth—the heart of Chinese civilization—where an American lands. Irving is on a special mission to China to "help" Chinese people during World War II, and the airplane crash arranges such a rendezvous. An Jie, a Chinese communist nurse, is portrayed as a glamorous and virtuous goddess through the

The second transracial/transnational romance in
Red River Valley (1997): Danzhu and Jones.

mise-en-scène and referred to as the "angel" sonically (her Chinese name, An Jie, sounds similar to "angel" in English) and figuratively throughout the film. She appears prominently in close-up and in high-key lighting. In the narrative, she is the "holy trinity" of maiden-lover-mother who provides sumptuous kindness, care, companionship, erotic passion, and even her own life to the Western advernturer-missionary. More strikingly, such a transnational engagement and collaboration on-screen between the two protagonists Ning Jing (who played An Jie in *Lover's Grief over the Yellow River* and Danzhu in *Red River Valley*) and Paul Kersey (the actor for the role of Irving in *Lover's Grief over the Yellow River* and for Jones in *Red River Valley*) sparked an off-screen romance and interestingly paralleled their love relationship in the post-Cold War, neoliberal-dominated reality.

All of these textual and intertexual nuances seem to affirm a long-standing geopolitical hierarchy of Western hegemony, or to borrow Pratt's words, the constitution of an ingrained "concubinage system," which is in fact "a romantic transformation of a particular form of colonial sexual exploitation."[71] It can be argued that a conflicting sentiment of love and hate and the ambivalent depiction of the Westerners as at once enemies and lovers have become universal themes in this specific Leitmotif genre. As such, a double vision suffused with a large degree of ambiguity has characterized the imagery of the West. *Red River Valley* presents two leading Western figures. Rockland, the British Commissioner to Tibet, is sketched as a stereotypically cunning and treacherous instigator who follows the clichéd pattern in socialist revolutionary pictures such as *Lin Zexu* (1959); on the other hand, his interpreter/correspondent, Jones, is a contrastively benign and helpless onlooker. Rockland, albeit directly accused as the vicious imperialist who launches the unjust war, is presented in a much more complex light rather than as merely a one-dimensional villain.

At the end of the war, the film crosscuts between close-ups of Rockland and his Tibetan friend/rival. The lit lighter, a gift from Rockland that, however, incurs and ultimately ends the war, is recaptured for a few times, looming large in the center of the frame. In conjunction with (and contrast to) the filmic imagery of the spinning prayer wheel, an emblem of Tibetan culture, Buddhism, and peace, the lighter is also a recurring motif and an important metaphor that suggests Western civilization and friendship, bringing modernity as well as war. The idyllic past and a sequence of wartime memories are presented in a flashback montage, accompanied by a melancholic piano score—the film's recurrent leitmotif. The last shot disclosing Rockland's dolorous confession—"You and I should have been friends"—in a prolonged, heightened cadence is captured with a zoom lens, lending a humanist touch to this largely negative character. In this light, the film can be understood as a neoliberal effort that interprets East-West conflict and warfare as prognostic to twentieth-century market economy, trading business, and the advent of globalization, a regnant theme that has its cinematic repercussion in another 1997 Leitmotif film, *The Opium War*.

Before the last scene of *Red River Valley*, a long shot reveals the Tibetan fort blown into pieces. It is a massive and actually bilateral wreck ignited by the small lighter that Geshang receives from Rockland. Wide shots of the torn fort with whirling, heavy smoke are intercut with images of howling British soldiers who are marred by fire and gunpowder of their own. The film's final sequence projects a last, sympathetic look at ruins of the war and the grandeur of the land (and the nation). Jones, one of only three survivors (in addition to the youngest Gaga and the oldest grandma), tearfully stands on the top of the hill in deep sorrow and regret. The camera follows his gaze; notwithstanding that the war has almost destroyed everything, the majestic, sublime nature (a commonplace trope standing in for the national spirit) will never perish. The immaculate Sacred Mountain is at last laid bare so closely and realistically upon his eyes: "I see the Sacred Mountain." Following Jones's interjection, the camera shifts to a close-up and then to a wide shot of the severed picture of the beautiful Danzhu, blown by the gust of wind and lost in the vast abyss of space, time, and history.

As Jones turns around, another splendor suddenly captivates him: in the enormous, mysterious land, myriads of Tibetan yaks gallop amidst the morning mist all around him. The land, through his look, is sutured into a magic world, fantastically bathed and enshrined in the radiant golden sunshine. At just this moment, an upbeat tune chimes in. It swells to a dashing ensemble of a large orchestra, with tremendous percussion and an exhilarating, thunderous chorus that pushes the film to its diegetic, audiovisual, and emotional zenith. As the director recalled, this design was the most expensive and difficult scene (certainly the best) he had handled. He rented thousands of yaks and reshot it many times, which turned the film into a hefty and affecting picture, a truly Chinese blockbuster, so to speak.[72]

The next reverse shot cuts back to a medium close-up of Jones who is utterly stunned, looking into the distance. From his perspective, we see once again the familiar imagery of the spinning prayer wheel, which is zoomed out from into a medium shot and subsequently a full shot of the two remaining characters, grandma and Gaga, mysteriously appearring on the faraway horizon. As if writing to his father, Jones murmurs to himself (in probably one of the most memorable speeches of all): "Father, why should we destroy their civilization with us? Why change their world with us? One thing is for certain. These people will never give in and never disappear. And the immense land behind them is the Oriental we shall never conquer." Apparently, such a grandiloquent annunciation, albeit from an alleged, diegetic Western point of view, is in fact the voice of the Chinese state that flaunts a propagandist message for the sake of nationalism. As the mythical pair slowly treads off into the far distance, the solemn voice of the grandma (in clear, perfect Mandarin Chinese) is heard almost for the first and the last time, reverberating through the end of *Red River Valley*: "When Goddess Qomolangma was born, she was a shell in the vast ocean. She became Goddess after many years. She had ten snow-mountain sisters. She had three sons who have been close to each other. The eldest was called Yellow River. The second was Yangtze River, and the youngest was Yarlung Zangbo River." In this way, China's national history has been squarely placed within the fanciful myth, personal tale, oral tradition, or safe container of what Jameson has called "national allegory." A freeze-frame of the lighter buried in the dust of history and a close-up of the spinning prayer wheel fade in and out, drawing the film to its noble, patriotic, and celebratory conclusion.

If one has to ask, "Who, in the end, is the winner?"—the key question that has been rigidly programmed into historical films, war epics, action films, and other blockbusters—I think *Red River Valley* presents a most satisfactory answer to the state. After his field trip to the anti-British museum in Gyantse, which features an exhibition of the British-Tibetan battle as depicted in *Red River Valley*, John Powers writes: "What appeared to a Western visitor as PRC propaganda was history to them, and most was clearly moved by what they read."[73] As a historian and scholar in Buddhism and Tibetan studies, Powers found many of the representations and claims in *Red River Valley* fairly unfounded and problematic. In his scathing dissection of the film, it is the historical inaccuracies and propagandist partial judgments that annoyed and disheartened him. In the film industry terrain, nevertheless, this colored, dubbed, and fabricated history has reinvigorated an outmoded genre, the revolutionary historical film, and spawned a refurbished genre, the Leitmotif blockbuster. Or, to borrow Adorno's most cited criticism of the culture industry,[74] *Red River Valley* is a Leitmotif paragon: a national anthem that lulls the masses into a cooperative, docile, and even appreciative "dupe" of the postsocialist system, which successfully plays a double-handed game with both the politics and the market in the post-Cold War, postnational era.

Leitmotif-Authorship-Blockbuster and Zhang Yimou in the Post-Heroic Era

Red River Valley, with its double imagery and vocal track, reflects the bifurcated dynamic of Western reconfiguration and Chinese self-representation that has permeated a large number of Leitmotif films. Both a corporate piece of government propaganda and a Chinese blockbuster, the film was produced and distributed via networks of transnational capital, political sponsorship, and amidst the social-cultural life that neoliberal reform had activated. After the film was released in 1997, many reviews lauded *Red River Valley* for its enthusiastic nationalism, revolutionary romanticism, and open-mindedness to the neoliberal transnational world. Following this pattern, *Purple Sunset*, the third piece in Feng's trilogy, recasts the transcultural journey and encounter into another remote forest in northeast China while extending the director's stylistic experimentation with flashbacks, voice-over, and a multilingual soundtrack. The central characters are a triad left stranded in the forest at the end of World War II: a male Chinese peasant, a female Russian soldier, and a Japanese schoolgirl. They have to depend on each other to find their way out of the forest, in spite of their distinct nationalities, political interests, social identities, and differing languages. Like Feng's previous works, a philosophical and at times platitudinous reflection on humanity and mutual understanding serves as the underlying message and leitmotif of the work.

Primarily funded by the Shanghai Yongle Film Company, *Red River Valley* and Feng's other epics all seem to support an emergent entrepreneurial spirit in collaboration and negotiation with the state order. Their production and commercial success are symptomatic of how the neoliberal principles of market and profitability in general, the mass entertainment value of film in particular, have been woven into China's postsocialist reality. When the market simultaneously serves as the regulation mechanism, technology, and tenet, profit-oriented film businesses emerge and proliferate quickly. Many of them, like the Shanghai Yongle Film Company, Beijing Forbidden City Film Company, and Imar Film Company, are joint ventures of private management and local government patronship. Historian Rebecca Karl aptly defines this convergence as "a state-market-world linkage."[75] Comparing *The Opium War*, a 1997 Leitmotif film, with its revolutionary predecessor made in 1959, *Lin Zexu*, Karl points out that modern Chinese history has been nostalgically recalled in recent Leitmotif pictures and this type of revisionist historiography, and that a reflection of the relationship between market and Chinese modernity brings new momentum to many contemporary cultural practices umder the impact of globalization.

The Opium War, *Red River Valley*, and similar works discursively grouped under the Leitmotif rubric suggest a state-sponsored and market-driven transnational formula in the postsocialist milieu. The double political and commercial stakes, nevertheless, have revealed their complicit, dubious position often fraught with contradictions and inconsistencies. Doubts were raised to question their blockbuster rationality aligned with state propaganda, their market hegemony that allegedly took an impartial guise, and their representational strategies of the Orientalist ideology. The problem lies in the narrative structure and soundtrack, too. *Red River Valley* represents the complex relationship between the Han people, Tibetans, and the West through the mediation of a Tibetan boy's vision and voice in parallel with that of a British soldier. Both Mandarin and English are chosen for important dialogue exchanges within the film, whereas the indigenous Tibetan (presumably spoken in the region) is muted and barely heard, with the exception of a handful of scenes featuring music and dance, as well as the closing credit sequence. This indicates the influence of revolutionary pictures in which ethnic minorities, in contrast to the civilized Han, are often portrayed as primitive people leading simple but rich lives with an abundance of jovial singing and dancing.

While the Leitmotif anthem has been widely circulated in the Chinese mainstream at the turn of the new century, the question of whether or not cinema can be at once political, commercial, and artistic remains a polemic topic. Not only is Leitmotif—often interchangeable with "cinema of propaganda"—a contingent and conflicting construction, but the market and neoliberal discourse that this film category is complexly associated with is ever-evolving and fluctuating in the postsocialist environment. As the US economy is undergoing a continual recession and global capitalist systems face a bottleneck, Li Minqi and other theorists assert that this current downturn and "demise of the neoliberal globalization" foreshadow a new surge of state regulated capitalism.[76] China, which once again survives this storm and rises undeniably as the next superpower and new epicenter of the world order, serves as a good role model. Does this mean that a particular mode of postsocialist neoliberalism that has been normalized and internalized within the Chinese structure may in turn become an alternative and supplementary solution to free market capitalism? Or is this perhaps a prime opportunity to be seized upon by the Chinese film industry, whose growth has been both dauntingly hindered and beneficially fostered by Hollywood's neoliberal expansion? How does and will this Chinese reconfiguration contribute to and rebuild the neoliberal sociopolitical order in general, and the world film market in particular?

To chart the precise direction and future-scape of the Chinese-global film culture is certainly not an easy task. Zhang Yimou's two big films of the new century—*Hero* (*Yingxiong*, 2002) and *The Flowers of War* (*Jinling shisan chai*, 2011)—may help cast some light on this set of questions. Both films were produced with extremely expansive budgets that far surpassed any of his previous works and any other previous Chinese pictures. In comparison to *The Opium War*, amply budgeted at $13 million, the so-called most expensive Chinese film made in the twentieth century, *Hero* hit the $30 million mark and *The Flowers of War*'s budget was set at $94 million. The cast and crew of *Hero* were just as impressive as the colossal budget, including Jet Li, Tony Leung, Maggie Cheung, Donnie Yen, Zhang Ziyi, and Chen Daoming—the best and most illustrious stars across Sinophone world. Tan Dun, a Grammy-and Academy Award-winning musician, composed the film music; Christopher Doyle, a preeminent cinematographer, created its ravishing visual style; and Quentin Tarantino introduced and presented the film when it was distributed by Miramax in the US.

The films' reception have been favorable: *Hero* received the Best Picture award at the Hundred Flowers Awards and was nominated for the Best Foreign Language Film at the 2003 Oscars; *The Flowers of War* was nominated for a Golden Globe and selected as China's entry for an Oscar in 2012. Box-office returns were more spectacular than ever: *Hero* totaled more than $177 million and *The Flowers of War* reaped over $311 million worldwide. What merits our attention in the astounding numbers is indeed the rabid response that these two films incited among audiences outside of mainland China. Among the total gross, 30.3 percent of *Hero*'s receipts (about $60 million) drew from the international market, where it enjoyed a wide release in as many as 2,175 US theaters. Although *The Flowers of War*'s world performance is comparatively pallid (which I will discuss shortly in more detail), it still grossed nearly $49 million in thirty locations in the US.[77]

What should, perhaps, be underscored here is that a reinvention or a reversal of Hollywood capitalism such as this, be it economically, culturally, or formally, is perpendicularly borne out of the Chinese mold of Leitmotif, as I have proven. The two pictures have been tenaciously tempered to bear much of the heaviness of the Leitmotif paradigm, particularly its epic responsibility to link up three mechanisms of the state, the market, the global through the fine-honed, auteurist apparatus of cinema. Whereas Chinese audiences and reviewers were still basking in the box-office glory of *Hero* and Zhang Yimou's "legendary" strike into and against Hollywood, the film inflamed an intense debate in the circle of Western critics and researchers.[78] Set in the imperial China of about 2,000 years ago, *Hero* was boasted to be another transnational martial arts masterpiece following the monumental *Crouching Tiger, Hidden Dragon* (*Wohu canglong*, dir. Ang Lee, 2000). It was, however, largely denounced by critics as yet another uncreative piece of propaganda, aestheticizing a fascist ideology and advancing a totalitarian, chauvinist view of what the Communist Party has disseminated as the centralized governance of *tianxia*—"under the heaven," despite all the differences. Drastically differing from the preceding era in which Zhang was "the most engaging, fiercely critical storyteller about the throttling hold of gerontocracy,"[79] *Hero* signifies the fall of a hero who religiously submitted himself to the regime on the one hand and vigorously succumbed to the temptations of transnational capitalism on the other.

In fact, at the close of the twentieth century, Zhang Yimou and his experimental projects, much like many other Fifth Generation filmmakers, *happily* ended his sojourns in the West. Probably, more than his peers, Zhang has quickly and competently assimilated himself into the mainstream culture and has indubitably become the regime's favorite filmmaker. Instead of being banned to reach out to his native audience, as was the case before, he has now been *seriously* invited to give talks, appear in media, and shoot films freely. Most significantly, Zhang was entrusted by the Chinese government with a pivotal and honorable mission to build China's new image for the global audience. He was chosen to make a short documentary for China's bid for the Olympics and to direct the opening and closing ceremonies for the 2008 Beijing Olympics. The privilege of signing agreements and contracts with the state office, as well as with multinational corporations, now enjoyed by the once most idiosyncratic and nonconformist Chinese auteur, is a striking but not uncommon occurrence in the postsocialist milieu.

Zhang Yimou, in his post-*Hero* period, has become a spokesperson and an ambassador who creates and promotes the new, ideal China and Chineseness in the public arena and on the global stage. Thus, treating Zhang Yimou and the Fifth Generation's recent mainstream commercial hits as a manifestation of Leitmotif, I appraise the Fifth Generation's transition to mainstream, central filmmaking. I will concentrate on *The Flowers of War*, because many of its formal devices have a deep resonance with Xie Jin's *The Opium War*, as well as Feng Xiaoning's trilogy. The most expensive film ever made in China, *The Flowers of War* is also among the top ten highest-grossing Chinese-language films to this day. Set during the Sino-Japanese War of the late 1930s, the film probes and recreates the Nanjing Massacre, one of the gravest, most insoluble, and controversial topics in Chinese-world history. The trauma of the war and revolutionary history are uncovered through the first-person narration of a schoolgirl, which, as in Feng Xiaoning's trilogy, functions as the bearer of memory and a cathartic device. The film's main actions, however, flippantly revolve around an American mortician-turned-priest's *heroic* act to save thirteen schoolgirls from rape and slaughter at the hands of the Japanese, with the assistance of a group of prostitutes.

The catchy plots, intense drama, and stunning cinematography fired up yet another Zhang Yimou fever. Zhang Yimou grabbed the world's spotlight again through his signature *mise-en-scène* of the primitive East and exotic womanhood. Critical reception was as mixed as it was for *Hero*.[80] Amid the crossfire as to whether or not *The Flowers of War* was government propaganda, Zhang Yimou defended himself: "This is not the sort of mainstream movie the Chinese government would usually approve. Topics about foreigners, about religion and about World War II are not well-received by the government, but because this movie is about who we are as humans, and what we would do to save other people, the government actually supported it."[81] Zhang may have a point, yet he presents only a half-truth. At least half of *The Flowers of War* is, I argue, for all intents and purposes, a compliant work aligning with the Leitmotif framework that "the Chinese government would usually approve." A prodigious entrepreneurial undertaking carefully handled by the Beijing New Picture Film Corporation (owned by Zhang Weiping, Zhang Yimou's longtime partner for all his films made after 1996), *The Flowers of War* was supported by many arms of the official apparatus, including banks for expendable capital, local governments, political organs, and cultural institutions who provided labor, set, and publicity, akin to Xie Jin's *The Opium War*. The film premiered at the National Political Consultative Hall near Tiananmen Square. That it premiered on December 11, 2011, was a salient move to commemorate the seventy-fourth anniversary of the Nanjing Massacre, which was accompanied by a plethora of patriotic and educational testimonials recounting the event.

While an imagined universal humanity is often touted by itself as the real "leitmotif" of the film, *The Flowers of War* struggles to find a balance between heroic patriotism and critical humanism, as it continually negotiates political intent, commercial appeal, and auteurist impulses. What comes out of the piece is a half-baked humanism that is wavering, maneuverable, and ready to sacrifice itself to the national cause whenever needed. A real humanist would find it hard to justify the film's pseudo-humanist logic to send the "bad" women to the butchery of the Japanese in place of the "good" girls, as is shown in its final moments. Rather, what is purveyed is the fully (and over-) cooked nationalism instilled into almost every character except the Japanese, including the Chinese soldiers led by Major Li, the convent girls centered around Shujuan, Yu Mo (translated to "jade and ink" in Chinese, which endues the character with a touch of elegance and civility despite her lower-class stature) and her fellow sisters with a stained past yet a true heart, the white hero John Miller, and even Shujuan's father, an unwilling traitor who is redeemed by his humanity of rescuing the schoolgirls at last. All of these factors testify that *The Flowers of War* is an ornate Leitmotif work, if not simply propagandist.

The film's English title, which ornaments violence and bloodshed with flowers, is somewhat disturbing and dangerously misleading.[82] While Zhang's intention was probably to soften the cruelty of war by injecting a feminine undertone, it could easily lead to an interpretation of the film as yet another signal of Zhang's post-heroic descent into fascism.[83] Critics frowned upon Zhang's frivolous fusion of prostitution, nudity, and sex scenes with a devastating national trauma. In an article published in *Southern Metropolis Daily*, Zhu Dake pinpoints *The Flowers of War*'s "discreditable" (*kechi*) commercial manipulations. Dismayed by the film's "erotic patriotism" (*qingse aiguozhuyi*), Zhu acerbically comments that it "turned the bloodbath cathedral into a love bed, the national trauma into an amorous nostalgia, the political discourse into the writing of body, the bloodshedding war into a sex scandal, the grave sufferings into a lucrative vehicle. Isn't such an abashed erotic patriotism a deadly lapse in moral orientation?"[84] To many, Zhang's "erotic" and "exotic" maneuvering of nationalism is highly problematic. However, it rightly betrays his uttermost attempt to consider market success and to synthesize a Chinese brand of blockbuster both for local consumption as well as global entertainment.

And this is precisely the second dynamic I want to tease out in *The Flowers of War*. A re-examination of Zhang's interview, in which he spoke of his ambitions explicitly, is helpful: "In the past, foreign characters were almost like decorations, they didn't have flesh and bones. This is the only movie so far that actually brings the West and East together organically. And this movie will really make China that much closer to the world on a global scale."[85] To meet these important goals, a first-rate Hollywood actor, Christian Bale, was hired and imported to China to star in *The Flowers of War*. A large transnational crew was also employed, most notably the special effects team of *Saving Private Ryan*. All of these choices seek to raise the film's global profile and appeal beyond national borders, something not entirely new in Chinese cinema but fully ripe in *The Flowers of War*. This conscientious construction of a China self in juxtaposition and linkage with the Western world has sprouted in the earlier Leitmotif model of Feng Xiaoning and Xie Jin. Here it is more organically integrated into Zhang's oeuvre thanks to his seasoned cinematic experience. Other Leitmotif-esque tactics involve the uncanny voice-over and point-of-view shot of an innocent child, genre hybridity of socialist revolutionary epic, Hollywood melodrama, and the Orientalist adventure story, as well as plots that turn upon the ambivalent relationship between China, Japan, and America.

Most indicative of *The Flowers of War*'s transnational engagement is, moreover, the urbane mixture of diverse tongues—Mandarin Chinese, Shanghainese, Nanjing dialect, English, and Japanese. Half of the dialogue in the film is delivered in English. The kind of romantic, visceral involvement between the Western hero Miller and Chinese prostitute Yu Mo, and the language proficiency of Yu Mo and the Chinese children in the cathedral to communicate freely in English, would perhaps lead to the question of the verisimilitude of the film. However, as Kinnia Yau Shuk-ting has noted, such a re-enactment—as opposed to that of the Japanese, most of whom "are depicted as unable to communicate with either the Chinese or the Americans"—can be "seen as reflecting or symbolizing China's contemporary relations with the West, and especially the USA."[86] Not only have the Chinese personalities on-screen joined the West and the world through the universal bonds of humanity, affection, and linguistic fluidity, but also the Chinese spectator in the theater is identified as a neoliberal, international citizen who could read, understand, and appreciate this English-inflected, subtitled film in the same way as they would for other Hollywood pictures shown next door.

Toward the end of *The Flowers of War*, in one of the most stirring, heart-melting scenes, Miller prepares to transform Yu Mo back to a virgin in lieu of the schoolgirls who are about to be sent to the Japanese and who are believed to be the hope of China's "future." When Miller woefully sees her off, he cannot help but comfort his lover with a slender promise to take her home after the war. After a couple of tight framings, the film cuts back to Yu Mo as she bursts into tears, beseeches in perfect, fluent English to "take me home now," and offers her body in bed. This amorous, affectionate moment is underscored by the melancholy folk song of "Qin Huai Legend" (*Qin huai jing*, composed by Qigang Chen), literally the leitmotif of the film. The idea of "taking me (Yu Mo) home" would seem dubious and especially absurd to contemporary viewers, as the US is addressed, no less, as home. Yu Mo's ironic, "odd reference to the US as home," as Yang Jing suggests, "recalled the staple Hollywood ending" and "unveiled a spiritual submission to the West."[87] While Yang's point is well taken, to pompously claim America home in the company of this homesick and distinctly vernacular music, "Qin Huai Legend," is, I think, also subversive and triumphant.

As opposed to the narrative and *mise-en-scène* of "take me home/US," home is sonically reconciled and reverberatingly specified as the Qin Huai River, the mother river of Nanjing that bears a rich historical past as well as the longings and paradoxes of the present. It bespeaks China and Chinese film's "dream" to merge into and restructure the world system as the country ascends to superpower status. It is the intersection of the disparate cultures, sexes, nationalities, languages, and home and the world in unison that allow Chinese viewers and Chinese films to transcend old barriers and build new relationships. Zhang Yimou is just one more example of how authorship is and has been annexed or straitjacketed by the modes of Leitmotif and blockbuster. In a highly fluctuating sociopolitical environment, when Chinese authors and artists empirically choose to ally themselves with concurrently official ideology as well as the Western gaze and transnational capitalism, it is important for us to reflect again on this last trembling inquiry Yu Mo propounds. Where does it—the war or the post-heroic cinema and era—take us to?

The Return of the Father and the (Re)founding of the Center

A special issue of *New Global Studies* in 2014 was devoted to a discussion of China's increasing interaction with the world. In particular, the extension of China's soft power is illustrated in the proliferation of Confucius Institutes across the world and the internationally engaged Chinese film, television shows, and popular media that promote a new image of China to the global audience.[88] This rightly echoes the Chinese leaders' call to cultivate the "cultural enterprises with Chinese characteristics"[89] and relates back to the question I posed earlier—what is cinema or Leitmotif's role in this blueprint of China's growing imperative on soft power and the China Dream? In a shift

Yu Mo and her prostitute sisters perform "Qin Huai Legend" in *The Flowers of War* (2011).

from 1980s liberalization and cultural renaissance to the *fin de siècle* materialization of the culture industry, Leitmotif and neoliberal-based philosophies, sensibilities, and interventions dominate the public domain and become visibly and sonically part of everyday life. My reading of *Red River Valley* and *The Flowers of War* in this chapter suggests that the historical, theoretical, and contextual understanding of popular mainstream Chinese cinema is inseparable from the evolving languagescape, ideoscape, and mediascape of post-socialist China and shall be always situated at the state-market-transcultural intersections.

The "founding" sequel, *The Founding of a Republic (Jianguo da ye*, 2009), and *The Founding of a Party (Jiandang wei ye,* aka *Beginning of the Great Revival,* 2011), self-evident as their titles appear, signal the apotheosis of this Leitmotif momentum. Co-directed and co-produced by the Fifth Generation veteran Huang Jianxin and the president of the China Film Group Corporation Han Sanping, the two films were made with enormous financial support to salute the sixtieth anniversary of PRC and the CCP's ninetieth birthday, respectively. Both proved to be huge box-office successes, albeit with considerable help from wholesale ticket sales to state units and institutions as a form of political-moral education. With significant reliance upon both state sponsorship and Hollywood star-system formula, these Chinese blockbusters embody the maturity of a "state-market-transcultural" synergy. It exhibits the ways in which the hard power of the statecraft may be turned into a soft power that infiltrates artifact, craftsmanship, individuality, and the popular consciousness of a post-heroic reality.

Thus, it should come as no surprise that nearly every star one can think of in the current Sinophone film world so eagerly lined up to play the heroes and founding fathers of PRC, even just for brief cameo appearances in these larger-than-ever pictures. Over 170 stars were cast in each of the two films, many of whom volunteered to play the roles entirely for free.⁹⁰ Local box-office personalities such as Tang Guoqiang, Zhang Guoli, Chen Daoming, Hu Jun, Liu Ye, Chen Kun, and Ning Jing; dashing transnational stars including Donnie Yen, Zhang Ziyi, Leon Lai, Daniel Wu, Andy Lau, Chow Yun-fat, Jet Li, Jackie Chan (who also directed and played the lead in *The 1911 Revolution*, another 2011 Leitmotif blockbuster in commemoration of the 100th anniversary of the Xinhai Revolution and the founding of the Republic of China); and filmmakers like Chen Kaige, He Ping, Jiang Wen, Feng Xiaogang, and John Woo all voluntarily offered their talents. Even American academics joined in the parade and commented on the significance of the productions:

> The making of the film *The Founding of a Republic* as well as its extraordinary box office success in 2009 underscores the convergence of the popular and the mainstream in contemporary Chinese culture. This robust mass culture, ever more integrated into the entertainment industry (especially TV programming), is not the subject of the many independent films that we are told we must see, but it reaches and entertains the general public, and generates its own star power.⁹¹

Drawing on the latest journal pulications, news stories, and blog essays related to the "founding" phenomenon, Tang Xiaobing has investigated the larger context and cultural system in which the film was conceived and circulated. He concludes: "It is high time that we reassessed these assessments. For that purpose, *The Founding* may be a good starting point, and my reflections here are meant to facilitate such a start. As a cultural event more than one particular contemporary revision of history, the film offers us a case study through which we may begin to fathom the historically determined and emotionally charged relationship between the Chinese public, its national consciousness, its collective memory and political imagination."⁹² Tang's enthusiastic praise of the new dynamic culminating in *The Founding of a Republic* vis-à-vis independent films may serve as a germane summation of cinema and the general landscape of popular mass culture in early twenty-first-century China. What he calls for is the "start" of a serious, conscientious, and more full deliberation on the complications of the "extraordinary box office success," the "convergence," "its own star power," and "the historically determined and emotionally charged relationship."

What, then, do such films mean to stars, filmmakers, viewers, and individuals in the new century, who are yet asked to serve the state almost in the same way as during the "founding" epoch? *The Founding of a Republic* marks a new height in Leitmotif's soft power reach and its fantasy of the China Dream. Yet what cannot be dismissed are the "historically determined" constraints from the top, "emotionally charged," unstable stardom, faltering cinematic quality, and many contradictions in the film. The generalist, flattened display of a wide gallery of historical figures has resulted in a muddled narrative, fragmented structure, and little aesthetic merit; in short, a tasteless, drowsy picture of state absolutism and the free market, where utilitarianism counts for the most. While an unprecedented number of film stars were involved in the productions and turned up *en masse* to promote an ostentatious vision of Chinese nationalism, interestingly, a great many of them were Chinese "foreign" actors and actresses who, having capitalized on the neoliberal power, have been naturalized to the US, UK, Singapore, Sweden, and other first-world countries.

Shelly Kraicer, an active programmer for international film festivals as well as a notable critic on Chinese cinema, presents a notion of "post-*zhuxuanlu* (Leitmotif) film" in his discussion of *City of Life and Death* (aka *Nanjing! Nanjing!*, dir. Lu Chuan, 2009), another war blockbuster released in 2009. Directed by the Sixth Generation member Lu Chuan, an indie-turned-mainstream filmmaker, the film similarly draws on historiography and the formal representation of national identity and, specifically, the Nanjing Massacre. *City of Life and Death* was a commercial and critical favorite despite its troubled relationship with the Chinese censors. Kraicer defines the film as "a sophisticated, post-*zhuxuanlu* movie," "negotiating within the genre's rules a more audience-appealing version of whatever party line is being sold."[93] This is all, Kraicer points out, well accomplished through Lu Chuan's meticulously modulated cinematic language. Kraicer's distinction between Leitmotif film and post-Leitmotif film is not entirely clear in the essay, but his perception of a collusion between the political regime, capitalism, artists, and intelligentsia in the postsocialist, post-Leitmotif field is compelling in a Žižekian thrust:

> Unlike a film such as *The Thin Red Line* (1998), *City of Life and Death* hides the gap and insists that the movie version is real, that what it shows is history. This is not history—it is ideology. Ideology that pins down the viewer, shuts down thought, and demands total emotional submission. Lu Chuan's film seeks to determine an audience's response to an issue of fundamental political importance, and determines it in a way entirely consonant with (at least one of) the current Communist Party line(s), precisely what typical Chinese zhuxuanlu and post-zhuxuanlu films do . . . In true Hollywood fashion, it substitutes spectacle for thought, mythology for history, and ideology for reality.[94]

Kraicer's claim echoes Slavoj Žižek's famous critique of ideology and the kind of political fantasy and constructiveness in a postmodern, neoliberal world. In a 2006 documentary *The Pervert's Guide to Cinema*, Žižek pronounces: "In order to understand today's world, we need cinema, literally. It's only in cinema that we get that crucial dimension which we are not ready to confront in our reality. If you are looking for what is in reality more real than reality itself, look into the cinematic fiction."

Inasmuch as cinema renders and covers the fiction of reality deceivingly with ideological and technological mastery, in the context of China, Leitmotif has become a quintessential fixture in contemporary fiction, reality, politics, arts, and popular culture. In a peculiarly transnational way, it revisits and replicates history and the past, domesticates them, and keeps them at a safe distance by means of popular mass culture consumption. In an effort to assuage the anxiety of warfare and subdue conflicts, it reinforces the established order of peace in reality. The heaviness of history, war, and national wounds has been replaced by the lightness of popular shows and mass entertainment. The China-scape at Tiananmen is suffused with a national anthem of Leitmotif that crystallizes the very alliance and interpenetration between state governmentality, market force, and personality.

One is left to wonder how much (free) room is left for subjectivity in this postsocialist velvet prison, or, in Žižek's term, in the wholeness of "ideological jouissance." As Žižek has elaborated, jouissance is not merely a Lacanian definition of phallic enjoyment vis-à-vis an immanent drive to go beyond the pleasure principle, but—like ideology—it serves as a screen which conceals an "inconsistency," a "void," and "serve[s] only its own purpose, that it does not serve anything."[95] He writes: "an ideology implies, manipulates, produces a pre-ideological enjoyment structured in fantasy."[96] The Chinese state-ordained mainstream productions discussed in this chapter embody precisely the jouissance of ideology achieved through the fantastic mechanisms of imaginary, blockbuster, and even artistic creavity. My investigation in chapter six continues these discussions and suggests that, as Žižek states above, "in order to understand today's world, we need cinema," and perhaps more than cinema. Cinema at the personal, grassroots level and its permutations into new, varied genres, forms, localities, audiovisual aesthetics, and media platforms in early twenty-first-century China present Žižek's ideas of fiction-reality and of jouissance at their best—the distinctive features of hip hop and Grass Mud Horse to be examined in the next chapter.

CHAPTER SIX

"Hip Hop Is My Knife, Rap Is My Sword": Hip Hop Network and the Changing Landscape of Image and Sound Making

> Let me rap, I will lead you to fight . . .
> Let me rap, do you fear to play with us?
> — **MC Hotdog,** "Let Me Rap" (2001)[1]

On the night of July 15, 2006, during his live unplugged concert in Beijing, China's foremost rock artist, Cui Jian made an opening remark prior to the performance of one of his rock anthems, "Like a Knife": "Twenty years ago, we said that while Western rock was analogous to the overwhelming flood, Chinese rock of the time can be described as a knife. Although what we faced then was a harder soil, the power and energy growing out of us was like a knife that pierced into this land so firmly." In this statement made on the twentieth anniversary of his—and China's—first rock song ("Nothing to My Name"), what is stressed is again the political and semiotic function of rock as a form of resistance against the totalitarian Chinese regime in particular and the authorities in general (as also conveyed in his songs)—a sentiment that defines Cui Jian and the rock 'n' roll generation. What is often overlooked is, however, the unique style of "Like a Knife" as one of the first works in China to appropriate and fuse a range of Western musical genres—among them, jazz, reggae, and rap—into this highly regarded rock 'n' roll classic.

In fact, Cui Jian is not only one of the first and paramount artists associated with the golden age of Chinese rock, but he also introduced a significant amount of experimentation and mixing of diverse musical elements in his musical palette. He utilized elements of rap as early as 1985, in "It Is Not That I Don't Understand" (*Bushi wo bu mingbai*). Cui Jian's keen interest in rap is evident in his early creations ("It Is Not That I Don't Understand" in *Rock 'n' Roll on the Long March*, 1989; "Like a Knife" in *Solution*, 1991; "Fly Away," "Beijing Story," and "Box" in *Balls Under the Red Flag*, 1994; "Buffer" and "Slackers" in *The Power of the Powerless*, 1998), and he has continued to develop conspicuously this interest in his later releases ("Country Surrounding the City," "Blue Bone," "Small Town Story v21," "Network Virgin," and "Exceeding That Day" in *Show You Color*, 2005). The performer's intrepid exploration and persevering innovation, nonetheless, provoked considerable ire from Chinese critics who came to ridicule these rap works as "powerless" and as "being merely derivative like a kind of conventional, platitudinous narration or reciting (*shuobai*)."[2]

At the beginning of the twenty-first century, a young college student and music aficionado, the self-proclaimed MC Hotdog, released his first eponymous EP album, which announced the arrival of "authentic" rap on Chinese soil. In "Let Me Rap" (*Rang wo rap*), one of the leading songs that marks his groundbreaking debut, MC Hotdog used this Western musical form to express a new dynamic of revolution and change in Chinese culture and the musical world by likening hip hop to a knife and rap to a sword:

> Hip hop is my knife
> Rap is my sword
> I rely on the strength of underground culture and act crazy everywhere ...
> I am going to eradicate the roots of social diseases ...

This song was recorded in three different versions on the same album, varying from an original "uncensored" performance to a "purified" track more suitable for public broadcasting to a subsidiary karaoke accompaniment. By telling a story about the disillusions, frustrations, and aspirations of a new generation of Chinese youth, the music in the three manifestations captures the bourgeoning youth culture and hip hop craze in China at the turn of the millennium. It also best illustrates the plural, fluid, and ambivalent characteristics of hip hop and rap—whether as an empowering, counter-hegemonic force for young rebels, or as an exploitative voice in close alignment with state control and media monopoly, or as a cultural commodity and entertaining product for fast consumption by the masses.

The academic study of hip hop, like hip hop itself, has been a subject of contention since its early days. Debates have mainly revolved around the following core issues: racial politics (hip hop in association with the black experience and the history of the civil rights movement and power struggle); forces of commercialization (hip hop has always been rife with materialism and hedonism in its compositions, expressions, and methods of diffusion);

spatial parameters (hip hop in relation to postmodern urban space and the simultaneous process of globalization and localization), and language determinants (a key component and important medium through which hip hop performances, practices, and ideologies are constructed and circulated). All of these factors converge in assessing the fundamental concerns of its authenticity and authorship—i.e., "how to keep it real" and "who creates it."

Tricia Rose, who wrote one of the earliest academic studies of hip hop in 1994, defined the culture as distinctly a "black noise" which was deeply ingrained within African American cultural codes, traditions, and sociohistorical constructions. The first generation of hip hop scholars shared a commonplace Afrocentric perspective in their early conceptions of hip hop.[3] However, this essentialist notion that invariably tied hip hop to African American conditions has since been challenged by many cultural critics and sociologists. With the rapid growth and global reach of hip hop, it is no longer considered merely "black noise" bracketed within African American histories and musical traditions. Scholars have begun to examine hip hop's expanding global influence and the network of national and regional interactions in which it is significantly entangled.[4] Global Hip Hop Studies rises as a new field, largely shaped by the edited volumes *Global Noise: Rap and Hip-Hop Outside the USA* (2001) and *Global Linguistic Flows: Hip Hop Cultures, Youth Identities, and Politics of Language* (2009), among others. Foregrounding the global-local interplay in hip hop's evolution, both of these works examine the trajectories and reconfigurations of hip hop beyond its origins, and across different national and geopolitical boundaries, in culturally and linguistically diverse places such as Italy, Germany, France, New Zealand, Korea, and Japan.[5] The widespread global hip hop movement is galvanized not only by an accelerated cultural and linguistic exchange in which vigorous forms of appropriation and hybridization occur between the West and the East, and the North and the South, but it also points to the many ambiguities and contradictions in the discourses of globalization, nationalization, and indigenization.

In the wake of Global Hip Hop Studies, research on Chinese hip hop culture has been undertaken, but it remains an under-explored field despite its enormous popularity and pervasive influence throughout China. The literature that does exist on Chinese hip hop tends to treat it as primarily a trendy, Western-originated cultural fad, giving a journalistic appraisal and a superficial gloss to events and performers such as the annual rap battle of Iron Mic in Shanghai; LMF, the first hip hop group in Hong Kong with a distinct invocation of Cantonese verbal art, "*fo*" (meaning "fire" or "rage" in Cantonese); TNT, a homegrown Chinese pop-rap group modeled after the popular dance-and-sing group HOT from South Korea.[6] While it may be true that hip hop in

China, particularly in its initial stage, often mimicked its American progenitor, or even Japanese and Korean predecessors, this discursive mapping of Chinese modality is far from rigorous and rather tendentious. Their visions are mainly fixed upon mainstream circuits, and writers such as Jeroen de Kloet and Anthony Fung dismiss Chinese hip hop as mostly a monolithic entity that attempts to "synchronize with the West"[7] while at the same time appearing "compromising, and non-confrontational to the state."[8] Meanwhile, Jin Liu's sociolinguist investigation of Chinese local-language rap music and alternative youth culture is another important addition to the field because it shifts emphasis from topics of the Westernization and authentication of Chinese hip hop to a more nuanced understanding of its local communities and protean nature as a plural and independent noise.[9]

In view of hip hop's substantial role in contemporary Chinese music landscape and cultural life, and the general paucity of thorough research thereof, I take a cultural-historical and cross-disciplinary approach to examine different aspects of hip hop music, cinema, and culture in contemporary China. When speaking of China or Chineseness, a clarification is needed here. While hip hop has been widely circulated throughout Greater China and the increasing globalization and permeability between mainland China, Hong Kong, and Taiwan have created specific types of interactions and integrations in hip hop culture, it is not the goal of this chapter to present a comprehensive picture of hip hop culture in all the three localities or to delineate the convergences and divergences between them. Given the complexity of the topic and the constraints of the space, I choose to focus my discussion mainly on hip hop on the mainland, with particular attention to its visual and musical interplay and interdependence, its formation and reconfiguration in relation to consumer culture, influences from America and other regions of Greater China, and social-cultural implications under the new age of digital reproduction.

MC Hotdog and Guerrilla Warfare

The opening account of MC Hotdog and his albums discursively touches upon a constellation of concerns and paradoxes that lie at the core of Chinese hip hop: marginal vs. mainstream, experimental vs. commercial, free vs. copyrighted, originality vs. appropriation, East vs. West, global vs. local, and guerrilla vs. orthodox. Highly acclaimed as the "godfather of Chinese rap" (*zhongwen raoshe jiaohu*) by his ardent admirers and fans, MC Hotdog's "free" hip hop songs were so widely circulated online and on campuses that they became fashionable across Taiwan, Hong Kong, and the mainland in the early 2000s. MC Hotdog was engaged in the entire process of music creation from composing, writing lyrics, performing live, recording demos, and even participating in publicity and distribution, but he did so outside of mainstream commercial channels at first. His homemade music was often uploaded to websites that provided easy access for amateurs and audiophiles to download songs, express opinions, and freely exchange ideas about music and other topics online. His handcrafted CDs from a one-man workshop then entered the black market. Following their quick sales, a great number of illegal and semi-legal bootleg versions quickly materialized.[10]

It was not until January 2001 (almost two years after his music was initially posted online) that he owned his first copyrighted album, *MC Hotdog*, through the Magic Stone Music Company (*moyan*). Within the same year he had four albums consecutively and exclusively released under his name: *MC Hotdog* (EP, January 2001), *Dog* (*Quan*, EP, April 2001), *MC Hotdog* (*Ha gou bang*, June 2001), and *Bottom of the Ninth* (*Jiu ju xia ban*, EP+VCD, October 2001), which sold more than 300,000 copies that year. This strikingly quantitative and qualitative music-making within such a short span of time not only elevated MC Hotdog to center stage, but also successfully introduced hip hop culture and rap music to the Chinese public. Of course, this did not happen overnight. MC Hotdog's persistent musical experiments, charismatic persona, and substantial youth following established at Web 2.0 helped spawn a string of hit albums.

Hailed as one of the greatest "blockbusters" (*juzuo*) from Magic Stone in the decade, MC Hotdog's rap became the bestseller that was no longer "free." During press releases, however, the record company constantly stressed MC Hotdog's "freedom" as the key to distinguishing his hip hop from other kinds of popular, overtly commercial—and thus uncreative—music. At a time when the Chinese music market and soundscape were flooded by Canto-pop from Hong Kong and Mandarin-pop of Taiwan (often grouped under the label of Gangtai pop altogether), MC Hotdog was marketed as a contrary artist-guerrilla who drew from the diasporic voice of African Americans at the margin of Western cosmopolitan centers to subvert the hegemony and hierarchy of the Chinese mainstream media and the popular culture circle. This neatly corresponded to the principal agendas of his production company, Magic Stone, arguably the earliest major Chinese music company with an independent hallmark.

Running from 1992 to 2001 under the loose control of its parent company, Rock Records (*gunshi*), Magic Stone, more than other record companies, was captivated by the surge of Chinese youth subculture and alternative music that reached a peak on the threshold of the twenty-first century. An avid supporter of experimental music, Magic Stone was lauded for its active role in

MC Hotdog's first eponymous album, produced by Magic Stone, 2001.

promoting Chinese rock artists such as Dou Wei, Zhang Chu, and He Yong, who were dubbed "The Three Heroes of Magic Stone" (*moyan sanjie*). Magic Stone's nonconformist propensity is also reflected in its name; by adopting the character of *mo* (meaning "magic," "devilish," or "heretic" in Chinese), it built a new musical identity charged with authenticity, diversity, dynamism, and freedom. Although the connotations of *mo* in Chinese are still largely pejorative, the primary founder of Magic Stone, Zhang Peiren, justified their unconventional acts and traced their creative spirit back to the roots of Chinese martial arts fictions whose legendary swordsmen and heroes are largely social outcasts, rebels, and exiles. A real musician, in Zhang's viewpoint, is a maverick in the vein of *mo*, that is, a daredevil spirit with a genuine mania for music and a longing for novelty and self-expression.[11] Magic Stone's avowal of *mo* would concur with Alfred Jarry's famous declaration that "it is conventional to call 'monster' any blending of dissonant elements . . . I call 'monster' every original, inexhaustible beauty."[12] Inexhaustible originality, said Zhang Piren, was then the path to "stripping off showiness, keeping it real (*qu wei cun zhen*),"[13] which, unsurprisingly, echoes MC Hotdog's monumental outcry to "rely on the strength of underground culture and act crazy everywhere" in "Let Me Rap."

In addition to the peculiarly *mo*-ish means of narrative, musical style, production, and distribution, MC Hotdog's hip hop campaign or warfare contains another challenge. He also celebrates defiance in his name. Many of his songs deploy a dialogic narrative, rather than a conventional linear perspective, where he frequently addresses his audience as if giving a live stage performance in which he refers to himself as *Laofuzi* (literally meaning "Old Master"). This notorious title instantly recalls the comic character *Laofuzi* (Old Master Q), who became a household name through the widespread circulation of the eponymous cartoon. A popular Chinese comic strip created by Alfonso Wang, it first appeared in Hong Kong newspapers and magazines in the mid-1960s and has been enormously popular in the Chinese world. As one of the longest-running cartoon series, which is still in print, it features Old Master Q in various geopolitical contexts and fluctuating scenarios that conspicuously serve as social commentaries and metaphors. The comic book inspired dozens of animated works, TV series, and films. Although MC Hotdog did not explicitly express an indebtedness to this popular character, his music is imbued with a similarly sarcastic, cynical tone and a good sense of black humor. Even his carefully cultivated appearance seems to mimic this fictional archetype: bald, overly skinny with strikingly long limbs and characteristic moustache, and perpetually dressed in a black suit with a black bowler hat and a pair of kung fu shoes.

If his nickname *Laofuzi* reminds us of MC Hotdog's Chinese origin in a way that at once evokes and challenges the deeply entrenched Confucian (which has a kindred name *Kongfuzi* in Chinese) hierarchy and social mores, then his other self-appointed name MC Hotdog is apparently another counter-gesture commenting on and contesting American popular culture, Western imperialism, and the sweeping imperatives of globalization. MC refers to his agency as a hip hop artist while hotdog points to the American-specific fast food that can be further extended as a metaphor of capitalist cultural trash. Moreover, hotdog's phallocentric symbolism corresponds to hip hop's chauvinist gendered view at large. All of these practices and appropriations have their corollary in guerrilla, an unexpected, improvised assault on the syntax of reality. To borrow Hebdige's terminology, MC Hotdog's rap music can be thus construed as an act of "semiotic guerrilla warfare" arrayed against parents and common sense.[14]

MC Hotdog is mainly a Taiwan-based artist, but he has become a figure of intertextual references and a polysemic icon in the imaginative construction of hip hop identity throughout Greater China, which is the case for other artists such as Jay Chou and David Tao (whom I will discuss shortly). In his hands, hip hop and rap become not merely a "knife" but a double-edged "sword"—a prism through which wide-ranging forces and ideologies are reflected. On the one side, hip hop is closely associated with the hegemony of leisure, fashion, and consumer culture shaped and exploited by a large network of mass media, ranging from the print industry, the music industry, radio, television to film. On the other side, a group of cinephiles, audiophiles, amateurs, and hackers have geared their work toward an alternative and subversive ideology that favors the local, the polyvocal, and the individual. These processes have opened up a space for indigenous and diversified Chinese voices, vernacular rap, and the proliferation of hip hop networks and cyber-activism in the wake of the digital revolution and new social media.

Innovation/Appropriation: Creating and Mediating Hip Hop in Everyday China

Unlike its Western predecessors, Chinese hip hop did not start out as an underground phenomenon. Rather, its embryonic development was in many ways a story of embracing American fads through the various channels of commercial enterprises, music stations, television publicity, and even the state apparatuses. Hip hop in China did not become a fully fledged movement until the dawn of the new millennium. But its roots can be traced back to the mid-to-late 1980s, when hip hop was first introduced to Chinese audiences as a Western style of dance through the imports of American television shows and some early hip hop pictures such as *Wild Style* (dir. Charlie Ahearn, 1983) and *Breakin'* (dir. Joel Silberg, 1984). It also capitalized on the momentum and sensational impact that Michael Jackson brought to China, when he, along with his iconic dance moves such as the robot and moonwalk, was imported as the first pop idol from the West to post-revolutionary China. Accordingly, Jackson's signature dance was named *pili wu* (Thunderbolt Dance) in Chinese, symbolizing a new way of moving. It was perceived as freestyle both in terms of body movement and ideology, standing in stark contrast to classical ballet and folk dance, the two officially sanctioned genres during Mao's era, which had become highly incompatible in the new epoch.

Tian Zhuangzhuang's *Rock Kids* (*Yaogun qingnian*), released in 1988, is one of the first films to address the subversive zeitgeist that early hip hop has provoked in reformist China. The film features Long Xiang, a young dancer in Beijing, who is discontented with his routine work as a traditional dancer in a state-run troupe and turns to hip hop dance for artistic freedom and personal inspiration. Long Xiang becomes obsessed with breakdance and decides to pursue a freelance life; in the process, he gives up steady employment (*tie fanwan*, literally meaning "iron rice bowl" in Chinese) and loses his girlfriend, Yuanyuan. The message *Rock Kids* aims to deliver is quite simple. In Tian Zhuangzhuang's own words, it is "a story about how young people [should learn to] live a light, relaxing and happy life; the film encourages them to pursue what they long for and dream after."[15] It is likely that the pursuits of youth, freedom, personal dreams, and individuality impel the filmmaker to advertise

A Thunderbolt dance craze took over China in the late 1980s after the screening of Breakin'. Source: "The Images of 1980s China," http://aohanshanwanziyuye.blog.163.com/blog/static /131330883201531910215227/?suggestedreading&wumii.

and associate *Rock Kids* with the late 1980s rock craze—as is obvious in its title—notwithstanding the actual focus on breakdance in the film.

Tian Zhuangzhuang had previously been an eccentric filmmaker, notorious for his arcane, polemic arthouse cinema, and was thus faced with the contradictions of grinding out a box-office winner at this moment. He openly admitted that "I still had to make a living and I didn't want to stray too far from cinema, so finally I decided I might as well work for whoever wanted to hire me—after all, I couldn't make my own films anyway. So my next four films . . . were all works commissioned by others: I came in only after there was a screenplay and funding."[16] It turns out that *Rock Kids* was a popular but artistically compromised piece; nonetheless, it shed crucial light on the raw reality of the early hip hop scene. Acclaimed as a representative of the best Chinese song-and-dance pictures (*gewu pian*), *Rock Kids* is noted for its refined choreography and throbbing music track, nuanced depiction of youthful desires and anxieties, and honest portrayal of the contradictions of a bourgeoning urban youth culture at the juncture of the postsocialist sea change. All of these are viewed through the vibrant angle of breakdance.

Rock Kids begins with a dreamlike sequence that showcases a flock of young kids doing spins, dives, and other characteristic breakdance moves. Exquisitely crafted through a combination of wide shots and close-ups, this scene is reminiscent of *Breakin'*, the American hip hop film that quickly took hold of youngsters and created a dance-cultural fever after landing in Chinese theaters in 1987.[17] After the opening scene becomes fully lit, the dance hall is revealed, however, to be the square in front of the Noon Gate of the Forbidden City in Beijing, an instantly recognizable public space and a national icon attached to Chinese history and traditional cultural values. The peculiar juxtaposition and contrast between hip hop dance and the Forbidden City is neither an accident nor a coincidence. During the course of the film, Long Xiang, in an illusionary montage (standing in stark contrast to the realistic scenes in other parts of the film), returns to the square from time to time and inaugurates a spontaneous, pre-marital sexual relationship with Xiaoxiao, an act still deemed a social taboo in 1980s China. Xiaoxiao is presented as a B-girl who shares Long Xiang's rebellious, carefree attitude and cheerful spirit.

The square's signification as an epitome of tradition and its modern reconfiguration for citizens' contemporaneous, everyday use reflect the dialectical logic fundamental to the new urban culture and hip hop in reformist China. The negotiations and politics of spatial-temporalities are also manifested and foregrounded by another set of visual representations. In *Rock Kids*, Long Xiang is enmeshed and deeply embroiled within complex social and political networks, such as state restriction, social responsibility, family bonding, and sexual relationships. The *mise-en-scène* conspicuously presents him in various frames of entrapment. The noirish composition of the depressing urban space, with its emphasis on the compressed apartment and enclosed living quarters, and the constant placement of Long Xiang against a wire cage and within the elevator, are all suggestive of his current captivity and longing for breaking away. Hence, breakdance symbolically becomes a life jacket, which saves him from this despondent, drowning circumstance and sets him free physically, artistically, sexually, and socially.

Through a distinctive point of view of hip hop dance, *Rock Kids* portrays the first generation of breakdancers, freelancers, or entrepreneurs (*getihu*) who "smash the iron rice bowl" (*dapo tie fanwan*) and "plunge into the business ocean" (*xiahai*), when Chinese society takes a critical turn from socialist centralization to a free market economy. An intertextual link is built between Long Xiang and Tao Jin, who plays the film role and was in fact one of the best-known modern dancers in 1980s China, dubbed "The King of Thunderbolt Dance." A substantial parallel is also drawn between Long Xiang, Tao Jin, and Cui Jian, who at the age of twenty-five left his post at the Beijing Symphony Orchestra to seek his dream of individual freedom and artistic autonomy through rock 'n' roll, as I explored in chapter three. In *Rock

"Hip Hop Is My Knife, Rap Is My Sword"

Film poster for *Rock Kids* (1988).

Kids, at the diegetic level, the relationship between Long Xiang and Da Lu, a B-boy and motorcycle performer who works in a circus troupe, is a recurrent theme that parallels and interweaves with his sexual and professional involvement with Yuanyuan, the lead dancer of the state troupe. All of these images and narrative threads revolve around a central paradox that comes to a head at this particular juncture—should he/they quit the state-secured job to pursue a new way of living? Apparently, the effervescent hip hop scene—in association with fast-paced, dynamic music, strong beats, and animated dance moves—signifies an exciting alternative to the rusty, dilapidated life of the "iron rice bowl" and a new outlet. At once a dance move, an urban youth culture, and a new lifestyle full of vigor and vitality, hip hop embodied a progressive, evolving force that reflected and heralded a surge of social mobility, a buttressing of consumer culture, and the broader social transformations of *fin-de-siecle* China.

It should be pointed out that dance is essential to understanding the history and formation of Chinese hip hop, although its role has been generally understated and neglected by critics who have music-centric biases. In the context of Chinese hip hop culture, however, it was dance and a fad of physical movement that arrived first and was then absorbed by contemporary youth cultures and further transformed. After the breakdance craze subsided in the early 1990s following the Tiananmen incident, hip hop was reshuffled and repackaged with more dimensions when it made a wider and more powerful resurgence in the late 1990s. Starting again with breakdance, hip hop created a cultural fever that captivated Chinese youth. In the popular market, hip hop journals, magazines, and videos proliferated. Most of them were pedagogy-oriented and pragmatic, with a concentration on teaching the fashion-eager young people how to perform dance moves such as popping, blocking, moonwalk, gliding, and spinning in the same manner as heard or seen in Western films. Hip hop knowledge became an important avenue for learning and adopting the Western styles and cultures that dominated the recording industry, television, and other entertainment sectors. A similar pattern flooded the airwaves when Chinese performers were seen singing and dancing in oversized jeans, baseball caps, and dreadlocks, which became a visual—much more than a musical—spectacle through their Western-simulated physical appearance and dance moves. According to a report by Elizabeth Rosenthal in the *New York Times* (2001), ten Chinese performers who defeated others in a dancing contest were selected by Korean investors and sent to Seoul to train as potential hip hop singers.[18] A 2004 report from CNN is also worth quoting:

> BEIJING, China (CNN)—In a rented hall in Beijing, a group of teenagers are taking turns to display their dance moves. Some are doing handstands along to those familiar western hip-hop beats. The music, and the gravity defying moves are also defying Chinese conventions. China's Generation-Y is seeking self-fulfillment and finding it in of all things, hip-hop.[19]

Although they were of limited scope and depth, these initial reports remain valuable as they provide historical insights into how hip hop was conceived and constructed in its nascent period, especially with regard to its symbiotic relationship with the systems of commerce and urban consumer culture.

From this perspective, it makes sense that when hip hop was introduced to China, it was first translated as *jiewu*, meaning "street dance." *Jie* (street), in Chinese, has a different connotation than it does in the US, which directly points to hip hop's roots in the impoverished ghetto. By contrast, *jie* in Chinese signifies an advanced, modernized, and Western lifestyle, whereas a vast majority of the rural areas are postulated as the other opposite—underdeveloped, disavantaged, and local. When hip hop took root in the mid-1990s, the terms "street dance" and "hip hop" were used interchangeably, with other elements largely downplayed and overshadowed by the prevailing impact of breakdance. However, as hip hop gradually evolved, the transliteration *xiha* became a new, substitute term for practitioners and journalists who had the goal of encompassing a larger scope of hip hop, including breakdancing (performance), rap (musical expression), DJ (social activity), and graffiti (visual arts). The deliberate use of the two onomatopoetic words *xi* and *ha* (both of which mean "happy" in Chinese) added to the rhythm of the name and endowed a lighthearted, entertaining tone to hip hop. However, it failed to invoke the resistant and oppositional consitituents essential to the American original and Chinese hip hop alike.

A passage conspicuously inscribed on the cover of *Hip Hop: Follow Me*, among the best-selling series of Chinese hip hop videos, illustrates the rationale:

> Hip hop dancing, if appearing on the party, is definitely a fashion, as well as a symbol of happiness. You don't need to think of the complaints that you have heard; you also don't need to know what these blacks have experienced; and you even don't need to know what it is. The only thing you need to do is just enjoy the relaxation and happiness that this culture has brought, because this is the hip hop in our concept.[20]

Tactically employing various marketing and advertising vocabularies, this provocative statement shows how hip hop, the formerly subcultural phenomenon, like other popular cultural products, can be eased up, remolded, and made into a fast-selling commodity with a totally *xiha* (joyful) attitude. In China, hip hop started as a trendsetter and grew rapidly, along with an increasingly exuberant mass culture and urban consumerism. Almost synonymous with fashion and pleasure, hip hop was first imported and promoted by Chinese mass media as the hippest dance, the most fun background music, and the coolest attitude for the young generation. With the slogan of "the way to learn hip hop is with your body, not your head," the mainstream media served a conventionally propagandist function by educating their audience to dress like breakdancers, to talk like a member of the hip hop generation, and develop a new hip hop personality by acquiring a range of modern goods. In this regard, hip hop became a model of the new hegemonic material culture or what Geremie R. Barme has called "Adcult PRC,"[21] where a form of corporate advertising forged through the intertwining of official agitprop and popular mass culture offers a "materialist" liberation in postrevolutionary China.

Jay Chou, a famous hip hop singer from Taiwan and Asia's hottest pop star, lends his name and music to numerous TV commercials, including China Mobile, Panasonic Electronics, Toyota, Coca-Cola, Pepsi, Youlemei milk tea, Tongyi instant noodle, Deerway sports apparel, and Sparking eye drops. His endorsements cover nearly a full range of product lines in everyday life, targeting Chou's diverse fanbase and Chinese youth in general. In order to minutely align the various merchandise with Chou's musical and public personae, the singer has been presented as the boy next door or a spokesperson for Chinese youth. He is relaxed, wholesome, sporty, fashion-sensitive, techno-savvy, open-minded to different music and cultures, and a wireless/internet fancier.

Chou's omnipresence in television advertising provides an excellent angle from which to examine the influence of hip hop on Chinese youth. His first highly publicized appearance on the CCTV New Year Gala of 2004, a sellout that year, reaffirms hip hop's significant role in Chinese cultural life. As the biggest and most-watched annual arts and performance event organized by the Chinese state, the basics of the gala have remained largely consistent with an emphasis on the promotion of traditional arts such as Chinese opera, traditional comedy, folk music, and dance. In response to a rapid decline in ratings, however, Jay Chou and his hip hop music were elevated to center stage with the intention of drawing Chinese youth back to the show—a move once deemed inappropriate for such a grand and formal occasion with billions of viewers. A more audacious approach was adopted by the party, with rap music incorporated into a reformulation of the revolutionary canon. In an attempt to revitalize revolutionary mythology under the new market economy, *Chairman Mao's Quotes* (*Mao Zedong yulu*) were overdubbed with hip hop music. Pop music versions of "The East is Red" (*Dongfang hong*) and "Serve the People" (*Wei renmin fuwu*) were also released in honor of the 110th anniversary of Mao's birth.[22]

More than simply a dance move or a musical style, hop hop in China evolved with the blooming urban youth culture and cosmopolitan subjectivity. It has become a vivacious avenue for creating, redefining, and reviving individuality and personal identities in the new postsocialist, transnational milieu. In a country where a majority of the Chinese population does not speak or use English, not to mention their slim knowledge of the cultural and historical backgrounds of hip hop culture, how does Chinese youth relate their own situation to that of African Americans? How does a Western cultural phenomenon resonate in a Chinese context? Why and how has hip hop captured the interest and buying power of so many people? The above instances of Jay Chou and the state's appropriation of rap music illustrate how hip hop has become integrated into the mainstream postsocialist mass culture, in conjunction with China's booming market economy and consumerism.

On the surface, having promised viewers and listeners an ecstasy of youthfulness, creativity, and a transnational cosmopolitan identity, what lies at the heart of the hip hop scenario is how this hypothetical "individualist" spirit has been translated into a set of identifiable merchandise. In a sense, the study of the trajectory of Chinese hip hop should begin from an anatomy of its incipient appropriation and programming into the marketplace, where the expression of the individual and so-called "consumer empowerment" needs

Jay Chou as a spokesperson for Sprite in the Chinese market.

to be extrapolated and reappraised. Wu Yi, a college student and part-time DJ, noted in an interview that "most of the rap I can't understand, but I have friends who tell me what the lyrics mean. The words become very personal to me."²³ What does "personal" mean here and how does it matter? Considering the language barriers that play an important part in this cultural encounter, how is hip hop justified and how can it be used to accommodate the desires and anxieties of the China self as opposed to the Western other? In this regard, is hip hop a classic Marxist case of the "fetishsized" object?²⁴ Or, is it a prototype of the "standardized" and "pseudo-individualist" practice of mass culture, as Adorno puts it?²⁵ Or, is there something more?

Sinicized/Synthesized: Chinese Hip Hop Linguistics, Codeswitching, and Mobile Identity

Commercial, standardized hip hop has become a front where a variety of ideological, geographical, and linguistic forces converge and what I call a "state-market-transcultural" synergy (a concept I framed in chapter five) is contentiously anchored. Another intriguing yet perplexing aspect of Chinese hip hop is rap. It represents an extension of a specific African American cultural tradition but, importantly, it also supplements and poses challenges to the premise of West-to-East cultural flow and the prevailing discourses of globalization and indigenization. In China, rap was initially consumed and circulated as a Western fashion to accompany dance. With the introduction of hip hop as a specific dance form, much of the rap scene was, in the first place, encountered as background music for clubbing and dance music albums. This is also due to the fact that Chinese rap, in a rigorous sense, only flourished in urban centers and was seldom identified with the lifestyle of the larger Chinese rural populations. It also implies that Chinese rap, to some extent, was heavily influenced by its neighbors of Japan and South Korea, who had earlier connections with American popular culture and adopted fast tempos and sharp rhythms for dance music. In its early phase, Chinese rap was a crude mingling of two different kinds of music. The lead vocal consisted of Chinese music and vernacular in a pop melody, while the accompaniment was often an amalgam of lyrics and rhythms that were typical of American rap music.

Strictly speaking, rap was not formed as an independent music category in China until much later. Language is the primary obstacle that makes it difficult to use Mandarin Chinese to produce a rap song. Compared to English, Mandarin Chinese is a tonal and monosyllabic language, making it awkward to create a striking rhythm. The intrinsic intonation and variations of pitch in English contribute a great deal to the rhythm of rap. By contrast, each syllable in Mandarin Chinese in a word receives the same amount of stress. Further, Mandarin Chinese is a language without final stops (e.g., the plosives /t/, /d/, /k/), which increases the difficulties of producing a catchy rhythm in the word stream. Different from other musical styles that largely rely on melodies, rap's uniqueness mostly lies in the peculiar style of verbal delivery. For a language such as Mandarin Chinese, whose natural sense of rhythm is fairly weak, rappers have to add artificial stress and staccatos to their performance in order to create specific punctuations. Hence, linguistic limitations often lead to awkward rhythms with a staccato flow in rap songs in Mandarin. Consequently, many singers seemed to have little confidence in executing an entire song in a rap style. They usually only rapped during the chorus while singing the main verses in a pop style. Even within the exiguous rap repertoire, English rather than Mandarin Chinese was likely to be the prioritized verbal tool.

Mandarin rap became a hybrid, highly ambivalent form plagued by problematics and difficulties since its adoption into the global rap lexicon. In spite of these sociolinguistic ramifications and technical complications, however, Mandarin rap had exerted significant aesthetic and sociocultural impact on the Chinese soundscape by the turn of the new millennium. In "To be different" (*Bu yiyang*, 1999),[26] David Tao, an eminent Taiwanese singer-songwriter who is notable for his music versatility and synthetic style, explicitly expresses the hip hop agenda as he and many Chinese youth have conceived:

> From the childhood I learned in history class that men are different . . .
> You need to liberate your mind
> To create a new life
> To be different

Although this song still fails to deliver a smooth and appealing hip hop rhythm, and the bizarre but innovative mixture of different musical elements may not qualify it as a rap song by some standards, it was passionately embraced by a large, appreciative audience who regarded it as a manifesto not only for hip hop devotees but also for the broader millennial generation. What is remarkable in this particular work is the seemingly sporadic, loose lineup of a vast array of names and categories—from countries to food to fashion to popular characters. In doing so, Tao reified and turned sampling—a core technique in rap practice—into a sampler that blends everything, especially everyday trivia, into a musical text. This neatly corresponds to his musical style and aesthetic philosophy, in which he publicly identified himself as a music liberalist and synthesis.[27] David Tao has often been lauded for his signature novelty act that fuses a wide variety of music genres and traditions, including Chinese opera, folk music, blues, R & B, rap, and rock. As an immigrant who was mostly raised and educated in the US, Tao linked this music syncretism to his ambiguous national and cultural identity. In press interviews, Tao repeatedly referred to his experience in Los Angeles, where he was exposed to and bonded with many African American musicians. The black music tradition and postmodern narrative and technology register even though they are recontextualized and reconfigured in his hybrid works that defy simple generic categorization.

This eclectic gesture earned Tao bountiful laurels of Best Singer, Best Artist, and so on, being acclaimed as "an all-around musical talent" (*yinyue quancai*) and "the most internationalized musician" (*zui guojihua yiren*).[28] Hip hop becomes formally and symbolically a nexus not only for addressing and connecting varieties, but also for marking differences. On the one hand, the song contradictorily celebrates and laments globalization and cultural homogeneity that bring transnational capital, modern goods, and a specific cosmopolitan subjectivity to China. On the other, cultural heterogeneity distinguishes and underscores the production of Chineseness and individuality in the globalization context, as encapsulated in the assertion "to be different." But is

David Tao's album *I Am OK* (Taipei: Xiake changpian, 1999).

there truly a difference? How different could Tao's music and Chinese hip hop be? Treading carefully between different ideologies and forms, Tao seemed to be mainly interested in pulling all of these sound fragments together to make a postmodern aural collage. His rap music elucidates the various ways in which the local entity appropriates, synthesizes, and internalizes the global. At the outset, it could be easily interpreted as another centrifugal instance attesting to the diffusion of Western music and capitalist consumer culture and the imposition of global upon local. However, these cross-cultural flows and aesthetic negotiations should not be simply viewed as a prototype of closed imitation and mindless mimicry. Rather, rap can serve as a vehicle that evokes alternative desires and identifications as opposed to the hegemonic paradigm of globalization, or rather Americanization.

The prominent role played by foreign singers in the Chinese hip hop scene, as epitomized in the Hidden (*Yincang*), one of the leading rap groups on the mainland, is a peculiar case in point. Unlike David Tao and many other rap singers, such as the members of Hi-Bomb (*Heibang*) and Red Star, who come from a returned Chinese expatriate's standpoint, the Hidden consisted of a cohort of global nomads: a native Beijinger, a Chinese Canadian, and two Americans who had recently relocated from the West to pursue a career in the lucrative Chinese market. Literally and metaphorically, their appearances on and off the stage have become a meeting ground in which a set of dialectics—such as global and local, West and East, tradition and modernity— converge. Their voices, however, did not mingle on equal terms. Each of the members used Mandarin Chinese to rap in a marked Beijing colloquial style. There was hardly a single trace of the West on the soundtrack. Jeremy and another MC from Chicago exhibited almost the same degree of proficiency in Beijing dialect as the other members, despite some subtle foreign inflections that were often masked by a chorus. The band has consistently and self-consciously performed Chineseness through the titles of their songs and names of their singers. By representing themselves as dedicated lovers and experts of Chinese language and culture, the two American "sinologists" adopted Chinese names and actively appeared on intercultural shows—for instance, *Modern English* (*Yanghua lianpian*, a popular program aired on the Beijing television station that, by adopting a sitcom style, succeeded in inaugurating a nationwide craze of English study at the beginning of twenty-first century). In this forum, they positioned themselves as mediators between languages, nations, and cultures. The debut album exhibits a distinct Chinese flavor, as reflected in its title *Serve the People* (*Wei renmin fuwu*, a parody of a notorious communist propaganda slogan) and the actual content of the songs, such as "In Beijing" (*Zai beijing*), "Beijing Beatbox" (*Beijing baozhu*), "S.A.R.S." (*Feidian*), and "Yellow Road" (*Huangpifu de lu*), which employ a range of geopolitical tropes and cultural allusions to speak to their Chinese awareness and experience.

This muted, sinicized foreignness on the soundtrack strikes an interesting contrast with their visible foreignness, which has been blatantly exploited on the airwaves and in their promotional campaigns. One of the posters introduced them and their first album *Serve the People* as a groundbreaking masterpiece created by "the allied forces of three nations" (*sanguo lianhe budui*). While this labeling may to some degree invoke the derogatory connotations of "the allied forces of eight powers" (*baguo lianjun*, the foreign military invasion and colonization of China at the beginning of the twentieth century), the implication of foreigners as the threatening other has been substantially downplayed and significantly changed in the context of their rap music in particular and contemporary Chinese popular culture in general. Playing with these racial and historical stereotypes—and placing themselves at the crossroads of the past and present, East and West, tradition and modern—allowed them to traverse territory the Chinese selves may not easily enter. This in-betweenness was also put to use in creating their discreteness and popularity. The press and large audiences seemed to be drawn by the unusual juxtaposition between their "exotic" faces and their "native" Chinese inflection. In an admiring tone, many journals paid homage to the Hidden's linguistic and cultural fluidity, applauding the moment of "the first released album by foreigners singing in Chinese" (*waiguoren chang zhongwenge, shouci luzhi chuban changpian*).[29] In this way, Chinese advertising and the popular music market not only manage to sell difference and otherness, but in doing so, to sell a new surge of consumer Orientalism at home—a trend exploded in the new millennium with the Asian economic boom and the rise of Asian popular culture.

Border-crossing thus becomes a catchword of the Hidden's reputation. More specifically, the Hidden crosses by means of rap as a music performance, cultural identity, and a way of living. Not only do they transcend national and linguistic boundaries with their language versatility and highly mixed demographics, they also break down and redefine cosmopolitanism by referring to themselves as a "Chinese hip hop band run by international people." Aihwa Ong notes that "the cultural logics of capitalist accumulation, travel, and displacement induce subjects to respond fluidly and opportunistically to changing political-economic conditions."[30] The Hidden is a sonic design of what Ong has called the "flexible citizenship," which is also visually paralleled and enhanced by their recorded migration inside the metropolis of Beijing from skyscrapers of the city center to the historical landmarks of the Forbidden City and the Temple of Heaven, and from the bustling marketplace to the peripheral wasteland. Repeatedly emphasizing Beijing as the place in which they work, and consistently identifying with a cohort of northern drifters (*beipiao*, a specific term referring to people who relocate to Beijing to pursue their artistic dreams and professional gains), the Hidden strategically position themselves at the intersections of global and local, mainstream and margin. As reflected in their name, the Hidden foregrounds their transnational cosmopolitan identity as well as their subversive and oppositional stance, which subtly refers back to the roots of hip hop culture.

While this kind of crossover and hybridity attracts special attention to the band, their visibility and salability depend significantly on the image of masculinity they deliberately construct in their music and with their body language. In the context of Chinese hip hop, representations of masculinity are based on two sources. Firstly, since martial arts and kung-fu have become a trademark and an integral part of Chinese hip hop, adopting these images and cultural emblems give the Hidden and many other Chinese hip hop groups an energetic, virile outloook as well as an indigenous sensibility. For instance, "Kung-fu," performed by CMCB (Chinese MC Brothers), became a huge hit in 2002. It was immediately made into a music video, the first of its kind on the mainland. Secondly, Chinese hip hop groups have adopted a Western look and displayed a fasciination with the West, in particular, the physicality, the open libido, and masculine prowess that African American

The Hidden's debut album, *Serve the People*
(Beijing: Haojiao changpian, 2003).

rappers embody. Blackness thus becomes a spectacle and a fetish, which is closely bound to and reaffirms the construction of selfhood.

China's Generation Y displays an enthusiastic respect for black creativity and empowerment, a move that has replaced the earlier sense of fear and distaste.[31] This black turn is manifested in the tag *hei* (the Chinese word for black) that has been so frequently affixed to the names of Chinese hip hop bands—to list a few: Hi-Bomb (*Hei bang* from Shanghai), Blakk Bubble (Wang Fan from Shanghai), Black Head (*Hei sa* from Xi'an), Feeling Black (*Hei guibang* from Chongqing), Black Pistol (*Hei qiang* from Xinjiang), Black Sound (Lil' Ray from Beijing), and Black Magic (*Hei du* from Hong Kong). By assuming a nominal "blackness" and by associating this token with hip hop symbols such as "pistol," "head," "bomb," "magic," and "sound," this collective group of young music makers express their yearnings for the dynamism and independent spirit that hip hop represents. A postsocialist aspiration to become a global citizen, capable of crossing borders and switching codes fluidly is further facilitated and electrified by the digital revolution and technological advancement in the new century. The cyber-public sphere not only provides such a platform for the formation of "flexible citizenship" or what I call "mobile identity," it also nourishes vernacular rap (*fangyan shuochang*), a grassroots-based, decentralized, pluralistic, democratic-participant medium and cultural phenomenon associated with diverse geographical locations and intonations.

Vernacular Rap, Hip Hop Network, and the Jouissance of the Masses

Technology has played a prominent role in the course of hip hop development, including turntable, mixer, vinyl record, compact disc, digital sampling, as well as the prodigious outpouring and circulation of hip hop music by the young generation in the virtual world. If my previous account maps out the primary constitution of hip hop and its signification as an arena in which many different visions and voices are represented and can express a youth-focused perspective, the infusion of digitalized production and new social media, then, is a major force that has accelerated hip hop's penetration into Chinese youth who now play a double role of audience and practitioner in today's market. Significantly, a large number of Chinese MCs and rap groups have begun to elbow their way onto the music stage via the internet. They find music partners who share the same interests and release their new albums through this virtual platform. For example, a rap group from Shanghai, Pen Peng, signed a contract with ShanghaiNing.com (a music and entertainment website dedicated to advancing Shanghainese culture) to make all their music tracks downloadable from this specific website. In an attempt to utilize contemporary technological resources to the fullest, Pen Peng made several music flashes concurrently with their rap songs, which initiated a new cycle of rap music and digital media collaboration and cross-promotion. This (r)evolution not only reflects and parallels the broad restructuring of media infrastructure and architecture in the new century, but also exhibits an important shift in the politics of Chinese hip hop, from its earlier phase, driven by commercial interests, to a more mature phase with diverse dimensions of multicultural, multilingual participations.

Hip hop's fluid and mutable presence in actual public venues—such as streets, parks, squares, and neighborhoods—parallels its variable trajectories in the cyber-public sphere, including chatrooms, forums, and microblogs (*weibo*). A traveling form of music and culture, it attracts millions of people from different cultural and national backgrounds into one symbolic concept, the Global Hip Hop Nation. This "nation" does not account for national consciousness; on the contrary, it challenges and defies purported national boundaries with its exceptional border-crossing capability. But the creative adoption of the nation trope foregrounds a sense of shared identification and collective activity, which has been intrinsic to hip hop practice since its inception. Moreover, the symbolic nationhood and bonding are more easily realized in an interconnected computer network where individual subjectivities and "imagined communities"[32] find an outlet and ideally converge. The internet thus becomes a new medium of communication for the hip hop generation. For instance, websites such as http://www.city.9sky.com; http://www.fm974.tom.com; http://www.2rapcity.com; http://www.chinese-forums.com; http://www.xici.net; http://www.southernexposure.com; http://www.comefromchina.com; and http://shanghaining.com have specific forums providing open dialogues and dynamic exchanges for hip hop artists and fans.

One of the largest and most influential hip hop channels is the Shanghai-based ZHONG.TV, which hosts hundreds of hip hop videos from Taiwan, Beijing, Chengdu, Shanghai, Changsha, Canton, Nanjing, and other places. It has also deployed China's most popular platform, *weibo* (microblogging, the Chinese equivalent of Twitter), to release new works, share information, and interact with hip hop enthusiasts. Popular hip hop artists—such as MC Hotdog (from Taiwan), AP Manchucker (from Taiwan), Sbazzo (a member of the Hidden from Beijing), Ablaze Crew (from Beijing), Nasty Ray (from Beijing), Tang King (a member of Red Star from Shanghai), Sha Zhou (from Qingdao), Big Zoo (from Chengdu), FatB (from Guangzhou), JR Fog (from Canton), Six-City (from Urumqi), MC Koz (from Xinjiang), Phat Chan, Kit, Lo Jim, and Kevin Jai (members of the now dis-banded LMF from Hong Kong), and GX6 Crew (an international group of rappers from China, Austrialia, and America, akin to the Hidden)—are all keen, active bloggers. The digital revolution advances and ultimately helps forge a real conception of a Hip Hop Nation in China in the new century.

Differing from traditional avenues, the internet has not only become the primary channel for hip hop production and distribution but it has also carved out a vitally new path for multiculturalism, free speech, and polyvocal practices in the postsocialist global milieu. Quick learners and avid devotees of music and new media, these Chinese rap musicians and groups use the internet as a means of subverting the authority of mainstream pop. The adoption of digital technology enables them to produce, operate, and circulate their work in an alternative, autonomous way. Furthermore, this cyberdemocracy has facilitated the proliferation of vernacular rap (*fangyan shuochang*), a diverse and decentralized voice drawn from the local masses and configured in a hip hop fashion.

The incorporation of a variety of local dialects into rap music is not a natural outcome but is overdetermined, in the Marxist sense, by relevant social and political economies. First, the diversification of music through the agency of language and its ramifications enriches and expands the Chinese rap repertoire. It adds new possibilities for producing a more appealing rap rhythm in Chinese local languages. As explained earlier, Mandarin, a standardized national language in mainland China, is inherently ill-suited to produce a characteristic rap rhythm and rhyme, whereas other dialects—such as the Shanghai dialect and a northeastern dialect with final plosives and intonations—are comparably better-suited to a hip hop speech style. As a consequence, these more audibly pleasant vernacular raps earn high regard not only inside the niche markets from which they originated and which they target, but also throughout the country.[33] The ubiquity of the internet, along with the bourgeoning of new social media, has played a decisive role in this transregional movement of vernacular rap.

Second, as an "accented" music,[34] vernacular rap is a diffused grassroots and participant-oriented cultural form quite often connected to a specific social class, locality, or ethnic group. In many ways, this new music pattern constitutes a challenge to the one-way, monopolistic, traditional media based upon a standardized national language and identity. With the imprint of a subculture, this accented music tends to be more privatized and decentralized in terms of production, circulation, and consumption. The internet, with its revolutionary technology and ideology, offers a greater potential for input and interaction from a mass audience in an imagined, virtualized public sphere. Flourishing in the more developed and modernized cities (e.g., Beijing, Shanghai, Xi'an, Canton, the northeast coast, etc.) under the pervasive force of the internet and of globalization, vernacular rap has become a secular, profane voice of critique that tightly mirrors the latest tendency in close correspondence with sociocultural change. Hence, the new music apparatus has brought about a topical and timely exploration of a wide spectrum of issues from divergent standpoints, which are now coming together at a virtual agora: from market reform and China's rise to superpower; the widening gap between rich and poor; large-scale migration; the divisions between city and rural areas; gender politics; to China's foreign policies and international relations. The list seems endless.

Happy (*Gaoxing*, dir. Ah Gan, 2009), a creative combination of musical and comedy film, capitalizes on the special appeal of hip hop and vernacular rap. Following the young rural migrants' humorous and tearjerking adventure to the city where they seek their cosmopolitan dreams, the film establishes its cinematic and musical foundations in the multicultural milieu of contemporary northwest China—specifically, the city of Xi'an. From the original novel to the film adaptation, the story was marketed under this distinct vernacular label and claims to be one of the first hip hop films to speak to and for the masses. Jia Ping'ao, the novel's author who is well-known for his enigmatic portrayal of northwestern Chinese culture and everyday reality, enthusiastically endorsed *Happy* as a truly groundbreaking film with a highlight of "grassroots carnival" (*jiceng renmin de kuanghuan*).[35] As Harry Kuoshu points out, the director names himself Ah Gan, which can be aptly translated as Dear Gump, revealing the impact of *Forrest Gump* in China.³⁶ The adoption is also, I argue, a tribute to the everyday man like Gump who remains honest, faithful, persevering, and blissful despite all his ordeals: "My momma always said, 'Life was like a box of chocolates. You never know what you're gonna get.'" The Gumpian wisdom, humor, and strength are at the very core of *Happy*, a small production that celebrates the victory of humble lives while ridiculing earlier privileged hierarchies. It inherits witty sacasm, hedonism, and a *flâneur* sensibility from Wang Shuo's hooligan subculture, a matter I exmined in chapter three. A deliberate evocation of the Broadway musical, *Happy* was shot in large part on a soundstage, but seeks to present a broad view of contemporary Chinese society from a hip hop-charged perspective. Both image and sound conjure up Bakhtin's conceptualization of the carnivalesque and the polyphonic text, in which many different voices mingle together in this paradoxical, liminal space of today's China.

Happy begins with a wide shot of the central character, Gaoxing (Happy), riding an airplane above a yellow earth plateau. When the camera zooms in to give a clearer picture of the airplane and its occupant, it is, however, revealed to be an utterly primitive, homemade tricycle-turned-aircraft maneuvered by a young Chinese farmer. The choice of music, a typical Northwest Wind solo track, provides an additional layer of meaning. Associated with a specific region, the melody, juxtaposed with the crude imagery, situates the narrative in northwest China. It also tactically alludes to the dilemma that Chinese rural youth like Gaoxing and his best friend, Wufu (Five Blessings), face. While their primary motivation is to improve their material status and to be assimilated into the dominant urban culture, what will they gain and what will they lose in this neoliberal, cosmopolitan expedition? Revealed to be a fleeting, unrealistic daydream, the opening sequence is abruptly followed by a realistic depiction of the two boys teaming up to leave their hometown for the city. Tracking shots and pans with a handheld camera create a raw, unsettled feeling. After Gaoxing and his rural migrant friends have been interrupted and interrogated by the meddling city police while they are on their way to the city, a dance performance of a rap song, "My Name is Liu Gaoxing" (*Wojiao liu gaoxing*), with a mixture of *Xintianyou* (a folk music genre popular in north Shaanxi region), comes in to articulate and foreshadow the ambivalent, complicated feelings they have toward dislocation and their imminent arrival in a new place.

The rap music track in *Happy* is significant because it endows Gaoxing and his friends, the marginal rural migrant workers, a prioritized voice and a privileged viewpoint. Equivalent to a voice-over explanation, the rap track directly communicates the yearnings, frustrations, and disillusions of the disenfranchised youth—a clever echo of the intrinsic concerns of rap music itself. As the narrative advances to disclose that this "happy king" is, in fact, a garbage king, who inhabits a small wasteyard where he discovers and builds his identity and dream, Gaoxing's singing becomes the predominant and pervasive voice in the diegesis—the theatrical, cinematic, and fictional representation of the postsocialist ghetto life. His fast rap and speech with heavy Xi'an inflection convey a sense of rawness and authenticity that aptly corresponds to the *mise-en-scène* of the wasteland. All varieties of trash (bottles, bags, cardboards, and tangled wires) are ingeniously deployed not only to serve the musical performance and a dramatic function but also to add critical commentary to the heated debates revolving around the issues of commodification, materialism, and urbanization in contemporary China.

A succession of rap songs—such as "Ode to Joy" (*Huanle song*), "I am a Happy Garbage King" (*Wo shi kuaile de polan wang*), "Getting up Earlier than Rooster" (*Qide bi ji zao*), "The Side Effect of Urban Night Life" (*Chengshi ye shenghuo de fu zuoyong*), "Shaanxi Delicacies" (*Shaanxi meishi*), and "The First Emperor's Accent" (*Qinshihuang de kouyin*)—further bring the thorny issues of marginalization and exile into sharp focus. Nearly all the rap songs in the film were created and performed by a local rap group, Black Head (*Heisa*), reaffirming the plural, polyphonic mechanism of the new Chinese hip hop culture. Retaining their musical and cultural roots in Xi'an, Black Head identifies itself as a real Xi'an music band run by native Xi'an people. A strong sense of local affiliation is stressed in their attempts to negotiate the double legacy of nationalism and regional culture. Both in the film and in their albums, Black Head employs the Xi'an dialect and (self-)consciously incorporates local elements such as *Xintianyou* and Shaanxi opera into their musical experiment. Their Chinese name—*Heisa*, which translates to angry man with blackface—refers to the male lead in Shaanxi opera. On top of such close attachments to their local origins, a handful of songs tap into the broader concerns of national identity. For example, their debut single "Fuck Japanese" (*Liansi xiao riben*) was widely circulated at the end of 2003, notably when Chinese students protested against the Japanese students' arrogant performance at Northwestern University in Xi'an, which incited a rapid escalation of nationalist and even xenophobic sentiments.

Black Head's rage and fierce rap style are motivated and charged by a resurgence of local and national pride, by discontent with the current status quo and social structure, by a call for communal consciousness, and by a desire for an alternative, public forum for free speech. How, then, do these black, inflammatory sonic signifiers harmonize in *Happy* with the variegated, elated characters of the film? What is the happiness in *Happy* that the Gumps are trying to seek? To pursue answers through the prism of ecstasy implies

Film poster for *Happy* (2009).

that ecstasy is a physical and psychological factor and a socioeconomic and political construction. One may find this logic of ecstasy or jouissance in Žižek's critique of modern society, as he has written:

> Modern society is defined by the lack of an ultimate transcendent guarantee, or, in libidinal terms, of total *jouissance*. There are three main ways to cope with this negativity: utopian, democratic, and post-democratic. The first (totalitarianisms, fundamentalisms) tries to reoccupy the ground of absolute *jouissance* by attaining a utopian and harmonious society which eliminates negativity. The second, democratic, enacts a political equivalent of "traversing the fantasy": it institutionalizes the lack itself by creating the space for political antagonisms. The third, consumerist post-democracy, tries

to neutralize negativity by transforming politics into apolitical administration: individuals pursue their consumerist fantasies in the space regulated by expert social administration. Today, when democracy is gradually evolving into consumerist post-democracy, one should insist that the democratic potential is not exhausted—"democracy as an unfinished project" could have been Stavrakakis' motto here. The key to the resuscitation of this democratic potential is to re-mobilize enjoyment: "What is needed, in other words, is *an enjoyable democratic ethics of the political.*"[37]

From the alternative viewpoint of the young rural migrants and rag-pickers, *Happy* explores how a set of value systems—the work ethic, social obligation, local identification, national identity, cosmopolitan awareness, and individual freedom—interact with current sociopolitical and cultural transformations. The protagonist, Gaoxing, leaves home and loses his money, his friends, and his girlfriend, but never loses himself in the vortex of a frantic, ever-changing world. Hence, *Happy* plays it safe and subscribes itself again to the mainstream ideology by neutralizing negativity and the hip hop grudge, by eulogizing the populist, Gump-esque smile for postsocialist life. *Happy* is a hip hop musical, but it is also a fairly conservative film that fits into Žižek's third category of "consumerist post-democracy," in which "individuals pursue their consumerist fantasies in the space regulated by expert social administration."[38] I, then, want to conclude this chapter by responding to Žižek's last call, "democracy as an unfinished project."[39] The case study I take up, the Grass Mud Horse Style, is symptomatic of "an enjoyable democratic ethics of the political" that "re-mobilize[s] enjoyment"[40] and that reorientates pain into pleasure, outcry into jouissance.

Grass Mud Horse Style and Social and Media Revolution in the Age of New Digital Globalization

While the diverse and multifaceted use of dialects and vernaculars may effectively construct rappers, migrant workers, and urban dwellers as decidedly local, an ambivalent and satirical undertone also characterizes this peculiar form of indigenous youth culture, indicating how Chinese nationality and provinciality negotiate the broader landscape of globalization and cosmopolitanism. Grass Mud Horse (*Cao Ni Ma*), a cultural fad and social phenomenon that emerged in Chinese cyberspace in the twenty-first century, provides a fresh twist on Chinese hip hop. It casts a new light on the fluctuating relations of globalization, cultural appropriation, and state regulation, which are essential to understanding audiovisual culture and popular aesthetics under the new digital conditions.

In 2009, an inflammatory posting of "Ten Mythical Creatures" (*Shi Da Shenshou*) originating from Baidu Baike—one of the most popular Chinese portal sites equivalent to Wikipedia—was promptly picked up, widely circulated, and massively reproduced among millions of Chinese netizens. Of particular interest was Grass Mud Horse, the central character of these ten virtually created imageries. What makes it intriguing and even contentious is its sardonic undertone and complex innuendoes referencing much more than just an animal species; it is a blasphemous rant synonymous with "fuck your mom." Intricately and tactfully designed in an effort to protest forms of internet censorship enforced by the Chinese authorities, this cult figure made a significant impact in cyberculture. Grass Mud Horse's counterhegemonic *style* fueled a national public outcry for freedom of speech in cyberspace as well as in postsocialist, globalized reality. Surprisingly, this was achieved through a quaint use of vernaculars and idioms, ingenious insinuation and simulacrum, and their radically defiant and audacious play on Chinese profanity. As Dick Hebdige explains:

> Style in subculture is, then, pregnant with significance. Its transformations go "against nature," interrupting the process of "normalization." As such, they are gestures, movements towards a speech which offends the "silent majority," which challenges the principle of unity and cohesion, which contradicts the myth of consensus. Our task becomes, like Barthes, to discern the hidden messages inscribed in code on the glossy surfaces of style, to trace them out as "maps of meaning" which obscurely re-present the very contradictions they are designed to resolve or conceal.[41]

If we follow Hebdige's logic and suggest that the radical, offensive practice of Grass Mud Horse is a *style* enacted to "interrupt the process of normalization," then what kind of formal, aesthetic, visual, acoustic, ideological, and technical *style* does Grass Mud Horse perform? What *contradiction* is it "designed to resolve or conceal"? My focus in this section is on politics and poetics—specifically, the resourceful *style* of concealing, pun, parody, and spoof in Grass Mud Horse. My objectives thus become, like Barthes and Hebdige, to decode the "hidden messages" and to delve into the complex ways and the highly audiovisual means in which nuanced sociopolitical messages are delivered to Chinese netizens and a wider civic society in the wake of digitization and new media culture.

It is believed that the upsurge of Grass Mud Horse was triggered by a lasting and aggravated history of censorship in CCP-led China. The beginning of 2009 witnessed another wave of tightened internet regulation in the country. Liu Xiaobo, a famous critic and dissident devoted to political reform and democracy, and an awardee of the 2010 Nobel Peace Prize, drafted Charter 08 and distributed it online in response to the government's escalating censorship legislation. Shortly after its publication, the government arrested Liu Xiaobo and sentenced him to a prison term of eleven years. Subsequently, the state inaugurated a nationwide campaign "against internet pornography and deviance" to "purify the internet sphere" and "build a harmonious society."[42] By mid-February 2009, the government had shut down thousands of websites and blogs containing "large amounts of low and vulgar content that violates social morality and damages the physical and mental health of youth."[43] The five most popular websites—Sina, Sohu, Tencent, Baidu, and Netease—were also charged with providing vulgar content on their webpages and were forced to issue public apologies. It was against this stringent environment that the unusual, whimsical Grass Mud Horse Style hatched and flourished in the cyber-public sphere.

After the original encyclopedia entry appeared online and attracted millions of clicks, numerous follow-up postings and writings poured into and flooded chat rooms, bulletin boards, and blogs instantly. New entries were added to give more complex twists on this cult figure. Most notable is a short film entitled *Special Program of Animal World: Grass Mud Horse in the Mahler Gobi Desert* (*Dongwu shijie tebie pian male gebi shang de cao ni ma*), which was quickly uploaded to some of the major portal sites specializing in mobile movies and internet videos, such as YouTube, Youku, and Tudou. This unauthored or perhaps multi-authored work runs just over six minutes. It gives an account of the life of Grass Mud Horses and their peaceful, idyllic homeland, which is subsequently threatened by alien invaders, called *He Xie* (River Crab). In a playful manner, the film adopts the format of a famous CCTV program, *Animal World* (*Dongwu shijie*). From its narrative structure to its visual design and sonic representation, this short video is meticulously fashioned after *Animal World*, yet furnishes the seemingly familiar story with new codes, metaphors, and signs.

The opening showcases the real world of animals with fast editing and a touch of dynamic music, closely resembling the conventional structure of *Animal World*. The superimposed words "Animal World" are repeatedly inserted into the frame and seem to deliberately emphasize its homage to this household television program. Following the opening title sequence, *Special Program of Animal World* begins with a television anchorman introducing a special kind of animal: "On a piece of bleak and beautiful Mahler Gobi Desert, there lives a flock of mighty animals named Grass Mud Horse." The film then fades into a wide shot of the desert landscape and progresses to show how the Grass Mud Horse, a species of alpaca, survives the harsh conditions. The first part of the video incorporates a great deal of stock footage of animals and natural landscapes to create a sense of realism and scientific objectivity that is often tied to CCTV's *Animal World*. Moreover, the male vocal narration in a low and deep voice recalls that of Zhao Zhongxiang, the longstanding host of *Animal World*, whose idiosyncratic aural-visual presence is another important hallmark of the program. In the second part, *Special Program of Animal World* shifts from a seemingly scientific illustration of the unique breed to a simulated interview as if the video was set on the real locale. A female reporter called *Ya Mie Die* brings the camera into the Gobi Desert and unveils the mysterious Grass Mud Horse from a first-person point of view. To supplement her in-person experience, she turns to another reporter, *Wei Shen Jin*, to conduct interviews with the local residents until the program is inexplicably cut off.

A first glimpse of this quasi-documentary short film gives the audience a Darwinist outlook of how *Cao Ni Ma* are severely endangered yet manage to survive in spite of *He Xie*, a mob of mythical intruders. All of this material is conspicuously modeled after the standard formula of CCTV's *Animal World*. However, it is much more than a sequel to *Animal World* or a simple story animated by animal characters. Relying heavily on various audiovisual effects and on the cultural awareness of its audience, the filmmakers cut and paste segments from documentary footage, stock photographic stills, folklore, and vernacular to create a seemingly informed yet unique context. Grass Mud Horse (*Cao Ni Ma*) is a homophone (the same pronunciation but with different tones and different writings) of the Chinese phrase "fuck your mom," whereas River Crab (*He Xie*) resembles "harmonization," a party slogan and a state project "designed to resolve or conceal"[44] conflicts and negativities in a time of postsocialist crisis. Other characters in the film, including the television anchor, reporters, and interviewees, are all associated with internet neologies; thus, they become cultural signifiers inscribed with symbolic meanings and a sense of irony. For instance, the two female reporters named *Ya Mie Die* and *Wei Shen Jin* derive their names from the Ten Mythical Creatures: "Small Elegant Butterfly" (referring to a Japanese word for "stop" that is commonly used in pornography) and "Stretch-Tailed Whale" (homophonous with "sanitary napkin" in Mandarin Chinese). Many terms invented in this mini-video—such as *Ma Le Ge Bi* (Mahler Gobi Desert), *Cao Ni Zu* (Grass Mud Tribe), *Cao Ni Xiao Huo* (Young Man of the Grass Mud Tribe), *Cao Ni Da Ye* (Old Man of the Grass Mud Tribe), *Wo Cao* (Fertile Grass, which is the only thing Grass Mud Horse can eat according to the film), *Wo Cao Ni Ma* (I Grass Mud Horse) and *Kuang Cao Ni Ma* (Wild Grass Mud Horse)—are all different variations of the Chinese f**k word.

The anchorman with the name of *Chun Ge* (Brother Chun) serves as a reference to another mythical creature, "Quail Pigeon." It is a popular term associated with Li Yuchun, a young girl who won a nationwide singing competition, Super Girl, in 2005 but quickly became the center of contention due to her androgynous appearance and allegedly ambiguous sexuality. More telling is the uncanny way in which the effeminate anchor mimics Zhao Zhongxiang in great detail, from his appearance to body gesture to intonation. This serves as a caricature of this formerly iconic figure of Chinese official media, whose reputation took a drastic downturn when he was allegedly involved in a sex scandal in 2004.[45] The caption on the upper left corner of the screen, "RPTV囧," further reveals the very nature and key concept of this quasi-documentary; that is, a farcical and burlesque imitation, or *E'gao* in Chinese. According to Bai Ruoyun in her critical study on the popular practice of "messing with the originals with a mischievous intention," *E'gao* exemplifies a new mode of internet-mediated activity that is at once entertaining and politically active from the grassroots level.[46] RP (an acronym for *Ren Pin* that literally means "personality" and "luck") and 囧 (pronounced as *Jiong*, which translates to "upset" or "frustrated") are two internet-coined phrases that cystallize a sensibility of parody and *E'gao* and an act of *bricolage* in the new millennial China.

In his theorization of subculture, Hebdige argues that "the concept of *bricolage* can be used to explain how subcultural styles are constructed . . . These magical systems of connection have a common feature: they are capable of infinite extension because basic elements can be used in a variety of improvised combinations to generate new meanings within them."[47] The aesthetic of *bricolage* is very relevant here. Soon after the quasi-documentary *Special Program of Animal World* appeared, numerous remakes, adaptations, reproductions, and spin-offs were spawned, inundating cyber-public space at an unprecedented speed. One of the most widely circulated remakes is a music video called *Song of Grass Mud Horse* (*Cao ni ma zhi ge*):

> There was a herd of Grass Mud Horses
> In the wild and beautiful Mahler Gobi Desert
> They were lively and intelligent
> They were cheerful and nimble . . .

A postmodern collage in the form of a children's chorus, *Song of Grass Mud Horse* borrows inventively not only from the previous video but also from other cultural resources (e.g., the widely known music of *The Smurfs*, a theme song that was scored and written in Chinese when the animated series was

The satirical internet video *Special Program of Animal World: Grass Mud Horse in the Mahler Gobi Desert* (2009).

imported and enjoyed immense popularity in 1980s China) in creating a new sonic and visual work. Unlike the abrupt, somber ending of *Special Program of Animal World: Grass Mud Horse in the Mahler Gobi Desert*, in which the interview is brutally cut off due to some "unanticipated" reasons (an allusion to the ubiquitous surveillance and the state's iron-handed censorship), *Song of Grass Mud Horse* presents, instead, a lighthearted and uplifting story, in which Grass Mud Horse strives to defeat the invasion of River Crab and protect their homeland. The song closes on a victorious note: "River crabs forever disappeared from Mahler Gobi Desert." The principal narrative and vivaciously humorous undertone echo the fantasy-comedy of *The Smurfs*, whose melody has been tactically appropriated and improvised in combination with new lyrics and implications. Many other internet films were spontaneously produced and disseminated around this peculiar imaginary of Grass Mud Horse. The most notable are a flash video that rewrites the tale by integrating the modern rhythm of hip hop and indigenous Uyghur folk music from northwest China, a humorous cartoon scoffing at River Crab (the official agenda of harmonization) ironically set against the familiar tune of the Chinese national anthem, and a music video entitled *Love of Grass Mud Horse* (*Cao ni ma de aiqing*) that makes further scathing remarks toward River Crab and pertinent social issues.

To be sure, this heterogenous, mixed palette embodies a kind of collective, symbolic action fueled and facilitated by new technology and the aesthetic of the internet. It is essentially a sarcastic critique of diverse social phenomena, including internet censorship, the right to free expression, and the order of "harmonious society" as it was propagated by the Chinese government when facing severe challenges of social unrest, political disillusionment, and ideological crisis in the new century. Grass Mud Horse pinpoints—instead of covering up—these conflicts. In a capricious, mocking, hip hop way, it transgresses the ordinariness and subverts these linguistic, social norms. The sounds, images, and entries were frequently cross-referenced and refabricated, ultimately inciting hundreds of "pirated," "illicit" copies loaded with vernacular and local interpretations. Such a cybercarnival has, moreover, fostered a broader interpretation of "Ten Mythical Creatures" (*Shi Da Shenshou*) that extends and pokes fun at a wide range of social phenomena by a clever use of euphemism and *E'gao*.[48]

Grass Mud Horse is a cultural symptom that emerges from within the subculture paradigm, but its critical, protesting edge has also been turned into a cooperative vogue, a cultural commodity generating considerable profits in the market-oriented, postsocialist material world. As Grass Mud Horse became a trendsetting buzzword in both Chinese virtual space and in real quotidian life, the market responded with the production of a variety of related merchandise, ranging from toys to T-shirts to everyday goods, all of which were churned out to capitalize on this frantic Grass Mud Horse fetish. Although its prominence has somewhat faded or dispersed into other cultural formations, a Google search with the keywords *Cao Ni Ma* (Grass Mud Horse) still yielded over 4,380,000 results in Chinese and approximately 1,090,000 results in English in January 2015.[49]

Grass Mud Horse is turned into an icon of popular dissent through *style* in the new century. It provides an alternative, vital outlet for a politically aware, technologically armed, and artistically cultivated public to express their opinions and disagreement with the regime and the current status quo in what remains an austere political environment in China. Cui Weiping, a cultural critic and professor at the Beijing Film Academy, published an article entitled "I am a Grass Mud Horse" (*Wo shi yizhi cao ni ma*) on her blog, blasting in outspoken terms the state's monopoly on information while celebrating what she envisioned as the arrival of the Grass Mud Horse era. She writes:

> I am thrilled and really want to applaud for the wisdom of euphemism and people who created Grass Mud Horse. The underlying tone is: I know you don't allow me to speak certain things. See, I'm completely cooperative, right? . . . What is Grass Mud Horse? It is a type of animal who survives through the harsh condition. Look, it comes from the vast and desolate desert. I like it and I love it. This is something too distant that is beyond your control. Moreover, why are you always keeping an eye on me? Am I really good? I am innocent and not controlled by the bad guy. I am not vulgar too. What do

you care? I am singing a cute children's song—I am a grass-mud horse! Even though it is heard by the entire world, you can't say I break the law.⁵⁰

To Chinese intellectuals and social activists, Grass Mud Horse signals "a particular kind of cultural contention in Chinese cyberspace—challenges by 'little people' against cultural power and authority," to borrow Yang Guobin's illation from his sociological study of Chinese society and online activism in the 2000s.⁵¹ Another digital contention that has further irritated the state authority is Ai Weiwei's performative work "Grass Mud Horse Covering the Middle" (*Cao Ni Ma Dang Zhong Yang*). In this telling self-portrait, Ai Weiwei captures himself posing against a blank wall, almost fully naked with only a stuffed toy of Grass Mud Horse to veil his genitals. The Chinese title, *Cao Ni Ma Dang Zhong Yang*, is tactfully sarcastic and boldly defiant, especially for the myriad Chinese netizens who are more or less acquainted with the popular imagery and context of Grass Mud Horse. It can be instantly linked to and apprehended as "Fuck your mother, the Communist Party Central Committee." Ai's many insolent, fierce attacks on the Chinese regime spread out across Twitter, blogs, and various digital platforms, likely leading to his arrest on April 3, 2011.⁵²

Named "China's most famous rebel artist" by the *New York Times*⁵³ and "the most powerful figure in the global art world" by *ArtReview*,⁵⁴ Ai Weiwei—with his visually striking and politically provocative artworks—has drawn significant attention and media coverage throughout the world. He is a visual artist and a documentary filmmaker who has produced a great number of works, including the Beijing National Stadium, the installation of Sunflower Seeds, the Sichuan Earthquake project, and dozens of documentaries. Most importantly, he is known as an activist and a dissident who avidly promotes human rights and democracy in China. In his experimental art and political protest, the internet has played a pivotal role in helping him reach a wide audience, forging a dialogic and democratic platform, and advancing his agenda of a "direct confrontation and enlightenment."⁵⁵ Ai has been an enthusiastic photographer and documentarian with a keen interest in capturing and exposing the human right conditions in China. He made over twenty videos and posted them on YouTube and Twitter for free access and public viewing. In most of the films, Ai is at once the filmmaker and a part of the narrative and sometimes the protagonist. Long takes, mobile cameras, natural lighting, and the use of raw footage with little editing contribute to a hyperrealistic, *cinema vérité* style, which corresponds to a bourgeoning interest in selfie-making and a new wave of digital video production. Targeting the internet as his primary space of screening and, in Perry Link's words, the "fart people"⁵⁶ (a jab at the

Chinese authorities who generally neglect and regard ordinary people as worthless) as his main audience, Ai's amateurish, homemade videos ally the populace with his empathic and engaged view and, most of all, through the easy accessibility of his works both practically and intellectually.

Before "Grass Mud Horse Covering the Middle" appeared in 2011, Ai Weiwei had made a short video *Grass Mud Horse, Motherland* after he was beaten by the local police during an investigation of student casualities during the Sichuan earthquake, which was recorded in his documentary *Disturbing the Peace* (*Lao ma ti hua*). As a result of the attack, the artist had to undergo brain surgery in Munich in 2009. The short film is a sampling of eight persons of different race, color, gender, and nationality against the singular backdrop of the Chinese characters "Grass Mud Horse, Motherland" (*Cao Ni Ma Zu Guo*), repeating the same phrase, "Fuck you, motherland" (sharing a similar pronunciation to "Grass Mud Horse, Motherland") with varying languages and inflections. Intended, according to Ai, as a "special tribute" to the sixtieth anniversary of the founding of the People's Republic of China, this short piece—lasting only one-and-a-half minutes and comprised of ten close-up shots—also acutely employs the rhetoric and symbolism of Grass Mud Horse.

Al Weiwei also organized a feast of River Crab to protest against the government order to demolish his studio in Shanghai. In a smiliar manner, he invoked the internet and announced an invitation on his Twitter account to communicate with and draw support from people who share the same degree of discontent. The posting immediately drew millions of clicks and replies, but it also caught the government's attention. Ai was consequently placed under house arrest. Despite his absence, a large-scale River Crab communal banquet ensued in which citizens literally and figuratively annihilated the River Crabs—apparently a daring challenge against the Chinese authorities. A documentary covering the event was shot and later posted online. Ai's recent work in his Grass Mud Horse oeuvre is another short video titled *Grass Mud Horse Style*. Capitalizing on the global appeal of "Gangnam Style," Ai's music video features himself and like-minded people dancing to the blaring music of "Gangnam Style" with few facial expressions and as though in handcuffs. One may sense that the representation poignantly alludes to Ai's eighty-one-day incarceration by the Chinese officials in 2011 and his current bail condition. Similarly, it is no surprise that this short video became the target of state censorship and was banned again in China.

From *Special Program of Animal World: Grass Mud Horse in the Mahler Gobi Desert* to "Ten Mythical Creatures," from "Song of Grass Mud Horse" to Ai Weiwei's "Grass Mud Horse Style," this cluster of Grass Mud Horse medleys embodies a sophisticated expression of social critique. It is a revolutionary, decentralized form of articulation, circulation, and exhibition, offering the prospect of evolving throughout the multifaceted micro-filmscape and mediascape in the twenty-first century. The distinctive *style* thrives on the digital conditions. It is predicated upon the creative, subcultural tactic of charade—a unique tongue-in-cheek parody with the postmodern aesthetics of appropriation and pastiche, as well as what I would call a discourse of "critical profanity." This term implies a thrust, as each of my examples illustrate, which is sociopolitically provocative and evocative rather than erotic, amusingly subversive rather than vulgar, and vernacular rather than standard. As Jacques Attali puts it, "Announcing the void, voicing insufficiency, refusing recuperation—that is blasphemy."[57] Hip hop and Grass Mud Horse capture the nuances and paradoxes of a blasphemous and liberatory postsocialist life, particularly its fluidity, mobility, and ambiguity, in the age of appropriation and networking.

The rise and development of hip hop culture in a Chinese context is an intriguing story. How it has been translated, reinterpreted, and reconfigured by various media offers clues on the interplay between global cultural flows, national manipulations, and local appropriations. In my narrative, China (and Chinese) is not just a passive recipient of this Western-originated paradigm. In fact, there has been a reverse flow from China to America in the form of martial arts and kung-fu that American hip hop groups such as the Wu-Tang Clan have embraced. Furthermore, Chinese martial arts and kung-fu have been appropriated by a number of Hollywood action movies in conjunction with hip hop soundtracks as vehicles for portraying cultural and ethnic conflicts. Such Hollywood blockbusters as *Romeo Must Die* (2000) and the *Rush Hour* series (1998, 2001, 2007) have employed the pairing of Chinese martial arts and American hip hop in a postmodern comingling of traditional Chinese values and African American contemporary lifestyles. This hybrid genre of hip hop/martial arts is an interesting phenomenon that requires further consideration.

While the specific case of Chinese hip hop in various ways actualizes and attests to our understandings of "glocalization,"[58] this multidimensional, polyphonic audiovisual construction also redefines and poses challenges to existing technological, aesthetical, and epistemological assumptions. If the work of art in general, to borrow Walter Benjamin's famous claim, has lost an aura of authenticity as a consequence of mechanical reproduction,[59] Chinese hip hop, as an exemplar of copying the West and mimicking the other, further deconstructs and reconceptualizes the ideology of authenticity in the new digital age. Rather than reading it as a manifestation of "inauthenticity," I see it as a dialectical form that has its roots in the discussion of authenticity; it turns authenticity into a parody and reifies it as a new fashion of appropriation. In a creative, self-reflective move, the intertextuality and postmodern pastiche of Chinese hip hop illustrate the critical possibilities of appropriation inherent in the rechanneling of myriad sources of words, sounds, and images. On the one hand, since imitation, copying, and paraphrasing is essential to such practices, they raise questions of what is original, copyrightable, and furthermore legitimate. On the other hand, hip hop counters the hegemony of the state and the traditional media apparatus, making the definition of originality as inbred in the individual author a contradictory discourse. It might well be that the word-music-video that plays with cultural authority and classical sources is what makes Chinese hip hop such a popular, albeit opaque, form.

As a cultural fashion, hip hop and popular culture's power is anchored in the present. However, if we sense the potential for hip hop's aura to dim (or, to be more accurate, if we sense that the original heterogenous and anarchic spirit has been undermined by commercialism at home and by the decline of the hip hop nation around the world, as exemplified by the famous black American rapper Nas in his provocative album *Hip-Hop Is Dead* at the end of 2006), it gives us occasion to question whether this sinicized and synthesized hip hop could survive, or how it has been changed and possibly reconceptualized, if not diminished, in present-day China. In an interesting way, the Grass Mud Horse Style responds to this dubious future by reinventing and revitalizing the form with more complex rhythms and visual images. To extend a number of confrontations and contradictions—authenticity/appropriation, authority/authorship—that are key to hip hop and to cultural (re)production in the new social and cultural environment, it is the debate about cultural fluidity and freedom both in economic and political terms that keeps the popular image and music alive. It further illustrates how new media and digital technology play an increasingly important role in shaping everyday life and in opening up an alternative public space—a grassroots-based, independent, and comparatively relaxed avenue—that offers views different from mainstream policies, perspectives, and ideologies.

At this important juncture, is it possible to reconcile global capital and state power with private interests? How can this be done? How does the sound and image of popular culture mediate and negotiate between these parties? To what extent are hip hop and the global lingua franca of popular culture and media mobile, free, and bordercrossing? Furthermore, how does this now-permeating imperative of new media enrich and restructure our understanding of cinema and the various audiovisual constructs in the new century? Chinese hip hop and the mixing questions it provokes await further exploration.

FINALE

A Shift in Perception

> Conceptualizing the coming order on the basis of the designation of the fundamental noise should be the central work of today's researchers. Of the only worthwhile researchers: undisciplined ones. The ones who refuse to answer new questions using only pregiven tools. Music should be a reminder to others that if *Incontri* was not written for a symphony orchestra, or the *Lamentations* for the electric guitar, it is because each instrument, each tool, theoretical or concrete, implies a sound field, a field of knowledge, an imaginable and explorable universe. Today, a new music is on the rise, one that can neither be expressed nor understood using the old tools, a music produced elsewhere and otherwise. It is not that music or the world have become incomprehensible; the concept of comprehension itself has changed; there has been a shift in the locus of the perception of things.
> —**Jacques Attali,** *Noise: The Political Economy of Music*[1]

Conceptualizing contemporary Chinese forms on the basis of sound is the central thesis of this book. When I take up a close and persistent examination of the largely neglected yet indispensable, multivalent roles of sound in the formation and transformation of Chinese cinema, media, and culture, sound thus becomes my new tool enabling me to reveal and reconceive the old and new relations between audio and visual, between cinema and other forms of representations, and between China and its global contacts. Its organic, constitutive roles are identified and depicted in my study as a specific "mixing" scenario, embodied by four principal cinematic modes and cultural phenomena in China since the mid 1980s: Northwest Wind, Chinese rock 'n' roll, Leitmotif, and hip hop. A primary subject that informs one or two chapters, respectively, each of these has been discussed as a popular music-film genre, intertwined with an extensive and creative use of dialects, vernaculars, other sources of sound.

I begin, in the first two chapters, with a reconception of the Chinese New Wave of the Fifth Generation and I revisit frequently discussed works to demonstrate my particular approach of viewing and listening to the film and medium texts. I go on to explore Chinese rock 'n' roll, which evokes a key activity by the Sixth Generation filmmakers and youth subgroups based in the city of Beijing. In these two chapters, I treat rock 'n' roll discursively as both a cinematic and musical discourse emblematic of urban youth identity in postsocialist China. The broader urban youth framework allows me to move beyond the traditional chronological classification of Chinese filmmakers and track rock's resonances across different generations, times, and spaces. The fifth chapter is devoted to a historiographical and political economy analysis of Leitmotif, an official production with Chinese characteristic in the market age. Such a corporate entity of political and commercial interests is quite often galvanized by a transnational imaginary and multilingual vocal track. That the cinema of Leitmotif represents a new mode of Chinese national film in response to and against Hollywood leads us to ask how film and culture industries play in the postsocialist political and social life, and to consider the complicated interplays between globalization, nationality, and local imperatives. The last chapter continues to highlight the intricate cultural reconciliations and image and musical exchanges that arise in the wake of globalization. It tackles the relatively underexplored ground of Chinese hip hop, and I recapitulate my critical methods and extend further to navigate the articulations and representations of hip hop in a wide range of domains, including film, popular music, and the newly emerged digital culture in the late twentieth and early twenty-first centuries.

The book, then, is about mixing, and its subject is the mixed multitude of filmmaking and media productions in postsocialist, globalized China. I show how the complex, evolving uses of sound (popular music, voice-over, silence, noise, audio mixing, etc.) in film and media reflect and engage the important cultural and socio-historical shifts in contemporary China and in an increasingly networked world. Likewise, the methodology I employ is mixing and demonstrably cross-disciplinary, ranging from close readings of popular music and multilingual soundtracks in relation to specific film texts and the broader socio-historical contexts, to an institutional analysis that tackles the process of administering, producing, and circulation of film and cultural products on the multiple levels of industry, nation-state, and global market, to an investigation of the role of spectator/listener and author/consumer in the context of the simultaneous and intertwined trends toward globalization, nationalization, and localization.

I have continued to use a mixed perspective and and a distinctive audiovisual palette to address and foreground moments of change in contemporary China in a transnational age. It is the audiovisual and multimedia approach that motivates this research and enables it to find its own unique niche in the current scholarship. Situated at the intersections of film and media studies, music studies, linguistics, Chinese studies, and transnational studies, my research aims to break down and bridge the traditional binaries of image/sound, high/low culture, experimental/commercial, and East/West. My purpose is not to single out sound but rather to resuscitate sound as part of an integrated audiovisual experience and of a complex sociocultural expression. It should also be pointed out that, throughout the book, I have endeavored to present these visual and sonic modalities as distinct yet interrelated discourses in parallel and negotiation with one another. Although they may appear in different chapters in a discursively chronological order, they are by no means understood as static and separate.

One of the best known Chinese filmmakers who had his film career inaugurated as early as 1983 and who still remains extremely active up to now is Zhang Yimou. His film trajectory comes to mind as a prime example of the developments and intersections of these audiovisual pratices. In such films as *Red Sorghum* (*Hong gaoliang*, 1987), *Keep Cool* (*You hua haohao shuo*, 1997), *Hero* (*Yingxiong*, 2002), *Riding Alone for Thousands of Miles* (*Qianli zou danqi*, 2005), *A Woman, a Gun and a Noodle Shop* (*Sanqiang pai'an jingji*, 2009), and *The Flowers of War* (*Jinling shisan chai*, 2011), Zhang Yimou exhibits an extraordinary knack to work with different genres and to capture the zeitgeist, be it Northwest Wind, rock 'n' roll, Leitmotif, or hip hop. Stunning color and visual spectacles are perhaps the most important attributes of Zhang Yimou's films. Less discussed, however, is his sapient use of popular music and local idioms. As my close analysis of *Red Sorghum*'s soundtrack illustrates, the original film music composed by Zhao Jiping (with lyrics co-written by the screenwriter Yang Fengliang, original author Mo Yan, and director Zhang Yimou) not only effectively serves as a narrative device and commercial attraction but also forges a new popular trend in the late 1980s, namely, Northwest Wind. After a long hiatus, the Red Sorghum tunes re-entered the market, likely through the zealous promotion of the director himself. In 2005, when Zhang Yimou premiered *Riding Alone for Thousands of Miles* (*Qianli zou danqi*) in Lijiang, Yunnan (the film's shooting location), he closed the show with "Ode to the Wine God" from his first directorial effort, *Red Sorghum*. This irresistibly led to a massive chorus in this otherwise peaceful and seclusive border town. As part of the promotional effort, a local hip hop band, Kung Fu Hustle (*Gongfu*), was invited to perform "Riding Thousands of Miles to Lijiang" (*Qianli zou lijiang*) at the opening of the ceremony, which provides an overview of the film and deliberately incorporates many of Zhang Yimou's previous works into their freestyle rap.

Hip hop with a quotidian, colloquial character was also carefully crafted into Zhang Yimou's recent work *A Woman, a Gun and a Noodle Shop*. Compared to Zhang's previous spectacular epics, the film appears somewhat bizarre and whimsical. In a hip hop fashion, it is a *mélange* and remix of a whole variety of cultural materials. The film draws extensively on popular resources from domestic and local loci while also functioning as a stylistic remake of Coen Brother's *Blood Simple* (1984). Both the narrative style and casting indicate the apparent influence of a popular TV series, *Legend of Martial Arts* (*Wulin waizhuai*, 2006), and of Zhao Benshan and Xiao Shenyang's comic sketches, which results in a unique mix of slapstick, satire, and parody. It should be noted that in all of these works, local language and folklore play a prominent role. They serve as a humorous and sarcastic device and furthermore articulate a distinct local identity. The song-and-dance sequence during the ending credits to a great extent recalls that of *Slumdog Millionaire* (dir. Danny Boyle and Loveleen Tandan, 2008), whereas the theme song "I Am Only a Legend" (*Wo zhishi ge chuanshuo*), written and co-performed by Zhang Yimou, is yet another joint venture that capitalizes on the immense popularity of hip hop in the new century. Delivered in nonstandard, colloquial dialects, notably in a northeastern accent and Xi'an dialect (the leading actor Xiao Shenyang's and Zhang Yimou's respective native tongues), the musical theme attests to what I have described in the last chapter as "vernacular rap," a signifier of how the local, indigenous culture negotiates with and plays into the broader landscape of globalization.

While *A Woman, a Gun and a Noodle Shop* has been accused as a platitudinous and kitschy work that panders to lowbrow taste, Zhang Yimou's next hit, *The Flowers of War*, has aroused an even wider discussion and more severe criticism due to its economically aggressive but politically conservative stance, as I detailed in the fifth chapter. A pragmatic and eclectic take that subscribes at once to the state's totalitarian ideology and the mechanism of neoliberal globalization, *The Flowers of War* is a Leitmotif product and a big picture with Chinese characteristic. More intriguingly, the Beijing Olympic Games' opening and closing ceremonies, certainly the highest-budget audiovisual extravaganza in the history of China, is another epitome of Leitmotif in which a variety of state apparatus, market forces, global media, and Zhang Yimou's artistic vision come into play. How this rigorously scripted yet highly stylized and globally televised blockbuster contributes to our understandings of national identity, globalization, and the interfacing across different media would be a promising topic for future inquiries.

In the wake of the social media boom and an all-pervasive cyber presence, artists and authors have started to play different roles in cultural productions that are triggered by new economic and social relations. The boundaries between producers, distributors, and consumers are blurred by the frequent circulation, exchange, and reappropriation of global vernaculars and images, as I have suggested throughout the book. The popularity of vernacular rap in the public sphere of cyberspace, which highlights local inflections by ordinary citizens, reaffirms image, sound, and cultural production as what I have cited in the opening of the book "the quintessential mass activity."[2] Recent years have seen a more intricate, multiauthored, and multimediatized evolvement of "the quintessential mass activity," which has decisively affected the big screen. Chen Kaige's *Caught in the Web* (*Sousuo*, 2012) and Jia Zhangke's *A Touch of Sin* (*Tian zhuding*, 2013) are two gritty realistic noirs by "serious," preeminent filmmakers grappling with contemporary Chinese circumstances. Undeniably essential to the works is how the narrative strands draw from headline news stories in China and their subsequent "petty" discussions in cyberspace and how the outbursts of digitalization and social media create the conditions, camerawork, and style for a polyvalent, multiscreen movement in present China. All of these practices, by and large, validate the fluid, conjugated, and sometimes elusive experience.

As I have been exploring the popular music-polyphonic dynamic in contemporary Chinese film and media, I argue that this audiovisual register is undivided from the afflux of mass popular culture and social transformation and should be always appraised with a state-market-transcultural linkage in mind. None of these shall be understood as *the* singular or *a* monolithic, uniform voice-noise. Rather, they are multifaceted, variable, and ambivalent, and they need to be brought to the forefront of scholarly study and questioned in a substantial manner. As such, many issues discussed in my book serve as a blueprint for future studies more than assertive conclusions. To attempt to answer them adequately would call forth another manuscript, or, in fact, new methods of study, new ways of thinking, reading, viewing, and listening, and "a shift in the locus of the perception of things," as Attali pronounces.[3] As cinema and media confront their polyglottic past, reality, and future and become inevitably 3D, 4D, and increasingly interactive, a mixed, relational, and multisensory study needs to be constituted in a broader sociocultural context and in a fuller dimension of perception—that of sight, sound, taste, smell, and touch.

APPENDIX I

Music and Sound in Jia Zhangke's *Platform* (*Zhantai*, 2000)

Time and Length of the Shot	Music and Sound Effect	Camera and Action
1:50–3:34, 1 min 44 sec.	*A Train Heading for Shaoshan* (*Huoche xiangzhe shaoshan pao*) **Style**: Diegetic revolutionary musical performance.	The play presents a group of passengers from various class, ethnic, and geographical backgrounds who are united in a sacred revolutionary pilgrimage to Chairman Mao. **Style**: Extreme long shot, long take, static camera.
13:40–14:00; 14:01–14:06; 14:07–15:10.	"Little Sister Looks for Brother with Tears" (*Meimei zhaoge leihua liu*, 1979, music by Wang Ming, lyrics by Kaichuan, performance by Li Guyi) **Style**: Diegetic theme song from a popular film, *Little Sister* (*Xiaohua*, dir. Zhang Zheng and Huang Jianzhong, 1979), played in the local theatre.	The first shot gives a quick overview of the theater that is playing *Little Sister* and then elicits a closer look at a ticket window swarming with enthusiastic young people. The third shot is a static shot of Yin Ruijuan and Zhong Ping in the foreground, eagerly waiting for Cui Mingliang and Zhang Jun to sprint to the theater on bicycles. **Style**: Long shot, static camera.

Appendix I

Time and Length of the Shot	Music and Sound Effect	Camera and Action
15:11–15:28; 15:29–16:02; 16:03–17:01.	"Awara Hoon" (Music by Shankar Jaikishan, lyrics by Shailendra, performance by Mukesh Chand Mathur) **Style**: Diegetic theme song and film clip from a classic Indian film, *Awara* (dir. Raj Kapoor, India, 1951), played in the local theater.	The first shot follows Yin and Cui as they arrive at the theater and find their seats. The film has already started and the lights are out. The camera then cuts to an excerpt of *Awara*, in which the tramp is released from prison and is back to his drifting old style. The show is interrupted by a call out to Rui, who is forced to leave the screening and is checked up on by her police father in the third shot. **Style**: Long shot, extreme long shot, static camera.
18:34–21:17, 2 min 43 sec.	Yoshihiro Hanno's musical score **Style**: The nondiegetic violin "leitmotif," appearing four times in the film (second appearance at 1:36:49 in the scene of Cui igniting a flame on the vast plateau during a forlorn night after seeing the passing train for the first time; third appearance at 2:27:22 at the end of the film where Cui finally gets back home and comes to see Yin in her apartment; last appearance at 2:34:43 in the last part of the closing credit sequence), gives the scene a melancholic feeling.	Cui and Yin meet at the old city wall to discuss their relationship. The musical score only glides into the scene during the last few seconds, when Cui hears of Yin's family's plan to set her up with a dentist and the conversation falls silent. **Style**: Extreme long shot, long take, static camera.
21:47–23:30, 1 min 43 sec.	"Wine and Coffee" (*Meijiu jia kafei*, music by Gu Yue, lyrics by Lin Huangkun, performance by Teresa Tseng, 1972) **Style**: Diegetic song emanating from a radio program in Taiwan.	A low-key shot depicts the young protagonists congregating at Zhang's home and listening to an "illegal" radio broadcast from Taiwan. **Style**: Extended medium shot, long take, static camera.

Appendix I

Time and Length of the Shot	Music and Sound Effect	Camera and Action
23:32–24:29; 24:30–24:43.	"Zeitgeist" (*Fengliu ge*, written by Ji Yu, 1980) **Style**: Diegetic poetry performance with musical accompaniment.	The first long shot depicts Yin's poetry recital in the room of the cultural troupe. The camera then turns around to reveal its musical source and frame the young accordionists and the flute player in a medium shot. **Style**: Long shot, medium shot, static camera.
28:39–29:08, 29 sec..	*Garrison's Gorillas* (US, 1967–68) **Style**: Diegetic soundtrack from *Garrison's Gorillas*, played on television.	The camera gazes back at the audience as they enjoy the show. **Style**: Medium shot, static camera.
31:21–31:35; 31:36–31:56; 31:57–32:26; 32:27–35:33.	"Young Friends Come Together" (*Nianqing de pengyou lai xianghui*, music by Gu Jianfen, lyrics by Zhang Meitong, 1980) **Style**: Diegetic song performance.	The sequence starts with a long shot of the troupe leader performing the song and then cuts to a medium shot that looks out at the audience from the back of the stage. The next shot is a tracking shot of the truck in the middle of the night after the performance, with the young protagonists shouting out a mockery of the song. After they return, the troupe leader calls a meeting to criticize their mischievous, "liberal" act, which also addresses the political culture of "modernization" and "one-child policy" dominant in 1980s China. **Style**: Extreme long shot.
38:30–39:08, 38 sec.	"Spanish Gypsy Dance" (written by Pascual Marquina Narro, 1921) **Style**: Diegetic music and dance performance.	The camera follows Zhong with her new "Western-style" permed hair while partaking in a hot Spanish flamenco dance to the worldwide famous tune. **Style**: Long shot.

Appendix 1

Time and Length of the Shot	Music and Sound Effect	Camera and Action
39:09–39:57, 48 sec.	CCP's issuing of the "Resolution on the Rehabilitation of Comrade Liu Shaoqi" (1980) **Style**: Diegetic announcement from the loudspeaker broadcast.	Zhong sees Zhang off for his expedition to Guangzhou. **Style**: Long shot.
39:58–45:05, 5 min 7 sec.	"Morning at School" (*Xiaoyuan de zaochen*, music by Gu Jianfen, lyrics by Gao Feng, 1980); "The Crystal and Clear Waterfall at the Frontiers" (*Bianjiang de quanshui qing you chun*, music by Wang Ming, lyrics by Kai Chuai, 1978); "Night at the Naval Port" (*Jungang zhiye*, music by Liu Shizhao, lyrics by Ma Jinxing, 1980). **Style**: Diegetic song performance.	While Zhang is away, Zhong kills time by reading a book and singing a few popular ballads. Yin drops by and gossips about an execution, boys, and make-up. **Style**: Long shot, long take, static camera.
49:06–51:56, 2 min 50 sec..	"Happiness is not Drizzle" (*Xingfu bushi maomaoyu*, music by Liu Shizhao, lyrics by Ma Jinxing, 1980); "Is Miss Taiwan or Miss Singapore better" (*Taiwan xiaojie hao haishi xinjiapo xiaojie hao*, music, lyrics, and performance by Zhang Di, 1985); "Genghis Khan" (*Chengjisihan*, music by Siegel Jun Ralph and Bernd Meinuger, lyrics by Zheng Guojiang, performance by George Lam, 1987) **Style**: Diegetic song performance and from the boom-box.	On a sunny afternoon, Cui pops out of the room, wandering about and humming a tune. The camera follows his point of view and pans to capture Zhang, who just returns from the affluent south, bearing the fruits of his cosmopolitan adventure: a fashionable shirt, sunglasses, a portable cassette boom-box that blasts the latest popular hits of Taiwan and Hong Kong. **Style**: Long shot.

Appendix I

Time and Length of the Shot	Music and Sound Effect	Camera and Action
51:57–52:33; 52:34–53:19; 53:20–53:45.	"Genghis Khan" (*Chengjisihan*, music by Siegel Jun Ralph and Bernd Meinuger, lyrics by Zheng Guojiang, performance by George Lam, 1987) **Style**: Diegetic and nondiegetic sound.	The popular hit glides into the next scene, in which the young people are having a celebrating dance party, and into the next shot, in which they are working to augment the exterior wall and add broken glass to prevent theft; both actions are done to the beat of the song. While the camera shifts to a closer shot of them at work, an English-study tape is heard. **Style**: Medium shot.
1:00:41–1:02:17, 1 min 36 sec..	"Little Secret" (*Xiao mimi*, music and lyrics by Lv Xiaodong, 1982) **Style**: Diegetic song performance.	After being rejected by Yin and learning about his father's extramarital affair, Cui hangs out with his male friends atop the wall and plays the guitar. The camera follows them as they throw stones at a bus (which his target presumably rides on), returns to him, and then extends his gaze towards Yin's house, dolefully. **Style**: Long shot, long take.
1:03:36–1:06:48, 3 min 2 sec.	Grand parade for China's thirty-fifth anniversary (1984) **Style**: Diegetic sound from the radio broadcast.	Zhang, Cui, and the leader talk about the privatization of the troupe outside the clinic where Zhong is going to have an abortion. The announcement of the parade is juxtaposed against the abortion scene to give an ironic twist. **Style**: Medium shot, long shot, long take.

Appendix I

Time and Length of the Shot	Music and Sound Effect	Camera and Action
1:12:35–1:13:07; 1:13:08–1:13:42.	"Goodbye Friends" (*Ah, pengyou zaijian*, a Chinese version based on the renowned song "Bella ciao" from *Most*, a 1969 Yugoslav war epic) **Style**: Diegetic song performance.	As the reformed troupe sets out on its "capitalist" journey, Cui looks out to the distance plaintively, hoping to see Yin one last time before they go. The camera then turns to a reverse tracking shot of the tractor loaded with troupe members passing through the street and city gate, singing "Goodbye Friends" to their family and hometown. **Style**: Medium shot, long shot.
1:21:37–1:23:57, 2 min 20 sec.	"On the Field of Hope" (*Zai xiwang de tianye shang*, music by Shi Guangnan, lyrics by Chen Xiaoguang, 1982) **Style**: Diegetic song performance.	When the troupe first arrives at a remote village where Cui's cousins live, the scene documents the monumental moment of the village getting connected to electric power and the performance that follows. **Style**: Extreme long shot, long take.
1:29:30–1:30:01, 31 sec.	"My Chinese Heart" (*Wo de zhongguoxin*, music by Wang Fuling, lyrics by Huang Zhan, 1984) **Style**: Diegetic song performance.	The scene depicts an open-air concert at a coal mine. **Style**: Extreme long shot, static camera.
1:32:19–1:33:13; 1:33:14–1:33:59; 1:34:00–1:34:57.	"Platform" (*Zhantai*, music, lyrics, and performance by Zhang Xing, 1987) **Style**: Diegetic song from the dashboard stereo of the truck.	When the troupe's truck breaks down on a bleak yellow plateau, Cui gets into the driver's seat and plays a tape of Zhang Xing's rock hit. The second shot is a reverse angle shot that reveals the troupe members surrounding him until they are attracted instead by a train horn. The camera then cuts to an extreme long shot of a passing train on the bridge over a dry riverbed in the highland. **Style**: Medium shot, extreme long shot.

Appendix I

Time and Length of the Shot	Music and Sound Effect	Camera and Action
1:48:31–1:50:14, 1 min 43 sec.	*River Elegy* (*Heshang*, a highly controversial documentary shown on CCTV in 1988 and subsequently banned after the Tiananmen Square protest of 1989) **Style**: Diegetic soundtrack from *River Elegy*, played on television.	Zhong breaks up with Zhang and disappears suddenly. Zhang and Cui come to request her whereabouts while her father is watching television indifferently. **Style**: Medium shot, long take, static camera.
1:50:15–1:52:19, 2 min 4 sec.	"Genghis Khan" (*Chengjisihan*, music by Siegel Jun Ralph and Bernd Meinuger, lyrics by Zheng Guojiang, 1987) **Style**: Recurrent diegetic song.	After a fruitless search for Zhong, Zhang gets drunk and cries out the song in despair. **Style**: Medium shot, long take.
1:52:20–1:53:24; 1:53:25–1:53:47; 1:53:48–1:56:10; 1:56:11–1:56:49; 1:56:50–1:57:21.	"Whether or Not" (*Shifou*, music and lyrics by Luo Dayou, performance by Su Rui, 1989) **Style**: Diegetic song.	This particular succession of five shots pivoting on "Whether or Not" is closely analyzed in chapter four. Of particular significance is Yin's extremely elaborate freestyle dancing to the song. **Style**: Long shot, extreme long shot, long take, static camera.
1:57:22–1:58:31; 1:58:32–1:59:24.	"Platform" (*Zhantai*, music and lyrics by Zhang Xing, 1987) **Style**: Recurrent diegetic song.	The first shot shows that as a member of the now-renamed Shenzhen All Stars Rock and Breakdance Electronic Band, Cui performs Zhang Xing's rock song in a tent to a rowdy audience. With the ill-received performance continuing on the soundtrack, the film cuts to the low-spirited Zhang Jun outside the tent, having now grown long hair in the fashion of a Chinese rock star. **Style**: Long shot, long take.

Time and Length of the Shot	Music and Sound Effect	Camera and Action
1:59:25–1:59:51, 26 sec.	A male voice brazenly touts business against the by-now extremely popular Northwest Wind music (for details, see my first chapter). **Style**: Diegetic sound.	The scene is shot from the far distance, with several individuals performing on the stage barely identifiable. **Style**: Extreme long shot, static camera.
2:04:58–2:05:58; 2:05:59–2:06:04; 2:06:05–2:06:25.	Clips of a sex education video. **Style**: Diegetic sound and video played in a video parlor (cassette cinema).	The scene shows a group of performers patronizing a seedy video parlor that plays a sex education film. **Style**: Long shot, close-up.
2:07:00–2:09:27; 2:11:53–2:12:39.	"Little Girls Under the Street Lamp" (*Ludeng xia de xiao nvhai*, a Chinese cover version and remix of Modern Talking's "Brother Louie," lyrics by Huang Pusheng, performance by Deng Jieyi, 1987) **Style**: Diegetic song and dance performance.	When the troupe travels to a mountainous area and attempts to talk to the local cultural bureau to secure a site to perform, they are manipulated by the treacherous villagers to give a free show. Having failed, the troupe has no choice but to perform on the open bed of their transport truck. The lyrics of the song comment on their misfortune and harsh reality. **Style**: Medium shot, long shot, long take, static camera.
2:13:25–2:15:41, 2 min 6 sec.	The weather bureau has issued a high wind and cold warning sweeping from the north. **Style**: Diegetic announcement from the radio broadcast.	The troupe finally takes a long, arduous journey back home across a crude terrain, during which they are caught in a gusty winter storm. **Style**: Long take.

Appendix I

Time and Length of the Shot	Music and Sound Effect	Camera and Action
2:15:42–2:16:21, 39 sec.	A female voice reads the list of student suspects and runaways. **Style**: Diegetic announcement from the official, public loudspeaker.	Cui and the rest of the troupe members are waiting in a bus station to return home. **Style**: Medium shot, static camera.
2:16:22–2:17:45, 1 min 19 sec.	Popular disco music. **Style**: Diegetic sound from a disco club.	A low-key shot of the young people enjoying a party at a disco club. **Style**: Medium shot, camera pan.
2:18:14–2:19:45, 1 min 31 sec.	"A Nice Day" (*Haorizi*, music by Li Xin, lyrics by Che Xing, 1998; this song was originally performed by Song Zuying at the 1998 CCTV Gala and later became very popular. In my view, the incorporation of this late 1990s song is probably an oversight, given the specific timeframe Jia Zhangke intends to depict in *Platform*) **Style**: Diegetic, off-screen song performance.	Cui returns home only to learn that his father has abandoned his family and moved in with a mistress. A group of women performing "A Nice Day" outside their apartment is heard throughout his conversation with his mother, giving a satirical dimension to the scene. **Style**: Medium shot, long take, static camera.
2:23:22–2:24:09, 2:24:26–2:24:46.	*Yearning* (*Kewang*, dir. Lu Xiaowei, 1990, one of the most influential television dramas in early 1990s China) **Style**: Clips and the eponymous theme song, "Yearning," played on television.	Cui and his mother sit at home and watch the popular television show, while Cui asks why she doesn't divorce his father. Two shots later, Cui is seen walking out of the apartment and onto the snowy street while *Yearning*'s theme song heard on the soundtrack. **Style**: Medium shot.

Time and Length of the Shot	Music and Sound Effect	Camera and Action
2:29:45–2:30:16; 2:30:17–2:32:07.	*The Killer* (*Diexue shuangxiong*, dir. John Woo, 1989) **Style**: Off-screen film soundtrack, both diegetic and nondiegetic. The particular song (and the soundtrack of the film) have also been appropriated in Jia Zhangke's *Xiao Wu*.	Cui looks out from the balcony of his apartment when we hear the playing of *The Killer*. The film soundtrack continues during the next shot (the final shot of the film), in which Cui is napping on a couch while his wife, Yin, is playing with their son and a kettle of boiling water comes to whistle. **Style**: Medium shot, long take, static camera.
2:32:20–2:34:42.	"Traveling in Suzou" (*Gusuxing*, music by Jiang Xianwei, 1962) **Style**: Traditional Chinese flute solo performance, which also appears earlier in the scene of Yin's poetry recital.	Closing credit sequence.

APPENDIX II
Box Office Overview of Mainland China, 1985–2012

Hollywood Imports		Chinese National Films		
Name	Box Office Revenue (million yuan)	Annul Output	Grand Total Box Office Revenue (million yuan)	Box Office Revenue of the Top 5 Grossing Films
1985				
		127	670	
1986				January 1986–November 1986 (million people)
		141	1410	1. *Juvenile Delinquents* 159.47 2. *Rescued from Desperation* 66.00 3. *Betrayal and Revenge* 64.44 4. *Bargain Under the Noose* 54.25 5. *The Little Black Box* 53.70
1987				(million people)
		149	1568	1. *King of Darts* 275.10 2. *The Battle of Taier'zhuang* 161.07 3. *Return of the Sword* 160.42 4. *The Loner* 144.70 5. *The Pairing of Love Birds* 141.02
1988				(million people)
		152	1806	1. *Yellow River Fighter* 184.96 2. *Lightning Action* 145.83 3. *Golden Dart Hero* 140.32 4. *The River Dragon* 118.92 5. *Swords Meet* 117.30
1989				(million people)
		154	2049	1. *Heroine Lv Siniang* 120.77 2. *The Last Duel of the Great Wall* 114.27 3. *The Village of Widows* 104.78 4. *Kaixi Upsets Wutai Mountains* 96.61 5. *Heorine Lv Siniang 2: The Dragon Swordswoman* 76.33

Appendix II

Hollywood Imports			Chinese National Films		
Name	Box Office Revenue (million yuan)	Annul Output	Grand Total Box Office Revenue (million yuan)	Box Office Revenue of the Top 5 Grossing Films	
1990					
		126	2225		
1991				(million people)	
		135.5	2365	1. *Jiao Yulu* 300 2. *Mao Zedong and His Sons* 136 3. *Warriors of China* 112 4. *Decisive Engagement 1* 95.05 5. *Decisive Engagement 2* 94.62	
1992					
		140.5	2003		
1993					
		154	123.48		
1994				(million yuan)	
The Fugitive	Shanghai 6 Chongqing 2.2	148	136.73	1. *Chongqing Negotiations* 7.57 2. *Painting Soul* 4.82 3. *The Long March* 4.20 4. *Green Snake* 3.89 5. *The New Legend of Shaolin* 3.81	
1995				Beijing Gross; Shanghai Gross (million yuan)	
True Lies	Shanghai 13 Beijing 9 PRC 120	146	1730	1. *In the Heat of the Sun* 4.25; 2.40 2. *Red Cherry* 4.12; 7.80 3. *The Peace Hotel* 3.12; 4.00 4. *Shanghai Triad* 2.53; 3.80 5. *My Father is a Hero* 2.12	
Speed	PRC 37.85				
Bad Boy	PRC 32.8				
Die Hard III	Beijing 6 PRC 47				
Forrest Gump	Shanghai 5.2 Beijing 4.2 PRC 19.6				
Lion King	Shanghai 13 Beijing 4.5 PRC 41.3				

Appendix II

Hollywood Imports			Chinese National Films	
Name	Box Office Revenue (million yuan)	Annul Output	Grand Total Box Office Revenue (million yuan)	Box Office Revenue of the Top 5 Grossing Films
1996				Beijing Gross; Shanghai Gross (million yuan)
Outbreak	Beijing 3.67 Shanghai 6 PRC 32.6	110	1740	1. *Kong Fansen* 1.55; 2.8 2. *The Emperor's Shadow* 2.93 3. *Rivalry* 1.85 4. *Her Majesty is Fine* 0.95 5. *The Bewitching Braid* 0.86
Walking in the Clouds	PRC 20.61			
The Bridges of Madison County	Beijing 7.86 Shanghai 8 PRC 39.5			
Broken Arrow	Beijing 4.34 Shanghai 10 PRC 50.57			
Twister	Beijing 7 Shanghai 12 PRC 54.55			
The Rock	Shanghai 9 PRC 47.7			
Mission Impossible	Beijing 6.4 Shanghai 7 PRC 45.1			
Jumanji	Beijing 7.03 Shanghai 9.1 PRC 47.7			
Toy Story	Beijing 4.5 Shanghai 10 PRC 31.8			
The Water World	Shanghai 6 PRC 34			
1997				Beijing Gross; National Gross (million yuan)
Sabrina	Beijing 4 Shanghai 3 PRC 20	88	1560	1. *The Opium War* 4.28; 80 2. *Red River Valley* 3.01; 30 3. *The Great Turn Around* 3.34 4. *Keep Cool* 7.12 5. *The Days Without Lei Feng* 5.76
Eraser	PRC 45.8			
Courage Under Fire	PRC 25.01			
Space Jam	PRC 24.1			
Dante's Peak	PRC 47.6			
Jurassic Park: The Lost World	Beijing 8.71 Shanghai 14 PRC 72.1			

Appendix II

Hollywood Imports			Chinese National Films	
Name	Box Office Revenue (million yuan)	Annul Output	Grand Total Box Office Revenue (million yuan)	Box Office Revenue of the Top 5 Grossing Films
Speed II	Beijing 3.37 PRC 30.47			
1998				National Gross; Beijing Gross (million yuan)
Titanic	Beijing 35 Shanghai 38 PRC 306.1	82	1450	1. *Zhou Enlai's Diplomacy Legends* 33.6; 3.5 2. *Party A, Party B* 33; 11.7 3. *A Time to Remember* 25 4. *Souls of the Sea* 5. *Spicy Love Soup*
Saving Private Ryan	Beijing 11 Shanghai 12 PRC 82.03			
Daylight	Beijing 1 Shanghai 2 PRC 16.25			
Home Alone III	Beijing 5 Shanghai 10 PRC 40.23			
Deep Impact	Beijing 7 Shanghai 6 PRC 51.58			
Volcano	Beijing 3 PRC 16.79			
1999				National Gross (million yuan)
Rush Hour	Beijing 5.2 PRC 25	102	850	1. *Be There or Be Square* 35 2. *No One Less* 30 3. *Lotus Lantern* 24 4. *National Anthem* 17 5. *Grief Over the Yellow River* 17
Mulan	Beijing 1.48 PRC 11.17			
Enemy of the State	Beijing 4 Shanghai 3 PRC 22.05			
Star Wars: Episode I-The Phantom Menace	Shanghai 5 PRC 33.94			
2000				
U-571	PRC 29.10	91	960	
Dinosaur	PRC 28.94			
Mission Impossible II	PRC 29.34			
Gladiator	PRC 27.96			
Matrix	PRC 17.94			
Perfect Storm	PRC 21.0			

Appendix II

Hollywood Imports			Chinese National Films		
Name	Box Office Revenue (million yuan)	Annul Output	Grand Total Box Office Revenue (million yuan)	Box Office Revenue of the Top 5 Grossing Films	
2001				Shanghai Gross (million yuan)	
Vertical Limit	Shanghai 3.8 PRC 26.53	88	800	1. *Out of Xibopo* 5.96　2. *Purple Sun* 3.41　3. *Cosmos and Human Beings* 3.36　4. *The Road Home* 3.11	
Antitrust	PRC 60.86				
Enemy at the Gates	Shanghai 5.2 PRC 21.30				
Pearl Harbor	Shanghai 15 PRC 106.27				
2002				National Gross (million yuan)	
Harry Potter and the Sorcerer's Stone	PRC 60		900	1. *Hero* 250　2. *Chinese Odyssey*　3. *The Touch* 28　4. *The Lion Roars* 22　5. *Out of Death Trap*	
The Lord of the Rings: The Fellowship of the Ring	PRC 50				
Spider-Man	PRC 40				
2003				National Gross (million yuan)	
Harry Potter and the Chamber of Secrets	PRC 52	140	1000	1. *Cell Phone* 55　2. *Warriors of Heaven and Earth* 38　3. *Infernal Affairs 3: End Inferno* 36　4. *Cat and Mouse* 22　5. *Zhou Yu's Train* 19	
The Matrix Revolutions	PRC 41.35				
The Matrix Reloaded					
2004				National Gross (million yuan)	
The Lord of the Rings: The Return of the King	PRC 71.91	212	1377	1. *House of Flying Daggers* 140　2. *A World Without Thieves* 87.57　3. *Kung Fu Hustle* 75.92　4. *New Police Story* 33.16　5. *2046* 25.70	
The Day After Tomorrow	PRC 71				
Troy	PRC 60.50				
Spider-Man 2	PRC 48.61				
Harry Potter and the Prisoner of Azkaban	PRC 33.88				

Appendix II

Hollywood Imports				Chinese National Films	
Name	Box Office Revenue (million yuan)	Annul Output	Grand Total Box Office Revenue (million yuan)	Box Office Revenue of the Top 5 Grossing Films	
2005				National Gross (million yuan)	
Harry Potter and the Goblet of Fire	PRC 83.55	260	2046	1. *The Promise* 140 2. *The Myth* 87.75 3. *The Seven Swords* 73.66 4. *Initial D* 57.25 5. *Seoul Raiders* 33.79	
Star Wars: Episode III-Revenge of the Sith	PRC 69.28				
Mr. and Mrs. Smith	PRC 58.67				
War of the Worlds	PRC 46.26				
National Treasure	PRC 33.38				
2006				National Gross (million yuan)	
The Da Vinci Code	PRC 105	330	2620	1. *Curse of the Golden Flowers* 281 2. *The Banquet* 130 3. *Fearless* 105 4. *Rob-B-Hood* 97 5. *Confession of Pain* 68	
King Kong	PRC 102				
Mission Impossible	PRC 81.20				
Poseidon	PRC 68.90				
2007				National Gross (million yuan)	
Transformers	PRC 282.31	402	3327	1. *The Warlords* 170.31 2. *Assembly* 143.54 3. *Lust, Caution* 137.57 4. *Protégé* 65 5. *Secret* 36.70	
Spider-Man 3	PRC 149.70				
Harry Potter and the Order of the Phoenix	PRC 145.14				
Pirates of the Caribbean 3	PRC 125.60				
Casino Royale	PRC 92.70				
Night at the Museum	PRC 64.84				
2008				National Gross (million yuan)	
Kung Fu Panda	PRC 182.36		3884	1. *Red Cliff* 321.24 2. *Painted Skin* 232.50 3. *If You Are the One* 214.55 4. *CJ7* 203.06 5. *The Forbidden Kingdom* 171.20 6. *Kung Fu Dunk* 110.63 7. *Forever Enthralled* 109.92 8. *The Mummy: The Tomb of the Dragon Emperor* 108.34	
Quantum of Solace	PRC 139.67				
Hancock	PRC 108.05				
Iron Man	PRC 90.63				
The Chronicles of Narnia: Prince Caspian	PRC 82.93				

Hollywood Imports				Chinese National Films
Name	Box Office Revenue (million yuan)	Annul Output	Grand Total Box Office Revenue (million yuan)	Box Office Revenue of the Top 5 Grossing Films
2009				National Gross (million yuan)
2012	PRC 465	456	6206	1. *The Founding of a Republic* 435
Transformers	PRC 430			2. *Red Cliff II* 265
Harry Potter and the Half-blood Prince	PRC 165			3. *A Simple Noodle Story* 230
				4. *The Message* 215
Ice Age: Dawn of the Dinosaurs	PRC 160			5. *Bodyguards and Assassins* 210
G.I. Joe: Rise of Cobra	PRC 135			6. *City of Life and Death* 175
2010				National Gross (million yuan)
Avatar	PRC 1378.70	526	10171	1. *Aftershock* 673.32
Inception	PRC 442.07			2. *Let the Bullets Fly* 479.81
Alice in Wonderland	PRC 226.40			3. *If You Are the One* 334.51
The Expendables	PRC 218.76			4. *Detective Dee and the Mystery of the Phantom Flame* 292.28
Harry Potter and the Deathly Hallows 1	PRC 205.81			5. *Ip Man 2* 234.04
Iron Man 2	PRC 176.37			6. *Sacrifice* 193.10
2011				National Gross (million yuan)
Transformers 3	PRC 1082.85	558	13115	1. *The Flowers of War* 467.14
Kung Fu Panda 2	PRC 617.11			2. *Beginning of the Great Revival* 422.90
Pirates of the Caribbean 4	PRC 467.27			3. *Flying Swords of Dragon Gate* 412.20
Harry Potter and the Deathly Hallows 2	PRC 404.41			4. *Love is Not Blind* 356.07
The Smurfs	PRC 261.00			5. *Shaolin* 216.23
2012				National Gross (million yuan)
Titanic (3D)	PRC 947.58	745	17073	1. *Lost in Thailand* 1004.61
Mission Impossible 4	PRC 674.71			2. *Painted Skin: The Resurrection* 704.51
Life of Pi	PRC 571.05			3. *CZ12* 535.33
The Avengers	PRC 567.92			4. *Back to 1942* 372.00
Men in Black 3	PRC 504.15			5. *Cold War* 253.61
				6. *The Silent War* 233.74

Note: All the data were collected from *Zhongguo dianying nianjian* [*China Film Yearbook*] (Beijing: Zhongguo dianying chubanshe, 1985–2012) and *Zhongguo dianying chanye yanjiu baogao* [*The Research Report on Chinese Film Industry*] (Beijing: Zhongguo dianying chubanshe, 2007–2013).

NOTES

Note on Names, Translation, and Publication

For the sake of clarity and consistency, I decided not to include Chinese characters in the main body of the text unless necessary. I chose to adopt the pinyin system of Romanization to transliterate the important Chinese terms, film titles, and names that appear in the text. Chinese sources used in the book are my own translations unless otherwise specified. In the case of person's name, I usually observe the Chinese custom to put family name in front of given name, unless another version of the name has been more commonly used and widely recognized.

Portions of some chapters were previously published elsewhere. All of these texts have been substantially revised, rewritten, and updated for this book. These essays are:

"Chinese Rock 'n' Roll and Cui Jian on Screen." In *The Oxford Handbook of New Audiovisual Aesthetics*, edited by Claudia Gorbman, John Richardson, and Carol Vernallis, 266–83. New York: Oxford University Press, 2013.
"'Hip Hop Is My Knife, Rap Is My Sword': Hip Hop, Cultural (Re)production and the Question of Authenticity and Authorship in Contemporary China." In *Three Asias: Japan, S. Korea, China*, edited by Takayuki Tatsumi, Jina Kim and Zhang Zhen. *Paradoxa: Studies in World Literary Genres* 22 (2010): 269–98.
"'Leitmotif': State, Market, and Postsocialist Chinese Film Industry under Neoliberal Globalization." In *Neoliberalism and Global Cinema: Capital, Culture, and Marxist Critique*, edited by Jyotsna Kapur and Keith B. Wagner, 157–79. London and New York: Routledge, 2011.

Overture

1. Jacques Attali, *Noise: The Political Economy of Music*, trans. Brian Massumi (Minneapolis: University of Minnesota Press, 1985), 14.

2. For more discussion, see Ting Wang, "Hollywood's Pre-WTO Crusade in China," *Jump Cut: A Review of Contemporary Media* 49 (Spring 2007), accessed August 25, 2015, http://www.ejumpcut.org/archive/jc49.2007/TingWang.

3. These numbers and data were obtained from two websites that specialize in the statistical documentation of box-office receipts in the US and many other countries including China: http://www.boxofficemojo.com/ (in English) and http://www.cbooo.cn/ (in Chinese), accessed August 25, 2015.

4. Germain Lussier, "Chinese Box Office Overtakes U.S. for First Time in History," *Slash Film*, March 3, 2015, accessed August 25, 2015, http://www.slashfilm.com/chinese-box-office-overtakes-america.

5. Zhang Yingjin, *Screening China: Critical Interventions, Cinematic Reconfigurations, and the Transnational Imaginary in Contemporary Chinese Cinema* (Ann Arbor: University of Michigan Press, 2002), 13.

6. In her influential article on "The Mass Production of the Senses: Classical Cinema as Vernacular Modernism," Miriam Hansen asserts that film became the "first global vernacular" after it was born and as it evolved in the twentieth century. Hansen argues that classical Hollywood, a dominant and hegemonic force in the entertaining business, has always been both international and vernacular in promoting a modernist sensibility. Furthermore, its global appeal to a wide, mass audience is based upon its association with the modern and the popular and everyday life. In "Fallen Women, Rising Stars, New Horizons: Shanghai Silent Film as Vernacular Modernism," Hansen further develops her arguments and calls Shanghai melodrama of the 1920s and 1930s "a distinct brand of vernacular modernism." To her, Shanghai cinema took form and thrived in its golden age under the impact of the powerful force of Hollywood "while drawing on and transforming Chinese traditions in theater, literature, graphic and print culture, both modernist and popular." See Miriam Hansen, "The Mass Production of the Senses: Classical Cinema as Vernacular Modernism," *Modernism/Modernity* 6. 2 (April 1999): 59–77; and "Fallen Women, Rising Stars, New Horizons: Shanghai Silent Film as Vernacular Modernism," *Film Quarterly* 54.1 (fall 2000): 10–22.

7. Michel Chion, *Audio-Vision: Sound on Screen*, trans. Claudia Gorbman (New York: Columbia University Press, 1994), 63.

8. Mikhail Bakhtin, *Problems in Dostoevsky's Poetics*, ed. and trans. Caryl Emerson (Minneapolis: University of Minnesota Press, 1993), 34.

9. Ibid., 36; emphasis in the original text.

10. Rick Altman, McGraw Jones, and Sonia Tatroe, "Inventing the Cinema Soundtrack: Hollywood's Multiplane Sound System," in *Music and Cinema*, eds. James Buhler, Caryl Flinn, and David Neumeyer (Hanover: Wesleyan University Press, 2000), 339–59.

11. Ibid., 341.

12. Ibid.

13. It is noteworthy that *Journal of Chinese Cinemas* launched a special issue, in 2013, on the research of Chinese film sounds; the issue pushed the study to a new stage. Along with Jean Ma and Matthew Johnson's "Introduction" (179–86), some of the important contributions selected into the issue are Nicole Huang's "Listening to Films: Politics of the Auditory in 1970s China" (187–206), Ying Bao's "Remembering the Invisible: Soundscape and Memory of 1989" (207–24), Lily Wong's "Moving Serenades: Hearing the Sinophonic in MP & GI's *Longxiang Fengwu*" (225–40), Evelyn Shih's "Getting the Last Laugh: Opera Legacy, Comedy, and Camp as Attraction in the Late Years of Taiyupian" (241–62), Mark Gallagher and Julian Stringer's "Reshaping Contemporary Chinese Film Sound: Dolby Laboratories and Changing Industrial Practices" (263–76), and Charles Kronengold's "Multitemporality and the Speed(s) of Thought in Jonnie To's Action Films" (277–95). See *Journal of Chinese Cinemas* 7.3 (2013).

14. This is not intended as an exhaustive list, but rather as an overview of the basic scholarship that contributes to and helps to define the field of Chinese film sound studies. Representative pieces include, in the order of publication date, Yueh-yu Yeh, "A National Score: Popular Music and Taiwanese Cinema" (PhD diss., University of Southern California, 1995); "A Life of Its Own: Musical Discourses in Wong Kar-wai's Films," *Post Script: Essays in Film and the Humanities* 19.1 (Fall 1999): 120–36; "Historiographic and Sinification: Music in Chinese Cinema of the 1930s," *Cinema Journal* 41.3 (Spring 2002): 78–97; Sue Tuohy, "Metropolitan Sounds: Music in Chinese Films of the 1930s," in *Cinema and Urban Culture in Shanghai, 1922–1943*, ed. Yingjin Zhang (Stanford: Stanford University Press, 1999), 200–21; "Reflexive Cinema: Reflection on and Representing the Worlds of Chinese Film and Music," in *Global Soundtracks: Worlds of Film Music*, ed. Mark Slobin (Middletown: Wesleyan

University Press, 2008), 177–213; Zhang Zhen, "*Song at Midnight*: Acoustic Horror and the Grotesque Face," in *An Amorous History of the Silver Screen: Shanghai Cinema, 1896–1937* (Chicago: University of Chicago Press, 2005): 298–344; Elena Pollacchi, "The Sound of the City: Chinese Films of the 1990s and Urban Noise," in *Cities in Transition: The Moving Image and the Modern Metropolis*, eds. Andrew Webber and Emma Wilson (London: Wallflower Press, 2008), 193–204; Ying Xiao, "More than a Mass Noise: Popular Music and Polyphonic Soundscapes in Postsocialist Chinese Cinema, Media, and Culture" (PhD diss., New York University, 2010); and Jean Ma, "Delayed Voices: Intertexuality, Music, and Gender in *The Hole*," *Journal of Chinese Cinemas* 5.2 (2011): 123–39, *Sounding the Modern Women: The Songstress in Chinese Cinema* (Durham: Duke University Press, 2015).

15. Chion points out that the unity of sound and image is fundamental to constituting and perceiving film as it is "the very signifier of the question of human unity, a cinematic unity, unity itself." See Chion, *Audio-Vision*, 97.

16. Edward M. Gunn, *Rendering the Regional: Local Language in Contemporary Chinese Media* (Honolulu: University of Hawaii Press, 2006) and Jin Liu, *Signifying the Local: Media Productions Rendered in Local Languages in Mainland China in the New Millennium* (Leiden: Brill, 2013).

17. Claudia Gorbman, *Unheard Melodies: Narrative Film Music* (Bloomington: Indiana University Press, 1987), 2.

18. Simon Frith, "Towards an Aesthetic of Popular music," in *Music and Society*, eds. Richard Leppart and Susan McClary (Cambridge: Cambridge University Press, 1987), 133.

19. As Appadurai explains: "I propose that an elementary framework for exploring such disjunctures is to look at the relationship among five dimensions of global cultural flows that can be termed (a) *ethnoscape*s, (b) *mediascape*s, (c) *technoscape*s, (d) *financescape*s, and (e) *ideoscape*s. The suffix *–scape* allows us to point to the fluid, irregular shapes of these landscapes, shapes that characterize international capital as deeply as they do international clothing styles. These terms with the common suffix *–scape* also indicate that these are not objectively given relations that look the same from every angle of vision but, rather, that they are deeply perspectival constructs, inflected by the historical, linguistic, and political situatedness of different sorts of actors: nation-states, multinationals, disaporic communities, as well as subnational groupings and movements (whether religious, political, or economic), and even intimate face-to-face groups, such as villages, neighborhoods, and families. Indeed, the individual actor is the last focus of the perspectival set of landscapes, for these landscapes are eventually navigated by agents who both experience and constitute larger formations, in part from their own sense of what these landscapes offer." Arjun Appadurai, *Modernity at Large: Cultural Dimensions of Globalization* (Minneapolis: University of Minnesota Press, 1996), 33.

20. Zhang Xudong, "Postmodernism and Postsocialist Society: Cultural Politics after the 'New Era,'" in *Postsocialism and Cultural Politics: China in the Last Decade of the Twentieth Century* (Durham: Duke University Press, 2008), 136.

21. For these terms, labels of periodization, and relevant discussions, see Zhang, "Postmodernism and Postsocialist Society," 136–77; Wang Hui, "The Year 1989 and the Historical Roots of Neoliberalism in China," *Position: East Asia Cultures Critique* 12.1 (2004): 7–69; and Li Minqi, "After Neoliberalism: Empire, Social Democracy, or Socialism," *Monthly Review* 55.8 (January 2004), accessed September 25, 2010, http://monthlyreview.org/01041i.htm.

22. Michel Foucault, "The Subject and Power," in *Power: Volume 3: Essential Works of Foucault 1954–1984*, ed. James D. Faubion, trans. Robert Hurley et al. (New York: New Press, 2000), 337.

23. Lisa Rofel, *Desiring China: Experiments in Neoliberalism, Sexuality and Public Culture* (Durham: Duke University Press, 2007).

24. Zhang Yingjin, "Rebel Without a Cause? China's New Urban Generation and Postsocialist Filmmaking," in *The Urban Generation: Chinese Cinema and Society at the Turn of the Twenty-first Century*, ed. Zhang Zhen (Durham: Duke University Press, 2007), 52.

25. Ibid., 50.

26. For historians and critics, the year 1989 marks a significant shift in Chinese history but also the shifting historical relationship between high culture and low culture, the public and the private, the political and the commercial, the elite and everyday life. In connection with the Frankfurt School's mode of consumerist mass culture but fundamentally different from it, Chinese mass culture, as Liu Kang argues, is modulated toward local needs and is deeply ingrained in the Chinese revolutionary past and socialist infrastructure. Propelled by the immensely social and economic reconstruction in the post-revolutionary reform, mass culture in contemporary China has undergone significant metamorphoses and "has increasingly become the site of dialogical contention of a variety of forces, among which the culture industry, or the commercial popular culture, and China's local and national forms and styles, including the revolutionary legacy of the culture of the masses, intersect and interpenetrate." See Liu Kang, "Popular Culture and the Culture of the Masses in Contemporary China," in *Postmodernism & China*, eds. Arif Dirlik and Xudong Zhang (Durham: Duke University Press, 2000), 141.

27. Lydia Liu elaborates the differences and connections between postsocialism amd transnationalism: "Postsocialism by no means constitutes resistance to transnational capitalism, although it is a direct response to it; however, the existence of residual socialist thought, state apparati, and historical memory do complicate the ways in which transnationalism and its critique operate in a postsocialist context." See Lydia H. Liu, *What's Happened to Ideology?: Transnationalism, Postsocialism, and the Study of Global Media Culture* (Durham: Asian/Pacific Studies Institute, Duke University, 1998), 14.

28. Rey Chow, *Primitive Passions: Visuality, Sexuality, Ethnography, and Contemporary Chinese Cinema* (New York: Columbia University Press, 1995), 26–28.

29. Ibid., 13.

30. Ibid., 26.

31. Hamid Naficy, *An Accented Cinema: Exilic and Diasporic Filmmaking* (Princeton: Princeton University Press, 2001).

Chapter One

1. Rey Chow, *Primitive Passions: Visuality, Sexuality, Ethnography, and Contemporary Chinese Cinema* (New York: Columbia University Press, 1995), 107.

2. In a meticulous delineation of how the term came about, Tony Rayns pointedly asserts: "Whatever, the nickname's underlying significance is that it implies some kind of new beginning and stresses the distance that separates the young directors from their 'Fourth Generation' predecessors. Calling them 'The Fifth Generation' is a characteristically Chinese way of saying that they represent a 'new wave.'" See Tony Rayns, "Chinese Vocabulary: An Introduction to King of the Children and the New Chinese Cinema," in *King of the Children and the New Chinese Cinema*, ed. and trans. Bonnie S. McDougall (London and Boston: Faber and Faber, 1989), 16.

3. André Bazin, "The Evolution of the Language of Cinema," in *What Is Cinema? Volume 1* (Berkeley and Los Angeles: University of California Press, 2005), 27.

4. The most influential studies on the Fifth Generation films and their artistic, social, and cultural implications are, among others, Rey Chow's *Primitive Passions: Visuality, Sexuality, Ethnography, and Contemporary Chinese Cinema* (New York: Columbia University Press, 1995), Ying Zhu's *Chinese Cinema during the Era of Reform: The Ingenuity of the System* (Westport: Praeger, 2003), Paul Clark's *Reinventing China: A Generation and Its Films* (Hong Kong: Chinese University Press, 2005), Zhang Xudong's *Chinese Modernism in the Era of Reforms: Cultural Fever, Avant-garde Fiction, and the New Chinese Cinema* (Durham: Duke University Press, 1997), and Dai Jinhua's "Severed Bridge: The Art of the Son's Generation," in *Cinema and Desire: Feminist Marxism and Cultural Politics in the Work of Dai Jinhua*, trans. Lisa Rofel and Hu Ying, eds. Jing Wang and Tani E. Barlow (London and New York: Verso, 2002).

5. Miriam Hansen, "The Mass Production of the Senses: Classical Cinema as Vernacular Modernism," *Modernism/Modernity* 6.2 (April 1999): 60.

6. Rayns, "Chinese Vocabulary," 24.

7. David Robinson, "Arts (Cinema): Touching Regard for Character/ Review of *Yellow Earth* at the ICA and *Survivors—The Blues Today* (PG) at the Cannon, Charing Cross Road," *Times*, August 8, 1986.

8. Clark, *Reinventing China*, 87–88.

9. Bai Tudi, "Dianying huang tudi bu zhide zanyang" [The Film *Yellow Earth* Does Not Deserve Praise], *Zhengming* [*Contention*] (August 1985): 78.

10. Shao Mujin, "Huashuo huang tudi" [Speaking of Yellow Earth], in *Huashuo huang tudi* [*Speaking of Yellow Earth*] (Beijing: Zhongguo dianying chubanshe, 1986), 258.

11. Esther C. M. Yau, "*Yellow Earth*: Western Analysis and a Non-western Text," *Film Quarterly* 41.2 (Winter 1987–88): 26.

12. Bonnie S. McDougall, *The Yellow Earth: A Film by Chen Kaige with a Complete Translation of the Filmscript* (Hong Kong: Chinese University Press, 1991).

13. For the film title, Chen sought something simple yet powerful until one afternoon the prevailing yellowness of the landscape suddenly dawned upon him. It took some time for the title to be accepted. According to Zhang Yimou, it was not officially adopted until the screening. See *Huashuo huang tudi*, 288.

14. McDougall, *The Yellow Earth*, 31.

15. *Suona* is a traditional Chinese musical instrument, used frequently in the folk music of northern China. In combination with other instruments such as drum, *gong*, and organ, it is often performed outdoors and has long been used for festival and military purposes.

16. McDougall, *The Yellow Earth*, 175–76.

17. See Karima Fumitoshi and Li He, "Chen Kaige yu da dao zhu duihua" [The Conversations Between Chen Kaige and Ogisha Oshima], *Dangdai dianying* [*Contemporary Cinema*] 6 (1987): 111–18.

18. Chen Kaige, "Qianli zou shanbei: pingqiong he xiwang de shouji" [A Thousand Miles Through Northern Shaanxi: Notes on Poverty and Hope], *Dianying yishu* [*Film Art*] 4 (1986): 31.

19. Zhang Yimou, "Huang tudi shying chanshu" [Explanation on the Cinematography of *Yellow Earth*], *Beijing dianying xueyuan xuebao* [*Journal of Beijing Film Academy*] 1 (1985): 116–19.

20. Related discussions can be found in Sue Tuohy, "The Social Life of Genre: The Dynamics of Folksong in China," *Asian Music* 30.2 (Spring/Summer 1999): 39–86; and Han Kuo-Huang, "Folk Songs of the Han Chinese: Characteristics and Classifications," *Asian Music* 20.2 (Spring/Summer 1989): 107–28.

21. Chow, *Primitive Passions*, 38–39.
22. Ibid., 38.
23. Ludwig Wittgenstein, *Tractatus Logico-Philosophicus*, trans. D. F. Pears and B. F. McGuiness (London: Routledge, 1961), 151.
24. Lu Xun, *Yecao* [*Wild Grass*], trans. Yang Xianyi and Gladys Yang (Hong Kong: Chinese University Press, 2003), 2.
25. Chen, "Qianli zou shanbei: pingqiong he xiwang de shouji," 29.
26. Chen Kaige construes some of the philosophical connotations and styles in this work: "I want our film to be rich and variable, free to the point of wildness; its ideas should be expressed with great ease, without any limitations or restrictions. However, most of the actual contours of the film must be mild, calm and slow . . . The quintessence of our style can be summed up in a single word: 'concealment.'" See Geremie Barme and John Minford, eds., *Seeds of Fire: Chinese Voices of Conscience* (New York: Hill and Wang, 1988), 259.
27. Chow, *Primitive Passions*, 171.
28. Zhang Wei, "New Film Sparks Controversy and Acclaim," *Beijing Review* 29.6–7 (February 1986): 31.
29. Chen Kaige later admitted that the use of a professional singer in *Yellow Earth* was a technical oversight. But he still insisted that music and sound effects in the film sprang from deliberate aesthetic experimentation and that he intended the film's sound to be as artistically revolutionary as his ambitious plans for the film's structure and cinematography.
30. See Tuohy, "The Social Life of Genre" and Han, "Folk Songs of the Han Chinese."
31. Clark, *Reinventing China*, 146.
32. Ryans, "Chinese Vocabulary," 31.
33. Clark, *Reinventing China*, 147.
34. See Rey Chow, "Male Narcissism and National Culture: Subjectivity in Chen Kaige's *King of Children*," in *Primitive Passions: Visuality, Sexuality, Ethnography, and Contemporary Chinese Cinema* (New York: Columbia University Press, 1995), 108–41; Zhang Xudong, "A Critical Account of Chen Kaige's *King of the Children*," in *Chinese Modernism in the Era of Reforms: Cultural Fever, Avant-garde Fiction, and the New Chinese Cinema* (Durham: Duke University Press, 1997), 282–305; Dai Jinhua, "Severed Bridge: The Art of the Son's Generation," in *Cinema and Desire: Feminist Marxism and Cultural Politics in the Work of Dai Jinhua*, eds. Jing Wang and Tani E. Barlow, trans. Lisa Rofel and Hu Ying (London and New York: Verso, 2002), 13–48.
35. Zhang, "A Critical Account of Chen Kaige's *King of the Children*," 284.
36. Chen Kaige was sent down as a *zhiqing* (educated youth) to a rubber farm in Yunnan during the Cultural Revolution. Many of his classmates, who are the backbones of the Fifth Generation and contribute to the Chinese New Wave, were also sent to the poor, less developed countryside. They had spent many years in exile before being admitted to Beijing Film Academy in 1978, when the Cultural Revoltion was over.
37. "Lao Gan" is literally translated as "Old Pole." The first word, *lao*, is a Chinese colloquialism used to address an old acquaintance. The second word, *gan*, serves as an indication of this character's thin and weak figure, perhaps the result of long-term malnutrition. Taken together, this phrase alludes to his *zhiqing* identity—an educated youth who has been assigned to the countryside for years of labor.
38. The term *Verfremdungseffekt* is a critical concept developed by Bertolt Brecht essential to his theory of theater. Translated into English as "defamiliarization effect," "estrangement effect," "alienation effect," or "distancing effect," Brecht used this term to assert a form

of performance and aesthetic "playing in such a way that the audience was hindered from simply identifying itself with the characters in the play." Artists may draw on the defamiliarization effect to create a work that can arouse the audience's reaction, interaction, observation, and an intellectual level of understanding. See John Willett, trans. and ed., *Brecht on Theatre: The Development of an Aesthetic* (New York: Hill and Wang, 1964), 91.

39. McDougall, *King of the Children and the New Chinese Cinema*, 62; my emphasis.
40. Chow, *Primitive Passions*, 118.
41. Rayns, "Chinese Vocabulary."
42. Friedrich Nietzsche, *The Birth of Tragedy*, trans. Walter Kaufmann (New York: Vintage Books, 1967), 136.
43. It is widely known among practitioners and scholars of Chinese music that mainland popular music has followed a different trajectory from that of Hong Kong and Taiwan. While the highly commercialized formula of Hong Kong and Taiwan is often used to evaluate the virtues and disadvantages of the mainland music industry, some critics contend that this monolithic classification of Hong Kong and Taiwan music as an undifferentiated whole is reductionist, as popular music from Taiwan arguably bears larger affinities to that of the mainland, particularly in the way that popular music therein serves as a vehicle of cultural reflection and for the construction of national identity. For an example of these polemics, see Dong Yajun, "Ta de ge heyi rang ni rumi: fang xianggang yingshi gequ dawang jiaguhui xiansheng" [How Does His Songs Captivate You?: An Interview With The Great Master of Hong Kong Film Music Mr. Gu Jiahui], *Dianying pingjie* [*Film Review*] 7 (1988): 26–27.
44. For further discussions, see Jin Zhaojun, *Guangtian huari xia de liuxing: qingli zhongguo liuxing yinyue* [*The Popular in High Profile: Experiencing Chinese Popular Music*] (Beijing: Remin yinyue chubanshe,) 2002.
45. Mercedes M. Dujunco, "Hybridity and Disjuncture in Mainland Chinese Popular Music," in *Global Goes Local: Popular Culture in Asia*, eds. Timothy J. Craig and Richard King (Vancouver: University of British Columbia Press, 2002), 32.
46. Michel Foucault, "The Subject and Power," in *Power: Volume 3: Essential Works of Foucault, 1954–1984*, ed. James D. Faubion, trans. Robert Hurley et al. (New York: New Press, 2000).
47. Nimrod Baranovitch, *China's New Voices: Popular Music, Ethnicity, Gender and Politics, 1978-1997* (Berkeley: University of California Press, 2003), 21.
48. Jin Zhaojun, "Zhongguo liuxing yinyue 30 nian huishou" [30 Years of Chinese Popular Music in Retrospect], *Nanfang zhoumo* [*Southern Weekend*], December 11, 2008; my translation.
49. Roland Barthes, "The Grain of the Voice," in *Image, Music, Text*, trans. Stephen Heath (New York: Hill and Wang, 1977), 179–89.

Chapter Two

1. Rey Chow, *Primitive Passions: Visuality, Sexuality, Ethnography, and Contemporary Chinese Cinema* (New York: Columbia University Press, 1995), 153–54; emphasis in the original text.
2. For discussions, see Zhang Xudong, "Ideology and Utopia in Zhang Yimou's *Red Sorghum*," in *Chinese Modernism in the Era of Reforms: Cultural Fever, Avant-garde Fiction, and the New Chinese Cinema* (Durham: Duke University Press, 1997), 306–28.

3. Dai Jinhua, "Severed Bridge: The Art of the Son's Generation," in *Cinema and Desire: Feminist Marxism and Cultural Politics in the Work of Dai Jinhua*, trans. Lisa Rofel and Hu Ying, eds. Jing Wang and Tani E. Barlow (London and New York: Verso, 2002), 29.

4. Ibid.

5. Qian Qian, "Dianying honggaoliang de shangyexing" [The Commercial Value of Film *Red Sorghum*] and Zhang Zhaohui, "Zai haizi wang yu jin naozhong jiang zhijian" [Between *King of the Children* and the Golden Alarm], *Dianying pinjie* [*Film Review*] (September 1988): 14.

6. For influential critiques of *Red Sorghum*, see Rey Chow, "The Forces of Surfaces: Defiance in Zhang Yimou's Films," in *Primitive Passions*, 142–71; Jerome Silbergeld, "Ruins of a Sorghum Field, Eclipse of a Nation: *Red Sorghum* on Page and Screen," in *China into Film: Frames of Reference in Contemporary Chinese Cinema* (London: Reaktion Books), 53–95; Zhang Xudong, "Ideology and Utopia in Zhang Yimou's *Red Sorghum*," in *Chinese Modernism in the Era of Reforms*, 306–28; Zhang Yingjin, "Ideology of the Body in *Red Sorghum*: National Allegory, National Roots, and Third Cinema," *East-West Film Journal* 4.2 (June 1990); and Wang Yuejin, "*Red Sorghum*: Mixing Memory and Desire," in *Perspectives on Chinese Cinema*, ed. Chris Berry (London: British Film Institute, 1991), 80–103. I also came across a brief discussion of the aural and visual elements in *Red Sorghum* by Yvonne Ng, "Imagery and Sound in *Red Sorghum*," *Kinema: A Journal for Film and Audiovisual Media* (Spring 1995), accessed March 21, 2015, http://www.kinema.uwaterloo.ca/article.php?id=354&feature.

7. Luo Xianrong, "Kuankuan de dalu, changchang de baochuan: qiantan dianying honggaoliang de sige yise" [Big Road, Long Boat: A Preliminary Discussion on Four Songs and One Color in *Red Sorghum*], *Dianying pinjie* [*Film Review*] (August 1988): 24–25.

8. Laura Mulvey remarks in her well-known article "Visual Pleasure and Narrative Cinema" that classical Hollywood cinema largely identifies the spectator as male, generating a dominant, masculine perspective and what she calls "the male gaze." Mulvey suggests that visual pleasure for all viewers is then inevitably drawn from the female characters in film being approached and constructed as image "to be looked at" and the object of desire, thereby serving as a projection of the larger patriarchy social structure. See Laura Mulvey, "Visual Pleasure and Narrative Cinema," *Screen* 16 (1975): 6–18.

9. Rey Chow, "The Forces of Surfaces: Defiance in Zhang Yimou's Films," in *Primitive Passions*, 142–71.

10. Yingjin Zhang, "Ideology of the Body in *Red Sorghum*: National Allegory, National Roots, and Third Cinema," *East-West Film Journal*, 4.2 (June 1990): 40.

11. Xu Linzheng, "Zhao Jiping gushi: 'diwudai' dianying yinyue zhangmen ren" [Legend of Zhao Jiping: A Great Master of the 'Fifth Generation' Film Music], *Dazhong dianying* [*Popular Cinema*] 4 (2006): 29; my translation.

12. The commentaries by the Hundred Flowers Awards committee (an audience-oriented award based on popular polls) represent such a popular view: "*Red Sorghum* eulogizes forcefully and boldly the indomitable will to freedom and the great, inexhaustible vitality of the Chinese nation." See Chen Haosu, "Guanyu gushipian honggaoliang de taolun" [Discussions on *Red Sorghum*], in *Zhongguo dianying nianjian 1989* [*China Film Yearbook 1989*] (Beijing: Zhongguo dianying chubanshe, 1989), 273–76.

13. Zhang Yimou, "Chang yizhi shengming de zange" [Sing a Paean to Life], *Dangdai danying* [*Contemporary Cinema*] 2 (1988): 81–83.

14. Ibid.

15. Friedrich Nietzsche, "The Birth of Tragedy from the Spirit of Music," in *Critical Theory Since Plato*, ed. Hazard Adams (New York: Harcourt Brace Jovanovich, 1977), 637.

16. Xu, "Zhao Jiping gushi," 28; my emphasis.

17. Ibid.

18. Jiao Xiongping, "Discussing *Red Sorghum*," in *Zhang Yimou: Interviews*, ed. Frances Gateward (Jackson: University Press of Mississippi, 2001), 5–10.

19. Zhang, "Chang yizhi shengming de zange," 81–83.

20. Andrew Jones, *Like a Knife: Ideology and Genre in Contemporary Chinese Popular Music* (Ithaca: East Asia Program, Cornell University, 1992), 57–58.

21. Jones, *Like a Knife*, 57–58.

22. Kaja Silverman, *The Acoustic Mirror: The Female Voice in Psychoanalysis and Cinema* (Bloomington and Indianapolis: Indiana University Press, 1988), 44.

23. Ibid.

24. Roland Barthes, "The Grain of the Voice," in *Image, Music, Text*, trans. Stephen Heath (New York: Hill and Wang, 1977), 188.

25. Jiao, "Discussing *Red Sorghum*," 5–10.

26. The so-called "cultural fever" (*wenhuare*) is a heated, nationwide discussion with respect to modernity and Chinese tradition at the historical threshold of reform. It emerged on the mainland in early 1985, blossomed into a pervasive sociocultural movement in the following years, and was brought to a sudden end with the crackdown of Tiananmen protest in 1989. See the related discussions in my introduction and first chapter.

27. Chow, *Primitive Passions*, 38.

28. Dai, "Severed Bridge," 30.

29. Lu Xun, "Silent China," in *Silent China: Selected Writings of Lu Xun*, ed. and trans. Gladys Yang (London: Oxford University Press, 1973), 164.

30. Ibid., 167.

31. Dai, "Severed Bridge," 27.

32. *Red Sorghum* proved to be a critical and commercial success, as I indicated earlier in the chapter. Its influence, moreover, goes far beyond the film and music circles and has influenced a full range of other domains, including performance, fashion, and foodways. All of these come to form what the critics term "the Red Sorghum Phenomenon" or "the Red Sorghum Effect." See discussions in Zhang Chunsheng, "Hong gaoliang xianxiang: yishu de rensheng jiazhi yu shenghuo jiazhi" [The Red Sorghum Phenomenon: The Life and Everyday Life Value of Arts], *Nanfang wentan* [*Southern Cultural Forum*] 5 (1988): 47–50; Lei Da, Zeng Zhengnan, Tong Daoming and Wang Dehou, "Yige hao 'xianxiang'" [A Good "Phenomenon"], *Dianying yishu* [*Film Art*] 8 (1988): 15–52; Ding Shaolun, "Wenhua xungen yu honggaoliang xianxiang" [Cultural Root-seeking and the Red Sorghum Phenomenon], *Shandong shida xuebiao* [*Journal of Shandong Normal University*] 2 (1989): 29–25; and Liu Mingqi, "Hong gaoliang xiaoying yu yishu minzhu" [The Red Sorghum Effect and Democracy of Arts], *Dianying pingjie* [*Movie Review*] 11 (1988): 14. When I was in Beijing in the 1990s, while "Red Sorghum" was still a big phenomenon, I frequently visited Summer Place, the Old Summer Palace, Beihai Park, the Temple of Heaven, and other historical sites and scenic spots of Beijing. I and other visitors were not surprised to often be approached by groups of people who simulated and acted out the wedding and sedan bouncing scenes as a way to sell us the so-called "authentic" Chinese experience. A replication of film, music, and ethnographic artifacts, therefore, became one of the great attractions in places that convene and are identified with Chinese culture, history, and a new sense of entertainment and everyday life in contemporary China.

Chapter Three

1. This is one of the first and foremost songs by Cui Jian, the so-called godfather of Chinese rock, from his most famous album of the same title. Released in 1989, the album is celebrated as the first rock album in China, and it also features "Nothing to My Name," China's first rock song and the one that made Cui Jian a legend. The album turned to be a big hit in music and cultural circles in late 1980s China. The song was performed in Mandarin Chinese.

2. Tim Brace and Paul Friedlander, "Rock and Roll on the New Long March: Popular Music, Cultural Identity, and Political Opposition in the People's Republic of China," in *Rockin' the Boat: Mass Music and Mass Movements*, ed. Reebee Garofalo (Boston: South End Press, 1992), 127.

3. Jeroen de Kloet, "Marx or Market: Chinese Rock and the Sound of Fury," in *Multiple Modernities: Cinemas and Popular Media in Transcultural East Asia*, ed. Jenny Kwok Wah Lau (Philadelphia: Temple University Press, 2003), 28–52.

4. For recent studies, see Zhang Yingjin, "Rebel Without a Cause? China's New Urban Generation and Postsocialist Filmmaking," in *The Urban Generation: Chinese Cinema and Society at the Turn of the Twenty-first Century*, ed. Zhang Zhen (Durham: Duke University Press, 2007), 49–80; Jenny Kwok Wah Lau, "Globalization and Youthful Subculture: The Chinese Six-Generation Films at the Dawn of the New Century," in *Multiple Modernities: Cinemas and Popular Media in Transcultural East Asia*, eds. Jenny Kwok Wah Lau (Philadelphia: Temple University Press, 2003), 13–27; and Zhou Xuelin, *Young Rebels in Contemporary Chinese Cinema* (Hong Kong: Hong Kong University Press, 2007).

5. Wang Jing, "Wang Shuo: 'Pop Goes the Culture,'" in *High Culture Fever: Politics, Aesthetics, and Ideology in Deng's China* (Berkeley: University of California Press, 1996), 261–86. For other primary texts on Wang Shuo, see Geremie Barme, "Wang Shuo and Liumang ('Hooligan') Culture," *Australian Journal of Chinese Affairs* 28 (July 1992): 23–64; Yusheng Yao, "The Elite Class Background of Wang Shuo and His Hooligan Characters," *Modern China* 30.4 (October 2004): 431–69; and Ying Zhu, "Commercialization and Chinese Cinema's Postwave," *Consumption, Markets and Culture* 5.3 (2002): 187–209.

6. The original titles and publication dates of Wang Shuo's novels each of these films was based upon are as follows in the order of how they appear in the text: *Half Is Water, Half Is Flame* (*Yiban shi haishui, yiban shi huoyan*, 1986), *Floating to the Surface of the Sea* (*Fuchu haimian*, 1985), *The Troubleshooters* (*Wanzhu*, 1987), *Rubber Man* (*Xiang piren*, 1986), *Half Is Water, Half Is Flame* (*Yiban shi haishui, yiban shi huoyan*, 1986), *Nobody Can Hurt Me* (*Ren mo yu du*, 1987), and *No One Cheers* (*Wuren hecai*, 1991). Feng Xiaogang's film *Gone Forever with My Love* (*Yongshi wo ai*, 1994) was adapted from the two novels of Wang Shuo: *Gone Forever with My Love* (*Yongshi wo ai*, 1989) and *Air Stewardess* (*Kongzhong xiaojie*, 1984).

7. Wang, "Wang Shuo," 262.

8. Mi Jiashan, "Discussing *The Troubleshooters*," *Chinese Education and Society* 31.1 (1998): 13.

9. Ibid., 12.

10. Ibid., 13.

11. *Xiahai* is one of the hottest topics in 1980s society after the Chinese state took the market initiatives. It is a popular metaphor that portrays an entrepreneurial craze among a massive number of Chinese who quit permanent jobs assigned by the state and started their own businesses.

12. See the discussions in Wang, "Wang Shuo" and Barme, "Wang Shuo and Liumang ('Hooligan') Culture."

13. See Geremie Barme, "Consuming T-shirts in Beijing," in *In the Red: On Contemporary Chinese Culture* (New York: Columbia University Press, 1999), 145–78.

14. Walter Benjamin, "Paris—the Capital of the Nineteenth Century," in *Charles Baudelaire: A Lyric Poet in the Era of High Capitalism*, trans. Harry Zohn (London: Verso, 1983), 170–71.

15. Yomi Braester, *Painting the City Red: Chinese Cinema and the Urban Contract* (Durham and London: Duke University Press, 2010).

16. Deborah Parsons, *Streetwalking the Metropolis: Women, the City and Modernity* (Oxford and New York: Oxford University Press, 2000), 3.

17. Susan Buck-Morss, "The Flaneur, the Sanwichman and the Whore: The Politics of Loitering," *New German Critique* 39 (Autumn 1986): 103–04.

18. Ibid., 103.

19. Barme, "Wang Shuo and Liumang ('Hooligan') Culture," 37.

20. Charles Baudelaire, *Oeuvres complètes* 2 (Paris: Gallimard, 1976), 639. See the translation of Susan Blood in *Baudelaire and the Aesthetics of Bad Faith* (Stanford: Stanford University Press, 1997), 164.

21. Barme, "Wang Shuo and Liumang ('Hooligan') Culture," 37.

22. Mi, "Discussing *The Troubleshooters*," 13–14.

23. Sergei Eisenstein, "Drafts of Introduction," in *Sergei Eisenstein, Selected Works, Volume 2, Towards a Theory of Montage*, eds. Michael Glenny and Richard Taylor, trans. Michael Glenny (London and New York: I. B. Tauris, 2010), 4.

24. Sergei Eisenstein, "The Montage of Attractions (1923)," in *The Eisenstein Reader*, ed. Richard Taylor, trans. Richard Taylor and William Powell (London: British Film Institute, 1998), 30.

25. Ibid.

26. Mi, "Discussing *The Troubleshooters*," 13.

27. Ibid., 14.

28. Barme, *In the Red*, 194.

29. Berenice Reynaud, "Zhang Yuan's Imaginary Cities and the Theatricalization of the Chinese 'Bastards,'" in *The Urban Generation: Chinese Cinema and Society at the Turn of the Twenty-first Century*, ed. Zhang Zheng (Durham: Duke University Press, 2007), 264–94.

30. Andrew Jones, *Like a Knife: Ideology and Genre in Contemporary Chinese Popular Music* (Ithaca: East Asia Program, Cornell University, 1992), 137.

31. Andrew Jones, "The Politics of Popular Culture in Post-Tiananmen China," in *Popular Protest and Political Culture in Modern China*, eds. Jeffery N. Wasserstrom and Elizabeth J. Perry (Boulder: Westview Press, 1994), 155.

32. See Dai Jinhua, *Wuzhong fengjing: zhongguo dianying wenhua, 1978–1998* [*Scenery in the Fog: Chinese Cinema Culture, 1978–1998*] (Beijing: Beijing daxue chubanshe, 2000), 408–411; and Cui Shuqin, "Working from the Margins: Urban Cinema and Independent Directors in Contemporary China," *Post Script* 20.2–3 (Winter/Spring-Summer 2001): 77–93.

33. Michel Chion, *Audio-Vision: Sound on Screen*, trans. Claudia Gorbman (New York: Columbia University Press, 1994), 129–31.

34. The film stirred up widespread discussions in various film forums and among popular audience. One good example is a film review, "*Wo de xiongdijiemei*: yige bei langfei de Cui Jian" [*Roots and Branches*: A Wasted Cui Jian], *Nanfang dushi bao* [*Southern Metropolis Daily*], June 26, 2001, accessed July 11, 2011, http://news.sohu.com/07/36/news145683607.shtml.

35. Yu Zhong, "*Wo de xiongdijiemei* daoyan shouji" [A Manuscript from the Director for *Roots and Branches*], *Dianying yishu* [*Film Art*] 5 (2001): 65–66.

36. Li Jiawei, "Cui Jian: Chengdu, wo ai ni" [Cui Jian: Chengdu, I Love You], *Zhongguo zhoukan* [*China Weekly*], September 28, 2009, accessed July 11, 2011, http://elite.youth.cn/zgzk/200910/t20091016_1052241.htm.

37. Michel Chion, *The Voice in Cinema*, trans. Claudia Gorbman (New York: Columbia University Press, 1999), 81.

38. Zhao Jianwei, *Cui Jian zai Yiwosuoyou zhong nahan: Zhongguo yaogun beiwanglu* [*Cui Jian Cries Out in "Nothing to My Name": A Memorandum on Chinese Rock*] (Beijing: Beijing shifan daxue chubanshe, 1992), 74.

39. Besides fiction films and documentaries, Zhang Yuan has worked extensively with Chinese rock artists to make music videos in the early-to-mid 1990s. Among them are Cui Jian's "Let Me Go Wild in the Snow" (*Kuai rang wo zai zhe xuedi shang sa dian ye*, 1991), "The Last Shot" (*Zuihou yi qiang*, 1992), "A Piece of Cloth" (*Yikuai hongbu*, 1992), and "Flying" (*Fei le*, 1994), Ai Jing's "My 1997" (*Wo de 1997*, 1992), Chen Jin's "Red Hair Band" (*Hong tousheng*, 1993), and Luo Qi's "Do As I Wish" (*Suixinsuoyu*, 1995), many of which have received international awards, such as the MTV Video Music Award (1991) and the Golden Gate Award at the San Francisco International Film Festival (1993).

40. Cui Chen, "Mishi de xuanlv: ping *wode xiongdi jiemei*" [Disconcerting Melody: A Film Review on *Roots and Branches*], *Beijing dianying xueyuan xuebao* [*Journal of Beijing Film Academy*] 4 (2001): 89–91.

41. Li, "Cui Jian."

42. Ibid.

43. For a definition of youth subculture and an analysis of its various configurations, see Dick Hebdige, *Subculture: The Meaning of Style* (London and New York: Routledge, 2002).

44. Wang Shuo, *Wo shi wang shuo* [*I am Wang Shuo*] (Beijing: Guoji wenhua chuban gongsi, 1992), 75.

45. Gregory B. Lee, "Chinese Trumpeters, French Troubadours: Nationalist Ideology and the Culture of Popular Music," in *Troubadours, Trumpeters, Troubled Makers: Lyricism, Nationalism, and Hybridity in China and Its Others* (Durham: Duke University Press, 1996), 171.

46. Chen Sihe, "Yaogun zhong de gexing yishi: yi wu suo you" [The Individual Consciousness in Rock 'n' Roll: "Nothing to My Name"], in *Zhongguo dangdai wenxueshi jiaocheng* [*A Guide to the History of Contemporary Chinese Literature*] (Shanghai: Fudan daxue chubanshe, 1999), 326–28.

47. Xie Mian and Qian Liqun, eds., *Bainian zhongguo wenxue jingdian 7* [*The Centennial Chinese Literature Classics, Volume 7*] (Beijing: Beijing daxue chubanshe, 1996), 62–65.

48. Tang Xiaobing, "In Search of the Real City: Cinematic Representations of Beiing and the Politics of Vision," in *Chinese Modern: The Heroic and the Quotidian* (Durham and London: Duke University Press, 2000), 270; my emphasis.

49. See Fredric Jameson, "The Cultural Logic of Late Capitalism," in *Postmodernism, or, the Cultural Logic of Late Capitalism* (Durham: Duke University Press, 1999), 1–55.

50. Walter Benjamin, "The Work of Art in the Age of Mechanical Reproduction," in *Illuminations: Walter Benjamin Essays and Reflections*, ed. Hannah Arendt, trans. Harry Zohn (New York: Schocken Books, 1968), 217–52.

51. Tang, "In Search of the Real City," 245–72.

52. Zhang Nuanxin, "*Beijing nizao* de daoyan chanshu" [The Director's Exposition of *Good Morning, Beijing*], *Dangdai dianying* [*Contemporary Cinema*] 39 (1990): 53–54.

53. Ibid.

54. *Rock 'n' Roll on the Long March* is still believed to be Chinese rock's best-selling album up to date, with estimated sales of over 1 million copies. It was a certified platinum album in both Hong Kong and Taiwan during the year of 1989, when it was released concurrently across the mainland, Hong Kong, and Taiwan.

55. Clifford Coonan, "'Also Rises' Not a Hemingway Film," *Variety*, August 31, 2007.

56. Jonathan Stewart, "Jiang's Sun Rises to Off-Beat Success," *China Daily*, September 30, 2007, accessed July 23, 2011, http://www.chinadaily.com.cn/ezine/2007-09/30/content_6148645.htm.

57. Miklós Haraszti, *The Velvet Prison: Artists Under State Socialism*, trans. Katalin and Stephen Landesmann with the help of Steve Wasserman (New York: Basic Books, 1987), 99.

58. Geremie Barme, "The Chinese Velvet Prison," in *In the Red: On Contemporary Chinese Culture* (New York: Columbia University Press, 1999), 2. An earlier version of the essay appeared as "The Chinese Velvet Prison: Culture in the 'New Age,' 1976–89," *Issues and Studies* 25.8 (August 1989): 54–79.

59. Ibid., 7.

60. Haraszti, *The Velvet Prison: Artists Under State Socialism*.

61. Barme, "The Chinese Velvet Prison," 7.

62. "Duihua Cui Jian: Rang wo zai dianying li sadianye" [A Dialogue with Cui Jian: Let Me Play a Bit Wild in the Film], *Shidai zhoubao* [*Time Weekly*], June 11, 2009, accessed August 5, 2011, http://culture.ifeng.com/special/shidaizhouba001/news/200906/0611_6743_1198729.shtml.

Chapter Four

1. Jia Zhangke, "Zai yinyue he dianying de jiacha zhichu" [At the Intersection of Film and Music], *Beijing dianying xueyuan xuebiao* [*Journal of Beijing Film Academy*] 2 (1994): 247–50.

2. Jason McGrath, "The Independent Cinema of Jia Zhangke: From Postsocialist Realism to a Transnational Aesthetic," in *The Urban Generation: Chinese Cinema and Society at the Turn of the Twenty-first Century*, ed. Zhang Zhen (Durham: Duke University Press, 2007), 82.

3. Besides Jason McGrath's "The Independent Cinema of Jia Zhangke," other important research includes Chris Berry, "*Xiao Wu*: Watching Time Go By," in *Chinese Films in Focus II*, ed. Chris Berry (London: Palgrave Macmillan, 2008), 250–57; and Lin Xiaoping, "Jia Zhangke's Cinematic Trilogy: A Journey Across the Ruins of Post-Mao China," in *Chinese-language Film: Historiography, Poetics, Politics*, eds. Sheldon H. Lu and Emilie Yueh-Yu Yeh (Honolulu: University of Hawaii Press, 2005), 186–209.

4. See Liu Jin, "The Rhetoric of Local Languages as the Marginal: Chinese Underground and Independent Films by Jia Zhangke and Others," *Modern Chinese Literature and Culture* 18.2 (2006): 163–205; and Sheldon Lu, "Dialect and Modernity in 21st Century Sinophone Cinema," *Jump Cut* 49 (Spring 2007), accessed November 1, 2011, http://www.ejumpcut.org/archive/jc49.2007/Lu/.

5. Although constantly referred to in the media as the "diva" (*tianhou*) of Chinese popular music, Faye Wong has been a maverick singer who has tried a variety of different styles and genres. Her personal life likewise displays an "anomalous," alternative style. She married Dou Wei, a famous rock singer from the mainland in the 1990s; had a second marriage with Li Yapeng, a television actor; and then restarted her controversial relationship with Nicholas Tse, a popular Hong Kong star who is eleven years younger than she is. For related discussions, see Anthony Fung and Michael Curtin, "The Anomalies of Being Faye

(Wong): Gender Politics in Chinese Popular Music," *International Journal of Cultural Studies* 5 (2002): 263–90.

6. McGrath, "The Independent Cinema of Jia Zhangke," 90.

7. Ibid.

8. Tony Rayns, "Review of *Xiao Wu*," accessed November 15, 2011, http://*www.usc.edu*/isd /archives/asianfil/china/xiaowu. Html.

9. Roger Ebert, "Pickpocket (1959)," *Chicago Sun-Times*, July 6, 1997.

10. Rayns, "Review of *Xiao Wu*."

11. Zhang Zhen, "Bearing Witness: Chinese Urban Cinema in the Era of 'Transformation' (*Zhuanxing*)," in *The Urban Generation: Chinese Cinema and Society at the Turn of the Twenty-first Century*, ed. Zhang Zhen (Durham: Duke University Press, 2007), 19.

12. Liu Jin, *Signifying the Local: Media Productions Rendered in Local Languages in Mainland China in the New Millennium* (Leiden: Brill, 2013), 196.

13. Lin Xudong, Zhang Yaxuan, and Gu Zheng, eds., *Jia Zhangke dianying: guxiang sanbuqu zhi zhantai* [*The Jia Zhangke Film: Hometown Trilogy—Platform*] (Beijing: Zhongguo mangwen chubanshe, 2003), 190.

14. Tony Rayns, "An Interview with Jia Zhangke: A Big Stone in My Heart," accessed November 28, 2011, http://www.asianfilms.org/china/zhantai/interviews.html.

15. McGrath, "The Independent Cinema of Jia Zhangke," 98.

16. Ibid.

17. For Fredric Jameson's widely influential definition of national allegory, see his "Third-World Literature in the Era of Multinational Capitalism," *Social Text* 15 (Autumn, 1986): 65–88.

18. McGrath, "The Independent Cinema of Jia Zhangke," 98–99.

19. Ibid.

20. Michel Chion, *Audio-Vision: Sound on Screen*, trans. Claudia Gorbman (New York: Columbia University Press, 1994), 8.

21. Ibid.

22. Rayns, "An Interview with Jia Zhangke."

23. McGrath, "The Independent Cinema of Jia Zhangke," 100.

24. Ibid.

25. Fredric Jameson, *Postmodernism, or, The Cultural Logic of Late Capitalism* (Durham: Duke University Press, 299).

26. Ibid., 279–96.

27. Dai Jinhua and Judy T. H. Chen, "Imagined Nostalgia," *Boundary* 2, vol. 24, no. 3, Postmodernism and China (Autumn 1997): 145.

28. McGrath, "The Independent Cinema of Jia Zhangke," 100–01.

29. In addition to McGrath's "The Independent Cinema of Jia Zhangke," see Michael Berry, *Xiao Wu, Platform, Unknown Pleasures: Jia Zhangke's "Hometown Trilogy"* (London: Palgrave Macmillian, 2009), 50–92.

30. Jameson, *Postmodernism, or, The Cultural Logic of Late Capitalism*, 29–31.

31. Stephen Teo, "Cinema with an Accent: Interview with Jia Zhangke, Director of *Platform*," *Senses of Cinema* 15 (2001), accessed November 28, 2011, http://sensesofcinema .com/2001/feature-articles/zhangke_interview/.

32. Berry, *Xiao Wu, Platform, Unknown Pleasures*, 64.

33. See Lv Shaoyong, "Houxiandai de liguizhe: yingpian zuotian pingxi" [Postmodernist Deviant: A Critical Analysis of *Quitting*], *Beijing dianying xueyuan xuebao* [*Journal of Beijing Film Academy*] 1 (2002): 103–106.

34. For the reception and genealogy of *How the Steel Was Tempered* in China, see Dai Jinhua, "Chongxie hongse jingdian" [Rewriting Red Classics], in *Dazhong chuanmei yu xiandai wenxue* [*Mass Media and Modern Literature*], eds. Chen Pingyuan et al. (Beijing: Xinshijie chubanshe, 2003), 524. A more detailed delineation is provided in Song Mingwei, "How the Steel Was Tempered: The Rebirth of Pawel Korchagin in Contemporary Chinese Media," *Frontiers of Literary Studies in China* 6.1 (March 2012): 95–111.

35. Mikhail M. Bakhtin, "The Bildungsroman and its Significance in the History of Realism (Toward a Historical Typology of the Novel)," in *Speech Genres and Other Late Essays*, eds. Caryl Emerson and Michael Holquist, trans. Vern W. McGee (Austin: University of Texas Press, 1986), 21–23; emphasis in the original text.

36. Gilles Deleuze, *Cinema 2: The Time-Image*, trans. Hugh Tomlinson and Robert Galeta (Minneapolis: University of Minnesota Press, 1989). By his conception of the "movement-image" versus the "time-image," Deleuze classifies two main forms of filmmaking. In a break with the "movement-image" that is commonly associated with Hollywood filmmaking, Deleuze finds the emergence of the "time-image" in postwar European art cinema that allows artists to preserve time and approximate the actual, pure image in an objective, crystalline form. The work of the "time-image" is often characterized by long takes and a loose narrative structure, rather than a classical pattern of plot development.

37. Ibid., 69.

38. See Lu Xuezhang's own account in "Lu Xuezhang: The Film Was Tempered in This Way," in *Wode sheyingji bu sahuang: xianfeng dianying ren dang'an, shengyu 1961–1970* [*My Camera Doesn't Lie: Archives of Avant-garde Filmmakers, Born Between 1961–1970*], eds. Cheng Qingsong and Huang Ou (Beijing: Zhongguo youyi chuban gongsi, 2002), 209.

39. Deleuze, *Cinema 2*, 201.

Chapter Five

1. Dai Jinhua, "Invisible Writing: The Politics of Mass Culture in the 1990s," in *Cinema and Desire: Feminist Marxism and Cultural Politics in the Work of Dai Jinhua*, eds. Jing Wang and Tani E. Barlow, trans. Jingyuan Zhang (London and New York: Verso, 2002), 213–17; my emphasis.

2. Paul Clark, *Reinventing China: A Generation and Its Films* (Hong Kong: Chinese University Press, 2005), 150.

3. Yomi Braester, *Painting the City Red: Chinese Cinema and the Urban Contract* (Durham and London: Duke University Press, 2010), 153–54; emphasis in the original text.

4. Ibid., 166.

5. Dai, "Invisible Writing," 213.

6. As Attali writes: "The game of music thus resembles the game of power: monopolize the right to violence; provoke anxiety and then provide a feeling of security; provoke disorder and then propose order; create a problem in order to solve it." Jacques Attali, *Noise: The Political Economy of Music*, trans. Brian Massumi (Minneapolis: University of Minnesota Press, 1985), 28.

7. The China Dream was a slogan put forth by President Xi Jinping after taking the office of general secretary and becoming the paramount leader of PRC in 2012. The phrase was formulated in part to replace the old saying of "socialism with Chinese characteristic" and thereby popularized to promote the soaring power, vitality, and ideals of the China self

against the predominant American dream in the new century. Xi described the China Dream as "national rejuvenation, improvement of people's livelihoods, prosperity, construction of a better society and military strengthening as the common dream of the Chinese people that can be best achieved under one party, Socialist rule." See Evan Osnos, "Can China Deliver the China Dream(s)?" *The New Yorker*, March 26, 2013, accessed March 30, 2014, http://www.newyorker.com/news/letter-from-china/can-china-deliver-the-china-dreams; and Geremie R. Barmé, "Chinese Dreams (*Zhongguo meng*)," *The China Story*, accessed March 31, 2014, https://www.thechinastory.org/yearbooks/yearbook-2013/forum-dreams-and-power/chinese-dreams-zhongguo-meng-%E4%B8%AD%E5%9B%BD%E6%A2%A6/.

8. A foundational work in film music studies, Claudia Gorbman's *Unheard Melodies* outlines and evaluates the guiding principles of classical Hollywood music. She discusses specifically how the repetition, variation, and interaction of leitmotif with other musical codes contribute to the construction of the film. The principles are, in her frame, that of "invisibility," "inaudibility," "signifier of emotion," "narrative cueing," "continuity," and "unity." Gorbman elaborates her notion of leitmotif via a close investigation of *Mildred Pierce* (dir. Michael Curtiz, 1945). She observes that the film score by Max Steiner can be discursively identified as five major tunes associated with the five protagonists; during the course of the film, they build and recall various thematic threads. Another leading scholar, Jeff Smith, also examines leitmotif from the angle of popular film music. He endorses the functionality of leitmotif bearing the following traits: 1) specificity: leitmotif must first be defined in conjunction with a particular character, scene, or emotion; 2) flexibility and textuality: it can be shaped, duplicated, and modified organically within a strong tie to its textual form; 3) organicity and harmony: the development of this musical idea stays within a stable, formulaic, and harmonic structure and provides a sense of unity through both repetition and diversity; 4) egalitarianism: from the point of view of ideology and reception, the emphasis on the repetitiveness, harmony, and brevity of the musical pattern functions specifically to evoke memory and a sense of familiarity, therefore entailing communication to a vast, heterogeneous audience. See Claudia Gorbman, *Unheard Melodies: Narrative Film Music* (Bloomington: Indiana University Press, 1987); and Jeff Smith, *The Sounds of Commerce: Marketing Popular Film Music* (New York: Columbia University Press, 1998).

9. See Ting Xue, "A Political Economy Analysis of Chinese Films (1979–1994)" (MA thesis, Chinese University of Hong Kong, 1995).

10. Zhai Jianlong, "Guanyu zhuxuanlv he duoyanghua de dawen: dianyingju juzhang teng jinxiang fangwenji" [Questions-and-answers about Leitmotif and Diversity: An Interview with Teng Jinxian, the Director of the Film Bureau], *Dianying yishu* [Film Art] 3 (1991): 8.

11. See Bonnie S. McDougall, "Mao Zedong's 'Talks at Yan'an Conference on Literature and Art': A Translation of the 1943 Text with Commentary," *Michigan Papers in Chinese Studies*, 39 (Ann Arbor: University of Michigan Center for Chinese Studies, 1980).

12. For discussions, see Dai, "Invisible Writing," 172–88; Dai Jinhua, "Rewriting the Red Classics," in *Rethinking Chinese Popular Culture: Cannibalizations of the Canon*, eds. Carlos Rojas and Eileen Chow (London and New York: Routledge, 2011), 151–78; and Geremie R. Barmé, "Totalitarian Nostalgia," in *In the Red: On Contemporary Chinese Culture* (New York: Columbia University Press, 1999), 316–45.

13. Paul Clark, "Two Hundred Flowers on China's Screens," in *Perspectives on Chinese Cinema*, ed. Chris Berry (London: British Film Institute, 1991), 40–61.

14. To urge work units and institutions to divest of their previously mandatory centralized planning, the document launched the following measures: (1) releasing the administrative

power from the central government to the individual enterprises; (2) stimulating the productivity and efficiency of industry and encouraging enterprises to increase their profits; (3) the establishment of a marketwise price system. It was against this backdrop of economic reform that reform within the film industry became inevitable and a rise of new entertainment films was made possible.

15. Although the doctrine that adheres to the political and educative value of cinema remained nominally unchanged, a considerable freedom was given to commercial efforts and entertaining trends, driven by market demands and audience expectations. This is substantially different from the first two waves of "Two Hundred Flowers," which were nevertheless fostered under a political hand inasmuch as the party dictated what the state and audience needed, and how filmmakers worked toward these goals. For further discussions, see Ying Zhu, *Chinese Cinema During the Reform Era: The Ingenuity of the System* (Westport: Praeger, 2003).

16. Liu Cheng, "Dui 1989 nian guishipian chuangzuo de huigu" [A Review on the Feature Productions of 1989], *Zhongguo dianying nianjian 1990* [*China Film Yearbook 1990*] (Beijing: Zhongguo dianying chubanshe, 1990), 23.

17. Zhai, "Guanyu zhuxuanlv he duoyanghua de dawen," 8.

18. Liu Cheng, "Guanyu zhuxuanlv duoyanghua jiqita" [A Reflection on Leitmotif, Diversity, and Other Issues], *Beijing dianying xueyuan xuebao* [*Journal of Beijing Film Academy*] 1 (1995): 49.

19. For more discussion, see Zhang Yingjin, *Screening China: Critical Interventions, Cinematic Reconfigurations, and the Transnational Imaginary in Contemporary Chinese Cinema* (Ann Arbor: University of Michigan Press, 2002), 191–94.

20. Sun Jiazheng, "Duochu youxiu zuopin, fanrong dianying shiye" [Produce More Excellent Works, Let the Film Industry Thrive], *Zhongguo dianying nianjian 1997* [*China Film Yearbook 1997*] (Beijing: Zhongguo dianying chubanshe, 1997), 8.

21. Aihwa Ong, *Neoliberalism as Exception: Mutations in Citizenship and Sovereignty* (Durham and London: Duke University Press, 2006).

22. For discussions on "New Mainstream Cinema," see Ma Ning, "Xin zhuliu dianying: dui guochan dianying de yige jianyi" [New Mainstream Cinema: A Suggestion on Domestic Filmmaking], *Dangdai dianying* [*Contemporary Cinema*] 4 (1999): 4–16; Ma Ning, "2000: xin zhuliu dianying zhenzheng de qidian" [2000: A Real Start for New Mainstream Cinema], *Dangdai dianying* [*Contemporary Cinema*] 1(2000): 16–18; Song Jialing, "Zhuxuanlv dianying de weiji yu huolu" [Crisis and Solution for Leitmotif Films], *Dianying yishu* [*Film Art*] 8 (2013): 53–55.

23. Li Yiming, "Cong diwudai dao diliudai" [From the Fifth Generation to the Sixth Generation], *Dianying yishu* [*Film Art*] 1 (1998): 15–22.

24. Hong Junhao, "The Evolution of China's War Movie in Five Decades: Factors Contributing to Changes, Limits, and Implications," *Asian Cinema* 10.1 (Fall 1998): 93–106.

25. Chris Berry, "A Nation T(w/o)o: Chinese Cinema(s) and Nationhood(s)," in *Colonialism Nationalism in Asian Cinema*, ed. Wimal Dissanayake (Bloomington: Indiana University Press, 1994), 49.

26. Ibid., 45.

27. Ying Zhu, "Commercialization and Chinese Cinema's Post-wave," *Consumption, Markets and Culture* 5.3 (2002): 187–209.

28. Chris Berry, "'What's Big About the Big Film?': 'De-Westernizing' the Blockbuster in Korea and China," in *Movie Blockbusters*, ed. Julian Stringer (London and New York: Routledge, 2003), 217.

29. Ibid., 222.

30. Ibid.

31. Li Erwei, "Yishujia yao you lishi shiminggan: xie jin tan yapian zhan zheng" [Artists Ought to Have a Sense of Historical Responsibility: An Interview with Xie Jin on *The Opium War*], *Dianying yishu* [*Film Art*] 5 (1997): 20–24.

32. For discussions, see Ma Ning, "Culture and Politics in Chinese Film Melodrama: Traditional Sacred, Moral Economy, and the Xie Jin Mode" (PhD diss., Monash University, 1992).

33. Dai Xiu and Zhuang Xin, *Xie Jin Zhuan* [*A Biography of Xie Jin*] (Shanghai: Huadong daxue chubanshe, 1997).

34. Ibid., 253–54.

35. Ibid., 243–301.

36. Berry, "'What's Big About the Big Film?'" 223.

37. Jason McGrath, "Metacinema for the Masses: Three Films by Feng Xiaogang," *Modern Chinese Literature and Culture* 17.2 (2005): 125.

38. Wu Ziniu, "Pai Guoge de chuzhong" [My Original Intentions on Shooting *The National Anthem*], *Dangdai dianying* [*Contemporary Cinema*] 5 (1999): 5.

39. Ibid.

40. Ibid.

41. Zhang Zhen, "Bearing Witness: Chinese Urban Cinema in the Era of 'Transformation' (*Zhuanxing*)," in *The Urban Generation: Chinese Cinema and Society at the Turn of the Twenty-first Century*, ed. Zhang Zhen (Durham: Duke University Press, 2007), 2.

42. For discussions, see Song, "Zhuxuanlv dianying de weiji yu huolu"; Lu Chunyan and Wang Zhanli, "Zhuxuanlv dianying de shangyehua yu shangye dianying de zhuxuanlv hua" [The Commercialization of Leitmotif Film and the Leitmotifization of Commercial Film], *Dangdai dianying* [*Contemporary Cinema*] 5 (1999): 106–109; Zhou Donglin, Kuang Xiaolan, and Zhang Qingsheng, "Guanyu zhuxuanlv dianying shichang yunying de sikao" [Reflections on the Market Strategies of Leitmotif Film], *Zhongguo dianying shichang* [*Chinese Film Market*] 1 (2012): 11–13.

43. Arjun Appadurai, *Modernity at Large: Cultural Dimensions of Globalization* (Minneapolis: University of Minnesota, 1996).

44. Examples of debates and discussions on *Saving Private Ryan* include Kang Baocheng, "Zhongguo ren zui xuyao shenme: cong zhengjiu dabin rui'en xiangdao de" [What the Chinese Need Most: Reflections on *Saving Private Ryan*], *Yue Hai Feng* [*Trend from the South Sea*] 6 (1998): 21–22; Dai Degang, "Leixing yishi xingtai yu chengxian fangshi xi yingpian zhengjiu babin rui'en" [Genre, Ideology, and Representational Style: An Analysis of *Saving Private Ryan*], *Dianying yishu* [*Film Art*] 1 (1999): 48–51; Long Xincheng, "Zhanzheng yu renxing de qianglie chongtu: kan zhengjiu babin rui'en" [The Intense Conflicts of War and Humanity: on *Saving Private Ryan*], *Dianying pingjie* [*Movie Review*] 1 (1999): 24.

45. See Hao Jian, "Taitannikehao zai zhong guo" [*Titanic* in China], *Dianying yishu* [*Film Art*] 4 (1998): 19–24.

46. Joseph S. Nye, "Why China Is Weak on Soft Power," *New York Times*, January 18, 2012, accessed May 3, 2013, http://www.nytimes.com/2012/01/18/opinion/why-china-is-weak-on-soft-power.html?_r=0.

47. Edward W. Said, *Orientalism* (New York: Pantheon Books, 1978).

48. Chen Xiaomei, *Occidentalism: A Theory of Counter-Discourse in Post-Mao China* (Lanham: Rowman & Littlefield, 2002), 5.

49. Ella Shohat and Robert Stam, *Unthinking Eurocentrism: Multiculturalism and the Media* (New York: Routledge, 1995), 3.

50. En Na, "Chongxin renshi meiguo dapian" [Re-understanding American Blockbusters], *Beijing qingnian bao* [*Beijing Youth Daily*], May 19, 1999.

51. Rey Chow, *Primitive Passions: Visuality, Sexuality, Ethnography, and Contemporary Chinese Cinema* (New York: Columbia University Press, 1995).

52. Ibid., 12–13.

53. Only a small number of films were made in mainland China featuring and addressing Tibet and Tibetan culture, for instance, *Serfs* (*Nongnv*, dir. Li Jun, 1963), *The Horse Thief* (*Daomazei*, dir. Tian Zhuangzhuang, 1986), *Mountain Patrol* (*Kekexili*, dir. Lu Chuan, 2004), and *The Silent Holy Stones* (*Lhing Vjags Kyi Ma Ni Rdo Vbum*, dir. Wanma-Caidan, 2005).

54. Nimrod Baranovitch, *China's New Voices: Popular Music, Ethnicity, Gender, and Politics, 1978–1997* (Berkeley: University of California Press, 2003), 100.

55. Janet L. Upton, "The Politics and Poetics of Sister Drum: 'Tibetan' Music in the Global Marketplace," in *Global Goes Local: Popular Culture in Asia*, eds. Timothy J. Craig and Richard King (Vancouver: University of British Columbia Press, 2002), 99–119.

56. *Red River Valley* was the winner of Best Picture at Hundred Flowers Awards in 1997. *Lover's Grief over the Yellow River*, which earned 20 million yuan at the box office, was the winner of Best Picture at Hundred Flowers Awards in 2000 and received several awards at Golden Rooster Awards in 1999, including Best Actress, Best Visual Effects, and Best Original Score.

57. *Red Valley River* was produced with a budget of 12 million yuan, and *Lover's Grief over the Yellow River* with a budget of 3.8 million yuan, compared to the average of 2.5 million yuan per feature in mainland China in the meantime.

58. Both films starred Ning Jing and Paul Kersey as the main attractions.

59. The two films offer breathtaking and magnificent scenery showing the Yellow River, Yellow Earth, the Great Wall, and Tibetan Plateau.

60. *Red Valley Rivers* and *Lover's Grief over the Yellow River* ranked no. 2 among national films in 1997 and 1999, respectively.

61. Feng Mei, "Ziji de dapian: caifang Feng Xiaoning" [Big Pictures of Our Own: An Interview with Feng Xiaoning], *Dazhong dianying* [*Popular Film*] 6 (1997): 22–23.

62. Dai, "Rewriting the Red Classics," 151–52.

63. Zhang Huiyu, *Mubei yu jiyi: geming lishi gushi de changhuan yu chongjian* [*Gravestone and Memory: The Redemption and Reconstruction of Revolutionary Historical Narratives*] (Taipei: Xiuwei chubanshe, 2012), 212–18.

64. Jonathan Crary, "The Cinema Obscura and Its Subject," *Techniques of the Observer: On Vision and Modernity in the Nineteenth Century* (Cambridge: MIT Press, 1990), 27.

65. Shohat and Stam, *Unthinking Eurocentrism*.

66. Robert Efird, "Rock in a Hard Place: Music and the Market in Nineties Beijing," in *China Urban: Ethnographies of Contemporary Culture*, eds. Nancy N. Chen, et al. (Durham: Duke University Press, 2001), 80.

67. Ibid.

68. Mary Louise Pratt, *Imperial Eyes: Travel Writing and Transculturation* (London and New York: Routledge, 1992), 7.

69. Ibid., 4.

70. Ibid., 97.

71. Ibid., 96.

72. Feng, "Ziji de dapian."

73. John Powers, *History as Propaganda: Tibetan Exiles Versus the People's Republic of China* (New York: Oxford University Press, 2004), 94.

74. Theodor Adorno and Max Horkheimer, "The Culture Industry: Enlightenment as Mass Deception," in *Dialectic of Enlightenment*, trans. John Cumming (New York: Continuum, 2001), 94–136.

75. Rebecca E. Karl, "The Burdens of History: Lin Zexu (1959) and *The Opium War* (1997)," in *Wither China: Intellectual Politics in Contemporary China*, ed. Zhang Xudong (Durham and London: Duke University Press, 2001), 229–62.

76. For further discussion, see Li Minqi, "After Neoliberalism: Empire, Social Democracy, or Socialism," *Monthly Review* 55.8 (January 2004), http://monthlyreview.org/010411.htm; Li Minqi, "An Age of Transition: The United States, China, Peak Oil, and the Demise of Neoliberalism," *Monthly Review* 59.11 (April 2008), http://monthlyreview.org/080401li.php; Immanuel Wallerstein, "The Demise of Neoliberal Globalization," *Monthly Review,* January 2, 2008, http://mrzine.monthlyreview.org/2008/wallerstein010208.html. Accessed September 25, 2010.

77. All of these numbers and data were obtained from two websites thats specifically assess and archive film box-office receipts: http://boxofficemjo.com/ (in English); and http://www.cbooo.cn/ (in Chinese), accessed January 05, 2014.

78. See Evans Chan, "Zhang Yimou's *Hero* and the Temptations of Fascism," *Film International* 2 (2004): 14–23; Wendy Larsen, "Zhang Yimou's *Hero*: Dismantling the Myth of Cultural Power," *Journal of Chinese Cinemas* 2.3 (2008): 181–96; Jenny Kwok Wah Lau, "*Hero*: China's Response to Hollywood Globalization," *Jump Cut* 49 (Spring 2007), accessed January 06, 2014, http://www.ejumpcut.org/archive/jc49.2007/Lau-Hero/; and Mark Brent Ellsworth, "The Hero Fallen: Zhang Yimou and the Question of Unstable Authorship" (MA thesis, Victoria University of Wellington, 2013).

79. Chan, "Zhang Yimou's *Hero* and the Temptations of Fascism," 18.

80. For a brief summary of the heated debate fueled by *The Flowers of War*, see Wang Jing, "Yichang guanyu jinling shisanchai de koushuizhan" [A Big Debate Revolving around *The Flowers of War*], *Qingnian cankao* [*The Elite Reference*], December 28, 2011, accessed May 30, 2013, http://qnck.cyol.com/html/2011-12/28/nw.D110000qnck_20111228_1-34.htm.

81. Pamela McClintock, "An Auteur + This Actor = Game Change," *Hollywood Reporter*, November 30, 2011, accessed January 25, 2014, http://www.hollywoodreporter.com/news/dark-knight-christian-bale-zhang-yimou-china-flowers-war-267220.

82. Director Zhang Yimou and producer Zhang Weiping had previously conceived two possible English titles for the film: *The 13 Women of Nanjing* or *Nanjing Heroes*. It was not until when the film premiered at the Toronto International Film Festival that they decided to change the film title to *The Flowers of War*. "Dianying jinling shisanchai liangxiang duolunduo: yingwen pianming queding" [*The Flowers of War* Premiered at Toronto: Its English Title Was Finalized], *Wangyi yuele* [*Netease Entertainment*], September 12, 2011, accessed January 28, 2014, http://ent.163.com/11/0912/09/7D072HUH00030oB1.html.

83. For examples of the film reviews, see Alex von Tunzelmann, "*The Flowers of War* Fails to Bloom for Chinese Film Industry," *Guardian*, August 2, 2012, https://www.theguardian.com/film/2012/aug/02/flowers-of-war-chinese-film; V. A. Musetto, "The Wilted Spoils of War," *New York Post*, December 21, 2011, http://nypost.com/2011/12/21/the-wilted-spoils-of-war/, accessed January 28, 2014.

84. Zhu Kade, "Shisanchai de qingse aiguozhuyi" [Thirteen Prostitutes' Erotic Patriotism], *Nafang dushibao* [*Southern Metropolis Daily*], December 13, 2011, accessed May 25, 2013, https://opinion.nfdialy.cn/content/2011-12/13/content_34896942.htm.

85. McClintock, "An Auteur + This Actor = Game Change."

86. Kinnia Yau Shuk-ting, "Meanings of the Imagined Friends: Good Japanese in Chinese War Films," in *Imagining Japan in Post-war East Asia: Identity Politics, Schooling and Popular Culture,* eds. Paul Morris, Naoko Shimazu, and Edward Vickers (New York: Routledge, 2014), 76.

87. Yang Jing, "The Reinvention of Hollywood's Classic White Saviour Tale in Contemporary Chinese Cinema: *Pavilion of Women* and *The Flowers of War*," *Critical Arts* 28.2 (March 2014): 257.

88. *New Global Studies,* Special Issue: Chinese Culture/Global Culture, 8.3 (December 2014).

89. See the discussions in "China Ambitious to Become Culture Power: CPC Decision," *Xinhua News,* November 15, 2013, accessed May 25, 2016, http://news.xinhuanet.com/english/china/2013-11/15/c_132892275.htm; and Anne-Marie Brady, "Hollywood with Chinese Characteristics," *Resurgent Dictatorship,* April 19, 2016, accessed May 26, 2016, http://www.resurgentdictatorship.org/hollywood-with-chinese-characteristics/.

90. Wang Nuan, "Jianguo da ye yanyuan ling pianchou de beihou" [Behind the Stars' Zero Salary in *The Founding of a Republic*], *Beijng qingnian bao* [*Beijing Youth Daily*], August 30, 2009, accessed January 25, 2014, http://news.163.com/09/0830/09/5HV4CoSQ00011SM9.html.

91. Tang Xiaobing, "Why Should 2009 Make a Difference? Reflections on a Chinese Blockbuster," *Modern Chinese Literature and Culture,* December 2009, accessed January 17, 2014, http://u.osu.edu/mclc/online-series/tangxb/.

92. Ibid.

93. Shelly Kraicer, "A Matter of Life and Death: Lu Chuan and Post-*Zhuxuanlu* Cinema," *Cinema Scope,* accessed January 28, 2014, http://cinema-scope.com/features/features-a-matter-of-life-and-death-lu-chuan-and-post-zhuxuanlu-cinema-by-shelly-kraicer/.

94. Ibid.

95. Slavoj Žižek, *The Sublime Object of Ideology* (New York: Verso, 1989), 79–84.

96. Ibid., 125.

Chapter Six

1. "Let Me Rap" (*Rang wo rap*), lyrics, music, and performance by MC Hotdog, in *MC Hotdog* (Taipei: Moyan changpian, 2001). Named after the young rap artist, *MC Hotdog* is an EP consisting of three singles—"Intro," "Let Me Rap," and "Where Are You Going?" (*Ni yao qu nali*)—and alternative versions of these featured songs.

2. For discussions, see Li Dongran, "Cui Jian: wo shenzhi ziji buzhi ruci" [Cui Jian: I Know from my Heart that I Can Go Beyond This], *Sanlian shenghuo zhoukan* [*Sanlian Life Weekly*], August 17, 2012, accessed August 23, 2013, http://www.lifeweek.com.cn/2012/0817/38284_2.shtml; and Wang Xiaofeng, "Cui Jian: ershi duonian lai" [Cui Jian: Since the Past Twenty Years], *Sanlian shenghuo zhoukan* [*Sanlian Life Weekly*], April 6, 2005, accessed August 01, 2013, http://www.lifeweek.com.cn/2005/0406/11445.shtml.

3. For discussions, see, among others, Tricia Rose, *Black Noise: Rap Music and Black Culture in Contemporary America* (Hanover: Wesleyan University Press, 1994); David Toop, *The Rap Attack: African Jive to New York Hip Hop* (Boston: South End Press, 1984); David Toop, *Rap Attack 2: African Rap to Global Hip Hop* (London: Serpent's Tail, 1991); and Russell A. Potter, *Spectacular Vernaculars: Hip-hop and the Politics of Postmodernism* (Albany: State University of New York Press, 1995).

4. Contributing significantly to the academic discourse on hip hop in relation to globalization, Paul Gilroy interrogates the unitary blackness of rap music and hip hop through his

proposition of African diaspora as a dynamic cultural force as well as a transformative influence on global popular culture. See Paul Gilroy, *The Black Atlantic: Modernity and Double Consciousness* (London: Verso, 1993).

5. Tony Mitchell, ed., *Global Noise: Rap and Hip-hop Outside the USA* (Middletown: Wesleyan University Press, 2001); and H. Samy Alim, Awad Ibrahim, and Alastair Pennycook, eds., *Global Linguistic Flows: Hip Hop Cultures, Youth Identities, and the Politics of Language* (New York: Routledge, 2009).

6. See Jeff Chang and S. Craig Watkins, "It's a Hip-Hop World," *Foreign Policy* 163 (Nov./Dec. 2007): 58–65; Angel Lin, "'Respect for Da Chopstick Hip Hop': The Politics, Poetics, and Pedagogy of Cantonese Verbal Art in Hong Kong," in *Global Linguistic Flows*, eds. Alim, Ibrahim, and Pennycook, 159–78; Tony Mitchell, "Another Root: Hip-Hop outside the USA," in *Global Noise*, ed. Mitchell, 1–38; and Eric Ma, "Translocal Spatiality," *International Journal of Cultural Studies* 5.2 (2002): 131–51.

7. Jeroen de Kloet, "Cultural Synchronization: Hip-hop with Chinese Characteristics?" *International Association of the Study of Popular Music* (July 25–29, 2005): 3, accessed January 30, 2010, http://home.tiscali.nl/jeroendekloeth.

8. Anthony Fung, "Western Style, Chinese Pop: Jay Chou's Rap and Hip-Hop in China," *Asian Music* 39.1 (Winter–Spring 2008): 79.

9. Jin Liu, "Alternative Voice and Local Youth Identity in Chinese Local-Language Rap Music," *Positions: East Asia Cultures Critique* 22.1 (Winter 2014): 263–92.

10. For instance, MC Hotdog's CDs were sold at Guang Hua Digital Plaza, an outlet in Taipei known for books, audiovisual, and electronics, especially for those out-of-print, censored, or unlicensed.

11. Zhang Peiren, "Xin yinyue xuanyan" [Manifesto of New Music], quoted from his interview with Shenzhen Radio Broadcasting on March 7, 2005, accessed March 03, 2010, http://music.yule.sohu.com/20050307/n224572949.shtml.

12. Roger Shattuck, *The Banquet Years: The Arts in France, 1885–1918: Alfred Jarry, Henri Rousseau, Erik Satie, Guillaume Apollinaire* (London: Faber and Faber, 1958), 239–40.

13. Zhang, "Xin yinyue xuanyan."

14. Dick Hebdige, *Subculture: The Meaning of Style* (London and New York: Routledge, 2002), 105.

15. Zhang Wei, "Xunzhao gexing zhangyang yu gewu yingpian de qihe duiying," [Seeking a Harmonious Expression of Personality in the Song-and-dance Movie], *Wenhui dianying shibao* [*Shanghai Film Times*], January 21, 1989.

16. Michael Berry, "Tian Zhuangzhuang: Stealing Horses and Flying Kites," in *Speaking in Images: Interviews with Contemporary Chinese Filmmakers* (New York: Columbia University Press, 2005), 65.

17. Li Yanze, "Cengjing fengmi zhongguo: dianying pili wu yuanyin zhuanji" [A Craze of Thunderbolt Dance Sweeping across China: The Motion Picture and Original Soundtrack of *Breakin'*], accessed March 03, 2010, http://www.360doc.com/content/11/1228/21/8021011_175693356.shtml.

18. Elisabeth Rosenthal, "Groomed to Hip-Hop," *South China Morning Post*, April 18, 2001.

19. Jaime Florcruz, "China's Hip-hop Dance Craze," *CNN Online*, accessed March 05, 2010, http://edition.cnn.com/2004/WORLD/asiapcf/01/05/trends.chinahiphop/.

20. *Hip Hop: Follow Me* was available from Joyo, the once-largest Chinese e-bookstore now being merged with amazon.cn, accessed March 25, 2010, http://www.joyo.com/hiphop.html.

21. Geremie R. Barme, "CCPTM and ADCULT PRC," in *In the Red: On Contemporary Chinese Culture* (New York: Columbia University Press, 1999), 235–54.

22. "Woguo nianqingren zai rap yinyue zhong ganshou Mao Zedong de meili" [Our Young People Appreciate Mao Zedong's Charisma Through Rap Music], accessed March 05, 2010, http://bbs.wh.sdu.edu.cn/ShowPost.asp?ThreadID=41943.

23. Martin Fackler, "Hip-hop Dancing Signals U.S. Influence in China," accessed March 10, 2010, http://thepost.baker.ohiou.edu/archives3/feb02/021802/n5.html.

24. Commodity fetishism is a central concept in Marx's critique of political economy. Marx holds that in a capitalist society, social relations, institutions, and superstructures are determined by economic relations and are motivated by the force of market exchange and value-relations of the products. "I call this the fetishism which attaches itself to the products of labour as soon as they are produced as commodities, and is therefore inseparable from the production of commodities." See Karl Marx, *Capital: Volume 1: A Critique of Political Economy* (London: Penguin Classics, 1990), 165.

25. Pseudo-individualization and standardization are a set of ideas that Adorno developed in his theory of the culture industry and critique of popular music. Adorno argues that a very important role the culture industry plays in a capitalist society is to promote "false needs" and deceive individuals into believing that they have free choices and that choosing among different products (which are actually mass-produced and standardized) will bring them happiness. Theodor Adorno, "On Popular Music," *Studies in Philosophy and Social Sciences* 9 (1941): 17–48.

26. David Tao, "To Be Different" (*Bu yiyang*), music by Deng Yuxian, lyrics by Li Linqu and Wa Wa, from David Tao's album, *I Am OK* (Taipei: Xiake changpian, 1999).

27. Lan Feng, "Taiwan xin yinyue jiafu taozhe beijing duihua lu" [A Conversation with David Tao in Beijing: the New Godfather of Taiwan Music], *Guoji yinyue jiaoliu* [*International Musical Movement*] 8 (2000): 114–15.

28. "David Tao," Great Entertainment, accessed April 1, 2010, http://www.great-great.com/atrists_detail.php?id=3.

29. "Shuochang zuhe yincang zai beijing MTV" [The MTV of "In Beijing" by a Rap Group, The Hidden], *Sina Entertainment*, November 6, 2003, accessed April 04, 2010, http://ent.sina.com.cn/p/i/2003-11-06/1621228635.html.

30. Aihwa Ong, *Flexible Citizenship: The Cultural Logics of Transnationality* (Durham: Duke University Press, 1999), 6.

31. Liu Hong, "Woguo shuochang yinyue de fazhan tanxi" [An Exploration of the Trajectory of Chinese Rap Music], *Liuxing yinyue* [*Popular Music*] 32 (2012): 8.

32. "Imagined communities" is a concept made by Benedict Anderson to explain his understanding of the nation and nationalism. In this theory, he contends that an awareness of nationalism or national identity is a sociopolitical construct—what he terms imagined communities, in which people perceive themselves belonging to the group. And this sense of belonging is largely created by the media through forms of images and vernaculars. Benedict Anderson, *Imagined Communities: Reflections on the Origin and Spread of Nationalism* (London and New York: Verso, 2006).

33. Hou Yan, "Fangyan changjin liuxing ge ni tingzhe sha ganjue" [How Do You Feel about the Adoption of Vernacular in Popular Music?], *Jinhua shibao* [*Beijing Times*], March 20, 2015, accessed May 3, 2015, http://epaper.jinghua.cn/html/2015-03/20/content_180622.htm; and Xi Ha Shen Jiao, "Lun zhongwen Rap de fazhan lishi" [A Brief History of Chinese Rap], *Hip*

Hop City, January 18, 2016, accessed March 1, 2015, http://www.51555.net/home/html/news/notes/2016/0118/12599.html.

34. See a discussion of the concept in Hamid Naficy, *An Accented Cinema: Exilic and Diasporic Filmmaking* (Princeton: Princeton University Press, 2001).

35. "Jia Ping'ao liting a gan: zhe shi shuyu jiceng renmin de kuanghuan" [Jia Ping'ao Endorses Ah Gan: This is a Grassroots Carnival], *Sina Entertainment*, January 21, 2009, accessed April 25, 2010, http://ent.sina.com.cn/m/c/2009-01-21/10092351892.shtml.

36. Harry Kuoshu, "Forrest Gump Becomes a Chinese Film Director: Idealism, Formalism, and an In-between Audience," *Global Studies Journal* 8.1 (March 2015): 1–11.

37. Slavoj Žižek, *In Defense of Lost Causes* (New York: Verso, 2008), 325; emphasis in the original text.

38. Ibid.

39. Ibid.

40. Ibid.

41. Dick Hebdige, *Subculture: The Meaning of Style* (London and New York: Routledge, 2002), 18.

42. "2009: zhongguo hulian wang fazhan dashi ji" [2009: The Important Events in the Development of China's Internet], *Cyberspace Administration of China*, February 24, 2014, accessed July 11, 2014, http://www.cac.gov.cn/2014-02/24/c_126182794.htm.

43. Michael Wines, "A Dirty Pun Tweaks China's Online Censors," *New York Times*, March 11, 2009, accessed May 05, 2010, http://www.nytimes.com/2009/03/12/world/asia/12beast.html?em.

44. Hebdige, *Subculture*, 18.

45. For decades, Chinese viewers and audiences have been very familiar with Zhao Zhongxiang and his signature broadcasting style. He joined CCTV and became one of the founding members in the late 1950s. His reputation grew as the principal Chinese broadcaster evolved and expanded in the second half of the twentieth century. He became the best-known TV anchor and a celebrity in mainland China in the 1980s and 1990s. However, his admirable image and credibility crashed when Rao Ying, a former medical staff at CCTV, went online and revealed her long-hidden extramarital affair with Zhao, as well as his immoral and abnormal sexual activities, through her personal blog. For more details, see Bai Ruoyun, "Disrobing CCTV: Scandals, *E'gao*, and Resistance in China's Cyberspace," in *Three Asias: Japan, S. Korea, China*, eds. Takayuki Tatsumi, Jina Kim, and Zhang Zhen, *Paradoxa: Studies in World Literary Genres* 22 (2010): 249–69.

46. Bai, "Disrobing CCTV," 249–69.

47. Hebdige, *Subculture*, 103.

48. Besides "Grass Mud Horse" (*Cao Ni Ma*), the other mythical creatures are: "Quail Pigeon" (*Chun Ge*), "Small Elegant Butterfly" (*Ya Mie Die*), and "Stretch-Tailed Whale" (*Wei Shen Jin*), as already mentioned earlier, "French-Croatian Squid" (*Fa Ke You*, a Chinese transliteration of "fuck you"), "Chrysanthemum Silkworm" (*Jiu Hua Can*, a vulgar slang referring to anal sex), "Lucky Journey Cat" (*Ji Ba Mao*, homophonous with hair around penis); "Singing Field Goose" (*Yin Dao Yan*, homophonous with viginitis), "Intelligent Fragrant Chicken" (*Da Fei Ji*, referring to a slang for masturbation), and "Hidden Fiery Crab" (*Qian Lie Xie*, a phonetic resemblance to prostatitis). While referencing some sort of animal in written form, all of these terms sound like profane phrases when spoken. Chinese netizens use them to make social commentary in a euphemistic and playful manner.

49. The results were based upon a quick search I conducted on Google with the key words "*Cao Ni Ma*" in Chinese and "Grass Mud Horse" in English on January 20, 2015.

50. Cui Weiping, "Wo shi yizhi cao ni ma" [I am a Grass Mud Horse], accessed May 5, 2010, http://www.hecaitou.net/?p=4723.

51. Yang Guobin, *The Power of the Internet in China: Citizen Activism Online* (New York: Columbia University Press, 2009): 81.

52. Ai Weiwei was taken by police from the Beijing airport as he was preparing to board a flight to Hong Kong on April 3, 2011. It was not until a few weeks later that the Chinese authorities made the charge against him for evading taxes and destroying financial documents. Ai's disappearance was immediately brought to the spotlight thanks to international media reports. His supporters believe that "the tax inquiry was a pretext to silence one of the most vocal critics of the Chinese Communist Party." He was released on June 22, 2011, after a three-month incarceration without specific legal explanations. See Edward Wong, "Dissident Chinese Artist is Released," *New York Times*, June 22, 2011, accessed January 21, 2015, http://www.nytimes.com/2011/06/23/world/asia/23artist.html.

53. Edward Wong, "China: An Artist Fights Back," *New York Times*, April 13, 2012, accessed January 21, 2015, http://www.nytimes.com/2012/04/14/world/asia/china-artist-ai-weiwei-fights-back.html.

54. "Ai Weiwei," *ArtReview*, accessed January 25, 2016, http://artreview.com/power_100/ai_weiwei/.

55. *Ai Weiwei: Fairytale* (documentary DVD), Jrp Ringier, 2011.

56. Perry Link and Xiao Qiang, "From Grass-Mud Equestrians to Rights-Conscious Citizens: Language and Thought on the Chinese Internet," in *Restless China*, eds. Perry Link, Richard P. Madsen, and Paul G. Pickowicz (Lanham: Rowman & Littlefield Publishers, 2013), 83–106.

57. Jacques Attali, *Noise: The Political Economy of Music*, trans. Brian Massumi (Minneapolis: University of Minnesota Press, 1985), 137.

58. Roland Robertson coined a new term "glocalization" to grapple with the contradictions and mutual dependency between globalization and localization. As he indicates, it is the complex dynamics of transnationalism, migration, hybridity, and indigenization that intersect to perpetuate and shape the scenario of what he defines "glocalization." See Roland Robertson, "Glocalization: Time-space and Homogeneity-Heterogeneity," in *Global Modernities*, eds. Mike Featherstone, Scott Lash, and Roland Robertson (London: Sage Publications, 1995), 25–44.

59. Walter Benjamin, "The Work of Art in the Age of Mechanical Reproduction," in *Illuminations: Walter Benjamin Essays and Reflections*, trans. Harry Zohu, ed. Hannah Arendt (New York: Schocken Books, 1968), 217–52.

Finale

1. Jacques Attali, *Noise: The Political Economy of Music*, trans. Brian Massumi (Minneapolis: University of Minnesota Press, 1985), 133.

2. Ibid., 14.

3. Ibid., 133.

CHINESE GLOSSARY
(in the order in which they appear in the text)

Hunyin zhongguo	混音中国		China in the Mix
Dianying	电影		cinema
Shengyin	声音		sound
Liuxing wenhua	流行文化		popular culture
Quanqiu hua	全球化		globalization
Dazhong wenhua	大众文化		mass culture
Sheng gui	声轨		soundtrack
Liuxing yinyue	流行音乐		popular music
Fangyan	方言		dialect
Hao lai wu	好莱坞		Hollywood
Shuyu/baihua	俗语/白话		vernacular
Hou sheihui zhuyi	后社会主义		postsocialism
Hou xiandai zhuyi	后现代主义		postmodernism
Hou xin shiqi	后新时期		post-New Era
Xin ziyou zhuyi	新自由主义		neoliberalism
You zhongguo tese de shehui zhuyi	有中国特色的社会主义		socialism with Chinese characteristic
Shichang jingji	市场经济		market economy
Gaige	改革		reform
Deng Xiaoping	邓小平		Deng Xiaoping
Xibei feng	西北风		Northwest Wind
Mingyao	民谣		folklore
Di wu dai	第五代		the Fifth Generation
Xin langchao	新浪潮		New Wave
Guojia yuyan	国家寓言		national allegory
Qiguan	奇观		spectacle
Wenhua re	文化热		cultural fever
Chen Kaige	陈凯歌		Chen Kaige
Zhang Yimou	张艺谋		Zhang Yimou
Tian Zhuangzhuang	田壮壮		Tian Zhuangzhuang
Huang Jianxin	黄建新		Huang Jianxin
Xi'an dianying zhipian chang	西安电影制片厂		Xi'an Film Studio

Tansuo pian	探索片	experimental film
Huang tudi	《黄土地》	*Yellow Earth*
Xungen	寻根	root-seeking
Shaanbei min'ge	陕北民歌	Shaanbei folk song
Suanqu'er	酸曲儿	sour tune
Xintianyou	信天游	roving around under the sky
Caifeng	采风	scouting around for folklores
Suona	唢呐	Suona
Huanghe	黄河	the Yellow River
Gongchan dang	共产党	the Communist Party
Dayin xisheng, daxiang wuxing	"大音希声，大象无形"	"The most majestic music would be inaudible; the most magnificent image would be formless."
Nv'er ge	《女儿歌》	"Song of the Daughter"
Da yuebing	《大阅兵》	*The Big Parade*
Haizi wang	《孩子王》	*King of the Children*
Zhiqing	知青	educated youth
Wenhua da geming	文化大革命	the Cultural Revolution
Huangtu gaopo	《黄土高坡》	"Hills of Yellow Earth"
Wusi yundong	五四运动	the May Fourth Movement
Wo relian de guxiang	《我热恋的故乡》	"My Beloved Homeland"
Jin Zhaojun	金兆钧	Jin Zhaojun
Hong gaoliang	《红高粱》	*Red Sorghum*
Zhao Jiping	赵季平	Zhao Jiping
Sige yise	四歌一色	four songs and one color
Dianjiao qu	《颠轿曲》	"Jolting Sedan"
Meimei, ni dadan de wang qianzou	《妹妹，你大胆的往前走》	"Sister, March Forward Bravely"
Jiushen qu	《酒神曲》	"Ode to the Wine God"
Mo Yan	莫言	Mo Yan
Dai Jinhua	戴锦华	Dai Jinhua
Lu Xun	鲁迅	Lu Xun
Xin changzheng lushang de yaogui	《新长征路上的摇滚》	"Rock 'n' Roll on the New Long March"
Yaogun yinyue	摇滚音乐	rock 'n' roll music
Cui Jian	崔健	Cui Jian
Yi wu suo you	《一无所有》	"Nothing to My Name"

Shangye wenhua	商业文化	commercial culture
Doushi dianying	都市电影	urban cinema
Xiaofei zhuyi	消费主义	consumerism
Wang Shuo re	王朔热	Wang Shuo fever
Pizi wenxue	痞子文学	hooligan literature
Mi Jiashan	米家山	Mi Jiashan
Wan zhu	《顽主》	*The Troubleshooters*
Wan'r	玩儿	to play
Kan	侃	fasting-talking/babbling
Xiahai	下海	plunging into the business ocean
Wenhua shan	文化衫	cultural T-shirts
Xianchang	现场	on the spot
Xianshi zhuyi	现实主义	realism
Zhenshixing	真实性	authenticity
Zhang Yuan	张元	Zhang Yuan
Beijing zazhong	《北京杂种》	*Beijing Bastards*
Di liu dai	第六代	the Sixth Generation
Dixia duli dianying	地下独立电影	underground independent film
Jilu pian	纪录片	documentary
Kuanrong	《宽容》	"Tolerance"
Dou Wei	窦唯	Dou Wei
He Yong	何勇	He Yong
Wang Xiaoshuai	王小帅	Wang Xiaoshuai
Beijing gushi	《北京故事》	"Beijing Story"
Wo de xiongdi jiemei	《我的兄弟姐妹》	*Roots and Branches*
Yu Zhong	俞钟	Yu Zhong
Yikuai hongbu	《一块红布》	"A Piece of Red Cloth"
Zuihou de baoyuan	《最后的抱怨》	"The Last Complaints"
Erhu	二胡	two-stringed fiddle
Pipa	琵琶	four-stringed lute
Guzheng	古筝	seven-stringed zither
Ganguang shidai	《感光时代》	*Age of Sensitivity*
Beijing, nizao	《北京，你早》	*Good Morning, Beijing*
Zhang Nuanxin	张暖忻	Zhang Nuanxin
Jiaxingseng	《假行僧》	"Fake Monk"
Taiyang zhaochang shengqi	《太阳照常升起》	*The Sun Also Rises*
Jiang Wen	姜文	Jiang Wen

Lanse gutou	《蓝色骨头》	*Blue Sky Bones*
Jia Zhangke	贾樟柯	Jia Zhangke
Guxiang sanbuqu	故乡三部曲	the Hometown Trilogy
Xiao wu	《小武》	*Xiao Wu* (aka *Pickpocket*)
Wang Fei	王菲	Faye Wong
Tian kong	《天空》	"Sky"
Xuanze	《选择》	"Choice"
Ai jiangshan geng ai meiren	《爱江山更爱美人》	"The Bold and the Beautiful"
Xin yu	《心雨》	"Heart Rain"
Bawang bieji	《霸王别姬》	"Farewell, My Concubine"
Zhan tai	《站台》	*Platform*
Deng lijun	邓丽君	Deng Lijun (aka Teresa Teng)
Shifou	《是否》	"Whether or Not"
Zuotian	《昨天》	*Quitting*
Zhang Yang	张扬	Zhang Yang
Jia Hongsheng	贾宏声	Jia Hongsheng
Lu Xuezhang	路学长	Lu Xuezhang
Gangtie shi zenyang liancheng de (aka Zhangda chengren)	《钢铁是怎样炼成的》	*How the Steel Was Tempered*
Zhuhelai	朱赫莱	Zhoukhrai
Tiananmen Guangchang	天安门广场	The Tiananmen Square
Guangchang	《广场》	*The Square*
Zhuxuanlv dianying	主旋律电影	Leitmotif film
Kuaguo xiangxiang	跨国想象	transnational imaginary
Zhongguo meng	中国梦	China Dream
Tuchu zhuxuanlv, jianchi duoyanghua	"突出主旋律，坚持多样化"	"Foregrounding Leitmotif, Persisting in Diversity"
Mao Zedong	毛泽东	Mao Zedong
Zai yanan wenyi zuotan hui shang de jianghua	《在延安文艺座谈会上的讲话》	Talks at the Yan'an Forum on Literature and Art
Guojia guangbo dianying dianshi zongju	国家广播电影电视总局	State Administration of Radio, Film and Television
Dianying chanye	电影产业	film industry
Wuge yi gongcheng	五个一工程	Five Ones Project
Jingpin dianying	精品电影	quality film

Chinese Glossary

Xin zhuliu dianying	新主流电影	New Mainstream Cinema
Shangye pian	商业片	commercial film
Dapian	大片	blockbuster / big picture
Xianli pian	献礼片	tribute to the nation
Liusi Tiananmen shijian	六四天安门事件	the Tiananmen incident of 1989
Xie Jin	谢晋	Xie Jin
Yanpian zhanzheng	《鸦片战争》	*The Opium War*
Hengdian yingshi cheng	横店影视城	Hengdian Film City
Jinji jiang	金鸡奖	the Golden Rooster Awards
Baihua jiang	百花奖	the Hundred Flowers Awards
Huabiao jiang	华表奖	the Huabiao Awards
Hesui pian	贺岁片	New Year Celebration Comedies
Feng Xiaogang	冯小刚	Feng Xiaogang
Feng Xiaoning	冯小宁	Feng Xiaoning
Wu Ziniu	吴子牛	Wu Ziniu
Guoge	《国歌》	National Anthem
Yangren yanzhong de zhongguo	"洋人眼中的中国"	"China Through Foreign Eyes"
Huanghe juelian	《黄河绝恋》	*Lover's Grief over the Yellow River*
Honghegu	《红河谷》	*Red River Valley*
Ziri	《紫日》	*Purple Sunset*
Zhengjiu dabing rui'en	《拯救大兵瑞恩》	*Saving Private Ryan*
Taitannike hao	《泰坦尼克号》	*Titanic*
Jiang Zemin	江泽民	Jiang Zemin
Hu Jintao	胡锦涛	Hu Jintao
Xizang re	西藏热	the Tibet craze
Huidao lasa	《回到拉萨》	"Return to Lhasa"
Huawaiyin	画外音	voice-over
Yingxiong	《英雄》	*Hero*
Jinling shisan chai	《金陵十三钗》	*The Flowers of War*
Jianguo daye	《建国大业》	*The Founding of a Republic*
Jiandang weiye	《建党伟业》	*The Founding of a Party* (aka *Beginning of the Great Revival*)
Nanjing! Nanjing!	《南京！南京！》	*City of Life and Death*

Hip Hop jiushi wo de dao, raoshe jiushi wo de jian	"Hip Hop 就是我的刀，饶舌就是我的剑"	"Hip hop is my knife, rap is my sword"
Xiang yiba daozi	《像一把刀子》	"Like a Knife"
Rang wo rap	《让我Rap》	"Let Me Rap"
Laofuzi	老夫子	MC Hotdog / Old Master
Kongfuzi	孔夫子	Confucius
Moyan changpian	魔岩唱片	Magic Stone Records
Quwei cunzhen	"去伪存真"	"Strip off showiness, keep it real"
Pili wu	霹雳舞	Thunderbolt Dance
Yaogun qingnian	《摇滚青年》	Rock Kids
Getihu	个体户	entrepreneur
Jiewu	街舞	street dance / breakdance
Xiha	嘻哈	hip hop
Zou Jielun	周杰伦	Jay Chou
Tao Zhe	陶喆	David Tao
Bu yiyang	《不一样》	"To be Different"
Yincang	隐藏	the Hidden
Wei renmin fuwu	《为人民服务》	Serve the People
Fangyan shuochang	方言说唱	vernacular rap
Weibo	微博	microblog
Gaoxing	《高兴》	Happy
Heisa	黑撒	Black Head
Cao ni ma	草泥马	Grass Mud Horse
He xie	河蟹	River Crab
Shi da shenshou	十大神兽	Ten Mythical Creatures
Dongwu shijie tebian pian male gebi shang de caonima	《动物世界特别篇：马勒戈壁上的草泥马》	Special Program of Animal World: Grass Mud Horse in the Mahler Gobi Desert
Cao ni ma zhi ge	《草泥马之歌》	Song of Grass Mud Horse
Qianli zou danqi	《千里走单骑》	Riding Alone for Thousands of Miles
Sanqiang pai'an jingji	《三枪拍案惊奇》	A Woman, A Gun and a Noodle Shop
Sousuo	《搜索》	Caught in the Web
Tian zhuding	《天注定》	A Touch of Sin

FILMOGRAPHY
(Listed in Chronological Order)

Note: In addition to the films discussed in the book, I have also included some other works that are known for their film music or have prominent acoustic features, including the use of dialect or multilingual soundtrack.

Sing-Song Girl Red Peony [*Genv hong mudan*]. 1930. Dir. Zhang Shichuan. Mingxing Film Company.
The Plunder of Peach and Plum [*Taoli jie*]. 1934. Dir. Ying Yunwei. Diantong Film Company.
Song of the Fisherman [*Yuguangqu*]. 1934. Dir. Cai Chusheng. Lianhua Film Company.
Big Road [*Dalu*]. 1935. Dir. Sun Yu. Lianhua Film Company.
Children of Troubled Times [*Fengyun ernv*]. 1935. Dir. Xu Xingzhi. Diantong Film Company.
City Scenes [*Dushi fengguang*]. 1935. Dir. Yuan Muzhi. Diantong Film Company.
Song of Triumph [*Kaige*]. 1935. Dir. Pu Wancang. Yihua Film Company.
Tuberose [*Yelaixiang*]. 1935. Dir. Cheng Bugao. Mingxing Film Company.
March of the Youth [*Qingnian jinxingqu*]. 1937. Dir. Shi Dongshan. Xinhua Film Company.
A New Year's Coin [*Yasuiqian*]. 1937. Dir. Zhang Shichuan. Mingxing Film Company.
Song at Midnight [*Yeban gesheng*]. 1937. Dir. Maxu Weibang. Xinhua Film Company.
Street Angel [*Malu tianshi*]. 1937. Dir. Yuan Muzhi. Mingxing Film Company.
New Song of the Fisherman [*Xin yuguangqu*]. 1941. Dir. Tu Guangqi. Dacheng Film Company.
Sing-Song Girl Red Peony [*Genv hong mudan*]. 1941. Dir. Wang Cilong. Haixing Film Company.
An All-Consuming Love [*Chang Xiangsi*]. 1947. Dir. He Zhaozhang. Da zhonghua Film Company.
Spring in a Small Town [*Xiaocheng zhichun*]. 1948. Dir. Fei Mu. Wenhua Film Company.
The White-Haired Girl [*Bai maonv*]. 1950. Dir. Shuihua, Wang Bin, and Wang Caixiang. Northeast Film Studio.
Awara. India. 1951. Dir. Raj Kapoor. All India Film Corporation and R.K. Films Ltd.
People on the Grasslands [*Caoyuan shang de renmen*]. 1952. Dir. Xu Tao. Northeast Film Studio.
Guerilla of the Train Trailer [*Tiedao youjidui*]. 1956. Dir. Zhao Ming. Shanghai Film Studio.
Heartbreak Ridge [*Shanggan ling*]. 1956. Dir. Shan Lin and Meng Sha. Changchun Film Studio.
The Story of Liubao [*Liubao de gushi*]. 1957. Dir. Wang Pin. August First Film Studio.
Women Basketball Player No. 5 [*Nvnan wu hao*]. 1957. Dir. Xie Jin. Tianma Film Studio.
San Mao Learns Business [*Sanmao xue shengyi*]. 1958. Dir. Huang Zuolin. Tianma Film Studio.
Five Golden Flowers [*Wuduo jinhua*]. 1959. Dir. Wang Jiayi. Changchun Film Studio.
Lin Zexu [*Lin zexu*]. 1959. Dir. Zheng Junli and Cen Fan. Haiyan Film Studio.
Pickpocket. France. 1959. Dir. Robert Bresson. Compagnie Cinématographique de France.
The Red Detachment of Women [*Hongse niangzijun*]. 1961. Dir. Jie Jin. Shanghai Film Studio.
Third Sister Liu [*Liusanjie*]. 1961. Dir. Su Li. Changchun Film Studio.

Guest on an Iceberg [*Binshan shang de laike*]. 1963. Dir. Zhao Xinshui. Changchun Film Studio.
Seizing Conscripts [*Zhua Zhuangding*]. 1963. Dir. Chen Ge and Shen Dan. August First Film Studio.
Heroic Sons and Daughters [*Yingxiong ernv*]. 1964. Dir. Wu Zhaodi. Changchun Film Studio.
Stage Sisters [*Wutai jiemei*]. 1965. Dir. Xie Jin. Shanghai Film Studio.
Taxi Driver. US. 1976. Martin Scorsese. Bill/Phillips and Italo/Judeo Productions.
Reverberations of Life [*Shenghuo de chanyin*]. 1979. Dir. Teng Wenji. Xi'an Film Studio.
Legend of Tianyun Mountain [*Tianyun shan chuanqi*]. 1980. Dir. Xie Jin. Shanghai Film Studio.
Drive to Win [*Sha ou*]. 1981. Dir. Zhang Nuanxin. Youth Film Studio of Beijing Film Academy.
My Memories of Old Beijing [*Chengnan jiushi*]. 1982. Dir. Wu Yigong and Wu Yonggang. Beijing Film Studio.
Narrow Street [*Xiaojie*]. 1981. Dir. Yang Yanjin. Shanghai Film Studio.
Wild Style. US. 1982. Dir. Charlie Ahearn. Wild Style.
A Symphony of Cooking Utensils [*Gouwan piaopen jiaoxiang qu*]. 1983. Dir. Teng Wenji. Xi'an Film Studio.
Papa, Can You Hear Me Sing [*Dacuoche*]. Hong Kong and Taiwan. 1983. Dir. Yu Kanping. Cinema City Film Productions.
Blood Simple. US. 1984. Dir. Coen Brothers. Foxton Entertainment.
Breakin'. US. 1984. Dir. Joel Silberg. Golan-Globus Productions.
Yellow Earth [*Huang tudi*]. 1984. Dir. Chen Kaige. Guangxi Film Studio.
Sacrifice of Youth [*Qingchun ji*]. 1985. Dir. Zhang Nuanxin. Youth Film Studio of Beijing Film Academy.
Song at Midnight [*Yeban gesheng*]. 1985. Dir. Yang Yanjin. Shanghai Film Studio.
The Big Parade [*Da yuebing*]. 1986. Dir. Chen Kaige. Guangxi Film Studio.
The Black Cannon Incident [*Heipao shijian*]. 1986. Dir. Huang Jianxin. Xi'an Film Studio.
Dislocation [*Cuowei*]. 1986. Dir. Huang Jianxin. Xi'an Film Studio.
Hibiscus Town [*Furong zhen*]. 1986. Dir. Xie Jin. Shanghai Film Studio.
The Horse Thief [*Daomazei*]. 1986. Dir. Tian Zhuangzhuang. Xi'an Film Studio.
The Old Well [*Lao jing*]. 1986. Dir. Wu Tianming. Xi'an Film Studio.
Angels and Demons [*Tianshi yu mogui*]. 1987. Dir. Ling Qiwei. Pearl River Film Studio.
Desperation [*Zuihou de fengkuang*]. 1987. Dir. Zhou Xiaowen. Xi'an Film Studio.
King of the Children [*Haizi wang*]. 1987. Dir. Chen Kaige. Xi'an Film Studio.
Let the World Be Filled with Love [*Rang shijie chongman ai*]. 1987. Dir. Teng Wenji and Weng Luming. Xi'an Film Studio.
Put Some Sugar in the Coffee [*Gei kafei jia dianr tang*]. 1987. Dir. Sun Zhou, Pearl River Film Studio.
Red Sorghum [*Hong gaoliang*]. 1987. Dir. Zhang Yimou. Xi'an Film Studio.
Sun Showers [*Taiyangyu*]. 1987. Dir. Zhang Zeming. Pearl River Film Studio.
Big Breath [*Dachuanqi*]. 1988. Dir. Ye Daying. Shenzhen Film Studio.
Half Is Water, Half Is Flame [*Yiban shi haisui, yiban shi huoyan*]. 1988. Dir. Xia Gang. Beijing Film Studio.
Obsession [*Fengkuang de daijia*]. 1988. Dir. Zhou Xiaowen. Xi'an Film Studio.
Rock Kids [*Yaogun qingnian*]. 1988. Dir. Tian Zhuangzhuang. Youth Film Studio of Beijing Film Academy.
Samsara [*Lunhui*]. 1988. Dir. Huang Jianxin. Xi'an Film Studio.

The Troubleshooters [*Wan zhu*]. 1988. Dir. Mi Jiashan. Emei Film Studio.
Ballad of the Yellow River [*Huanghe yao*]. 1989. Dir. Teng Wenji. Xi'an Film Studio.
The Birth of New China [*Kaiguo dadian*]. 1989. Dir. Li Qiankuan and Xiao Guiyun. Changchun Film Studio.
Bethune: The Making of a Hero [*Baiqiu'en: yige yingxiong de chengzhang*]. 1990. Dir. Phillip Borsos and Wang Xingang. Filmline International, Inc., and August First Film Studio.
Black Snow [*Ben Mingnian*]. 1990. Dir. Xie Fei. Youth Film Studio of Beijing Film Academy.
Good Morning, Beijing [*Beijing, ni zao*]. 1990. Dir. Zhang Nuanxin. Youth Film Studio of Beijing Film Academy.
Jiao Yulu [*Jiao yulu*]. 1990. Dir. Wang Jixing. Emei Film Studio.
Ju Dou [*Ju dou*]. 1990. Dir. Zhang Yimou. Xi'an Film Studio, Tokuma Shoten, China Film Co-Production Corporation, and Cineplex Odeon Films.
A Mysterious Couple [*Shenmi fuqi*]. 1991. Dir. Li Ziyu. Beijing Film Studio.
Raise the Red Lantern [*Dahong denglong gaogao gua*]. 1991. Dir. Zhang Yimou. Nian Dai International, China Film Co-Production Corporation, Century Communications, and ERA International.
After Separation [*Da saba*]. 1992. Dir. Xia Gang. Beijing Film Studio.
The Story of Qiu Ju [*Qiuju da guansi*]. 1992. Dir. Zhang Yimou. Youth Film Studio of Beijing Film Academy and Sil-Metropole Organisation Ltd.
Beijing Bastards [*Beijing zazhong*]. 1993. Dir. Zhang Yuan. Beijing Bastards Group Production.
The Days [*Dongchun de rizi*]. 1993. Dir. Wang Xiaoshuai. Image Studio.
Dirt [*Toufa luanle*]. 1993. Dir. Guan Hu. Inner Mongolia Film Studio.
Farewell, My Concubine [*Bawa bieji*]. 1993. Dir. Chen Kaige. Beijing Film Studio, China Film Co-Production Corporation, Maverick Picture Company, and Tomson Films.
The Fugitive. US. 1993. Dir. Andrew Davis. Warner Bros.
In a Distant Land [*Zai na yaoyuan de defang*]. 1993. Dir. Teng Wenji. Jianian Film Ltd. and Xi'an Film Studio.
No One Cheers [*Wuren hecai*]. 1993. Dir. Xia Gang. Beijing Film Studio.
Rocking Killer [*Yaogun shashou*]. 1993. Dir. Cheng Ke. Changchun Film Studio.
Age of Sensitivity [*Ganguang shidai*]. 1994. Dir. Ah Nian. Pearl River Film Studio.
Chungking Express [*Chung Hing sam lam*]. Hong Kong. 1994. Dir. Wong Kar-wai. Jet Tone Production Co.
Ermo [*Ermo*]. 1994. Dir. Zhou Xiaowen. Shanghai Film Studio and Hong Kong Ocean Film Ltd.
Gone Forever with My Love [*Yongshi wo ai*]. 1994. Dir. Feng Xiaogang. Beijing Film Studio.
In the Heat of the Sun [*Yangguang canlan de rizi*]. 1994. Dir. Jiang Wen. China Film Co-Production Corporation and Dragon Film.
Lost My Love [*Yongshi wo'ai*]. 1994. Dir. Feng Xiaogang. Beijing Film Studio.
To Live [*Huo zhe*]. 1994. Dir. Zhang Yimou. ERA International and Shanghai Film Studio.
The Square [*Guangchang*]. 1994. Dir. Duan Jinchuan and Zhang Yuan.
True Lies. US. 1994. Dir. James Cameron. Lightstorm Entertainment.
Kong Fansen [*Kong Fansen*]. 1995. Dir. Chen Guoxing. Beijing Film Studio.
How the Steel Was Tempered [*Gangtie shi zenyang liancheng de*, aka *Zhangda chengren*]. 1995. Dir. Lu Xuezhang. Beijing Film Studio.
The Phantom Lover [*Yeban gesheng*]. 1995. Dir. Yu Rentai. Dongfang Company.

Red Cherry [*Hong Yingtao*]. 1995. Dir. Ye Daying. Youth Film Studio of Beijing Film Academy.
Weekend Lover [*Zhoumo qingren*]. 1995. Dir. Lou Ye. Fujian Film Studio.
Xian Shan Going Home [*Xiao Shan huijia*]. 1995. Dir. Jia Zhangke. Beijing Film Academy.
Frozen [*Jidu hanleng*]. 1996. Dir. Wang Xiaoshuai. International Film Circuit.
I Am Your Dad [*Woshi ni baba*]. 1996. Dir. Wang Shuo. Beijing Film Studio, Beijing Good Dreams, and Beijing Shanhe Yingshi Yishu.
Rainclouds Over Wushan [*Wushan yunyu*]. 1996. Dir. Zhang Ming. Beijing Film Studio.
Red River Valley [*Honghegu*]. 1996. Dir. Feng Xiaoning. Shanghai Film Studio.
So Close to Paradise [*Biandan guniang*]. 1996. Dir. Wang Xiaoshuai. Beijing Film Studio.
A Symphony of Graduation [*Biye jiaoxiang qu*]. 1996. Dir. Hua Ke. Changchun Film Studio.
Temptress Moon [*Fengyue*]. 1996. Dir. Chen Kaige. Shanghai Film Studio and Tomsen Films.
The Days of Leaving Leifeng [*Likai leifeng de rizi*]. 1997. Dir. Lei Xianhe. Youth Film Studio.
Dream Factory [*Jiafang yifang*]. 1997. Dir. Feng Xiaogang. Beijing Film Studio.
How the Steel Was Tempered [*Gangtie shi zenyang liancheng de*, aka *Zhangda chengren*]. 1997. Dir. Lu Xuezhang. Beijing Film Studio.
Keep Cool [*Youhua haohao shuo*]. 1997. Dir. Zhang Yimou. Guangxi Film Studio.
The Opium War [*Yapian zhanzheng*]. 1997. Dir. Xie Jin. The Opium War Production Ltd.
Titanic. 1997. US. Dir. James Cameron. Twentieth Century Fox, Paramount Pictures, and Lightstorm Entertainment.
Xiao Wu [*Xiao Wu*, aka *Pickpocket*]. 1997. Dir. Jia Zhangke. Hong Kong Hutong Production Company.
Be There, Be Square [*Bujian busan*]. 1998. Dir. Feng Xiaogang. Beijing Film Studio and Beijing Forbidden City Film Company.
The Beautiful New World [*Meili xin shijie*]. 1998. Dir. Shi Runjiu. Xi'an Film Studio and Imar Film Company Ltd.
The Emperor and the Assassin [*Ciqin*]. 1998. Dir. Chen Kaige. Beijing Film Studio and New Wave Company.
Rhapsody of Spring [*Chuntian de kuangxiang*]. 1998. Dir. Teng Wenji. Beijing Film Studio and Film Satellite Channel Production Center.
Rush Hour. US. 1998. Dir. Brett Ratner. Roger Birnbaum Productions.
Saving Private Ryan. 1998. Steven Spielberg. Amblin Entertainment and Mutual Film Company.
A Tree in House [*Meishi touzhe le*]. 1998. Dir. Yang Yazhou. Xi'an Film Studio, Beijing Dayu Culture Company, and Shenzhen Zhengfangzheng Ltd.
The Birth of Atomic Bomb [*Hengkong chushi*]. 1999. Dir. Chen Guoxing. Beijing Film Studio and CCTV Film Channel.
Crash Landing [*Jinji pojiang*]. 1999. Dir. Zhang Jianya. Shanghai Film Studio.
The Flag of PRC [*Gongheguo zhi qi*]. 1999. Dir. Wang Jixin and Lei Xianhe. Beijing Forbidden City Film Company and CCTV Film Channel.
Love's Grief over the Yellow River [*Huanghe juelian*]. 1999. Dir. Feng Xiaoning. Shanghai Yongle Film Company.
My 1919 [*Wo de yijiu yijiu*]. 1999. Dir. Huang Jianzhong. Beijing Film Studio, Xi'an Film Studio, and CCTV Film Channel.
National Anthem [*Guoge*]. 1999. Dir. Wu Ziniu. Xiaoxiang Film Studio.
No One Less [*Yige dou buneng shao*]. 1999. Dir. Zhang Yimou. Guangxi Film Studio, Columbia Pictures Film Production Asia, and Beijing New Picture Film Company.

The Road Home [*Wode fuqin muqin*]. 1999. Dir. Zhang Yimou. Guangxi Film Studio and Columbia Pictures Film Production Asia.
Shower [*Xizao*]. 1999. Dir. Zhang Yang. Xi'an Film Studio and Imar Film Company.
Crouching Tiger, Hidden Dragon [*Wohu canglong*]. Hong Kong, Taiwan, China, and US. 2000. Dir. Ang Lee. Asia Union Film and Entertainment Ltd., China Film Co-Production Corporation, Columbia Pictures Film Production Asia, Edko Films, Good Machine, Sony Pictures Classics, United China Vision, and Zoom Hunt International Productions.
Crucial Choices [*Shengsi jueze*]. 2000. Dir. Yu Benzheng and Zhang Pin. Shanghai Film Studio.
In the Mood for Love [*Fa yeung nin wa*]. Hong Kong. 2000. Dir. Wong Kar-wai. Block 2 Pictures, Jet Tone Production, and Paradis Films.
Platform [*Zhantai*]. 2000. Dir. Jia Zhangke. Hong Kong Hutong Production Company, Japan T-Mark, Artcam International, and Bandai Entertainment, Inc.
Romeo Must Die. US. 2000. Andrzej Bartkowiak. Warner Bros. and Silver Pictures.
Shadow Magic [*Xiyangjing*]. 2000. Dir. Hu An. Beijing Film Studio.
Suzhou River [*Suzhou he*]. 2000. Dir. Lou Ye. The Coproduction Office and Essential Filmproduktion GmbH.
Balzac and the Little Chinese Seamstress [*Baier zake he xiao caifeng*]. 2001. Dir. Dai Sijie. Phil International Company.
Beijing Bicycle [*Shiqisui de danche*]. 2001. Dir. Wang Xiaoshuai. Arc Light Films Company.
Beijng Rocks [*Beijing le yu lu*]. 2001. Dir. Mabel Cheung. Huangya Film Ltd.
Big Shot's Funeral [*Dawan*]. 2001. Dir. Feng Xiaogang. Columbia and Samsung Company.
Orphan of Anyang [*Anyang ying'er*]. 2001. Dir. Wang Chao. Les Films du Paradoxe.
Rush Hour 2. US and Hong Kong. 2001. Dir. Brett Ratner. Roger Birnbaum Productions and Salon Films.
Quitting [*Zuotian*]. 2001. Dir. Zhang Yang. Xi'an Film Studio and Imar Film Company.
Purple Sun [*Ziri*]. 2001. Dir. Feng Xiaoning. Shanghai Yongle Film Company and Beijing Forbidden City Film Company.
Roots and Branches [*Wo de xiongdi jiemei*]. 2001. Dir. Yu Zhong. Tianshan Film Studio.
Charging out Amazon [*Chongchu yamaxun*]. 2002. Dir. Song Yaming. August First Film Studio and CCTV Movie Channel.
Hero [*Yingxiong*]. 2002. Dir. Zhang Yimou. Beijing New Picture Film Company and Elite Group Enterprises.
Missing Gun [*Xunqiang*]. 2002. Dir. Lu Chuan. Cape of Good Hope Cultural Ltd.
Together with You [*He ni zai yiqi*]. 2002. Dir. Chen Kaige. 21 Century Shengkai Film, China Movie Channel, Chinarunn Entertainment, and China Film Group Corporation.
Unknown Pleasures [*Ren Xiaoyao*]. 2002. Dir. Jia Zhangke. Hong Kong Hutong Production Company, Japan T-Mark, Lumen Films, and E-Pictures.
Blind Shaft [*Mangjing*]. 2003. Dir. Li Yang. Shengtang Film Production Ltd.
Peacock [*Kongque*]. 2004. Dir. Gu Changwei. Zhongkai Company.
The World [*Shijie*]. 2004. Dir. Jia Zhangke. Xstream Pictures, Office Kitano, Lumen Films, Xinghui Production, and Shanghai Film Group.
Riding Alone for Thousands of Miles [*Qianli zou danqi*]. 2005. Dir. Zhang Yimou. Beijing New Picture Film Co., China Film Co-Production Corporation, Edko Films, Elite Group Entertainment, Gilla Company, Toho Company, and Zhang Yimou Studio.
Shanghai Dreams [*Qing hong*]. 2005. Dir. Wang Xiaoshuai. Xingmei Media, Beijing Debo Film Company, and Beijing Mengzhou Culture Ltd.
The Age of Repairing Virginity [*Xiufu chunvmo shidai*]. 2006. Dir. Cui Jian. Zonbo Media.

The Pervert's Guide to Cinema. UK, Austria, and Netherlands. 2006. Dir. Sophie Fiennes. Amoeba Film, Kasander Film Company, Lone Star Productions, and Mischief Films.
Rush Hour 3. US and Germany. 2007. Dir. Brett Ratner. Roger Birnbaum Productions and Arthur Sarkissian Productions.
The Sun Also Rises [*Taiyang zhaochang shengqi*]. 2007. Dir. Jiang Wen. Taihe Film Investment, Beijing Bu Yi Le Hu Film Company, Lotus Entertainment, and Emperor Motion Pictures.
Forever Enthralled [*Mei Lanfang*]. 2008. Dir. Chen Kaige. China Film Group Corporation, Emperor Motion Pictures, and CMC Entertainment.
Slumdog Millionaire. UK and US. 2008. Dir. Danny Boyle and Loveleen Tandan. Warner Bros., Celador Films, Film4, and Pathé Pictures International.
Chengdu, I Love You [*Chengdu, wo ai ni*]. 2009. Dir. Cui Jian. Zonbo Media.
City of Life and Death [aka *Nanjing! Nanjing!*]. 2009. Dir. Lu Chuan. China Film Group, Chuan Films, Media Asia Films, Jiangsu Broadcasting System, and Stellar Megamedia.
Disturbing the Peace [*Lao ma ti hua*]. 2009. Dir. Ai Weiwei. Ai Weiwei Studio.
The Founding of a Republic [*Jianguo da ye*]. 2009. Dir. Han Sanping and Huang Jianxin. China Film Group, China Movie Channel, Media Asia, Emperor Motion Pictures, Beijing Hua Lu Bai Na Film Company.
Grass Mud Horse, Motherland [*Cao Ni Ma Zu Guo*]. Dir. Ai Weiwei. Ai Weiwei Studio.
Happy [*Gaoxing*]. 2009. Dir. Ah Gan. Filmko Pictures and Shenzhen Jin Hai An Film Ltd.
Love of Grass Mud Horse [*Cao ni ma de aiqing*]. 2009.
Song of Grass Mud Horse [*Cao ni ma zhi ge*]. 2009.
Special Program of Animal World: Grass Mud Horse in the Mahler Gobi Desert [*Dongwu shijie tebie pian male gebi shang de caonima*]. 2009.
A Woman, A Gun and a Noodle Shop [*Sanqiang pai'an jingji*]. 2009. Dir. Zhang Yimou. Beijing New Picture Film Co., EDKO Film Ltd., and Sony Pictures Classics.
The 1911 Revolution [*Xinhai geming*]. 2011. Dir. Jackie Chan and Zhang Li. Changchun Film Studio, Hebei Film Studio, Shanghai Film Group, Xiaoxiang Film Ltd, and Jiangsu Broadcasting System.
Ai Weiwei: Fairytale. 2011. Dir. Ai Weiwei. Jrp Ringier.
The Flowers of War [*Jinling shisan chai*]. 2011. Dir. Zhang Yimou. Beijing New Picture Film Company, Jiangsu Broadcasting-Film-Television Bureau, and EDKO Film Ltd.
The Founding of a Party [*Jiandang wei ye*, aka *Beginning of the Great Revival*]. 2011. Dir. Han Sanping and Huang Jianxin. China Film Group, China Movie Channel, Shanghai Film Group, Jiangsu Broadcasting-Film-Television Bureau, and Hunan Television Station.
Caught in the Web [*Sousuo*]. 2012. Dir. Chen Kaige. 21 Century Shengkai Film.
Grass Mud Horse Style [*Cao ni ma style*]. 2012. Dir. Ai Weiwei. Ai Weiwei Studio.
A Touch of Sin [*Tian zhuding*]. 2013. Dir. Jia Zhangke. Xstream Pictures, Shanghai Film Group, Bandai Visual Co. Ltd., Bitters End, and Office Kitano.
Blue Sky Bones [*Lanse gutou*]. 2014. Dir. Cui Jian. Beijing Dongxi Music Art Production Company, Liaoning Ougu Digital Technology Ltd., Shenzhenshi Zhongshu Wenchuang Capital Management Ltd., and Dongyue International Media.

BIBLIOGRAPHY

Adorno, Theodor. "On Popular Music." *Studies in Philosophy and Social Sciences* 9 (1941): 17–48.
———, and J. M. Bernstein, eds. *The Culture Industry: Selected Essays on Mass Culture*. New York: Routledge, 2001.
———, and Hanns Eisler. *Composing for the Films*. London and New York: Continuum, 2007.
———, and Max Horkheimer. "The Culture Industry: Enlightenment as Mass Deception." In *Dialectic of Enlightenment*. Translated by John Cumming, 94–136. London and New York: Continuum, 2001.
Alim, H. Samy, Awad Ibrahim, and Alastair Pennycook, eds. *Global Linguistic Flows: Hip Hop Cultures, Youth Identities, and the Politics of Language*. New York: Routledge, 2009.
Altman, Rick, McGraw Jones, and Sonia Tatroe. "Inventing the Cinema Soundtrack: Hollywood's Multiplane Sound System." In *Music and Cinema*. Edited by James Buhler, Caryl Flinn, and David Neumeyer, 339–59. Hanover: Wesleyan University Press, 2000.
Anderson, Benedict. *Imagined Communities: Reflections on the Origin and Spread of Nationalism*. London and New York: Verso, 2006.
Appadurai, Arun. *Modernity at Large: Cultural Dimensions of Globalization*. Minneapolis: University of Minnesota, 1996.
Attali, Jacques. *Noise: The Political Economy of Music*. Translated by Brian Massumi. Minneapolis: University of Minnesota Press, 1985.
Bai, Ruoyun. "Disrobing CCTV: Scandals, *E'gao,* and Resistance in China's Cyberspace." In *Three Asias: Japan, S. Korea, China*. Edited by Takayuki Tatsumi, Jina Kim, and Zhang Zhen. *Paradoxa: Studies in World Literary Genres* 22 (2010): 249–69.
Bakhtin, Mikhail. *Problems in Dostoevsky's Poetics*. Edited and translated by Caryl Emerson. Minneapolis: University of Minnesota Press, 1993.
———. *Speech Genres and Other Late Essays*. Edited by Caryl Emerson and Michael Holquist. Translated by Vern W. McGee. Austin: University of Texas Press, 1986.
Bao, Ying. "Remembering the Invisible: Soundscape and Memory of 1989." *Journal of Chinese Cinemas* 7.3 (2013): 207–24.
Baranovitch, Nimrod. *China's New Voices: Popular Music, Ethnicity, Gender, and Politics, 1978–1997*. Berkeley: University of California Press, 2003.
Barme, Geremie. "Chinese Dreams (*Zhongguo meng*)." *The China Story*. Accessed March 31, 2014. https://www.thechinastory.org/yearbooks/yearbook-2013/forum-dreams-and-power/chinese-dreams-zhongguo-meng-%E4%B8%AD%E5%9B%BD%E6%A2%A6/.
———. *In the Red: On Contemporary Chinese Culture*. New York: Columbia University Press, 1999.
———. "Wang Shuo and Liumang ('Hooligan') Culture." *Australian Journal of Chinese Affairs* 28 (July 1992): 23–64.
———, and John Minford, eds. *Seeds of Fire: Chinese Voices of Conscience*. New York: Hill and Wang, 1988.

Barthes, Roland. "The Grain of the Voice." In *Image, Music, Text*. Translated by Stephen Heath, 179–89. New York: Hill and Wang, 1977.
Baudelaire, Charles. *Oeuvres complètes 2*. Paris: Gallimard, 1976.
Bazin, André. *What is Cinema? Volume 1*. Berkeley: University of California Press, 2005.
———. *What is Cinema? Volume 2*. Berkeley: University of California Press, 2005.
Benjamin, Walter. *Charles Baudelaire: A Lyric Poet in the Era of High Capitalism*. Translated by Harry Zohn. London: Verso. 1983.
———. "The Work of Art in the Age of Mechanical Reproduction." In *Illuminations: Walter Benjamin Essays and Reflections*. Edited by Hannah Arendt. Translated by Harry Zohn. 217–52. New York: Schocken Books, 1968.
Berger, Harris M., and Michael Thomas Carroll, eds. *Global Pop, Local Language*. Jackson: University Press of Mississippi, 2003.
Berry, Chris. "A Nation T(w/o)o: Chinese Cinema(s) and Nationhood(s)." In *Colonialism and Nationalism in Asian Cinema*. Edited by Wimal Dissanayake, 42–64. Bloomington: Indiana University Press, 1994.
———. "'Race' (*minzu*): Chinese Film and the Politics of Nationalism." *Cinema Journal* 31.2 (1992): 45–58.
———. "What's Big about the Big Film? 'De-Westernizing' the Blockbuster in Korea and China." In *Movie Blockbusters*. Edited by Julian Stringer, 217–29. London and New York: Routledge, 2003.
———. "*Xiao Wu*: Watching Time Go By." In *Chinese Films in Focus II*. Edited by Chris Berry, 250–57. London: Palgrave Macmillan, 2008.
———, ed. *Perspectives on Chinese Cinema*. London: British Film Institute, 1991.
———, and Mary Farquhar. *China on Screen: Cinema and Nation*. New York: Columbia University Press, 2006.
Berry, Michael. *Speaking in Images: Interviews with Contemporary Chinese Filmmakers*. New York: Columbia University Press, 2005.
———. *Xiao Wu, Platform, Unknown Pleasures: Jia Zhangke's "Hometown Trilogy."* London: Palgrave Macmillian, 2009.
Blood, Susan. *Baudelaire and the Aesthetics of Bad Faith*. Stanford: Stanford University Press, 1997.
Brace, Timothy. "Modernization and Music in Contemporary China: Crisis, Identity, and the Politics of Style." PhD diss., University of Texas at Austin, 1992.
———. "Popular Music in Contemporary Beijing: Modernism and Cultural Identity." *Asian Music* 22.2 (Spring/Summer 1991): 43–63.
———, and Paul Friedlander. "Rock and Roll on the New Long March: Popular Music, Cultural Identity, and Political Opposition in the People's Republic of China." In *Rockin' the Boat: Mass Music and Mass Movements*. Edited by Reebee Garofalo, 115–28. Boston: South End Press, 1992.
Braester, Yomi. "Chinese Cinema in the Age of Advertisement: The Filmmaker as a Cultural Broker." *China Quarterly* 183 (September 2005): 549–64.
———. *Painting the City Red: Chinese Cinema and the Urban Contract*. Durham and London: Duke University Press, 2010.
Brady, Anne-Marie. "Hollywood with Chinese Characteristics." *Resurgent Dictatorship*, April 19, 2016. Accessed May 26, 2016. http://www.resurgentdictatorship.org/hollywood-with-chinese-characteristics/.

Brown, Royal S. *Overtones and Undertones: Reading Film Music*. Berkeley: University of California Press, 1994.

Buck-Morss, Susan. *Dreamworld and Catastrophe: The Passing of Mass Utopia in East and West*. Cambridge: MIT Press, 2002.

———. "The Flaneur, the Sanwichman and the Whore: The Politics of Loitering." *New German Critique* 39 (Autumn 1986): 99–140.

Cai, Shangwei. *Yingshi chuanbo yu dazhong wenhua: wenhua gongye shidai de yingshi fangfa lun* [*Film, Television and Popular Culture: The Methodology of Film and Television in the Time of Culture Industry*]. Chengdu: Sichuan daxue chubanshe, 2005.

Chan, Evans. "Zhang Yimou's *Hero* and the Temptations of Fascism." *Film International* 2 (2004): 14–23.

Chang, Jeff, and S. Craig Watkins. "It's a Hip-Hop World." *Foreign Policy* 163 (Nov./Dec. 2007): 58–65.

Chen, Gang. *Dazhong wenhua yu dangdai wutuobang* [*Mass Culture and Contemporary Utopia*]. Beijing: Zuojia chubanshe, 1996.

Chen, Haosu, "Guanyu gushipian honggaoliang de taolun" [Discussions on *Red Sorghum*]. In *Zhongguo dianying nianjian 1989* [*China Film Yearbook 1989*], 273–76. Beijing: Zhongguo dianying chubanshe, 1989.

Chen, Kaige, "Qianli zou shanbei: pingqiong he xiwang de shouji" [A Thousand Miles Through Northern Shaanxi: Notes on Poverty and Hope]. *Dianying yishu* [*Film Art*] 4 (1986): 29–31.

Chen, Nancy N. et al., eds. *China Urban: Ethnographies of Contemporary Culture*. Durham: Duke University Press, 2001.

Chen, Sihe. "Yaogun zhong de gexing yishi: yi wu suo you" [The Individual Consciousness in Rock 'n' Roll: "Nothing to My Name"]. In *Zhongguo dangdai wenxueshi jiaocheng* [*A Guide to the History of Contemporary Chinese Literature*], 326–28. Shanghai: Fudan daxue chubanshe, 1999.

Chen, Xiaomei. *Occidentalism: A Theory of Counter-Discourse in Post-Mao China*. Lanham: Rowman & Littlefield, 2002.

Cheng, Qingsong, and Huang Ou, eds. *Wode sheyingji bu sahuang: xianfeng dianying ren dang'an, shengyu 1961–1970* [*My Camera Doesn't Lie: Archives of Avant-garde Filmmakers, Born Between 1961–1970*]. Beijing: Zhongguo youyi chuban gongsi, 2002.

Chion, Michel. *Audio-Vision: Sound on Screen*. Translated by Claudia Gorbman. New York: Columbia University Press, 1994.

———. *The Voice in Cinema*. Translated by Claudia Gorbman. New York: Columbia University Press, 1999.

Chow, Rey. "Listening Otherwise, Music Miniaturized: A Different Type of Question About Revolution." *Discourse* 13.1 (1992): 129–48.

———. *Primitive Passions: Visuality, Sexuality, Ethnography, and Contemporary Chinese Cinema*. New York: Columbia University Press, 1995.

———. *Sentimental Fabulations, Contemporary Chinese Films: Attachment in the Age of Global Visibility*. New York: Columbia University Press, 2007.

———. *Writing Diaspora: Tactics of Intervention in Contemporary Cultural Studies*. Bloomington: Indiana University Press, 1993.

Chun, Allen, Ned Rossiter, and Brian Shoesmith, eds. *Refashioning Pop Music in Asia: Cosmopolitan Flows, Political Tempos and Aesthetic Industries*. London and New York: Routledge, 2004.

Clark, Paul. *Reinventing China: A Generation and its Films*. Hong Kong: Chinese University Press. 2005.

———. "Two Hundred Flowers on China's Screens." In *Perspectives on Chinese Cinema*. Edited by Chris Berry, 40–61. London: British Film Institute, 1991.

———. *Youth Culture in China: From Red Guards to Netizens*. New York: Cambridge University Press, 2012.

Coonan, Clifford. "'Also Rises' Not a Hemingway Film." *Variety*, August 31, 2007.

Craig, Timothy J., and Richard King, eds. *Global Goes Local: Popular Culture in Asia*. Vancouver: University of British Columbia Press, 2002.

Crary, Jonathan. "The Cinema Obscura and Its Subject." In *Techniques of the Observer: On Vision and Modernity in the Nineteenth Century*, 25–66. Cambridge: MIT Press, 1990.

Cui, Chen. "Mishi de xuanlv: ping wode xiongdi jiemei" [Disconcerting Melody: A Film Review on *Roots and Branches*]. *Beijing dianying xueyuan xuebiao* [Journal of Beijing Film Academy] 4 (2001): 89–91.

Cui, Shuqin. *Women Through the Lens: Gender and Nation in a Century of Chinese Cinema*. Honolulu: University of Hawaii Press, 2003.

———. "Working from the Margins: Urban Cinema and Independent Directors in Contemporary China." *Post Script* 20.2–3 (Winter/Spring-Summer 2001): 77–93.

Cui, Weiping. "Wo shi yizhi cao ni ma" [I am a Grass Mud Horse]. Accessed May 05, 2010. http://www.hecaitou.net/?p=4723.

Curtin, Michael. *Playing to the World's Biggest Audience: The Globalization of Chinese Film and TV*. Berkeley: University of California Press, 2007.

Dai, Degang. "Leixing yishi xingtai yu chengxian fangshi xi yingpian zhengjiu babin rui'en" [Genre, Ideology, and Representational Style: An Analysis of *Saving Private Ryan*]. *Dianying yishu* [Film Art] 1 (1999): 48–51.

Dai, Jinhua. *Cinema and Desire: Feminist Marxism and Cultural Politics in the Work of Dai Jinhua*. Edited by Jing Wang and Tani E. Barlow. Translated by Lisa Rofel and Hu Ying. London and New York: Verso, 2002.

———. "Rewriting the Red Classics." In *Rethinking Chinese Popular Culture: Cannibalizations of the Canon*. Edited by Carlos Rojas and Eileen Chow, 151–78. London and New York: Routledge, 2011.

———. *Wuzhong fengjing: zhongguo dianying wenhua, 1978–1998* [Scenery in the Fog: Chinese Cinema Culture, 1978–1998]. Beijing: Beijing daxue chubanshe, 2000.

———. and Judy T. H. Chen. "Imagined Nostalgia." *Boundary* 2, Vol. 24, No. 3, Postmodernism and China (Autumn 1997): 143–61.

Dai, Xiu, and Zhuang Xin. *Xie Jin Zhuan* [A Biography of Xie Jin]. Shanghai: Huadong daxue chubanshe, 1997.

de Certeau, Michel. *The Practice of Everyday Life*. Berkeley: University of California Press, 1984.

de Kloet, Jeroen. *China with a Cut: Globalization, Urban Youth and Popular Music*. Amsterdam: Amsterdam University Press, 2010.

———. "Cultural Synchronization: Hip-hop with Chinese Characteristics?" *International Association of the Study of Popular Music* (July 25–29, 2005). Accessed January 30, 2010. http://home.tiscali.nl/jeroendekloeth.

———. "Popular Music and Youth in Urban China: The Dakou Generation." *China Quarterly* 183 (September 2005): 609–26.

———. "Sonic Sturdiness: The Globalization of 'Chinese' Rock and Pop." *Critical Studies in Media Communication* 22.4 (Nov. 2005): 321–38.

Deleuze, Gilles. *Cinema 2: The Time-Image*. Translated by Hugh Tomlinson and Robert Galeta. Minneapolis: University of Minnesota Press, 1989.

DeNora, Tia. *Music in Everyday Life*. Cambridge: Cambridge University Press, 2000.

Dikotter, Frank. *Exotic Commodities: Modern Objects and Everyday Life in China*. New York: Columbia University Press, 2006.

Ding, Guangen. "Duochu youxiu zuopin, fanrong dianying shiye" [Produce More Excellent Works, Let the Film Industry Thrive]. In *Zhongguo dianying nianjian 1997* [*China Film Yearbook 1997*], 7–10. Beijing: Zhongguo dianying chubanshe, 1997.

Ding, Shaolun, "Wenhua xungen yu honggaoliang xianxiang" [Cultural Root-seeking and the Red Sorghum Phenomenon]. *Shandong shida xuebiao* [*Journal of Shandong Normal University*] 2 (1989): 29–25.

Dirlik, Arif, and Zhang, Xudong, eds. *Postmodernism & China*. Durham: Duke University Press, 2000.

Dong, Yajun. "Ta de ge heyi rang ni rumi: fang xianggang yingshi gequ dawang jiaguhui xiansheng" [How Does His Songs Captivate You?: An Interview With The Great Master of Hong Kong Film Music Mr. Gu Jiahui]. *Dianying pingjie* [*Film Review*] 7 (1988): 26–27.

Efird, Robert. "Rock in a Hard Place: Music and the Market in Nineties Beijing." In *China Urban: Ethnographies of Contemporary Culture*. Edited by Nancy N. Chen, et al., 67–88. Durham: Duke University Press, 2001.

Eisenstein, Sergei. *The Eisenstein Reader*. Edited by Richard Taylor. Translated by Richard Taylor and William Powell. London: British Film Institute, 1998.

Ellsworth, Mark Brent. "The Hero Fallen: Zhang Yimou and the Question of Unstable Authorship." MA thesis, Victoria University of Wellington, 2013.

En, Na. "Chongxin renshi meiguo dapian" [Re-understanding American Blockbusters]. *Beijing qingnian bao* [*Beijing Youth Daily*], May 19, 1999.

Feng, Jinfang. *Quexi yu zaichang de pianzheng tujin: xin shiqi zhongguo dianying guanzhong wenti yanjiu* [*Dialectics of Absence and Presence: Studies of Spectatorship of Chinese Cinema in the New Era*]. Beijing: Beijing guangbo xueyuan chubanshe, 2006.

Feng, Mei, "Ziji de dapian: caifang Feng Xiaoning" [Big Pictures of Our Own: An Interview with Feng Xiaoning]. *Dazhong dianying* [*Popular Film*] 6 (1997): 22–23.

Fore, Steve. "From *Rock Kids* to *Beijing Bastards*: P.R.C. Youth Subcultures on Film Before and After June 4." *Screening the Past* 18 (2005). Accessed April 6, 2008. http://www.latrobe.edu.au/screeningthepast/firstrelease/fr_18/SFfr18a.html.

Foucault, Michel. *Power: Volume 3: Essential Works of Foucault, 1954–1984*. Edited by James D. Faubion. Translated by Robert Hurley et al. New York: New Press, 2000.

Frith, Simon. "Towards an Aesthetic of Popular music." In *Music and Society: The Politics of Composition, Performance, and Reception*. Edited by Richard Leppart and Susan McClary, 133–49. Cambridge: Cambridge University Press, 1987.

———. ed. *Popular Music: Critical Concepts in Media and Culture Studies*. London and New York: Routledge, 2004.

Fumitoshi, Karima, and Li He, "Chen Kaige yu da dao zhu duihua" [The Conversations Between Chen Kaige and Ogisha Oshima]. *Dangdai dianying* [*Contemporary Cinema*] 6 (1987): 111–18.

Fung, Anthony. "Western Style, Chinese Pop: Jay Chou's Rap and Hip-Hop in China." *Asian Music* 39.1 (Winter–Spring 2008): 69–80.

———, and Michael Curtin. "The Anomalies of Being Faye (Wong): Gender Politics in Chinese Popular Music." *International Journal of Cultural Studies* 5 (2002): 263–90.

Gallagher, Mark, and Julian Stringer. "Reshaping Contemporary Chinese Film Sound: Dolby Laboratories and Changing Industrial Practices." *Journal of Chinese Cinemas* 7.3 (2013): 263–76.
Gary, Xu, *Sinascape: Contemporary Chinese Cinema*. Lanham: Rowman & Littlefield, 2007.
Gateward, Frances, ed. *Zhang Yimou: Interviews*. Jackson: University Press of Mississippi, 2001.
Gilroy, Paul. *The Black Atlantic: Modernity and Double Consciousness*. London: Verso, 1993.
Gorbman, Claudia. *Unheard Melodies: Narrative Film Music*. Bloomington: Indiana University Press, 1987.
Gunn, Edward M. *Rendering the Regional: Local Language in Contemporary Chinese Media*. Honolulu: University of Hawaii Press, 2006.
Hall, Stuart, and Paddy Whannel. *The Popular Arts*. New York: Pantheon Book, 1965.
Han, Kuo-Huang. "Folk Songs of the Han Chinese: Characteristics and Classifications." *Asian Music* 20.2 (Spring/Summer 1989): 107–28.
Hansen, Miriam. "Fallen Women, Rising Stars, New Horizons: Shanghai Silent Film as Vernacular Modernism." *Film Quarterly* 54.1 (Fall 2000): 10–22.
———. "The Mass Production of the Senses: Classical Cinema as Vernacular Modernism." *Modernism/Modernity* 6.2 (April 1999): 59–77.
Hao, Jian, "Taitannikehao zai zhong guo" [Titanic in China]. *Dianying yishu* [*Film Art*] 4 (1998): 19–24.
Haraszti, Miklós. *The Velvet Prison: Artists Under State Socialism*. Translated by Katalin and Stephen Landesmann with the help of Steve Wasserman. New York: Basic Books, 1987.
Harootunian, Harry. *History's Disquiet: Modernity, Cultural Practice, and the Question of Everyday Life*. New York: Columbia University Press, 2000.
Hebdige, Dick. *Subculture: The Meaning of Style*. London and New York: Taylor and Francis, 2002.
Hong, Junhao. "The Evolution of China's War Movie in Five Decades: Factors Contributing to Changes, Limits, and Implications." *Asian Cinema* 10.1 (Fall 1998): 93–106.
Hou, Yan. "Fangyan changjin liuxing ge ni tingzhe sha ganjue" [How Do You Feel about the Adoption of Vernacular in Popular Music?] *Jinhua shibao* [*Beijing Times*], March 20, 2015. Accessed May 3, 2015. http://epaper.jinghua.cn/html/2015-03/20/content_180622.htm.
Huang, Huilin, ed. *Dangdai zhongguo dazhong wenhua yanjiu* [*A Contemporary Chinese Mass Culture Reader*]. Beijing: Beijing shifan daxue chubanshe, 1998.
Huang, Nicole. "Listening to Films: Politics of the Auditory in 1970s China." *Journal of Chinese Cinemas* 7.3 (2013): 187–206.
Inglis, Ian, ed. *Popular Music and Film*. London: Wallflower Press, 2003.
Jameson, Fredric. *Postmodernism, or, the Cultural Logic of Late Capitalism*. Durham: Duke University Press, 1999.
———. "Third-World Literature in the Era of Multinational Capitalism." *Social Text* 15 (Autumn 1986): 65–88.
Jia, Zhangke. "Zai yinyue he dianying de jiacha zhichu" [At the Intersection of Film and Music]. *Beijing dianying xueyuan xuebao* [*Journal of Beijing Film Academy*] 2 (1994): 247–50.
Jin, Zhaojun. *Guangtian huari xia de liuxing: qingli zhongguo liuxing yinyue* [*The Popular in High Profile: Experiencing Chinese Popular Music*]. Beijing: Remin yinyue chubanshe, 2002.
———. "Zhongguo liuxing yinyue 30 nian huishou" [30 Years of Chinese Popular Music in Retrospect]. *Nanfang zhoumo* [*Southern Weekend*], December 11, 2008.
Jones, Andrew. *Like a Knife: Ideology and Genre in Contemporary Chinese Popular Music*. Ithaca: East Asia Program, Cornell University, 1992.

———. "The Politics of Popular Culture in Post-Tiananmen China." In *Popular Protest and Political Culture in Modern China*. Edited by Jeffery N. Wasserstrom and Elizabeth J. Perry, 148–65. Boulder: Westview Press, 1994.

Kang, Baocheng. "Zhongguo ren zui xuyao shenme: cong zhengjiu dabin rui'en xiangdao de" [What the Chinese Need Most: Reflections on *Saving Private Ryan*]. *Yue Hai Feng* [*Trend from the South Sea*] 6 (1998): 21–22.

Karl, Rebecca E. "The Burdens of History: *Lin Zexu* (1959) and *The Opium War* (1997)." In *Wither China: Intellectual Politics in Contemporary China*. Edited by Zhang Xudong, 229–62. Durham and London: Duke University Press, 2001.

Kato, M. T. *From Kung Fu to Hip Hop: Globalization, Revolution, and Popular Culture*. Albany: State University of New York Press, 2007.

Kraicer, Shelly. "A Matter of Life and Death: Lu Chuan and Post-*Zhuxuanlu* Cinema." *Cinema Scope*. Accessed January 28, 2014. http://cinema-scope.com/features/features-a-matter-of-life-and-death-lu-chuan-and-post-zhuxuanlu-cinema-by-shelly-kraicer/.

Kronengold, Charles. "Multitemporality and the Speed(s) of Thought in Jonnie To's Action Films." *Journal of Chinese Cinemas* 7.3 (2013): 277–95.

Kuoshu, Harry. "Forrest Gump Becomes a Chinese Film Director: Idealism, Formalism, and an In-between Audience." *Global Studies Journal* 8.1 (March 2015): 1–11.

Lan, Feng. "Taiwan xin yinyue jiafu taozhe beijing duihua lu" [A Conversation with David Tao in Beijing: The New Godfather of Taiwan Music]. *Guoji yinyue jiaoliu* [*International Musical Movement*] 8 (2000): 114–15.

Larsen, Wendy. "Zhang Yimou's *Hero*: Dismantling the Myth of Cultural Power." *Journal of Chinese Cinemas* 2.3 (2008): 181–96.

Lau, Jenny Kwok Wah. "*Hero*: China's Response to Hollywood Globalization." *Jump Cut* 49 (Spring 2007). Accessed January 06, 2014. http://www.ejumpcut.org/archive/jc49.2007/Lau-Hero/.

———. ed. *Multiple Modernities: Cinemas and Popular Media in Transcultural East Asia*. Philadelphia: Temple University Press, 2003.

Lee, Gregory B. *Troubadours, Trumpeters, and Troubled Makers: Lyricism, Nationalism, and Hybridity in China and Its Others*. Durham: Duke University Press, 1996.

Lei, Da, Zeng Zhengnan, Tong Daoming, and Wang Dehou. "Yige hao 'xianxiang'" [A Good "Phenomenon"]. *Dianying yishu* [*Film Art*] 8 (1988): 15–52.

Li, Dongran. "Cui Jian: wo shenzhi ziji buzhi ruci" [Cui Jian: I Know from my Heart that I Can Go Beyond This]. *Sanlian shenghuo zhoukan* [*Sanlian Life Weekly*], August 17, 2012. Accessed August 23, 2013. http://www.lifeweek.com.cn/2012/0817/38284_2.shtml.

Li, Erwei, "Yishujia yao you lishi shiminggan: xie jin tan yapian zhan zheng" [Artists Ought to Have a Sense of Historical Responsibility: An Interview with Xie Jin on *The Opium War*]. *Dianying yishu* [*Film Art*] 5 (1997): 20–24.

Li, Jiawei, "Cui Jian: Chengdu, wo ai ni" [Cui Jian: Chengdu, I Love You]. *Zhongguo zhoukan* [*China Weekly*], September 28, 2009. Accessed July 11, 2011, http://elite.youth.cn/zgzk/200910/t20091016_1052241.htm.

Li, Minqi. "After Neoliberalism: Empire, Social Democracy, or Socialism." *Monthly Review* 55.8 (January 2004). Accessed September 25, 2010. http://monthlyreview.org/01041i.htm.

———. "An Age of Transition: The United States, China, Peak Oil, and the Demise of Neoliberalism." *Monthly Review* 59.11 (April 2008). Accessed September 25, 2010. http://monthlyreview.org/080401li.php.

Li, Yanze. "Cengjing fengmi zhongguo: dianying pili wu yuanyin zhuanji" [A Craze of Thunderbolt Dance Sweeping across China: The Motion Picture and Original

Soundtrack of *Breakin'*]. Accessed March 3, 2010. http://www.360doc.com/content/11/1228/21/8021011_175693356.shtml.

Li, Yiming, "Cong diwudai dao diliudai" [From the Fifth Generation to the Sixth Generation]. *Dianying yishu* [*Film Art*] 1 (1998): 15–22.

Lin, Xiaoping, "Jia Zhangke's Cinematic Trilogy: A Journey Across the Ruins of Post-Mao China." In *Chinese-language Film: Historiography, Poetics, Politics*. Edited by Sheldon Hsiao-peng Lu and Emilie Yueh-Yu Yeh, 186–209. Honolulu: University of Hawaii Press, 2005.

Lin, Xudong, Zhang Yaxuan, and Gu Zheng, eds. *Jia Zhangke dianying: guxiang sanbuqu zhi zhantai* [*The Jia Zhangke Film: Hometown Trilogy—Platform*]. Beijing: Zhongguo mangwen chubanshe, 2003.

Link, Perry, Richard P. Madsen, and Paul G. Pickowicz, eds. *Popular China: Unofficial Culture in a Globalizing Society*. Lanham: Rowman & Littlefield, 2002.

———. and Xiao Qiang. "From Grass-Mud Equestrians to Rights-Conscious Citizens: Language and Thought on the Chinese Internet." In *Restless China*. Edited by Perry Link, Richard P. Madsen, and Paul G. Pickowicz, 83–106. Lanham: Rowman & Littlefield Publishers, 2013.

Lipsitz, George. *Dangerous Crossroads: Popular Music, Postmodernism, and the Poetics of Place*. New York: Verso, 1994.

Liu, Cheng. "Dui 1989 nian guishipian chuangzuo de huigu" [A Review on the Feature Productions of 1989]. In *Zhongguo dianying nianjian 1990* [*China Film Yearbook 1990*], 18–24. Beijing: Zhongguo dianying chubanshe, 1990.

———. "Guanyu zhuxuanlv duoyanghua ji qita" [A Reflection on Leitmotif, Diversity, and Other Issues]. *Beijing dianying xueyuan xuebao* [*Journals of Beijing Film Academy*] 1 (1995): 47–57.

Liu, Hong, "Woguo shuochang yinyue de fazhan tanxi" [An Exploration of the Trajectory of Chinese Rap Music]. *Liuxing yinyue* [*Popular Music*] 32 (2012): 8.

Liu, Jin. "Alternative Voice and Local Youth Identity in Chinese Local-Language Rap Music." *Positions: East Asia Cultures Critique* 22.1 (Winter 2014): 263–92.

———. "The Rhetoric of Local Languages as the Marginal: Chinese Underground and Independent Films by Jia Zhangke and Others." *Modern Chinese Literature and Culture* 18.2 (2006): 163–205.

———. *Signifying the Local: Media Productions Rendered in Local Languages in Mainland China in the New Millennium*. Leiden: Brill, 2013.

Liu, Kang. *Globalization and Cultural Trends in China*. Honolulu: University of Hawaii Press, 2004.

———. "Popular Culture and the Culture of the Masses in Contemporary China." In *Postmodernism & China*. Edited by Arif Dirlik and Xudong Zhang, 123–44. Durham: Duke University Press, 2000.

Liu, Lydia H. "Translingual Practice: The Discourse of Individualism between China and the West." *Positions* 1 (Spring 1993 1): 160–93.

———. *What's Happened to Ideology?: Transnationalism, Postsocialism, and the Study of Global Media Culture*. Durham: Asian/Pacific Studies Institute, Duke University, 1998.

Liu, Mingqi. "Hong gaoliang xiaoying yu yishu minzhu" [The Red Sorghum Effect and Democracy of Arts]. *Dianying pingjie* [*Movie Review*] 11 (1988): 14.

Long, Xincheng, "Zhanzheng yu renxing de qianglie chongtu: kan zhengjiu babin rui'en" [The Intense Conflicts of War and Humanity: on *Saving Private Ryan*]. *Dianying pingjie* [*Movie Review*] 1 (1999): 24.

Lu, Chunyan, and Wang Zhanli, "Zhuxuanlv dianying de shangyehua yu shangye dianying de zhuxuanlv hua" [The Commercialization of Leitmotif Film and the Leitmotifization of Commercial Film]. *Dangdai dianying* [*Contemporary Cinema*] 5 (1999): 106–109.

Lu, Sheldon Hsiao-peng. *China, Transnational Visuality, Global Postmodernity*. Stanford: Stanford University Press, 2001.

———. "Dialect and Modernity in 21st Century Sinophone Cinema." *Jump Cut* 49 (Spring 2007). Accessed November 1, 2011. http://www.ejumpcut.org/archive/jc49.2007/Lu/.

———. ed. *Transnational Chinese Cinema: Identity, Nationhood, Gender*. Honolulu: University of Hawaii Press, 1997.

Lu, Xun. *Silent China: Selected Writings of Lu Xun*. Edited and translated by Gladys Yang. London: Oxford University Press, 1973.

———. *Yecao* [*Wild Grass*]. Translated by Yang Xianyi and Gladys Yang. Hong Kong: Chinese University Press, 2003.

Luo, Xianrong. "Kuankuan de dalu, changchang de baochuan: qiantan dianying honggaoliang de sige yise" [Big Road, Long Boat: A Preliminary Discussion on Four Songs and One Color in *Red Sorghum*]. *Dianying pinjie* [*Film Review*] (August 1988): 24–25.

Luo, Zhanfeng. *Dianying ×yinyue* [*Film × Music*]. Beijing: Sanlian shudian, 2005.

Lussier, Germain. "Chinese Box Office Overtakes U.S. for First Time in History." *Slash Film*, March 3, 2015. Accessed August 25, 2015. http://www.slashfilm.com/chinese-box-office-overtakes-america.

Lv, Shaoyong. "Houxiandai de liguizhe: yingpian zuotian pingxi" [Postmodernist Deviant: A Critical Analysis of *Quitting*]. *Beijing dianying xueyuan xuebao* [*Journal of Beijing Film Academy*] 1 (2002): 103–06.

Ma, Eric. "Translocal Spatiality." *International Journal of Cultural Studies* 5.2 (2002): 131–51.

Ma, Jean. "Delayed Voices: Intertexuality, Music, and Gender in *The Hole*." *Journal of Chinese Cinemas* 5.2 (2011): 123–39.

———. *Sounding the Modern Women: The Songstress in Chinese Cinema*. Durham: Duke University Press, 2015.

———. and Matthew Johnson. "Introduction." *Journal of Chinese Cinemas* 7.3 (2013): 179–86.

Ma, Ning. "2000: xin zhuliu dianying zhenzheng de qidian" [2000: A Real Start for New Mainstream Cinema]. *Dangdai dianying* [*Contemporary Cinema*] 1(2000): 16–18.

———. "Culture and Politics in Chinese Film Melodrama: Traditional Sacred, Moral Economy, and the Xie Jin Mode." PhD diss., Monash University, 1992.

———. "Xin zhuliu dianying: dui guochan dianying de yige jianyi" [New Mainstream Cinema: A Suggestion on Domestic Filmmaking]. *Dangdai dianying* [*Contemporary Cinema*] 4 (1999): 4–16.

Marx, Karl. *Capital: Volume 1: A Critique of Political Economy*. London: Penguin Classics, 1990.

McClintock, Pamela. "An Auteur + This Actor = Game Change." *Hollywood Reporter*, November 30, 2011. Accessed January 25, 2014. http://www.hollywoodreporter.com/news/dark-knight-christian-bale-zhang-yimou-china-flowers-war-267220.

McDougall, Bonnie S. "Mao Zedong's 'Talks at Yan'an Conference on Literature and Art': A Translation of the 1943 Text with Commentary." *Michigan Papers in Chinese Studies* 39. Ann Arbor: University of Michigan Center for Chinese Studies, 1980.

———. *The Yellow Earth: A Film by Chen Kaige with a Complete Translation of the Filmscript*. Hong Kong: Chinese University, 1991.

McGrath, Jason. "Metacinema for the Masses: Three Films by Feng Xiaogang." *Modern Chinese Literature and Culture* 17.2 (2005): 90–132.

———. *Postsocialist Modernity: Chinese Cinema, Literature, and Criticism in the Market Age.* Stanford University Press, 2008.

Meng, Fanhua. *Zhongshen kuanghuan: shiji zhi jiao de zhongguo wenhua xianxiang* [*Carnival: Chinese Culture Phenomena at the Turn of the Twenty-first Century*]. Beijing: Zhongyang Bianyi chubanshe, 2003.

Mi, Jiashan. "Discussing *The Troubleshooters.*" *Chinese Education and Society* 31.1 (1998): 8–14.

Mitchell, Tony, ed. *Global Noise: Rap and Hip-hop Outside the USA.* Middletown: Wesleyan University Press, 2001.

Mulvey, Laura. "Visual Pleasure and Narrative Cinema." *Screen* 16 (1975): 6–18.

Musetto, V. A. "The Wilted Spoils of War." *New York Post*, December 21, 2011. Accessed January 28, 2014. http://nypost.com/2011/12/21/the-wilted-spoils-of-war/.

Naficy, Hamid. *An Accented Cinema: Exilic and Diasporic Filmmaking.* Princeton: Princeton University Press, 2001.

Ng, Yvonne. "Imagery and Sound in *Red Sorghum.*" *Kinema: A Journal for Film and Audiovisual Media* (Spring 1995). Accessed March 21, 2015. http://www.kinema.uwaterloo.ca/article.php?id=354&feature.

Nietzsche, Friedrich. *The Birth of Tragedy Out of the Spirit of Music.* Edited by Michael Tanner. Translated by Shaun Whiteside. London and New York: Penguin, 1993.

Nye, Joseph S. "Why China Is Weak on Soft Power." *New York Times,* January 18, 2012. Accessed May 3, 2013. http://www.nytimes.com/2012/01/18/opinion/why-china-is-weak-on-soft-power.html?_r=0.

Ong, Aihwa. *Flexible Citizenship: The Cultural Logics of Transnationality.* Durham: Duke University Press, 1999.

———. *Neoliberalism as Exception: Mutations in Citizenship and Sovereignty.* Durham and London: Duke University Press, 2006.

Osnos, Evan. "Can China Deliver the China Dream(s)?" *New Yorker,* March 26, 2013. Accessed March 30, 2014. http://www.newyorker.com/news/letter-from-china/can-china-deliver-the-china-dreams.

Pang, Laikwan. "Piracy/Privacy: The Despair of Cinema and Collectivity in China." *Boundary 2* (Fall 2004): 101–24.

Parsons, Deborah. *Streetwalking the Metropolis: Women, the City and Modernity.* Oxford and New York: Oxford University Press, 2000.

Pollacchi, Elena. "The Sound of the City: Chinese Films of the 1990s and Urban Noise." In *Cities in Transition: The Moving Image and the Modern Metropolis.* Edited by Andrew Webber and Emma Wilson, 193–204. London: Wallflower Press, 2008.

Potter, Russell A. *Spectacular Vernaculars: Hip-hop and the Politics of Postmodernism.* Albany: State University of New York Press, 1995.

Powers, John. *History as Propaganda: Tibetan Exiles Versus the People's Republic of China.* New York: Oxford University Press, 2004.

Pratt, Mary Louise. *Imperial Eyes: Travel Writing and Transculturation.* London and New York: Routledge, 1992.

Qian, Qian. "Dianying honggaoliang de shangyexing" [The Commercial Value of Film *Red Sorghum*]. *Dianying pinjie* [*Film Review*] (September 1988): 14.

Rayns, Tony. "Chinese Vocabulary: An Introduction to King of the Children and the New Chinese Cinema." In *King of the Children and the New Chinese Cinema.* Edited by Chen Kaige, Wan Zhi, and Tony Rayns, 1–58. London and Boston: Faber and Faber, 1989.

———. "An Interview with Jia Zhangke: A Big Stone in My Heart." Accessed November 28, 2011. http://www.asianfilms.org/china/zhantai/interviews.html.

Robertson, Roland. "Glocalization: Time-space and Homogeneity-Heterogeneity." In *Global Modernities*. Edited by Mike Featherstone, Scott Lash, and Roland Robertson, 25–44. London: Sage Publications, 1995.

Robinson, David. "Arts (Cinema): Touching Regard for Character/ Review of *Yellow Earth* at the ICA and *Survivors—The Blues Today* (PG) at the Cannon, Charing Cross Road." *Times*, August 8, 1986.

Rofel, Lisa. *Desiring China: Experiments in Neoliberalism, Sexuality, and Public Culture*. Durham: Duke University Press, 2007.

Romney, Jonathan, and Adrian Wootton, eds. *Celluloid Jukebox: Popular Music and the Movies Since the 50s*. London: British Film Institute, 1995.

Rose, Tricia. *Black Noise: Rap Music and Black Culture in Contemporary America*. Hanover: Wesleyan University Press, 1994.

Rosen, Stanley. "The Wolf at the Door: Hollywood and the Film Market in China." In *Southern California and the World*. Edited by Eric J. Heikkila and Rafael Pizarro, 49–78. Westport: Praeger, 2002.

Rosenthal, Elisabeth. "Groomed to Hip-Hop." *South China Morning Post*, April 18, 2001.

Said, Edward W. *Orientalism*. New York: Pantheon Books, 1978.

Shao, Mujin. "Huashuo huang tudi" [Speaking of Yellow Earth]. In *Huashuo huang tudi* [Speaking of Yellow Earth], 256–58. Beijing: Zhongguo dianying chubanshe, 1986.

Shen, Yun. *Zhongguo dianying chanye shi* [History of Chinese Film Industry]. Beijing: Zhongguo dianying chubanshe, 2005.

Shih, Evelyn. "Getting the Last Laugh: Opera Legacy, Comedy, and Camp as Attraction in the Late Years of Taiyupian." *Journal of Chinese Cinemas* 7.3 (2013): 241–62.

Shohat, Ella, and Robert Stam. *Unthinking Eurocentrism: Multiculturalism and the Media*. New York: Routledge, 1995.

Siefert, Marsha. "Image/Music/Voice: Song Dubbing in Hollywood Musicals." *Journal of Communication* 45.2 (1995): 46–59.

Silbergeld, Jerome. *China into Film: Frames of Reference in Contemporary Chinese Cinema*. London: Reaktion Books.

Silverman, Kaja. *The Acoustic Mirror: The Female Voice in Psychoanalysis and Cinema*. Bloomington and Indianapolis: Indiana University Press, 1988.

Smith, Jeff. *The Sounds of Commerce: Marketing Popular Film Music*. New York: Columbia University Press, 1998.

Song, Jialing. "Zhuxuanlv dianying de weiji yu huolu" [Crisis and Solution for Leitmotif Films]. *Dianying yishu* [Film Art] 8 (2013): 53–55.

Song, Mingwei. "How the Steel Was Tempered: The Rebirth of Pawel Korchagin in Contemporary Chinese Media." *Frontiers of Literary Studies in China* 6.1 (March 2012): 95–111.

Stewart, Jonathan. "Jiang's Sun Rises to Off-Beat Success." *China Daily*, September 30, 2007. Accessed July 23, 2011. http://www.chinadaily.com.cn/ezine/2007-09/30/content_6148645.htm.

Tang, Xiaobing. *Chinese Modern: The Heroic and the Quotidian*. Durham and London: Duke University Press, 2000.

———. "Why Should 2009 Make a Difference? Reflections on a Chinese Blockbuster." *Modern Chinese Literature and Culture*, December 2009. Accessed January 17, 2014. http://u.osu.edu/mclc/online-series/tangxb/.

Teo, Stephen. "Cinema with an Accent: Interview with Jia Zhangke, Director of *Platform*." *Senses of Cinema* 15 (2001). Accessed November 28, 2011. http://sensesofcinema.com/2001/feature-articles/zhangke_interview/.

Toop, David. *The Rap Attack: African Jive to New York Hip Hop.* Boston: South End Press, 1984.

———. *Rap Attack 2: African Rap to Global Hip Hop.* London: Serpent's Tail, 1991.

Tunzelmann, Alex von. "*The Flowers of War* Fails to Bloom for Chinese Film Industry." *Guardian,* August 2, 2012. Accessed January 28, 2014. https://www.theguardian.com/film/2012/aug/02/flowers-of-war-chinese-film.

Tuohy, Sue. "Metropolitan Sounds: Music in Chinese Films of the 1930s." In *Cinema and Urban Culture in Shanghai, 1922-1943.* Edited by Yingjin Zhang, 200-21. Stanford: Stanford University Press, 1999.

———. "Reflexive Cinema: Reflection on and Representing the Worlds of Chinese Film and Music." In *Global Soundtracks: Worlds of Film Music.* Edited by Mark Slobin, 177-213. Middletown: Wesleyan University Press, 2008.

———. "The Social Life of Genre: The Dynamics of Folksong in China." *Asian Music* 30.2 (Spring/Summer 1999): 39-86.

Wallerstein, Immanuel. "The Demise of Neoliberal Globalization." *Monthly Review,* January 2, 2008. Accessed September 25, 2010. http://mrzine.monthlyreview.org/2008/wallerstein010208.html.

Wang, Hui. "The Year 1989 and the Historical Roots of Neoliberalism in China." *Position: East Asia Cultures Critique* 12.1 (2004): 7-69.

Wang, Jing "Bourgeois Bohemians in China?: Neo-Tribes and the Urban Imaginary." *China Quarterly* 183 (September 2005): 532-48.

———. *High Culture Fever: Politics, Aesthetics, and Ideology in Deng's China.* Berkeley: University of California Press, 1996.

———. "Yichang guanyu jinling shisanchai de koushuizhan" [A Big Debate Revolving around *The Flowers of War*]. *Qingnian cankao* [*The Elite Reference*], December 28, 2011. Accessed May 30, 2013. http://qnck.cyol.com/html/2011-12/28/nw.D110000qnck_20111228_1-34.htm.

Wang, Ning. *Globalization and Cultural Translation.* New York: Cavendish Square Publishing, 2004.

Wang, Nuan. "Jianguo da ye yanyuan ling pianchou de beihou" [Behind the Stars' Zero Salary in *The Founding of a Republic*]. *Beijng qingnian bao* [*Beijng Youth Daily*], August 30, 2009. Accessed January 25, 2014. http://news.163.com/09/0830/09/5HV4CoSQ0o011SM9.html.

Wang, Shujen. *Framing Piracy: Globalization and Film Distribution in Greater China.* Lanham: Rowman & Littlefield, 2003.

Wang Shuo, *Wo shi wang shuo* [*I am Wang Shuo*]. Beijing: Guoji wenhua chuban gongsi, 1992.

Wang, Ting. "Hollywood's Pre-WTO Crusade in China." *Jump Cut: A Review of Contemporary Media* 49 (Spring 2007). Accessed August 25, 2015. http://www.ejumpcut.org/archive/jc49.2007/TingWang.

Wang, Wenhe. *Zhongguo dianying yinyue xuezong* [*Looking for the Trace of Chinese Film Music*]. Beijing: Zhongguo guangbo dianshi chubanshe, 1995.

Wang, Wuming. "The Identity of Chinese Film in the Situation of Globalization." *New Films* 5 (2001): 48-54.

Wang, Xiaofeng. "Cui Jian: ershi duonian lai" [Cui Jian: Since the Past Twenty Years]. *Sanlian shenghuo zhoukan* [*Sanlian Life Weekly*], April 6, 2005. Accessed August 01, 2013. http://www.lifeweek.com.cn/2005/0406/11445.shtml.

Willett, John, trans. and ed. *Brecht on Theatre: The Development of an Aesthetic.* New York: Hill and Wang, 1964.

Williams, Raymond. *The Long Revolution.* New York: Columbia University Press, 1961.

Wines, Michael. "A Dirty Pun Tweaks China's Online Censors." *New York Times*, March 11, 2009. Accessed May 5, 2010. http://www.nytimes.com/2009/03/12/world/asia/12beast.html?em.
Wittgenstein, Ludwig. *Tractatus Logico-Philosophicus*. Translated by D. F. Pears and B. F. McGuiness. London: Routledge, 1961.
Wojcik, Pamela Robertsonk, and Arthur Knight, eds. *Soundtrack Available: Essays on Film and Popular Music*. Durham: Duke University Press, 2001.
Wong, Edward. "China: An Artist Fights Back." *New York Times*, April 13, 2012. Accessed January 21, 2015. http://www.nytimes.com/2012/04/14/world/asia/china-artist-ai-weiwei-fights-back.html.
———. "Dissident Chinese Artist is Released." *New York Times*, June 22, 2011. Accessed January 21, 2015. http://www.nytimes.com/2011/06/23/world/asia/23artist.html.
Wong, Lily. "Moving Serenades: Hearing the Sinophonic in MP & GI's *Longxiang Fengwu*." *Journal of Chinese Cinemas* 7.3 (2013): 225–40.
Wu, Ziniu. "Pai Guoge de chuzhong" [My Original Intentions on Shooting *The National Anthem*]. *Dangdai dianying* [*Contemporary Cinema*] 5 (1999): 5–6.
Xi Ha Shen Jiao. "Lun zhongwen Rap de fazhan lishi" [A Brief History of Chinese Rap]. *Hip Hop City*, January 18, 2016. Accessed March 01, 2015. http://www.51555.net/home/html/news/notes/2016/0118/12599.html.
Xiao, Ying. "Chinese Rock 'n' Roll and Cui Jian on Screen." In *The Oxford Handbook of New Audiovisual Aesthetics*. Edited by Claudia Gorbman, John Richardson, and Carol Vernallis, 266–83. New York: Oxford University Press, 2013.
———. "'Hip Hop Is My Knife, Rap Is My Sword': Hip Hop, Cultural (Re)production and the Question of Authenticity and Authorship in Contemporary China." In *Three Asias: Japan, S. Korea, China*. Edited by Takayuki Tatsumi, Jina Kim, and Zhang Zhen. *Paradoxa: Studies in World Literary Genres* 22 (2010): 269–98.
———. "'Leitmotif': State, Market, and Postsocialist Chinese Film Industry under Neoliberal Globalization." In *Neoliberalism and Global Cinema: Capital, Culture, and Marxist Critique*. Edited by Jyotsna Kapur and Keith B. Wagner, 157–79. London and New York: Routledge, 2011.
Xiao, Zhiwei. "Nationalism in Chinese Popular Culture: A Case Study of the Opium War." In *Exploring Nationalisms of China: Themes and Conflicts*. Edited by C. X. George Wei and Xiaoyuan Liu, 41–56. Westport: Praeger, 2002.
Xiao, Zhiwei, and Hong Yin. "The First Official Finding Report of China's Film Market and Hollywood's Globalizing Tactics." *Film Art* 1 (2002): 119–21.
Xie, Mian, and Qian Liqun, eds., *Bainian zhongguo wenxue jingdian 7* [*The Centennial Chinese Literature Classics, Volume 7*]. Beijing: Beijing daxue chubanshe, 1996.
Xu, Linzheng, "Zhao Jiping gushi: 'diwudai' dianying yinyue zhangmen ren" [Legend of Zhao Jiping: A Great Master of the 'Fifth Generation' Film Music]. *Dazhong dianying* [*Popular Cinema*] 4 (2006): 29.
Xue, Ting. "A Political Economy Analysis of Chinese Films (1979–1994)." MA thesis, Chinese University of Hong Kong, 1995.
Yang, Guobin. *The Power of the Internet in China: Citizen Activism Online*. New York: Columbia University Press, 2009.
Yang, Jing. "The Reinvention of Hollywood's Classic White Saviour Tale in Contemporary Chinese Cinema: *Pavilion of Women* and *The Flowers of War*." *Critical Arts* 28.2 (March 2014): 247–63.

Yang, Mayfair. "State Discourse or a Plebeian Public Sphere: Film Discussion Groups in China." *Visual Anthropology* 10.1 (1994): 112–25.

Yao, Yusheng. "The Elite Class Background of Wang Shuo and His Hooligan Characters." *Modern China* 30.4 (October 2004): 431–69.

Yau, Esther C.M. "*Yellow Earth*: Western Analysis and a Non-western Text." *Film Quarterly* 41.2 (Winter 1987–88): 22–33.

Yau, Kinnia Shuk-ting. "Meanings of the Imagined Friends: Good Japanese in Chinese War Films." In *Imagining Japan in Post-war East Asia: Identity Politics, Schooling and Popular Culture*. Edited by Paul Morris, Naoko Shimazu, and Edward Vickers, 68–84. New York: Routledge, 2014.

Yeh, Yueh-yu. "A Life of Its Own: Musical Discourses in Wong Kar-wai's Films." *Post Script: Essays in Film and the Humanities* 19.1 (Fall 1999): 120–36.

———. "A National Score: Popular Music and Taiwanese Cinema." PhD diss., University of Southern California, 1995.

———. *Gesheng meiying: gequ xushi yu zhongwen dianying* [Phantom of the Music: Song Narration and Chinese-language Cinema]. Hong Kong: Yuanliu chuban gongsi. 2000.

———. "Historiographic and Sinification: Music in Chinese Cinema of the 1930s." *Cinema Journal* 41.3 (Spring 2002): 78–97.

Yin, Hong. *Shiji zhuanzhe shiqi de zhongguo yingshi wenhua* [Chinese Film and Media Culture at the Turn of the Twenty-first Century]. Beijing: Beijing chubanshe, 1998.

Yu, Zhong, "*Wo de xiongdijiemei* daoyan shouji" [A Manuscript from the Director for *Roots and Branches*]. *Dianying yishu* [Film Art] 5 (2001): 65–66.

Zha, Jianying. *China Pop: How Soap Operas, Tabloids, and Bestsellers Are Transforming a Culture*. New York: New Press, 1995.

Zhai, Jianlong. "Guanyu zhuxuanlv he duoyanghua de dawen: dianyingju juzhang teng jinxiang fangwenji" [Questions-and-answers about Leitmotif and Diversity: An Interview with Teng Jinxian, the Director of the Film Bureau]. *Dianying yishu* [Film Art] 3 (1991): 4–8.

Zhang, Boqing, and Wei Zhang. "Construction of Audience-Orienting Film Criticism." *Film Art* 3 (2001): 48–51.

Zhang, Chunsheng. "Hong gaoliang xianxiang: yishu de rensheng jiazhi yu shenghuo jiazhi" [The Red Sorghum Phenomenon: The Life and Everyday Life Value of Arts]. *Nanfang wentan* [Southern Cultural Forum] 5 (1988): 47–50.

Zhang, Huiyu. *Mubei yu jiyi: geming lishi gushi de changhuan yu chongjian* [Gravestone and Memory: The Redemption and Reconstruction of Revolutionary Historical Narratives]. Taipei: Xiuwei chubanshe, 2012.

Zhang, Nuanxin. "*Beijing nizao* de daoyan chanshu" [The Director's Exposition of *Good Morning, Beijing*]. *Dangdai dianying* [Contemporary Cinema] 39 (1990): 53–54.

Zhang, Wei. "New Film Sparks Controversy and Acclaim." *Beijing Review* 29.6–7 (February 1986): 31.

———. "Xunzhao gexing zhangyang yu gewu yingpian de qihe duiying," [Seeking a Harmonious Expression of Personality in the Song-and-dance Movie]. *Wenhui dianying shibao* [Shanghai Film Times], January 21, 1989.

Zhang, Xudong. *Chinese Modernism in the Era of Reforms: Cultural Fever, Avant-Garde Fiction, and New Chinese Cinema*. Durham: Duke University Press, 1997.

———. *Postsocialism and Cultural Politics: China in the Last Decade of the Twentieth Century*. Durham: Duke University Press, 2008.

Zhang, Yimou. "Chang yizhi shengming de zange" [Sing a Paean to Life]. *Dangdai danying* [*Contemporary Cinema*] 2 (1988): 81–83.

———. "Huang tudi shying chanshu" [Explanation on the Cinematography of *Yellow Earth*]. *Beijing dianying xueyuan xuebao* [*Journal of Beijing Film Academy*] 1 (1985): 116–19.

Zhang, Yingjin. "Ideology of the Body in *Red Sorghum*: National Allegory, National Roots, and Third Cinema." *East-West Film Journal* 4.2 (June 1990): 38–53.

———. *Screening China: Critical Interventions, Cinematic Reconfigurations, and the Transnational Imaginary in Contemporary Chinese Cinema*. Ann Arbor: Center for Chinese Studies, University of Michigan, 2002.

Zhang, Yiwu. "Hou xinshiqi: Xinde wenhua kongjian" [Post-New Era: A New Cultural Space]. *Wenyi zhengmin* [*Literature and Art Forum*] 6 (1992): 9–12.

———. "Hou xinshiqi zhongguo dianying: Fenglie de tiaozhan" [Chinese Cinema in the Post-New Era: The Challenge of Fragmentation]. *Dangdai dianying* [Contemporary Cinema] 5 (1994): 4–11.

———. "Rethinking China: The Challenge of Globalization and 'New Internal Trend.'" *Film Art* 1 (2001): 16–18.

Zhang, Zhaohui. "Zai haiziwang yu jin naozhong jiang zhijian" [Between *King of the Children* and the Golden Alarm]. *Dianying pinjie* [*Film Review*] (September 1988): 14.

Zhang, Zhen. *An Amorous History of the Silver Screen: Shanghai Cinema, 1896–1937*. Chicago: University of Chicago Press, 2005.

———. ed. *The Urban Generation: Chinese Cinema and Society at the Turn of the Twenty-first Century*. Durham: Duke University Press, 2007.

Zhao, Jia. "Chinese National Cinema in the New Situation." *New Films* 3 (2001): 45–55.

Zhao, Jianwei, *Cui Jian zai Yiwosuoyou zhong nahan: Zhongguo yaogun beiwanglu* [*Cui Jian Cries Out in "Nothing to My Name": A Memorandum on Chinese Rock*]. Beijing: Beijing shifan daxue chubanshe, 1992.

Zhao, Yiheng. "'Houxue' yu zhongguo xin baoshou zhuyi" [Post-isms and Chinese Neo-conservatism], *Ershi yi shiji* [*Twenty-First Century*] 27 (February 1995): 4–15.

Zheng, Yongnian. *Globalization and State Transformation in China*. New York: Cambridge University Press, 2004.

Zhou, Donglin, Kuang Xiaolan, and Zhang Qingsheng. "Guanyu zhuxuanlv dianying shichang yunying de sikao" [Reflections on the Market Strategies of Leitmotif Film]. *Zhongguo dianying shichang* [*Chinese Film Market*] 1 (2012): 11–13.

Zhou, Xuelin. *Young Rebels in Contemporary Chinese Cinema*. Hong Kong University Press, 2007.

Zhu, Kade. "Shisanchai de qingse aiguozhuyi" [Thirteen Prostitutes' Erotic Patriotism]. *Nafang dushibao* [*Southern Metropolis Daily*], December 13, 2011. Accessed May 25, 2013. https://opinion.nfdialy.cn/content/2011–12/13/content_34896942.htm.

Zhu, Ying. *Chinese Cinema During the Era of Reform: The Ingenuity of the System*. Westport: Praeger, 2003.

———. "Commercialization and Chinese Cinema's Post-wave." *Consumption, Markets and Culture* 5.3 (2002): 187–209.

Žižek, Slavoj. *In Defense of Lost Causes*. New York: Verso, 2008.

———. *The Sublime Object of Ideology*. New York: Verso, 1989

INDEX

acousmêtre, 100, 109, 139, 174
Adorno, Theodor, 183, 209, 279n25
Appadurai, Arun, 10, 162, 259n19
Attali, Jacques, 3, 144, 231, 233, 237, 271n6
"audiovisual contract," 7–8, 121–22, 125, 128

Bakhtin, Mikhail, 6, 61, 138, 219
Barthes, Roland, 70–71, 223
Beijing Bastards (1993), 15, 77–78, 93–99, 101–2, 118, 133–35, 137, 141
Benjamin, Walter, 85–87, 231
Big Parade, The (1986), 14, 38–41, 66, 142–43
Black Head, 17, 215, 220
blockbuster, 4, 156–62, 169, 172, 182–84, 188, 190, 192–94, 236
breakdance, 202–6
Brecht, Bertolt, 114, 262n38

Chen Kaige, 18, 20, 23–24, 26, 34, 37, 45, 65, 68, 72, 79, 142–43, 192, 262n26, 262n29, 262n36
China Dream, the, 16, 145, 190, 193, 271n7
"China through Foreign Eyes," 16, 145, 160–62, 167, 169, 172
Chion, Michel, 5, 7–8, 100, 121, 124, 139, 259n15
Chou, Jay, 17, 201, 207–9
cinema *vérité,* 14–15, 93, 99, 112–13, 116–18, 124, 134, 229
Cui Jian, 15, 75, 78, 93, 95–111, 112, 139, 195, 204, 266n1
cultural fever, 11, 41, 47, 71, 75, 84, 148, 205, 265n26
Cultural Revolution, the, 18, 22, 24, 34, 42–43, 72, 108, 137, 262n36
culture industry, 16, 153, 175, 183, 191, 260n26, 279n25

Dai Jinhua, 72–73, 99, 131, 142–43, 175
Deleuze, Gilles, 139, 141, 271n36

dialect, 19, 132, 189, 213, 218, 220, 236
documentary, 28, 36, 39, 81–82, 91, 93–95, 97–98, 102, 107, 122, 135, 143, 186, 194, 225–26, 229–30
Dou Wei, 95, 200, 269n5

Eisenstein, Sergei, 89–90

"Fake Monk," 105–6, 135
Feng Xiaogang, 80, 151, 159, 192, 266n6
Feng Xiaoning, 16, 145, 160–62, 167, 169, 171–72, 176, 179, 187, 189
Fifth Generation, the, 4, 7, 11, 14, 18–21, 24, 26, 35, 37, 39, 47, 49, 52–53, 65–66, 68, 71–74, 76–77, 79, 132, 134, 136–37, 139, 140, 151–52, 159, 169, 174, 186, 191, 234, 260n2, 261n4, 262n36
film industry, 4, 13, 16, 144, 146–47, 149, 153–55, 165, 172, 183, 185, 273n14
flâneur, 14–15, 85–87, 89, 92, 94, 96, 99, 106, 219
Flowers of War, The (2011), 16, 145, 185, 187–91, 235–36, 276n82
folklore, 17, 20, 23, 29, 37–38, 43, 45–47, 66, 71, 75, 225, 236
Foucault, Michel, 11, 14, 146
Founding of a Party, The (2011), 16, 191
Founding of a Republic, The (2009), 16, 191–92

globalization, 3, 5, 10, 78, 137, 142–43, 145, 153, 157, 162, 176, 181, 184–85, 197–98, 201, 210–12, 218, 222, 234, 236, 281n58
Good Morning, Beijing (1990), 15, 77, 104–7, 134–35
Grass Mud Horse, 17, 194, 222–32, 280n48, 281n49

Hansen, Miriam, 5, 19, 258n6
Happy (2009), 17, 218–22

Hero (2002), 151, 185–87, 235
He Yong, 95, 200
Hidden, the, 17, 212, 214, 217
"Hills of Yellow Earth," 47–48, 74
hip hop, Chinese, 6, 12, 16, 197–98, 202, 205, 207, 208–9, 212–16, 220, 222, 231–34
Hollywood, 4–5, 13, 16, 56, 144–46, 153–72, 186, 189–93, 231, 234, 258n6, 264n8, 271n36, 272n8
hooligan literature, 15, 80, 149
How the Steel Was Tempered (1997), 15, 77, 92, 137–41, 170, 271n34
Huang Jianxin, 16, 20, 79, 191
Hu Jintao, 165

independent film, 112, 133–34, 150
internet, the, 14, 17, 111, 208, 216–18, 223–30

Jackson, Michael, 202
Jameson, Fredric, 35, 106, 119, 130–32, 182
Jia Hongsheng, 105, 135–37, 140–41
Jiang Wen, 15, 80, 108–9, 178, 192
Jiang Zemin, 163
Jia Zhangke, 15, 112–13, 116–17, 122, 153, 237
"Jolting Sedan," 54–56, 62, 64
jouissance, 194, 216, 221–22

King of the Children (1987), 14, 20, 24, 38–46, 52–53, 73, 79, 108, 174, 260n2

Leitmotif films, 6, 12–17, 143–94, 233–36
"Let Me Rap," 195–96, 200, 277n1
"Like a Knife," 97, 195–96
Lover's Grief over the Yellow River (1999), 16, 145, 160, 162–67, 171–72, 176, 179–80, 275nn56–57, 275n60
Lu Xuezhang, 15, 77, 137–38, 140–41, 170
Lu Xun, 34, 73

Mao Zedong, 149, 208
market reform, 10–11, 18–19, 79–80, 105–7, 113, 123, 138, 144, 148, 218
MC Hotdog, 17, 195–96, 198–201, 217, 277n1
Mi Jiashan, 15, 77, 80–81
mise-en-bande, 7, 29
mise-en-scène, 7, 9, 18, 29, 37, 58, 81, 95, 108, 114, 124, 131, 164, 172, 180, 187, 190, 204, 220

Mo Yan, 71, 235
MRFT (Ministry of Radio, Film and Television), 148, 151, 158–59, 161
Mulvey, Laura, 54, 178, 264n8

national allegory, 35, 119, 169, 179, 182
National Anthem (1999), 159–60
neoliberalism, 11, 14, 145, 152–53, 161–62, 185
New Mainstream Cinema, 152–53, 273n22
New Wave, Chinese, 4, 13, 14, 17–18, 22, 35, 77, 234, 262n36. *See also* Fifth Generation, the
New Year Celebration Comedies, 159
Northwest Wind, 6, 12, 14, 17, 18, 20–21, 47–51, 58, 64–66, 69, 71, 74, 75–76, 79, 81, 219, 233, 235
"Nothing to My Name," 75, 97, 103, 195, 266n1

"Ode to the Wine God," 54, 59, 61, 64, 235
Opium War, The (1997), 16, 145, 156–59, 181, 184–85, 187
Orientalism, 132, 168, 170, 214

"Piece of Red Cloth, A," 101–4, 135
Platform (2000), 15, 112, 118–34, 137, 140
postmodernism, 10, 131
postsocialism, 10–12, 162, 260n27. *See also* "socialism with Chinese characteristic"
Purple Sunset (2001), 145, 162, 172, 183

Quitting (2001), 15, 77, 134–37, 140–41

realism, 15, 36, 78–79, 89, 108, 112–13, 124, 126, 131–32, 134, 225
Red River Valley (1996), 16, 145, 162, 167, 170–84, 191, 275n56
Red Sorghum (1987), 14, 20, 51, 52–74, 78–79, 174, 235, 264n12, 265n32
"Return to Lhasa," 170, 177
Riding Alone for Thousands of Miles (2005), 235
rock, Chinese, 15, 75–78, 93–95, 97, 99, 102–3, 107–8, 111, 118, 134, 195, 200, 233–34, 266n1, 268n39
Rock Kids (1988), 77, 202–5
"Rock 'n' Roll on the New Long March," 75, 97–98
Roots and Branches (2001), 15, 100–102, 108, 134

"root-seeking," 14, 20–21, 39, 41, 47–49, 53, 56, 71, 79, 169

Saving Private Ryan (1998), 16, 155, 160, 162–63, 169, 189, 274n44
"Sister, March Forward Bravely," 54, 57–58, 62–64, 69
Sixth Generation, the, 4, 7, 15, 76–77, 93–94, 99, 102, 105, 108, 132, 134–37, 139, 143, 150, 152, 170, 193, 234. *See also* urban cinema
"socialism with Chinese characteristic," 11, 271n7. *See also* postsocialism
"Song of the Daughter," 37–38, 66
soundscape, 5–13, 19, 97, 103–4, 112, 122, 126, 199, 210
soundtrack, 6–12, 23–24, 33, 36–37, 40, 45–46, 54, 58, 65, 90, 95, 97, 99, 107, 113, 118, 120, 124–25, 130, 133, 146, 163, 171, 174, 183–84, 213, 235
Special Program of Animal World: Grass Mud Horse in the Mahler Gobi Desert (2009), 224–27, 230
Square, The (1994), 143
subculture, 17, 74, 95, 97–98, 102, 107, 134, 199, 218–19, 223, 226, 228
Sun Also Rises, The (2007), 15, 108–10, 134

Tao, David, 17, 201, 211–12
Teng, Teresa, 123–24, 133, 137
Ten Mythical Creatures, 223, 225, 228, 230
Thunderbolt Dance, 202–4
Tiananmen Square, 40, 75, 97, 133, 142–43, 187
Tian Zhuangzhuang, 18, 20, 72, 79, 139–40, 203, 275n53
Tibet, 170–74, 176–80, 275n53
Titanic (1997), 4, 16, 155, 160, 163–65, 169
"To Be Different," 211, 279n26
transnational imaginary, 16, 145, 154, 234
Troubleshooters, The (1988), 15, 77–78, 80–92, 99, 134, 266n6

urban cinema, 14, 17, 77, 134. *See also* Sixth Generation, the

vernacular modernism, 5, 19, 21, 258n6
vernacular rap, 17, 202, 215, 217–18, 236–37

voice-over, 6, 12, 54, 138, 139–40, 162, 173–74, 183, 189, 219, 234

Wang Shuo, 15, 78, 80, 84, 86, 88, 92, 102, 149, 266n6
Wang Xiaoshuai, 96, 135, 141
"Whether or Not," 124–30
Woman, a Gun and a Noodle Shop, A (2009), 235–36
Wong, Faye, 114, 269n5
Wu Ziniu, 18, 39, 159

Xi'an Film Studio, 20, 37, 68–69, 79
Xiao Wu (1997), 15, 112–18, 121–22, 126, 134
Xie Jin, 16, 145, 156–58, 189

Yellow Earth (1984), 4, 14, 21–38, 39, 41–42, 47, 50, 52–53, 62, 65–66, 69, 73–74, 172, 174, 262n29
Yellow River, the, 25–27, 31–32, 38, 47, 72, 162, 164, 172, 177, 182, 275n59
Yu Zhong, 15, 100

Zhang Nuanxin, 15, 77, 104, 107
Zhang Yang, 15, 77, 134–36
Zhang Yimou, 15, 18, 20, 26, 53, 60, 63, 65, 68–69, 71–72, 79, 186–87, 190, 235–36, 261n13
Zhang Yuan, 15, 77, 93–98, 101, 112, 143, 268n39
Zhao Jiping, 37, 58–59, 65, 67–68, 235
Žižek, Slavoj, 194, 221–22

www.ingramcontent.com/pod-product-compliance
Lightning Source LLC
Chambersburg PA
CBHW030607230426
43661CB00053B/1879